THE NATIONAL INSTITUTE OF
ECONOMIC AND SOCIAL RESEARCH

Economic and Social Studies
XXXIV

WORLD INFLATION
SINCE 1950

An International Comparative Study

WORLD INFLATION
SINCE 1950

An International Comparative Study

BY

A. J. BROWN

ASSISTED BY

JANE DARBY

The right of the
University of Cambridge
to print and sell
all manner of books
was granted by
Henry VIII in 1534.
The University has printed
and published continuously
since 1584.

CAMBRIDGE UNIVERSITY PRESS

CAMBRIDGE

LONDON   NEW YORK   NEW ROCHELLE

MELBOURNE   SYDNEY

CAMBRIDGE UNIVERSITY PRESS
Cambridge, New York, Melbourne, Madrid, Cape Town, Singapore,
São Paulo, Delhi, Dubai, Tokyo, Mexico City

Cambridge University Press
The Edinburgh Building, Cambridge CB2 8RU, UK

Published in the United States of America by Cambridge University Press, New York

www.cambridge.org
Information on this title: www.cambridge.org/9780521154864

First published 1985
Reprinted 1988
First paperback edition 2010

A catalogue record for this publication is available from the British Library

Library of Congress Catalogue Card Number: 84-29252

ISBN 978-0-521-30351-4 Hardback
ISBN 978-0-521-15486-4 Paperback

CONTENTS

v

LIST OF TABLES

LIST OF CHARTS

PREFACE

Thirty years ago, I wrote a book which, with what can now be seen as excessive optimism, I entitled 'The Great Inflation, 1939–51'. The present work is an attempt to make sense of the greater inflation which has occurred since then. Like Goethe, returning in his mature years to finish 'Faust', I might well ask of the shadowy forms I had tried to grasp:

Versuch ich wohl, euch diesmal fest zu halten?
Fühl ich mein Herz noch jenem Wahn geneigt?

There are, indeed, reasons for caution. In the literary field, sequels are not always a success. The scene to be depicted, in my case, has been greatly broadened, in that the period is longer, and the relevant literature is vastly greater than it was in 1955. Since one reputable journal reviewed the earlier book under the heading 'A canvas too broad', I cannot say I was not warned. I have, however, not resisted the temptation to try to make a single picture of a worldwide process, most of the best treatments of which, in recent years, have taken the form rather of sets of conference papers than of works of one or two pairs of hands.

To make such a picture, one could, at the one extreme, write a survey of the literature or, at the other, start from the basic data and apply a mode of analysis of one's own choice. The treatment here lies somewhere between the extremes. It is not a systematic, econometric one, nor does it come near to surveying the whole of the immense literature; but it rests on direct examination of the data and also appeals to what seem to be the most important and relevant of the systematic studies which others have made. The general form which it takes, and its rather elastic geographical scope, are outlined in the last section of chapter 1. The main features of the inflationary processes which seem to me to emerge are drawn together in chapter 13. Whether I have grasped the substance, or only the shadow, the reader must decide.

Shortcomings in the finished product cannot be blamed on any lack of encouragement and help that I have received in working on it. The late Andrew Shonfield was one of those who encouraged me to take up the story where I had left it in 1955, and the Royal Institute of International Affairs (under whose auspices the earlier study was produced) kindly agreed that this could most appropriately be done under the roof of the National Institute of Economic and Social Research. This scheme was made possible by a most generous grant from the Leverhulme Trust Fund, to which – and to its then Director, Ronald Tress, in particular – my warmest thanks are due.

I have been especially fortunate in having the help, in the National Institute, of Jane Darby. Not only was her work in compiling and processing data and in searching and appraising the literature indispensable, but the writing has benefited at every stage from her good judgement and economic expertise. It has benefited, also, from the comments and encouragement of the successive Directors of the Institute, David Worswick and Andrew Britton. The supporting services of the Institute, under the expert eye of Kit Jones, have, as always, been excellent; Anne Wright typed most of the earlier drafts and Fran Robinson prepared the final version for the printer. Any mistakes (and any outrageous views) that remain are my sole responsibility.

Finally, I have some acknowledgements to make nearer home. The University of Leeds, and its School of Economic Studies, have continued to provide me with invaluable library, and other facilities long after I have disappeared from their payroll; I am greatly indebted to my son, William Brown, then Director of the Industrial Relations Research Unit in the University of Warwick, for comments and suggestions on chapter 8, and my wife has added to the infinite debt of gratitude I owe her, not only by much help with the index, but by bearing with my retreat into my study at a time when retirement might have been expected to make me more useful about the house.

October, 1984   A. J. BROWN

1

RECONNAISSANCE AND PLAN

THE RECORD OF INFLATION

The years 1950–79, over which we have chosen to study experience of inflation, clearly provide us with plenty of raw material. Before embarking on our main analysis it will be useful to make a preliminary reconnaissance and to set the period in context.

Inflation is not a very rare phenomenon in economic history; the ancient world was very well acquainted with it; in the Middle Ages it was not unknown, despite the constraints of a general scarcity of the precious metals; the discovery of the New World produced a protracted inflationary episode of at least West European extent, and each of the world wars since the late eighteenth century has brought inflation on an international scale. There have been, in addition, a fair number of more local occurrences, often, but not always, connected with physical conflict.

The inflation of our period was both extensive and severe (see table 1.1). No market economy avoided it, and none seems to have escaped with less than a doubling of its consumer price index. Only the official prices of some centrally planned economies (the USSR, Bulgaria, Czechoslovakia) showed virtually no increase, and those of some others (Poland, Hungary) only a small one. The International Monetary Fund gives a 'world' (weighted) average increase of 5.3-fold, and the median country increase is about the same. The United Nations indices for US dollar prices of internationally traded goods show a 3.6-fold increase in the case of manufactures, and a 4.8-fold one in that of primary products. The greater number of market economies show increases between two- and seven-fold; not many (Spain, 10.6-fold, being one) show higher increases than that until we come to very much higher ones, ranging from between 30 and 80-fold (Colombia, Ghana, Israel, Peru, Turkey) to 12,000-fold (Uruguay) and 100,000-fold (Argentina).

This suggests a bigger total price rise, by most criteria, than that of the second world war and its immediate aftermath (say July, 1939 to August, 1948), when the median increase among 45 countries for which indices are available, mostly of wholesale prices, but some of cost of living, appears to have been a little more than a

1

Table 1.1 *Consumer price index levels, 1979*   1950 = 1

Argentina	100,000.0	Australia	5.5
Uruguay	12,058.0	Denmark	5.5
Bolivia	719.0	Philippines	5.5
Brazil	275.0	Sweden	5.0
South Korea	183.0	Norway	4.9
Israel	80.5	South Africa	4.9
Iceland	60.4	India	4.3
Paraguay	54.0	Austria	4.1
Ghana	50.0	Morocco	4.1
Peru	45.3	Costa Rica	3.6
Turkey	40.3	Netherlands	3.4
Colombia	29.2	El Salvador	3.4
Yugoslavia	15.0	Burma	3.4
Spain	10.6	Canada	3.2
Mexico	9.7	Tunisia	3.2
Portugal	7.9	Belgium	3.1
Ireland	7.0	United States	3.0
Finland	6.7	Dominican Republic	3.0
Greece	6.6	Egypt	2.9
Iran	6.5	Malta	2.7
United Kingdom	6.3	Guatemala	2.7
New Zealand	6.2	Sri Lanka	2.6
Italy	5.9	Switzerland	2.5
Japan	5.7	West Germany	2.4
France	5.7	Malaysia	2.1

Source: *International Financial Statistics.*

three-fold one (see Brown, 1955). There is, however, the noteworthy difference that our period affords no cases of really full-blooded hyperinflation, wheareas the second world war does. With the striking examples before us of Argentina, Uruguay, and even some of the other very high inflation countries just mentioned, this may seem a surprising statement. Our justification must be that it is best to reserve the term hyperinflation for those cases where a currency virtually blows itself out of most of its normal uses as a medium of exchange and a store of value and, usually, has to be replaced with a new one, as happened with the Greek currency in 1944 and the Hungarian in 1946. The criterion of a currency having put itself largely out of use is that its velocity of circulation has increased to many times its normal value (or, to put it in the opposite way, the real value of the money stock is only a small fraction of what it has normally been). The circumstances in which this happens vary greatly from one case to another (see Brown, *op. cit.*, chapter 8), but drastic rises in velocity do not seem to occur unless inflation has reached some high level such as a quadrupling of prices in a year. Cagan, in his classic study (1956), defines hyperinflation, arbitrarily, as setting in when prices rise 50 per cent in a month – equivalent to 130-fold in a year. There has been nothing like that in our period.

A glance at the course of velocity of circulation in Argentina, the star case of very high inflation in our period, shows a rise of velocity by about 60 per cent after a year of 100 per cent inflation in 1959, but no great variation thereafter, even when prices more than quintupled in 1976. Money was still very much in business in 1979. There is a sharp contrast here with the Greek and Hungarian hyperinflations connected with the second world war in which, at their peaks, with prices in the former case rising nearly 60 per cent a day, in the latter case trebling each day, the aggregate real values of the currency in circulation fell to fractions of 1 per cent of their pre-hyperinflation levels.

A similar comparison may be made between the inflation of our period and that of the first world war and its immediate aftermath. By 1920 consumers' prices had more than doubled in the United Kingdom and nearly doubled in the United States; wholesale prices had doubled or trebled in most countries except the belligerents of continental Europe, where much larger increases had occurred. True hyperinflations (on Cagan's definition) either had arrived, or were shortly to arrive, in Austria, Hungary, Poland, Russia and, most notoriously, Germany.

The French Revolutionary and Napoleonic wars had also produced widespread inflation which varied from a doubling of prices in the United Kingdom and the United States to much higher increases in central Europe. France had already, by 1796, suffered and recovered from the episode of the paper assignats, which had fallen to $\frac{1}{2}$ per cent of their individual face value in terms of silver (see Bresciani-Turroni, 1937) (and collectively to about a thirtieth of the silver value of the amount of them in circulation) two years earlier – perhaps only marginal as an example of hyperinflation, but a notable example of flight from a paper currency.

In comparison with world war periods, therefore, our period produced larger price increases for the generality of countries, but no truly hyperinflationary fireworks. Although two wars – in Korea and Viet Nam – powerfully influenced events within it, it was far from being a period of war economy; it was, indeed, unusual for a period of its length in that no major country was fully mobilised for war within it. But also, in comparison with the two periods earlier in the twentieth century which were dominated by war economy or reconversion, it was much longer – roughly three times as long – though the relevance of this may be modified when we consider the way in which inflation was concentrated within particular sub-periods of it.

How does it compare with the other major and widespread inflation not connected with world war, the 'price revolution' of the sixteenth–seventeenth centuries? Keynes, in a famous passage in the 'Treatise on Money' characterised the inflationary results of New World gold and silver as being a five-fold increase of Spanish prices over about 80 years (to 1600), a 2.5-fold increase in French prices over a similar, but slightly later period, and, in England, a rise which he did not precisely quantify during the 90 or 100 years ending in 1650. (According to the later studies of Knoop and Jones (1933) and of Phelps Brown and Hopkins (1956), English cost of living rose perhaps five- or six-fold between the beginning of the sixteenth century and the middle of the seventeeth, a particularly sharp rise occurring in the two middle decades of the sixteenth.) We again have evidence, therefore, of a fairly widespread inflation of the size typical of the middle range of experience in our period – but spread over three or more times as long.

If, instead of looking at total price increases over a period, we have regard to average annual rates of price increase, we can say that the rate for the median market economy in our period was about 6 per cent, and the corresponding figure for 1939–48 a little over twice as great. For 1914–20 (which excludes the hyperinflations in some countries where they subsequently developed), the median for the United States, Canada, Australia, Japan and twelve European countries was a little higher (15 per cent) though the figures for those countries range from 8 per cent (Australia) to 93 per cent (Austria). In contrast, the annual rates for the price revolution of the sixteenth–seventeenth centuries work out at between 1 and 2 per cent, though it is possible that the trend rate in England over a couple of decades in the middle of the sixteenth century may have been as high as 3 per cent per annum. In average annual rate, therefore, the inflation of our period stands somewhere between that of the longest seriously upward price trend of modern history and those of the short, sharp shocks imparted by world wars and their immediate aftermaths.

In considering that period, however, there are two further things to remember. The first is that it is only part of a longer inflationary period. It followed immediately after one of the world war inflations just referred to, which in turn, had followed with little or no intermission on a cyclical upswing in prices and it has itself been succeeded, up to the time of writing, by further inflation, not yet over. The second is that it was a far from homogeneous period, during which the rates and circumstances of inflation underwent important changes. Let us look briefly at each of these things.

In the United Kingdom, both the consumer price index and the

GDP deflator show, as this is written, strong promise of celebrating in 1984 their fiftieth successive annual increases. In the United States, the price increase is not quite continuous, but it has been broken since 1934 only by minor decreases in 1937–9 and 1948–9 and, for the consumer price index, marginally in 1955. A review of the corresponding experience of other countries over this half century would be tedious. At least for the industrial ones, it would certainly show continuous increase with few and unimportant interruptions, if any. The United Kingdom can look back on fifty years of continuous inflation in the course of which the price level has risen more than twenty-fold, an average rate of 6¼ per cent (not much below the figure for the war period, 1939–48, alone); in the United States, the only slightly less continuous rise of the half-century has brought a more than eight-fold price increase; an annual average of some 4¼ per cent.

This near continuity of year-to-year average price increase over long periods deserves to be stressed; it contrasts markedly with the experience of any earlier time. The available indicators of consumers' prices and the GDP deflator suggest that, in the United States from 1820, and the United Kingdom as far back as the thirteenth century, runs of more than half a dozen consecutive annual changes in the same direction have been very rare until relatively recently. The United States GDP deflator showed eight successive falls from 1872–9 and nine successive rises from 1912–20; then another nine rises 1940–8, followed by 34 (to the time of writing) starting in 1950. The United Kingdom's GDP deflator, from 1868, did not show runs of more than six years in either direction until the succession of eleven rises from 1910–20. This was prevented only by a less than ½ per cent fall in 1909 from being a run of seventeen; though even that would have been unimpressive in comparison with the still unbroken succession of increases which began in 1935.

Quite apart from the recent prevalence of near continuous inflation, the courses of the available (and, indeed, the appropriate) indicators of general price levels have, over the generations and centuries, certainly come to show less and less irregular year-to-year movement. Before the mid-eighteenth century, the predominant weights in such indicators belonged to the prices of agricultural products, which varied more or less randomly with local (not even world) variations of climate, in addition to the usual manmade disturbances. The development of trade cycles may have served to reduce the irregularity, if not the amplitude, of variations, and it was, of course, accompanied by growth of international trade which spread the risk of natural supply changes. But the growing weight in output and consumption of manufactures and services has certainly been the main factor in smoothing general price indices; one has only to compare the indices for manufactures with those for primary products to appreciate this. The sudden arrival on the scene of nearly uninterrupted inflation is attributable to other factors besides the strength of the inflationary impulse.

If we look at the 48 countries for which *International Financial Statistics* (IFS) gives annual changes in consumers' price indices throughout our period, we find that, collectively, they have experienced increases for all but a twelfth of the time. No industrial country has had decreases of price in more than three years during the period; those countries which have had more are, naturally enough, mostly (not all) those with moderate average rates of inflation, but they are also, all of them, primary producers. At the end of the period, none of the twenty 'industrial' countries had experienced an annual fall in the index since Australia, which is classed as industrial in this context, did so marginally, in 1962. On the other hand, Saudi Arabia, Haiti and Burma had experienced falls in consumer prices as recently as 1978, as had Singapore, Nepal, India and Bangladesh in 1976. The continuity of inflation in the industrial countries is thus a new and striking phenomenon, likely to have had an important effect on attitudes and expectations, but it does not extend to at least some of the primary producers, or of the countries which, like Singapore, are closely bound up with them. The 'baskets' of goods and services which are priced to obtain the index are no doubt very different in these latter cases from the industrial countries' baskets.

Consumers' prices and prices of traded goods: whole period
This brings us to the extent to which the inflation of our period was manifested to different extents in different broad classes of goods or services, as well as in different countries. Here it will suffice for the present if we consider the 'Big Six' OECD countries, the United States, United Kingdom, Japan, Germany, France and Italy, plus India and Australia, and the world markets. Of course, goods which have nearly uniform market prices throughout the world, when those prices are measured in, say, United States dollars, will show divergences of prices measured in different national currencies in so far as the exchange rates of those currencies against the dollar diverge.

We can start from the fact that the IFS index of 'world' export prices, expressed in dollars, rose about 3.8-fold during our period. If we turn now to the unit values of imports of the sample countries, expressed in dollars, we find a range from a 2.6-fold rise for India, and a 3.2-fold rise for Japan to a 4.3-fold increase for the United Kingdom, and a 4.9-fold one for Australia, with the United States ratio (4.1) nearer to the British and Australian, the French and German nearer to the Japanese, and the Italian in the middle. These differences must be affected by the different commodity compositions of the countries' imports, but that probably does not explain all of them (Japan, for instance, is notoriously an importer of raw materials and fuels rather than manufactures, and should on that ground have experienced a large rise in import prices). For a wide variety of reasons, changes in relative prices were not perfectly reflected by alterations in exchange rates.

The discrepancies, however, are smaller than the differences in the extents to which the US dollar had changed value in relation to the respective national currencies, thus affecting the relative movements of their national currency prices of imports. The dollar had appreciated by about 70 per cent against the Indian Rupee, about a third in relation to both the British and Italian currencies; it had remained about constant in terms of the Australian, but fallen in value by 38 per cent in relation to the Japanese and 56 per cent in relation to the German. As a combined result of changes in dollar import prices and exchange rates, the local currency unit values of United Kingdom imports had risen 5.6-fold, those of Italian 4.9-fold, of Indian 4.5-fold, while those of German and Australian imports had increased less than 1.6-fold and of Japanese also less than two-fold. (The details are given in chapter 9, table 9.1 where the relation between national and international price inflation is more fully discussed.)

How do the rises in consumer prices, with which we started, compare with those in national currency prices of international goods? We can make the comparison using either the prices the respective countries paid for their imports (import unit values in national currency) or with the world price index of traded goods (exports) converted into the relevant national currency. There is not a very great deal of difference between the two. In either case, the CPI in 1979, with 1950 as base, stands higher than the prices of international goods do, in every country of this sample except the United States and India. In Japan it stands $2\frac{1}{2}$ times as high. Traded goods, in general, had risen in price markedly less than non-traded goods and services, mainly, no doubt, because productivity in the industries producing them had advanced faster than that in other industries. The case of Japan, with very rapid progress in manufacturing, and much less rapid advance in, for instance, service industries whose products enter substantially into domestic consumption, is outstanding. In the United States, the smaller absolute difference between productivity growth in traded and non-traded output provides some, though not all, of the story. The same is probably true for India.

Table 1.2 *Price indices*

		1953	1968	1979
Consumer price index (national currencies)				
US	a	111	145	302
	b		130	271
	c			209
UK	a	119	185	633
	b		156	533
	c			344
Japan	a	130	229	567
	b		175	435
	c			248
Germany	a	108	148	242
	b		137	225
	c			164
France	a	129	227	566
	b		176	439
	c			249
Italy	a	116	183	594
	b		158	511
	c			324
Australia	a	147	209	548
	b		143	373
	c			261
India	a	105	213	427
	b		202	407
	c			201
Export unit values, world index, US dollars				
Manufactures	a	118	126	364
	b		107	309
	c			290
Primary products	a	100	91	481
	b		91	481
	c			531

Note: a, 1950 = 100; b, 1953 = 100; c, 1968 = 100.

Two sub-periods
In these remarks, we have been treating our period as a whole. It is, however, plain that, with regard to inflation, it was far from uniform (see table 1.2). This is very obvious from the course of the world index of dollar prices of traded goods, which, after rising by some 25 per cent in 1951, under the influence of the Korean war, followed a gently declining trend until the late 1950s or early 1960s, and was at about the same level (13 per cent above 1950) in 1968 as in 1953. Between then and 1979 it rose 3½-fold. A sharper contrast between sub-periods is seen in the course of primary product (dollar) prices, which were at

the same level in 1953 as in 1950 (they had reached their Korean war peak in 1951), fell 9 per cent by 1968 and proceeded to rise 5.3-fold by the end of our period. The contrast is sharpest of all for fuels, (largely petroleum) which rose only 6 or 7 per cent in this first sub-period, but more than ten-fold in the second. Prices of traded manufactures had never come all the way down from their Korean peak – they were 18 per cent higher in 1953 than in 1950 – and, in aggregate, they rose another 6 per cent by 1968, after which they rose 2.9-fold by 1979.

This record might seem to raise the question whether it is sensible to speak of our period, as a whole, as one of inflation; whether one should not reserve that description for post-1968. But it will be recalled that consumer price indices in the main countries rose faster than the dollar prices of traded goods, and this was so in the period up to 1968, as well as over the whole thirty years. By 1968, consumers' prices in national currency, as compared with their levels in 1950, had risen 44 per cent in the United States and a little more in Germany, but in Australia, Japan, France, and India they had more than doubled and were not far from having done so in Italy and the United Kingdom. In every country of this sample, consumers' prices had risen more than the unit value (in local currency) of either the country's imports or its exports. Indeed, the local currency prices of Japanese exports and imports, Italian exports and German imports had actually fallen. Once more, what we have up to 1968 is inflation mainly in the prices of goods and services not internationally traded.

We have just seen that, in the second sub-period, 1968–79, dollar prices of traded goods rose nearly three-fold for manufactures and more than five-fold for primary products (for these excluding petroleum the increase was still more than three-fold), and about $3\frac{1}{3}$-fold for primary products and manufactures together. With these great increases it is perhaps not surprising, though it is still noteworthy, that national currency unit values of traded goods generally rose more than consumers' prices (McCracken, OECD, 1977). The only exception in our present sample of countries is Japan, where consumers' prices again rose more than those of either imports or exports.

There seems to be a hint here that, whereas inflation in the first sub-period came mainly from within countries, in the second sub-period it was something largely imposed from outside. That, of course, could not be so for the whole world; inflation did not come from outer space. More precisely, the first impulse of higher inflation in the second sub-period came, as we have seen, from the world markets of primary products, and, in fact, some semi-manufactured products, such as non-ferrous metals. This explains why the import prices of the industrial countries, and the export prices of the primary producers (Australia, and in some degree India) rose more than their consumer prices. The main reason why some primary producing countries' imports also rose more is to be found in the spectacular rise of petroleum prices already referred to. (Statistics such as we have been using for our sample countries are not available over our whole period, or even over the second half of it, for a typical oil exporter.) But why did the unit values of exports from most of the manufacturing countries in this sub-period rise more than their consumer price indices, in such marked contrast to what had happened before 1968?

The main part of the answer is probably that domestic factor costs, other than those of primary products (which in any case came partly from abroad) rose less than primary product prices, and that they form higher proportions of the retail costs of final consumers' goods and services than of exports from these countries. A further part of the answer may be that, from some time in the second sub-period, labour-productivity in manufacturing began in several industrial countries to grow less rapidly than before in relation to its rate of growth in the service industries which enter more heavily into provision of consumers' goods and services than of exports. In any case, the growth of export prices does not exceed that of the consumers' price index by a very large margin in most industrial countries – it is the rise of import prices that shows the bigger excess.

Finally, in this connection, it should be emphasised that though the rise in consumers' prices in the second sub-period was smaller, in general, than that in prices of internationally traded goods, it was, absolutely, large. In all our sample countries except India it was larger than that in the first sub-period; in the United States it was twice, and in the United Kingdom and Italy nearly three times as large. The first sub-period amply justifies its claim to be considered one of major inflation in terms of consumers' goods and services; the second was in these terms a time of still greater inflation, though the contrast between the two was very much less sharp than that concerning wholesale prices of traded goods.

THE HIGH INFLATION COUNTRIES

Leaving this introductory survey of inflation in the great majority of countries, in which prices rose between two- and seven-fold during our period, let us glance briefly at those in which it was far more severe. They are a mixed bag, with a number of different circumstances which seem likely, on the face of it, to have been responsible for their inflationary record. The most obvious special cause is war, and its aftermath of dislocation and reconversion. South Korea showed something like a fifty-fold increase in prices between 1948 and 1953, followed by a ten- or eleven-fold one in the following fifteen years, after which she settled down to a 4.5-fold increase during 1968–79 – still high, but not so very much higher than the increases in a good many other countries at that time. Israel, with a continuously high (at times very high) military expenditure, recurrent conflicts, and an open economy with a precarious external balance, showed a high inflation rate, going with a four-fifths reduction in the dollar value of the currency, in the early 1950s, and an accelerating inflation from the early 1970s which produced a fifteen-fold price increase in our second sub-period. The South Viet Nam index of consumers' prices rose more than twenty-fold between 1961 and July, 1974. These inflations were presumably connected with the relevant governments' (and in some instances allied forces') urgent needs to acquire domestic resources by expenditure not wholly matched by internal revenue, coupled in varying degrees with the effect of war or postwar dislocation in reducing the domestic resources available.

It is, however, notable that a large proportion of the cases of very high inflation are Latin American – Argentina, Brazil, Chile, Bolivia, Uruguay, with increases ranging from several hundred to many thousand-fold – though Venezuela showed one of the two or three lowest inflations among all the market economies of the world in our period, and most of the smaller Caribbean countries fell well below the world average. The high inflation in some of the larger and more developed South American countries is of special interest in that it was the subject of a diagnosis (by the Economic Commission for Latin America, Seers (1962), and others) under the name of 'structuralism'. The diagnosis takes various forms, but the feature common to all of them is that inflexibility of the structure of the economy, in some respect, presents it with a choice between substantial inflation and unacceptable sacrifice of real income and growth, especially where the population is increasing rapidly. Stated as generally as this, it is applicable to inflation in a large variety of economies; it is, moreover, not very obviously and specially applicable to some of the more severe Latin American cases of inflation, including Brazil, to which we give further attention in future chapters. Argentina, however, is one where this cap seems to fit. (See Maynard and van Ryckeghem (1976), chapter 9). In the briefest possible terms, her exports were, and still are, largely grain and meat, which are also (meat especially) her most prominent wage goods. There was a determined policy of industrialising, under the shelter of high protection. Whenever negative external balances occurred, and the external value of the currency fell, the consequent diversion of home and foreign demand towards foodstuffs was not able sufficiently to increase the supply of them. More could not be exported without creating scarcity at home, to which prices are sensitive. A rise in domestic food prices provoked wage demands and created political unrest. Domestic manufacturing did not benefit from devaluation, because it had not yet become able to compete substantially abroad, and the extra protection provided for it at home tended to be offset by the diversion of consumers' expenditure to food. Alternatively, if wage-claims succeeded in maintaining home spending power, costs were raised and the effects of devaluation cancelled.

The removal of a deficit in a country's current external balance always requires, of course, that it should wipe out the excess of its absorption of goods and services over its production of them by reducing the one and/or increasing the other. If circumstances throw nearly the whole weight of adjustment not only on reduction of absorption, but on the particular reductions that hurt most, socially and politically, then effective removal is apt to be avoided, so that the currency depreciates and domestic prices rise more or less indefinitely.

There are, as we have noted, many variants on this mechanism, right down to the simplest of all (to which we have referred in connection with countries at war) where the 'rigidity' in the situation is the inability of the government to collect enough tax revenue, so that it meets what it sees as the compelling needs for expenditure by, in effect, printing money. There has been much of this in Latin America – and in other areas too.

THE ZERO INFLATION COUNTRIES

As we remarked at the beginning of this chapter, no market economy has avoided very substantial inflation in our period. Indeed, some economies which are normally thought of as 'planned' have not avoided it either; Yugoslavia's consumer price index rose more than fifteen-fold between 1951 and 1979. But the increases reported from the USSR, Bulgaria, Czechoslovakia, Romania and East Germany have been nil, negligible, or even negative.

In centrally planned economies (the adverb is important) such as those just mentioned, prices of finished consumers' goods are, of course, administratively fixed at a figure representing estimated cost of production plus a surplus or profit and a turnover tax which between them provide, substantially, for every form of expenditure except private consumption and imported materials – that is, for public consumption and all investment. The distinction between turnover tax and surplus is for this purpose unimportant; the surplus (or some of it) may be at the disposal of enterprises for investment, as opposed to the state, but that is a secondary matter. The distribution or relative incidence of tax *plus* surplus between different goods is rather more to the point. It is presumably designed so that each separate market will clear, as nearly as possible. Failure to achieve this ideal will mean that some consumable goods accumulate unsold, while others are sold out before replacements arrive, and some intending buyers are always frustrated. If prices were freed to move under market forces (as many have been, to varying extents, in the later part of our period, in Bulgaria, Hungary, Czechoslovakia, East Germany and Yugoslavia), some will rise, some will fall. If official prices are rigid, the same will happen in any unofficial markets that exist. The main point is that, so long as aggregate disposable household incomes do not exceed the aggregate value, at official prices, of consumable output, the general level of prices of consumer goods will not be under pressure to increase.

Even under central planning, there are, however, pressures tending to make disposable incomes exceed the planned value of output. One is the natural tendency towards optimism about the growth of output; the more serious if (as seems to have happened in a number of countries during our period) the incremental capital–output ratios actually realised turned out to be larger than anticipated, as possibilities of recruiting and redeploying labour reached their limits. Another is the pressure for higher wages and the (sometimes excessive) hope that they will act as incentives to higher output and as general lubricants of the system. The serious inflation in Yugoslavia dates mainly from 1963, when enterprises gained free wage determination. In any case, there is probably a tendency for planners to think moderate scarcity of goods less damaging than equivalent scarcity of demand for them; so long as the main physical and conventional necessities of life are not scarce, or are thought to be fairly rationed, this view may well be justified.

Yet the dam of official price control seems generally to have held. Moreover, Portes (1977) quotes the ratios of free market prices (which exist for limited classes of goods in most of the relevant countries) to official prices as evidence that repressed inflation has usually been moderate, and has not increased over our period, at least in the USSR or Hungary. In Poland, the gap has increased; between 1955 and 1975, official prices rose by a quarter, free market prices by three times as much. In Yugoslavia, as we have noted, the dam was not maintained. In China there seem to have been price rises of about 20 per cent in the early 1950s and the early 1960s, and retail price inflation varying between 2 and 6 per cent a year began again from

1978 (see Balassa (1982), Peebles (1984)). It is the combination of liberalisation with the avoidance of inflation that seems generally to have been difficult, though by no means uniformly unsuccessful.

THE GENERAL SETTING

Finally, in this preliminary survey of our field, it may be useful to sketch the general setting of world economic development into which the inflation of our period fits. Even when taken as a whole, it counts as by far the most rapid burst of economic growth in recorded history. According to Angus Maddison (1977, 1980), the aggregate real gross national product of sixteen principal OECD countries[1] grew over the three decades at an average rate of about 4.3 per cent a year, which may be compared with 2.6 per cent in the previous longish period of relatively undisturbed growth, 1879–1913, and only 1.9 per cent in the intervening period, 1913–50, which, of course, encompasses two world wars and the great depression of the 1930s. The two decades 1950–70 show an average growth rate of 4.9 per cent, not far short of twice the 1870–1913 rate. The brilliance was somewhat clouded after 1970; nevertheless, the average annual growth 1970–9 was still 3.2 per cent and, even if one measures from the peak year 1973, still 2.4 per cent.

Moreover, the prosperity that this implies was remarkably uninterrupted, in contrast with previous times. Maddison shows that there were only half a dozen years between 1871 and 1913 when output of at least one of the countries in question did not fall absolutely and only three years between 1913 and 1950 when no fall was registered; but only seven between 1951 and 1973 (inclusive) when *any* of the countries showed a fall. Half of them, including France, Italy and Japan, showed no year-to-year fall, according to his data, in that period of almost a generation.

The sixteen OECD countries referred to are, of course, among the more advanced market economies. For the less developed, statistics are often not available for our whole period but the United Nations Organisation (1969–70), in its assessment of progress during the 'Development Decade' of the 1960s, estimated the median annual rate of growth over the period 1960–8 as 4.6 per cent for developing (that is, less developed) countries, against 5.1 per cent for the rest of the world (the more developed). It is true that the dispersion of growth rates was greater among the countries of the former group (lower quartile rate 2.7 per cent, as compared with 4.0 per cent in the latter

[1] Australia, Austria, Belgium, Canada, Denmark, Finland, France, Germany, Italy, Japan, Netherlands, Norway, Sweden, Switzerland, United Kingdom and United States.

group), so that high rates were far from universal, but the general record, on a world scale, is impressive. A useful compilation of *per capita* real annual growth rates for 123 countries during the years 1960–73, by R. J. Tyrrell (1976), shows a median value of 2.9 per cent, with upper quartile 3.6 per cent and lower quartile 1.9 per cent. For comparison, the *best* performances on record among the advanced countries over the 43 years 1870–1913 (United States, Canada, Sweden, Denmark, Austria) seem to have been annual rates of a little over 2 per cent. The median rate then among Maddison's sixteen countries was about 1.4 per cent. The rate in, at all events, the central part of our period thus seems to have been roughly twice that of what, before it, had often been thought of as the golden age of modern growth. Sir Arthur Lewis (1978) has characterised our period as that in which the tropical countries, in particular, emerged from what he calls 'The Greatest Depression'; the forty years from 1913. Speaking very generally, the same might be said of the world as a whole, except that, for it, the surge of growth into which it emerged was far greater than anything experienced before.

How does our period stand in relation to the fluctuations that some observers have discerned in world growth and prosperity? The shortest of these, the roughly four-year Kitchin fluctuation is, as we shall see, fairly prominent in most of the countries that we shall examine in detail for most of the period, though not well synchronised between them. It is too short to concern us at the moment. The Juglar cycle, something like twice as long, was the classic trade cycle of most discussion before the second world war, against the immediate background of cyclic peaks in 1929 and 1937; though on later consideration it appeared to be, over the longer run, less well marked in the United States than in the United Kingdom. For the sixteen-country OECD group as a whole, it is less clear than for most of its members separately; in any case it is hard to detect any sign of it for them collectively in our period unless, extending that period, we deem it to have re-emerged in the two growth troughs of 1975 and 1982. The most prominent longer fluctuation in the United States seemed to have been one of about twenty years' period, sometimes described as the Kuznets cycle, which had brought alternate decades of high and low prosperity; the 1870s, 1890s and 1930s low (the first world war having smudged the record in the second decade of this century), the 1880s, 1900s and the 1920s high. For a whole group of advanced countries, such as the OECD sixteen (and presumably for the whole world), this alternation is less clear, because United States prosperity went to some extent with immigration from Europe which reduced growth there; but traces of it can, nevertheless, be made out. The

1920s and 1930s, at least, fit the pattern. On this reckoning, the 1940s should have been a decade of high growth, at least in the United States, and the second world war may reasonably be supposed to have postponed much development which, in its absence, might have happened then, besides creating, especially in Europe and Japan, a great need for making good war damage and wartime neglect of non-military needs and opportunities. Twenty years, or even more, of high activity and growth fit, *prima facie*, well enough into a Kuznets pattern thus modified. Only, it is so different from what happened after the first world war.

There is, however, a longer cycle still which has received some serious attention, the Kondratiev cycle, about half a century long. This, at least as originally described, is a cycle not of real growth or output, but of prices -- in the first place of commodity prices, on a world scale. This is, on the face of it, nearer to the purpose of a study of inflation. The shorter cycles to which we have referred have been discussed mainly in connection with growth or the level of real output, though they have been presumed to take the general price level in some degree with them. (This is not a perfectly straightforward matter, as we shall see later. Friedman and Schwartz (1982), in their study of monetary trends in the United States and the United Kingdom, observed, apparently with some surprise, that the correlation between changes in output and in prices is generally negative, even when the shorter cycles are smoothed out. But, in any cyclical pattern, a delayed or lagged relation between one variable and another can make all the difference to the sign of their relationship. We return to this later on.) With the Kondratiev cycle, however, it was real income and growth that arose as secondary matters.

At first sight some degree of long-term fluctuation in world prices appears plain. Both British and American wholesale prices trended downwards from 1815 to the 1840s, then up to the 1870s (ignoring the American Civil War peak in 1865), then down to the 1890s and up to 1920. After that, it is still possible to maintain that the *trend* was downwards from 1920 to the second world war: the price peaks of 1920, 1929 and 1937 form a descending series, even though the lowest point was reached about 1933. One can imagine (if one enjoys such flights of fancy) that in the absence of Adolf Hitler the 1938 downturn might have led to a lower (trend) turning point in the early 1940s, followed by an upper turning point around 1970; indeed, one astute economic journalist greeted the beginning of that year as a scheduled Kondratiev peak. But the upswing of prices has now, as we have noted, lasted fifty years – twice the 'normal' length of a rising Kondratiev phase – and to blame the second world war for extending the scheduled upward phase, at both ends, by such a large total amount, when the first world war has been fitted into the scheme without such allowances, seems arbitrary, especially as what in fact happened around 1970 was an actual and major acceleration of inflation.

Some date around 1970 can, however, be claimed as a turning point of another kind; the end of the continuous postwar period of high prosperity. This raises the question whether the Kondratiev fluctuations apply (as is often claimed) to prosperity or growth, as well as to prices.

If one uses Maddison's figures for the average real GDP growth rates in sixteen OECD countries, one does, indeed, find some connection of the ascending Kondratiev phases with faster growth and of the descending phases with slower growth. From 1875 to 1896 and from 1924 to 1937 the rate is less than $2\frac{1}{2}$ per cent; for 1897–1913 it is over 3 per cent and for 1950–70, as we have seen, nearly 5 per cent. If we allow the period from, say, 1975 to 1982 to count as an honorary part of a new descending phase, despite the continued inflation, its average growth rate of under 2 per cent fits in with the pattern, though with some exaggeration, since 1973 was a peak of activity and 1982 a trough. (1973–9, peak-to-peak, as we have noted, gives 2.4 per cent, which still fits.)

All this is to be treated with caution. GDP data over such periods are far from perfect. We have, moreover, Sir Arthur Lewis's (1978) very careful study of industrial output in the Big Four industrial countries of that day, the United Kingdom, the United States, France and Germany, in which he sees no change of trend corresponding to the Kondratiev turning point of the 1890s. Nevertheless, the growth rate manifestation of the Kondratiev cycle seems to have stuck to its schedule better than the originally observed manifestation in terms of prices. There is, moreover, some evidence that unemployment rates have (inversely) kept it company. United States unemployment rates were unusually high in the 1870s and the mid 1890s and much lower in the following, ascending, phase to 1913. United Kingdom rates were high in the 1880s and earlier 1890s, considerably lower on average from then until the first world war. The general levels of rates in those of the OECD sixteen for which there are data, were exceptionally high for the interwar period as a whole, exceptionally low from 1950 until the 1970s and have been substantially higher since the middle of that decade. Faster growth and lower unemployment, very broadly, seem to go together and for over a hundred years to have alternated with periods of slower growth and higher unemployment in something like a fifty-year cycle. International prices, of primary products especially, have most notably failed to keep in phase with prosperity and growth by their near constancy in the 1950s and 1960s, though one might say that they made up for it in the 1970s. (Consumers' retail prices, as we have noted, behaved differently.) Consequently, another magnitude which broadly followed the Kondratiev cycle for three-quarters of a century – the price of primary products in terms of manufactures – behaved anomalously by falling in the twenty years of fastest growth and lowest unemployment ever recorded. Once again, the mid-1970s brought a sharp reversal.

PLAN OF THE BOOK

Such are the general features of the period to which this book is devoted. In it we propose to confine ourselves almost entirely to experience in a sample of thirteen countries; the United States, United Kingdom, Japan, Germany, France, Italy, Canada, Sweden, the Netherlands, Denmark, Australia, India and Brazil. The first six, the major OECD countries to which we shall refer from time to time as the 'Big Six', are an obvious choice. The next five, smaller, economies were originally selected because of the availability for them of data from an OECD study of manufacturing profits. India and Brazil are included for their intrinsic importance and as examples of quite different kinds of economy, the latter with experience of inflation outside the broad modal range within which it lies for the rest of our sample.

We do not propose to discuss the experiences of all the countries in this sample all the time. On some topics the Big Six provide us with as much as seems necessary, or as much as the energy of the authors, and perhaps that of the readers, can reasonably cope with. On others, we draw on the whole sample, sometimes with a less systematic (or, at least, different) treatment for India and Brazil necessitated by the nature of their data sources. References to countries outside the sample are incidental, except to some extent in the discussion of inflation and growth.

We begin with the income version of the Fisher identity, $MV = PQ$, in a year-to-year incremental form, that is to say, with proportional changes (measured, actually, as changes of logarithms) of the stock of money, its average velocity of circulation, the price level and real income or output. Since the convenient indicator of the last named is the real gross domestic product, the price data with which we work are not indices of consumers' prices, which we have used in this preliminary survey, but gross (market price) domestic product deflators. These differ from consumers' price indices in two respects;

they are broader, covering goods and services which fall under the headings of capital formation, public consumption and exports, as well as private consumption and they exclude the *direct* effects of changes in prices of imports (in contrast with indirect effects, through percentage mark-up of import elements in cost, or higher wage settlements induced by raised import prices). For most of the time, the differences between movements of GDP deflators and those of consumers' price indices are not very great; but they become important on occasion when the terms of trade change suddenly. Chart 1.1. shows the two series for the United States (a relatively closed economy) and for the United Kingdom, where, since its economy is rather more open than the average for our sample, the difference is also probably rather greater than in the average case.

Having the year-to-year changes in the four Fisher variables before us, we proceed to note the similarities and differences which each one of them displays between different countries and then the more obvious relations between the different variables in each country.

We proceed in finer detail to the relation (for each sample country separately) between two of these variables, changes in output and in price, supplemented by that between price change and the departure of output from its long-term trend. We consider both the cyclical and non-cyclical movements that appear, seeking to interpret them in terms of shifts in aggregate supply and demand curves.

Next we turn to a diagnosis of different kinds of inflationary and disinflationary impulse in our sample countries; monetary impulses where growth of the money stock accelerates or decelerates ahead of expenditure, expenditure impulses where that variable accelerates or decelerates apparently ahead of costs, wage-push (and the negative equivalent) where wage inflation accelerates or decelerates to the detriment (or advantage) of the profit share, and import price-push (and its negative version), where the rate of inflation of import prices changes enough to make an appreciable impact on the economy. Each of these four kinds of impulse is then explored more thoroughly in the following chapters; one concerned with the sources and effects of changes (especially those diagnosed as providing 'impulses') in money supply, one on monetary and other sources of the crucial changes in growth of expenditure, one on labour markets and the impulses they provided and one on the behaviour of the world markets for internationally traded goods, especially primary products. A short separate treatment is also given of the evidence relating to expectations of inflation in some of the principal countries. Finally, in this main section of our study, we examine the formation of prices within each of the Big Six and discuss some aspects of the process in

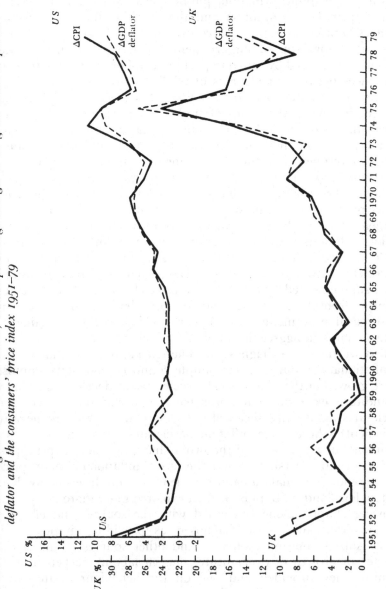

Chart 1.1 *United Kingdom and United States; annual percentage changes in the gross domestic product deflator and the consumers' price index 1951–79*

Source: *International Financial Statistics, Annual Supplement, various years*

the smaller OECD countries of our sample. Having thus completed what we have to say about the causes and processes of inflation, we turn to its effects on the working of the economy, limited for our purposes mainly to those, so far as we are able to discern them, on inequality of income distribution, level of income in relation to trend, and rates of economic growth. We then briefly survey events in the depression or recession which followed the end of our 'official' period in 1979, and we endeavour to draw our main conclusions together.

2

MONEY, VELOCITY, PRICE AND OUTPUT

We begin with an application to our sample countries of the Fisher Identity of Exchange (Fisher, 1911). In its original form, this merely states, in effect, that the value of goods and services exchanged against money in any period must be equal to the value of the money given in exchange for them and that each side of the identity can be regarded as the product of two factors; on the money side the number of units of money in existence and the average number of times each unit changes hands; on the side of goods and services, the number of unit transactions performed with these (handings-over of a physical unit of goods and services) and the average price of a unit. The price in question is, of course, an index number, which can be interpreted as the price of a 'parcel' of goods and services, so composed as to be representative of the totality of such things changing hands against money. The number, or physical volume, of transactions can similarly be interpreted as the number of such representative parcels contained in the totality of goods and services exchanged.

This original, Fisher, form of the identity thus relates to the total transactions of all kinds, involving money, in the economy and the period under discussion. It includes not only the income payments to owners of factors of production for their contribution to total output and the payments made in purchasing the final goods and services produced, but also payments made when intermediate products pass from one stage of production to another, or when the finished products pass from one stage to another of distribution. It also includes, in principle, all the transactions not immediately connected with the production and distribution of the national product, involving existing assets, both real and financial.

Annual estimates (or, in most countries, any estimates) of the total value of transactions are lacking. Where estimates have been made (for the United Kingdom and the United States) it appears, moreover, that the transactions in financial assets are so large in total as to swamp all the others, while their relevance to the total demand for money is much smaller than their size would suggest. The transactions aggregates of which reliable annual estimates are available are, of course, the usual social accounting aggregates, national or domestic income or expenditure, and they relate more or less directly to both the concepts of total physical output and the price levels which are of greatest interest in themselves. In practice, therefore, the Identity of Exchange is usually recast into an 'income' rather than a 'transactions' form, in which either the national or the domestic product (in current values) is taken to stand for the total of transactions, or of the transactions in which we are interested for our present purpose. This means that, so far as intermediate and financial transactions vary differently from income transactions, there will be disturbances to the income velocity of circulation of money as deduced from the Identity by dividing the money stock into the nominal GDP (for instance). Vertical integration of industry, by reducing intermediate transactions in relation to income, might be expected to produce an apparent increase in income velocity (less money required to finance a given nominal income); increasing sub-division of operations between different firms as products become more complex might be supposed to have the opposite effect. These changes are likely to be gradual; over a long period they could have considerable effects, though it is not easy to say, *a priori*, in which direction the net movement is likely to be at any given time. Increases and decreases in the amount of money used in the financial circulation, in proportion to that in the income circulation, might be expected to be variable in a shorter run but, as we have hinted above, the balances involved may be relatively small. Over the years 1927–9, for instance, when increased demand for money in the financial circulation in the United States might have been expected to reduce the ratio of nominal income to total money stock, that ratio (the simply measured income velocity of circulation) in fact rose to a peak. Income velocity, as we shall see, is variable in the short run, but varying *transactions* demands not closely related to nominal income do not seem to be the major creators of the variability. Changes in desire to *hold* money for precautionary or speculative purposes, plus simple inertia (delay in adjusting money supply to changing transactions demand) may be more important.

We propose, then, to start from the income form of the Identity:

$$MV = PQ$$

(using Q to stand for real income, since Fisher's T signified total transactions, and we shall find it convenient to use Y for *nominal* income, equal by definition both to MV and to PQ). We are, however, concerned with year-to-year changes, preferably proportionate changes. It will therefore be convenient to use the differential logarithmic form of the Identity:

$$\Delta\log M + \Delta\log V = \Delta\log P + \Delta\log Q = \Delta\log Y,$$

which we can write more briefly:

$$m + v = p + q = y.$$

(This convention will be used henceforward.)

The income aggregate (Y) with which we propose to work is, where available, the gross domestic product at market prices. The price index that naturally goes with this is the implicit deflator derivable from the GDP at current prices and at the prices ruling in the base year. As we have noted in Chapter 1, this differs from an index of the prices of final goods and services available in the country, in that it takes no *direct* account of changes in the prices of imports; if a rise in prices of imported materials is simply added on to prices of domestic products incorporating them, there is no change in the deflator. A difference appears only if, for instance, domestic wages are increased or profits augmented by a percentage mark-up on costs of the imported materials. The implicit GDP deflator is thus essentially an index of domestic factor costs, taking account of changes in productivity, plus effects of changes in net indirect taxation.

The choice of a statistic representing total money stock is more difficult. We shall return to the problem in a later chapter. Ideally, several different monetary aggregates might be considered, but for practical reasons of simplicity and availability the choice is reduced to two; the 'broad money' and 'narrow money' aggregates compiled by the Bureau of Statistics of the International Monetary Fund and published in *International Financial Statistics*. The 'narrow money' aggregate, commonly referred to as M1, consists of currency in the hands of the public (outside the banks) together with private sector demand deposits. The 'broad money' aggregate (M2) includes also the time, savings and foreign currency deposits of residents in the country. In what follows, we take account of both these aggregates but with the greater emphasis on the broader one.

Charts 2.1.1–2.1.13 show the courses of year-to-year change in the five variables of the Identity for each of our 13 sample countries, from 1951 (where possible) to 1979. The change dated 1951, for instance, is that between the years 1950 and 1951 and the vertical axes are calibrated in differences of natural logarithms × 100, which for small changes are close to percentages. We shall use this convention throughout in referring to changes between one year and the next.

The figures raise two groups of questions. The first concerns international similarities and differences relating to each of the five series. The second is about the interrelations of the five series within each sample country. We start by looking at the similarities and differences between the thirteen series of price changes.

PRICES

It is perhaps not surprising that the international similarities between price changes are greater than those between output changes, or those in any other of our five variables, even though one might expect this to be truer of (for instance) consumer goods prices than of the GDP deflators which we are using. Apart from shifts in exchange rates, the existence of world markets should do something to bring such a result about. Over the period as a whole (1953–79 for this purpose), eight countries, the United States, United Kingdom, Germany, France, Italy, Sweden, Canada and Denmark, constitute a 'club' in which every country's price changes are correlated at the 1 per cent level of significance with those of every other. The Netherlands very nearly qualifies; Australia fails only by virtue of inadequate correlation with Germany and Denmark (and the Netherlands). Of the outsiders, India and Brazil show correlations at this level with no country: Japan shows them only with Canada and Australia, countries with which her trading relations are no more than moderately close.

It must, however, be remembered that the correlation significant at 1 per cent level here leaves more than three-quarters of one country's variance 'unexplained' by its relation with another. There is a smaller inner group, the United States, United Kingdom, Italy, Canada (and, very nearly, Sweden and Denmark) for which $r^2 = 0.64$ or more (where r^2 is the squared correlation coefficient, which equals the proportion of the variance 'explained' by the correlation). The highest single correlation ($r^2 = 0.82$) is, reassuringly, that between Canada and the United States.

A different story begins to emerge, however, if one looks at the first part of the period, 1953–67, in which exchange rates were mostly constant and inflation rates mostly relatively low (mean for the median country 3.5 per cent). For those fifteen years, correlations significant at the 1 per cent level between one country's price changes and another's are hard to find; of the 78 country pairs in our sample, only four achieve it, Germany–Sweden, Canada–India, Brazil–Italy and Brazil–Denmark. Only the first of these pairs has any obvious trade affinity. A further ten reach the 5 per cent level of significance but in two of these (Australia's correlations with Germany and Denmark) the coefficient is negative.

Chart 2.1 *First differences of the logarithms of money stock, velocity, prices and output, 1951–79*

Chart 2.1.1 *United States*   Chart 2.1.2 *United Kingdom*

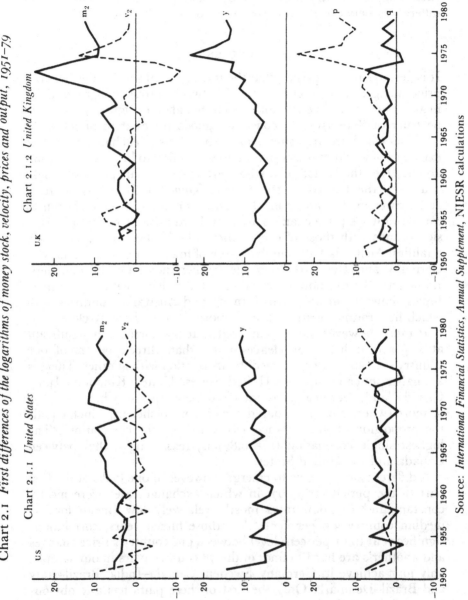

Source: *International Financial Statistics, Annual Supplement,* NIESR calculations

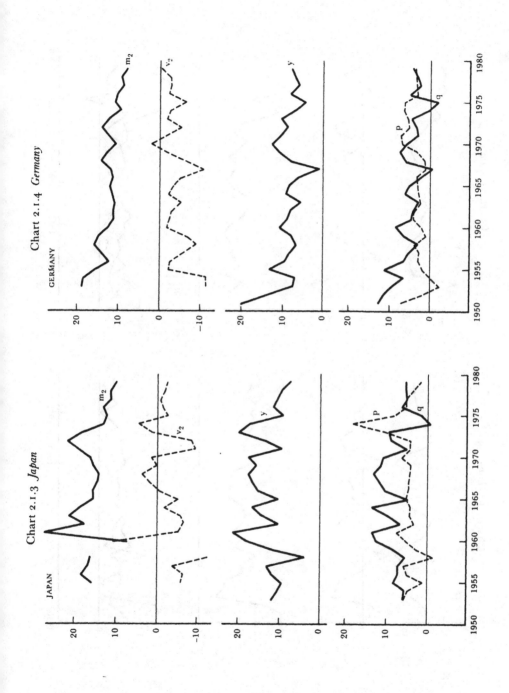

Chart 2.1.3 *Japan*

Chart 2.1.4 *Germany*

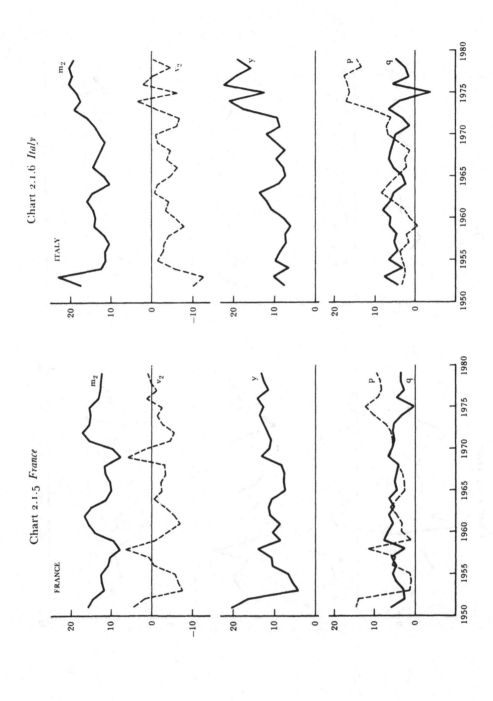

Chart 2.1.5 *France*

Chart 2.1.6 *Italy*

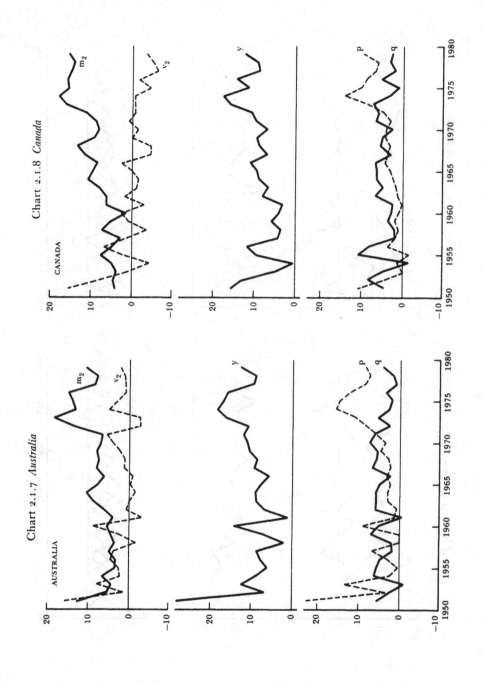

Chart 2.1.7 *Australia* Chart 2.1.8 *Canada*

Chart 2.1.9 *Denmark*

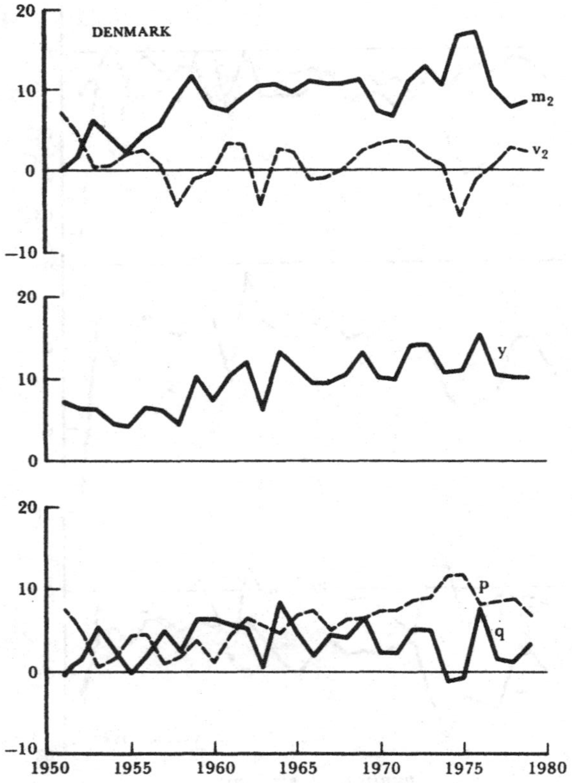

Chart 2.1.10 *The Netherlands*

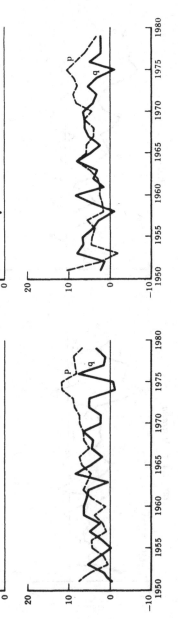

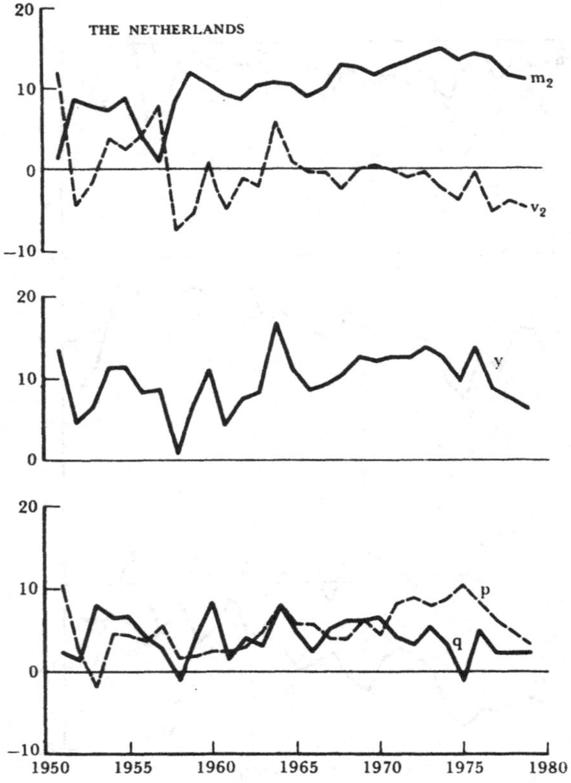

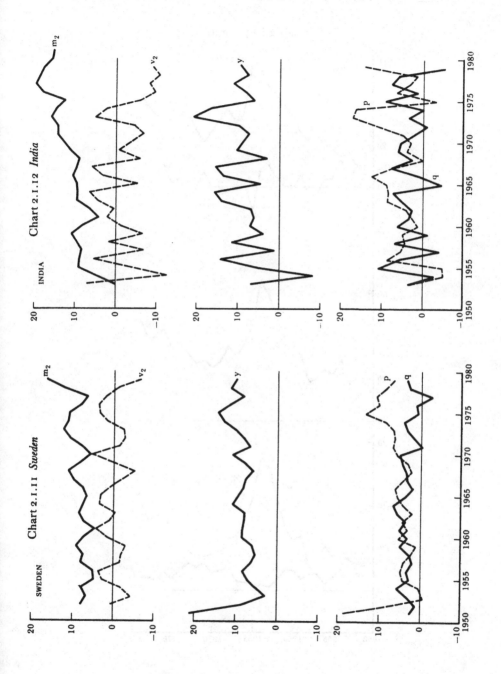

Chart 2.1.11 *Sweden*

Chart 2.1.12 *India*

SWEDEN

INDIA

Chart 2.1.13 *Brazil*

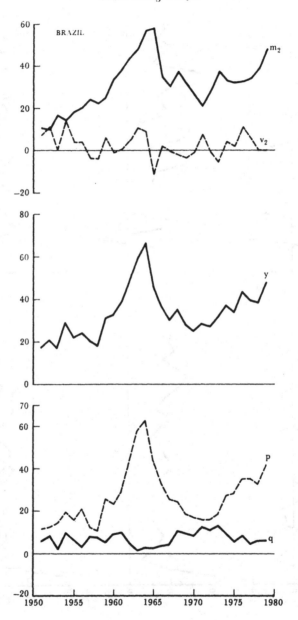

The remainder of the period, 1968–79, in which inflation rates were higher (mean for the median country about 7½ per cent) has more similarities to offer. There is a '1 per cent significance club' consisting of United States, United Kingdom, France and Italy, with Canada, Australia, Sweden and Denmark nearly qualifying for membership. Germany, correlated with nobody at 1 per cent level, and only with the Netherlands at 5 per cent level, is the most complete outsider, except for India, with no correlations significant at 5 per cent or better. Japan shows correlations at the 1 per cent level with Australia and Canada. The highest single correlation ($r^2 = 0.84$) is between the United Kingdom and France.

So far as GDP deflators are concerned, therefore, it seems that international links emerge more clearly, exchange variations notwithstanding, in the stormy period when the world price level made dramatic movements. What the United States, United Kingdom, France, Italy, Canada and Australia have in common in the later, more disturbed period are the high peak of 1974 or 1975, lower peaks around 1970, and fresh accelerations of inflation in 1979, making an upward trend over the period as a whole. Japan, Sweden, Denmark and the Netherlands share the 1974 or 1975 peak, but not the generally upward trend. Germany's chief peculiarity is in having her main peak of inflation in 1970–1. In the earlier Bretton Woods period, there was very little significant correlation at all between the relatively mild national price evolutions.

REAL INCOME GROWTH

The similarities between national patterns of real income growth are much smaller than those between inflation patterns. For the period 1953–79 as a whole, only three countries, Germany, Italy and France, show correlation with each other significant at the 1 per cent level, though correlations at this level prevail between fourteen out of our 78 country pairs. France shows the greatest number of links at this level (six); Sweden, Brazil and India show none; the United States only one (with Canada). The highest correlation is that between Germany and the Netherlands ($r^2 = 0.496$).

Once more, the first sub-period, 1953–67, yields very few significant similarities; two (United States–Canada, United Kingdom–Netherlands) at the 1 per cent level, three (United Kingdom–Sweden, Germany–Netherlands, France–Australia) at 5 per cent, plus two *negative* correlations at 5 per cent level, Brazil with the United States and Canada.

The sub-period 1968–79, however, again does better. There is an inner group consisting of the original EEC members of our sample, France, Germany, Italy and the Netherlands all showing mutual similarities significant at the 1 per cent level, and Japan, Australia and Denmark are not far from qualifying to join them. The United States shows no link at the 1 per cent level with any member of the sample, but links at the 5 per cent level with the United Kingdom and Denmark. Only India and Sweden show no correlation at the 5 per cent level or above with anyone. Brazil provides the highest single coefficient of the table (with Canada; $r^2 = 0.84$), besides links at the 5 per cent level with France, Australia and the Netherlands.

In this later sub-period, the main features of what one might call the Old EEC pattern are the sharp minimum of growth in 1975 and the generally downward trend of growth rate. The United States and United Kingdom show minima a year earlier and there is an absence of downward trend in the former country. Sweden's minimum falls in 1977, India's in 1978, with little obvious trend, there being a good recovery in 1979. The extent to which something like general variations of growth are displayed is, however, in marked contrast with the earlier sub-period.

NOMINAL INCOME GROWTH

Over the whole period, the United States, United Kingdom, Canada and Italy form a club with mutual correlations at 1 per cent level, France, Australia and Denmark almost qualifying. Germany, Japan and Brazil on the other hand, show no correlations significant at this level and India achieves one only with Canada. When the division into our two sub-periods is made, however, the connections within them become much rarer. From 1953 to 1967 there are only five correlations significant at the 1 per cent level out of the 78 possibilities; from 1968 to 1979 only two. The result for the former period is hardly unexpected in view of the poor correlations achieved with each of the two factors, price change and output change, of which changes in nominal income are composed. That for the period after 1967, however, is poorer than might have been looked for on these grounds. It is no doubt connected with the fact, to which we come presently, that quantity and price changes tend to be negatively correlated.

GROWTH OF MONEY STOCK

When we come to changes in money stock (starting with 'broad money'), the contrast over the whole period[1] between the members of

---

[1] Since the data for Japan start only in 1955, the 'whole period' in this case is taken as 1955–79.

the club and the outsiders becomes particularly clear. The German series is negatively correlated with that of every other country in our sample and significantly (at 1 per cent) with an index of changes in 'world' money supply. Japan also shows negative correlations with eight other countries, though not significant ones. An important, perhaps the main, part of the reason for this result is, apparently, that the trends of rate of money growth in Germany and Japan are downward, whereas for most if not all other countries in the sample they are upward. Brazil shows no correlations significant at 1 per cent, France shows one only with Italy. The Netherlands, Sweden, the United States, the United Kingdom, Italy, Australia, Canada and India, however, form a club with all mutual correlations significant at the 1 per cent level, except for that between the two first-named.

On breaking the period up into two parts, we again see a great deterioration in the degree of international similarity. The first sub-period, 1955–67, retains some of the characteristics of the whole period. Germany again shows a significant *negative* correlation with the 'world' series and with every sample country except, in this case, India. Only the United States, Australia, Canada and Brazil show correlations significant at 1 per cent with 'the world' (Denmark shows one significant at 5 per cent). The United Kingdom shows negative (though not significant) correlations not only with Germany and Japan, but with France and Italy, too.

Relations are weaker still in the second sub-period. No sample country shows a correlation significant at the 1 per cent level with the 'world' series; only the United Kingdom and the United States show one significant at the 5 per cent level. The negative German correlation with that series is replaced by a non-significant positive one; Denmark and the Netherlands show non-significant negative coefficients with the 'world' series. The United States, the United Kingdom and France, however, show correlations significant at the 1 per cent level with each other.

If we use the 'narrow money' (M1) statistics instead of the 'broad' ones, we get a rather similar result for the whole period, though the number of significant connections is somewhat smaller. For 1955–67, the results are broadly similar to those with 'broad' money, though the identities of the countries showing significant positive correlations with the 'world' are not quite the same. Germany still shows a significant negative one. For 1968–79, the connections are poorer than with the 'broad' money series. Only two coefficients significant at 1 per cent appear in the table, those of France with Sweden and with the United Kingdom. Germany, however, shows a positive coefficient significant at the 5 per cent level with the 'world' series, the only other

country to do so being the United States. In general, it would appear
that similarities between national patterns of money growth do not
survive very well the weakening of trend elements which is produced
by dividing our period into two parts.

VELOCITIES

Although velocities of circulation of money (or, more exactly, changes
in them) make an impressive appearance in our diagrams, seeming to
play a systematic part not much less (to say the least) than that of
variations in money growth, there is very little relation between their
courses in different countries. Whether we use the 'broad' or 'narrow'
definition of money, we get only three connections significant at the 1
per cent level for our whole period, out of our 78 possible ones (plus
three or four more significant at 5 per cent). When the period is
broken up, the score for each separate sub-period is seen to be lower
still. Some of the correlations, however, suggest associations that are
not merely fortuitous (United States and Canada, Sweden with
Germany and Denmark at 1 per cent significance, 1955–67). The
similar correlations of the United States with France and of the
Netherlands with Canada, 1968–79, carry a little less conviction. The
results are much the same whether the broad money or narrow money
velocities are used. Clearly, the time pattern of velocity changes is in a
high degree peculiar to the circumstances of each country and the
degree in which international transmission of changes in prices or in
demand achieves international coordination of such patterns is nar-
rowly limited.

More generally, the international similarities of pattern which we
have indicated by Pearsonian correlation coefficients deserve a further
word of interpretation. Some of them make obvious economic sense;
the 'clubs' of countries with similar time patterns of inflation are
mostly economies with strong mutual trading links, subject to common variations in world (or, at least, international) prices. The same
is true, to some extent, of the 'clubs' with similar time patterns of
growth in output, nominal income and money stock. Some of the
similarities between two countries, not shared with others have,
however, less obvious economic meaning (for example, Canada–
India, Brazil–Italy). Nor can much economic meaning be attached to
the negative correlations that occur. It should be remembered that,
when one is dealing with 78 pairs of countries, there is a good chance
of finding one or two correlations significant at the 1 per cent level and
several at the 5 per cent level without any implication of a systematic
connection. But the differences in the general levels of international

interconnection displayed by our five variables, and the closer interconnections within the 'clubs' which we have distinguished, are reasonable *prima facie* evidence of economic reality. Whether one is more impressed by the apparent strength of interconnection or by its partial nature depends on one's initial expectations about world markets and the world economy.

MONEY AND NOMINAL INCOME

Let us now pass from the relation (or lack of it) between the same variables in different countries to the correlations between different variables within each country. Perhaps the most natural starting point here is the relation between money stock and nominal income (or rather, between their year-to-year rates of change). The simplest form of the Quantity Theory is that which asserts that these two variables move together. The stronger version of this would be that M and Y move proportionately, that 'Cambridge k' (the ratio of M to Y) and its inverse, V, are constant. The weaker version, more appropriate to our annual difference approach, would be that the annual first difference of k, or of V, is constant, though not necessarily zero. We can check these hypotheses directly. The standard deviation of $\Delta\log_e V2$ ranges across our sample countries from 2.4 to 6.4. That of $\Delta\log_e M2$ ranges from 2.0 to 10.7. In six countries it is the standard deviation of velocity that is the greater. Velocity change from year to year is certainly not so much less variable than money growth that we can treat it as a constant while treating money growth as a variable.

The alternative approach, of course, is to look directly at the correlations between annual changes in money aggregates and those in nominal income. Increments of both money aggregates, broad and narrow, are correlated with those of income at the 1 per cent level or better, over our period as a whole, in the United States, United Kingdom, Italy, Australia, Denmark and Brazil. In Germany, France and India the coefficients for both are well below the 5 per cent point of significance. In Japan and Sweden, the narrow money relation achieves 1 per cent significance, the broad money one falls below the 5 per cent point. In Canada the reverse is true. In the Netherlands, the broad money relation just achieves 5 per cent significance, the narrow one fails. In a word, the results are mixed. Of thirteen countries, eight achieve significance at the 5 per cent level or better using the narrow money aggregate and eight achieve it with the broad aggregate, each group including six countries which achieve it in both.

If we divide the period up, the scores drop. In 1953–73, the growths of the two money aggregates, together, achieve only twelve correlations with nominal income growth significant at 5 per cent (out of 26), and in the remaining brief period 1974–9 they achieve only five. For the six larger OECD economies (United States, United Kingdom, Japan, Germany, France, Italy) a division into the sub-periods 1953–67 and 1968–79 yields only two coefficients significant at that level in the former one and three in the latter (in each case out of twelve). These six countries, taken together, achieved seven significant coefficients out of twelve for the whole of our period. It is plain that the relation in question is a highly unstable one with regard to the period selected.

The considerable, and changing, variability of velocity is somewhat in conflict with the emphasis given to its relative constancy in Friedman and Schwartz's monumental study (Friedman and Schwartz, 1982). Two things should be said about this. The first is that Friedman and Schwartz work, not with annual data, but with 'phase averages', averages for upswings and for downswings of 'standard' business cycles. It is plain that much of our year-to-year variation is of a cyclical nature and this part of it Friedman and Schwartz mostly eliminate. The second thing to be said is that, even with cyclical variations so far eliminated, Friedman and Schwartz do not demonstrate constancy of broad money velocity (with which they work) over our period, or the major part of it which their study covers. This is particularly so with the United Kingdom. Between their Phase 26, centred in 1949, and Phase 35, centred in 1970, on the evidence of their Table 5.8, both velocity and the money stock nearly doubled; they made nearly equal contributions to the near quadrupling of money income over that hardly short period. The case is less extreme with the United States (their Table 5.7), where between Phase 40, also centred on 1949, and Phase 48, centred on 1967, velocity rose by 36 per cent while money stock more than doubled; but a 36 per cent rise is still not negligible.

Friedman and Schwartz deal with these departures from constancy of velocity mainly by introducing two dummy variables, one supposed to express high liquidity preference over a period extending from before the second world war to the mid-1950s, the other a postwar shift variable describing an upward shift of liquidity preference immediately after the end of the war, retraced gradually until the variable vanishes, also in the mid-1950s. These *descriptions* of variations in velocity acknowledge its non-constancy, even after elimination of cyclical fluctuations, in the period we are dealing with. A further criticism of these authors' treatment of the United Kingdom data is given in Brown (1983) and an econometric critique in Hendry and Ericsson (1983).

Since the relation between simultaneous changes in money stock and money income is not very close, it may be useful to see whether they are better related when a lag of one or other of them is allowed for. We confine ourselves to lags of one year in each direction. Table 2.1 shows, for the six large OECD countries, the correlation coefficients, first with money changes leading, then with no lead or lag (the figures already considered), then with income change leading. Correlations are given, first for the whole period, then for the two sub-periods 1953–67 and 1968–79, then for the sub-periods 1953–73 and 1974–9.

Over the period as a whole, somewhat better fits are obtained with $m2$ (but not $m1$) leading income in the United States, United Kingdom and, less decisively, France and (on the edge of 5 per cent significance) with both $m1$ and $m2$ doing so in Germany. Japan goes the other way so far as $m2$ is concerned; there is some indication that it lags. In the sub-period 1953–67, both monetary aggregates rise to significance in the United States, as does $m1$ in the United Kingdom, Germany and Italy, in leading income by a year, but Japan (with $m2$) again goes the other way. The later period, 1968–79, however, shows some evidence that money (both aggregates) leads in Japan, and also that $m1$ does so in France, $m2$ in Germany and Italy. If the whole period is divided at 1973/4, the first sub-period shows results not differing very much from those for 1953–67; the short remaining period gives some evidence of $m2$ lagging in the United States, but of $m2$ leading income in Japan and $m1$ possibly doing so in Germany and France.

Counting only the correlations significant at 5 per cent level, we find that, among the six big OECD countries, taking both money aggregates in each case, we have $14\frac{1}{2}$ cases of money leading income, $14\frac{1}{2}$ of simultaneity and 5 of income leading money (the halves refer to a dead heat). The cases involving $m1$ show a majority in which simultaneity rules ($10\frac{1}{2}$, against $6\frac{1}{2}$ where $m1$ leads and 1 where y does), those involving $m2$ include 8 in which that variable leads, along with four in each of the other categories. If we confine our attention to $m2$, the evidence for it leading is strongest in the United States (with a slight indication also from Germany); Japan shows a slight balance in favour of y leading, rather than the reverse, the United Kingdom and Italy favour simultaneity, though each with one significant case of $m2$ leading. France presents no significant cases. We are, however, dealing with very small numbers here and it is really safe to say only that these very simple tests of leads and lags between money growth and nominal income growth yield results which vary from country to country and according to the period or sub-period tested, with some

Table 2.1 *Correlations between changes in money stock and money income*

		United States		United Kingdom		Japan	
		m1	m2	m1	m2	m1	m2
1953–79	1	0.66	0.68*	0.73	0.73*	0.26	−0.15
	2	0.75*	−0.64	0.81*	0.59	0.51*	0.26
	3	0.51	0.42	0.74	0.51	0.34	0.46*
1953–67	1	0.52	0.53*	0.51	0.12	0.01	−0.51
	2	0.45	0.40	0.31	0.59*	0.60*	0.22
	3	0.15	0.24	−0.30	0.10	0.49	0.65*
1968–79	1	0.18	0.41	0.43	0.48	0.62*	0.71*
	2	0.72*	0.43	0.63	0.12	0.40	0.41
	3	0.17	−0.06	0.67*	0.07	0.16	0.08
1953–73	1	0.61	0.70*	0.75*	0.73	0.09	−0.36
	2	0.67*	0.61	0.71	0.78*	0.43	0.17
	3	0.34	0.27	0.50	0.69	0.35	0.51*
1974–79	1	0.10	−0.69	−0.54	0.12	0.88*	0.93*
	2	0.90*	0.08	0.16	0.56	0.88*	0.76
	3	0.63	0.84*	0.16	−0.47	0.68	0.52
		Germany		France		Italy	
		m1	m2	m1	m2	m1	m2
1953–79	1	0.41*	−0.40	0.09	0.37	0.51	0.65
	2	0.09	0.11	−0.04	0.15	0.59*	0.72*
	3	−0.03	−0.08	−0.03	0.14	0.41	0.68
1953–67	1	0.61	0.44	0.17	0.19	0.67*	0.12
	2	0.39	0.09	−0.03	−0.04	−0.56	0.39
	3	−0.06	−0.28	−0.18	−0.18	0.07	−0.11
1968–79	1	0.20	0.65*	0.64*	0.53	0.10	0.80*
	2	−0.36	0.38	0.32	0.08	0.23	0.79
	3	0	−0.03	0.45	0.34	0.06	0.67
1953–73	1	0.39	0.30	−0.02	0.23	0.47	0.18
	2	0.20	−0.07	−0.13	0.03	0.58*	0.50*
	3	0.08	−0.29	−0.12	0.02	0.23	0.03
1974–79	1	0.80	0.14	0.78	0.62	−0.13	0.38
	2	−0.48	−0.50	0.23	0.25	0.20	0.05
	3	−0.48	−0.20	−0.02	0.32	−0.09	−0.23

Note: Correlation coefficients which are both the highest in their 'triad' and significant at the 5 per cent level are marked *.
Source: IFS annual supplements, NIESR calculations.

indication that $m2$ leading y is rather more common than the reverse, or than simultaneity, whereas using $m1$ makes simultaneity appear the most common time character of the relation.

MONEY AND PRICES

An alternative simple formulation of the Quantity Theory is that quantity of money and price move together. This takes more for granted than the 'constant velocity' form, since it requires that V should change to offset any changes in Q; less probable, *a priori*, than the simple requirement that money should be held in a constant relation to nominal income. A number of systematic investigations of money–price relationships have been made (see, for example, Sims (1972), Williams *et al.* (1976), Wren-Lewis (1984)). It is, indeed, the case that, over our period as a whole, the correlations of changes in both $M1$ and $M2$ are closer with those in Y than with those in P, apart from France and India, where both coefficients are very low and Germany, where the substantial correlation of $m2$ with p is negative.

Table 2.2 sets out the correlations of p with $m1$ and $m2$ first with money leading by a year, then without lag and finally with price leading by a year. Selecting those coefficients which are both significant at the 5 per cent level and also the highest of their triad (that is, which represent the best relation between the two variables in the country concerned, given our range of lags), it emerges that, altogether, there are $11\frac{1}{2}$ cases where m leads ($6\frac{1}{2}$ with $m1$, 5 with $m2$), 5 with no lag (3 with $m1$, 2 with $m2$), and $9\frac{1}{2}$ with p leading ($3\frac{1}{2}$ with $m1$, 6 with $m2$). The honours appear, therefore, to be rather more nearly equal between relations with m leading and those with p leading than they were in the corresponding investigation for m and y. There is also some evidence that simultaneous connections are somewhat rarer than either of those with a lag. There is, on the face of it, a slight suggestion that $m1$ is the money variable more likely to show a lead, the opposite of the suggestion where y was concerned, but one should probably not rest much weight on it. The United States again emerges as the country where money is most likely to lead the other variable, but this time the strongest probability of the opposite lead is not in Japan but in the United Kingdom. The evidence about the propensities of money to lead, or to be led by the other variable concerned in separate sub-periods does not match very well between our income and price observations, except that its tendency to lead in the brief sub-period 1974–9 is visible in both. It may well be that leads and lags are different in separate brief inflationary episodes, a matter to which we shall return in later chapters.

Table 2.2 *Correlations between changes in money stock and in price*

		United States		United Kingdom		Japan	
		m1	m2	m1	m2	m1	m2
1953–79	1	0.79*	0.66*	0.63	0.71*	0.32	0.05
	2	0.58	0.52	0.70	0.48	0.22	0.09
	3	0.49	0.41	0.76*	0.44	−0.01	0.17
1953–67	1	0.47	0.16	0.15	−0.05	0.15	−0.32
	2	0.01	−0.06	−0.48	−0.32	0.54*	0.26
	3	−0.25	0.19	−0.24	−0.06	0.39	0.68*
1968–79	1	0.33	0.31	0.28	0.48	0.50	0.56
	2	−0.38	−0.07	0.52	−0.05	0.04	0.02
	3	−0.47	−0.26	0.70*	−0.06	−0.26	−0.28
1953–73	1	0.82*	0.52*	0.51	0.47	0.34	−0.10
	2	0.65	0.47	0.47	0.51	0.48*	0.26
	3	0.52	0.42	0.56*	0.72*	0.40	0.66*
1974–79	1	0.54	0.98*	−0.74	0.44	0.98*	0.98*
	2	−0.47	0.58	−0.15	−0.23	0.84	0.69
	3	−0.58	−0.92	0.48	−0.80	0.49	0.52

		Germany		France		Italy	
		m1	m2	m1	m2	m1	m2
1953–79	1	−0.17	−0.43	0.12	0.38	0.57*	0.70
	2	−0.03	−0.60*	0	0.16	0.54	0.68
	3	−0.01	−0.49	−0.08	0.05	0.46	0.79*
1953–67	1	−0.12	−0.60	0.15	0.15	0.64*	0.23
	2	−0.16	−0.77	−0.16	−0.20	0.24	−0.03
	3	−0.40	−0.71	−0.33	−0.38	−0.09	−0.37
1968–79	1	−0.18	0.13	0.70*	0.54	0.10	0.87
	2	0.10	0	0.56	0.29	0.11	0.87
	3	0.41	0.05	0.42	0.21	0.13	0.89*
1953–73	1	−0.03	−0.45	0	0.21	0.66*	0.23
	2	−0.06	−0.64	−0.19	−0.04	0.61	0.28
	3	−0.01	−0.46	−0.24	−0.15	0.66*	0.17
1974–79	1	−0.74	0.45	0.50	0.60	−0.56	−0.28
	2	0.03	0.48	0.90*	0.85*	−0.66	−0.41
	3	0.04	0.83*	−0.28	−0.10	−0.04	0.72

Note: Correlation coefficients which are both the highest in their 'triad' and significant at the 5 per cent level are marked *.

OTHER RELATIONS

What other relations between our variables are visible in the charted time series and in the correlation tables? One of the strongest and most constant is the negative correlation between m and v. For our period as a whole, this is significant for all our sample countries except Brazil (both m_1 and m_2), Australia (m_2), Italy (both) and the United States (m_1). The negative correlation is also strong in nearly all the sub-periods we have distinguished, the later ones providing the greater number of exceptions. Money growth (m_2) is, as we have seen, in every case positively correlated with y. Over the period as a whole, it may seem anomalous at first sight that v_2 also manages to be in every case positively correlated with the latter. There are, of course, limits to the extent to which both m_2 and v_2 can be positively correlated with y while remaining negatively correlated with each other. One can divide our countries into those in which m_2 is more closely correlated with y than v_2 is, and those where the reverse is true. The greater correlation with y also goes with the greater variance, so that the variable in question may be said to dominate y, or to take most of the strain of its variation. On this criterion, the United States, United Kingdom, Italy, Canada, Australia, Denmark and Brazil are 'm' countries, as opposed to the 'v' countries, Japan, Germany, France, Sweden, the Netherlands and India, where variations of v have taken most of the strain. There is some tendency for the countries of highest mean inflation to be 'm' countries; the five highest in our sample are, but the United States and Canada, which are among the least inflationary, are in this group also. It may be noted that Italy, showing high correlations of both m and v with y, reconciles these two coefficients by having a very low negative correlation between m and v.

The other noteworthy consistency is the universally negative correlation in our sample between p and q, which holds over the period as a whole and also for each sub-period we have distinguished in every country except the United States; there the coefficient is non-significantly positive for 1953–67 and virtually zero for 1953–73. This negative relationship, clearly one of the widespread facts of economic life, was the source of some speculation by Friedman and Schwartz. We shall return to it in a future chapter. The two variables concerned in this case show very different relations with their sum, y. The price variable, p, is significantly correlated, positively, with y over our period as a whole in every country except Germany (and there the coefficient is still positive). On the other hand, q shows no generally valid relation with y; the correlation is positive and significant in the

United States, Japan, Germany, Canada, Denmark and the Netherlands but elsewhere it is non-significant and mostly negative. We shall have occasion later to consider how far this irregularity of connection between real output and nominal income springs, in part at least, from the existence of cost–push factors (which may be expected to discourage output while, possibly, inflating its money value), as well as demand–pull forces, which might be expected to act in the same direction on both output and price.

It is only one step beyond this to the relation, or absence of it, between the money and real output variables. Absence of it was one of the most emphasised of Friedman and Schwartz's findings from the (de-cycled) United States and United Kingdom data and Charles Goodhart (1982) subsequently showed that, even without the removal of cyclical fluctuations, there is little trace of such a relation in those two countries. If we confine ourselves to the relation involving $M2$, what we find is far from impressive. There is a significant positive relation for the whole period only in Germany. Some significant ones for sub-periods (the United Kingdom, 1953–73, Italy, 1953–67) do not go far to redeem the situation. We shall have to consider later whether this does, indeed, mean, as Friedman and Schwartz imply, that money supply makes itself felt through price, real output being determined by quite other factors. Perhaps the monetary factors which, with others, influence real output are not to be captured simply by measuring the rate of increase of the money stock.

3

QUANTITY–PRICE RELATIONS

In the following chapter, we explore the relations in our sample countries between real output and price. First, we consider the relevant formulations of aggregate supply and demand curves, and note that, in view of the predominance over our period of trend in the presumed movement of both curves, it will be most useful to consider either first differences of quantity and price, or the first differences of the latter along with the deviations of the former from trend. Both of these courses are pursued.

We examine short-term cyclical relations, the incidence and conditions of apparent major shifts, and for some countries the relation between deviation of output from trend and the incremental ratio of price increase to output increase. Finally, we consider the relation (or lack of it) between the general variability of growth rate of output and that of price.

AGGREGATE SUPPLY AND DEMAND

Of the relations between the four series of year-to-year incremental changes, m, v, p and q, which we have been examining, the one that first invites closer inspection is that between p and q. It will be simplest to start on the more familiar ground of the relation between the integral magnitudes of price and quantity, P and Q, rather than their rates of change. The basic relationships here, on which light would be welcome, are the aggregate supply and demand relationships, and it may be useful at this point to define the terms which we shall use in connection with them.

Keynes, in the *General Theory* (p. 25) first put forward the aggregate supply function as the relation between employment and the aggregate supply price (that is, aggregate expenditure on factors of production) required to call forth that employment. It can thus be visualised (Chart 3.1(A)) as a rising curve, presumably starting from the origin, with employment in person-hours measured horizontally and expenditure on factors of production measured vertically. The

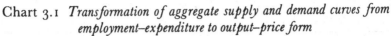

Chart 3.1 *Transformation of aggregate supply and demand curves from employment–expenditure to output–price form*

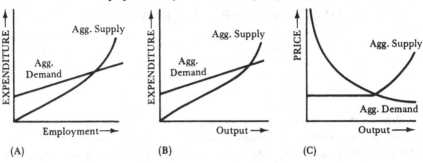

Keynesian aggregate demand function (defined in the same para-graph of the *General Theory* as the relation between employment and the aggregate proceeds expected by entrepreneurs from that employ-ment) can be visualised as a second curve in chart 3.1(A). The presumption is that it will start above the origin and have a slope shallower than that of the aggregate supply function, because saving, social security payments, income-sensitive taxation, and other in-fluences make expenditure on goods and services vary less sharply with employment than factor incomes do. Aggregate demand is therefore cut from below by aggregate supply at some level of expenditure which Keynes calls 'the effective demand'.

These relations between expenditures and employment are not, however, directly relevant to prices and quantities of output; we need to transform them into terms of those variables. If there is a short-term relation (not necessarily a proportional one) between employment and output, then we can readily transform the horizontal measurements, subject to index-number problems which we have in any case accepted by using the concept of aggregate output at all (chart 3.1(B)).

So far as the supply function is concerned, we now have aggregate supply price as a function of output. The slope of the function is marginal cost, which (with some adjustments where competition is imperfect) we can regard as equal in equilibrium to price, and can re-plot against output to get what we need – an aggregate supply curve in the same form as the familiar Marshallian curve for a single firm or industry, unit supply price against output (chart 3.1(C)). It is not unlikely that a good deal of the left-hand part of such a short-term aggregate supply curve will be horizontal, or of only slight positive slope since, where there is excess capacity, marginal costs may well be nearly constant (as well as being relatively low), especially in manufacturing and many service industries. It seems likely also that it will steepen sharply near its right-hand end, where bottlenecks in either labour, raw materials or plant-capacity become important. The degree of steepening, however, will depend on the assumptions we make about the labour market. If we take money wage rates as being constant in the short run, then the upward slope, and steepening, of the curve will be largely due to diminishing physical returns; any change in wages will then have to be treated as requiring a *shift* of the curve – a convenient approach if the labour market does not adjust promptly and regularly to the pressure of demand in the economy.

It has to be remembered that, as soon as prices of output rise, and so long as any of the products enter into wage-earners' consumption, the real wage falls. It is obvious that, if labour were the only variable factor, its real reward per person-hour, in terms of the product, would be directly related to real marginal cost by its marginal physical productivity. Thus, if this productivity fell with rising pressure on capacity, the real product wage would necessarily fall correspondingly, so long as price remained equal to marginal cost. The conclusion is reinforced if real costs of imported materials rise with cyclical expansion. In fact, we shall see later that productivity in most countries moves pro-cyclically. Leaving this and related complications aside for the moment, let us proceed with aggregate supply curves specific to a particular money-wage level, and shifting, therefore, if the money wage rate changes.

The aggregate demand function can be translated to quantity-price axes in a similar way. The only important difference in procedure concerns the step from aggregate expenditure to price as an ordinate (stage B to C in chart 3.1). Price is *average* revenue, so that for this step we simply divide aggregate expenditure by quantity of output for each point of the function in chart 3.1(B), to get the prices at which the market should clear, given the total expenditures to be expected from the aggregate factor incomes associated with the various hypothetical output levels.

For our present purpose, however, we need not be much concerned with the quantity–price aggregate demand curve. We are dealing, on the whole, with countries in which monetary and fiscal policy of governments and vicissitudes of foreign demand play an active part, and it will usually do to treat expenditure as largely given extraneously by these agencies. We can then conduct the discussion in terms of simple expenditure lines; since we are measuring quantity and price logarithmically, the line showing all the combinations of price and quantity corresponding to a particular expenditure will be a straight one sloping negatively at 45° to the axes.

Chart 3.2 *Quantity and price level in the United States, 1950–79*

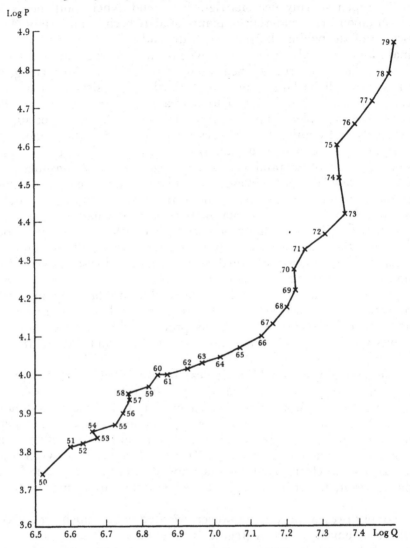

If aggregate supply curves could be relied upon to remain stationary, and if markets could be regarded as being fairly close to
equilibrium states, then movement of the expenditure line would, of
course, trace an aggregate supply curve out on a plot of price against
quantity. Similarly, if the authorities held aggregate expenditure
constant for a time, any movements of the aggregate supply curve
(because of, for example, autonomous changes in wages or import

prices) would trace out part of the relevant expenditure line. What do we see in the actual plot for one country? Chart 3.2 is such a plot for the United States.

INTEGRAL AND DIFFERENTIAL VARIABLES

This figure makes it clear that the chief thing the quantity–price (or rather, log quantity, log price) points are doing is receding from the origin at a great rate. The path they trace is not a straight one, and it presents quite an interesting view of the varying relations between output change and price change, along with the concomitant changes in total expenditure, which are measured by increases in the (either vertical or horizontal) intercepts of negatively sloping lines drawn through successive annual points at 45° to the axes. It shows the changes in the elasticity of price with respect to output, $\Delta\log P/\Delta\log Q$, which is, of course, the slope of the curve. In the 1950s this elasticity was about 0.8. From 1960 to 1966, its average value was lower, between 0.3 and 0.4; but thereafter it rose steeply – to about 1.5 between 1966 and 1973 and 3.0 between 1973 and 1979. The interesting question whether this elasticity is smaller downwards than upwards – whether a fall in expenditure is liable to involve a smaller change in price and a larger change in output than an equal rise in expenditure – cannot be answered from our data, since there were no falls in annual money expenditure in our period. It is noteworthy that, as this implies, all the years in which real output was virtually stationary or falling (1954, 1958, 1970, and the two-year period 1974–5) showed considerable rises in price – in the two last-mentioned cases, peak values.

But the strong trends both of output and of price dominate this picture. In particular, whatever the shape of the short-term supply curve, it is presumably moving bodily to the right all the time as capacity increases. We need, therefore, to give short-term changes greater prominence, and the simplest way to do this is to plot against each other the annual first differences of output and price, which we have already charted over time.

There is an alternative – namely to plot first differences of price against the movements by which output deviates from its long-term growth trend – but we will come to this later.

We have been discussing the plotted relations between integral quantities. What difference does it make if instead we discuss those between their first differences? What we should expect to see, given specified behaviour of aggregate supply functions and expenditure lines, can be worked out, but the process is a little tiresome. A short cut can save some trouble. For large parts of the time, apart from trends, the movements of both price and quantity approximate to sinusoidal fluctuations, broken by some sudden shifts. (Strictly speaking, the non-linear shape we have been led to expect for the aggregate supply curve suggests that if one of our series moved in a simple sine curve, the other would not, but for our broad purposes this probably does not matter much.) We will return to the shifts presently; at first sight it is the cyclical movements that are hard to interpret. If, however, the integral variables, with or without linear trends, described sine curves, so would their first differences, growth rate and price inflation. These would lead their integral values by a quarter of a period. A cyclical relation that appears between the first differences of quantities and prices should reflect a broadly similar relation between the integral variables a quarter-period later.

We have already noted that the equilibrium relation between output and price can be either positive or negative, according to whether the aggregate supply curve or the expenditure line is nearly stationary while its companion shifts. We have now seen that, in so far as the shifts in question are oscillatory, the same will be true of the equilibrium relation between the first differences of output and price. But what is actually observed may not be a set of equilibrium positions, since one variable or the other may take an appreciable time to reach the appropriate equilibrium value when the latter has changed. Suppose that the aggregate supply curve is stationary and the expenditure line shifts in an oscillatory fashion (it will not matter if this oscillation is superimposed on a uniform upward or downward shift). With instantaneous adjustment of price and quantity to equilibrium, our first difference data would give us a positive linear relationship between q and p, (where, it will be remembered, $q = \Delta \log Q$ and $p = \Delta \log P$) but if either of the variables took, for instance, half a period of the expenditure line's oscillation to reach its equilibrium value, the relation actually observed would be a linear *negative* one. Similarly, a quarter-period's lag by either variable would produce zero correlation, the points in the scatter diagram moving round a loop (a 'hysteresis loop') with horizontal and vertical axes of symmetry. A lag of less than a quarter-period would produce a positively inclined hysteresis loop corresponding to a positive but imperfect correlation; a lag of between a quarter- and a half-period would give a negatively inclined loop. In all the looped plots, the direction of movement round the loop would depend on the direction of the lag between the variables – clockwise if p leads q, anti-clockwise if q leads p.

If the equilibrium relation is a negative one (expenditure line

Chart 3.3 *Hypothetical lag relations between q and p*

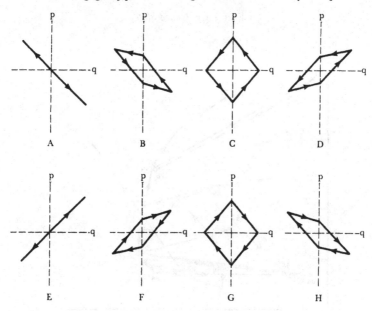

	Positive relation between q and p	*Negative relation between q and p*
A	q leads (and lags on) p by $\frac{1}{2}$ period	q moves with p
B	q leads p by more than $\frac{1}{4}$, less than $\frac{1}{2}$ period	p leads q by less than $\frac{1}{4}$ period
C	q leads p by $\frac{1}{4}$ period	p leads q by $\frac{1}{4}$ period
D	q leads p by less than $\frac{1}{4}$ period	p leads q by more than $\frac{1}{4}$, less than $\frac{1}{2}$ period
E	q moves with p	p leads (and lags on) q by $\frac{1}{2}$ period
F	p leads q by less than $\frac{1}{4}$ period	q leads p by more than $\frac{1}{4}$, less than $\frac{1}{2}$ period
G	p leads q by $\frac{1}{4}$ period	q leads p by $\frac{1}{4}$ period
H	p leads q by more than $\frac{1}{4}$, less than $\frac{1}{2}$ period	q leads p by less than $\frac{1}{4}$ period

NB The diagrams are drawn for the case where the period is 4 years, and where the maximum and zero values of q occur at mid-year

stationary, aggregate supply curve shifting), adjustment lags produce corresponding complications; a half-period lag by either variable gives a *positive* observed relation, and so forth. The range of possibilities with both positive and negative equilibrium relations is set out in chart 3.3. It is plain, however, that each of the observed relationships can, if we admit the possibility of lags of up to half a period in one or other of the variables, be explained in either of two ways. Every picture tells two stories, between which, given regular fluctuations,

Chart 3.4 *Output growth and price inflation, 1951–79*

Chart 3.4.1 *United States*

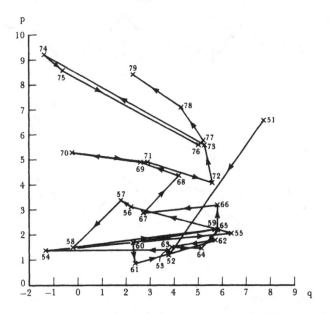

there is no way of discriminating, except by judgement based on the inherent plausibilities of the rival lag structures concerned.

The interpretation of non-cyclical movements is rather less complicated because appearances of lags are less ambiguous. It is, however, still important to remember that we are dealing with first differences, not with integral quantity and price variables, so that, for instance, a once-for-all rise in prices means a vertical displacement of one point only, while a once-for-all rise in the rate of inflation means a once-for-all move of the action to a higher level. And, of course, a shift to a higher 45° expenditure line (one further from the origin to the north-east) means a shift to a higher *rate of growth* of nominal income.

Interpreting recorded changes in quantity and price in terms of shifts in aggregate supply and demand curves, or even aggregate supply curves and autonomous 45° expenditure lines, is bound to be hazardous. That does not, however, forbid a cautious reconnaissance of the problem.

With these considerations in mind, let us take a first look at our scatter diagrams (charts 3.4.1–3.4.13) of price increase against real growth.

Chart 3.4.2 *United Kingdom*

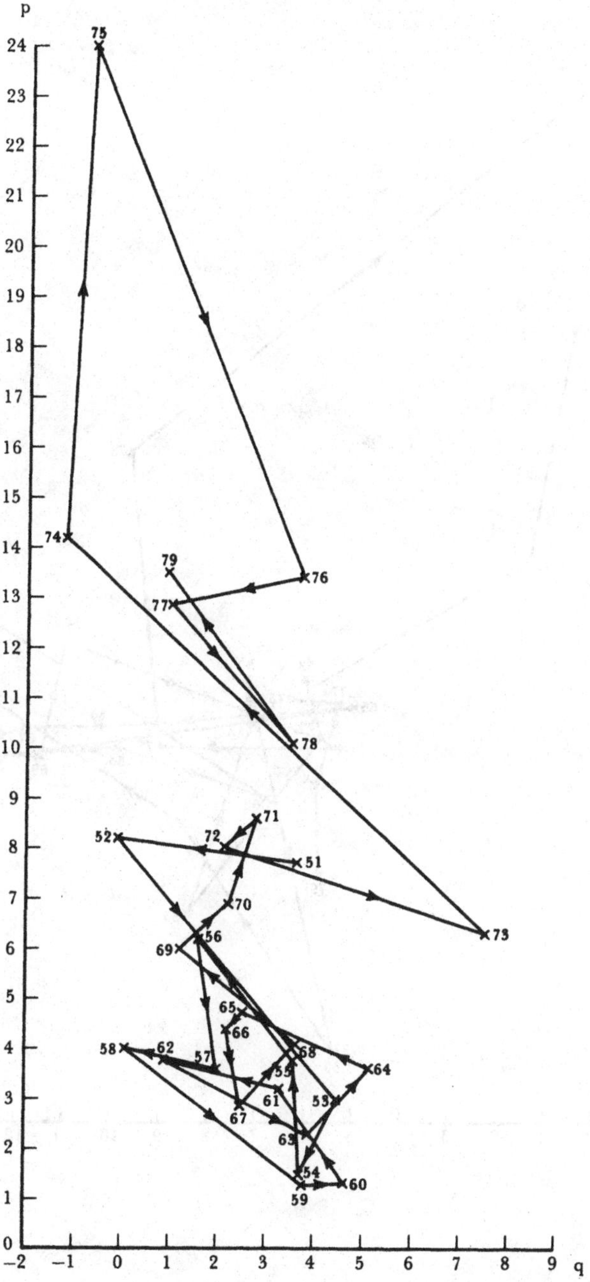

Chart 3.4.3 *Japan*

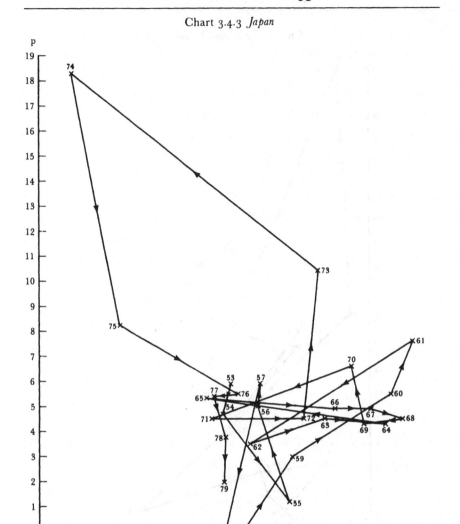

Chart 3.4.4 *Germany*

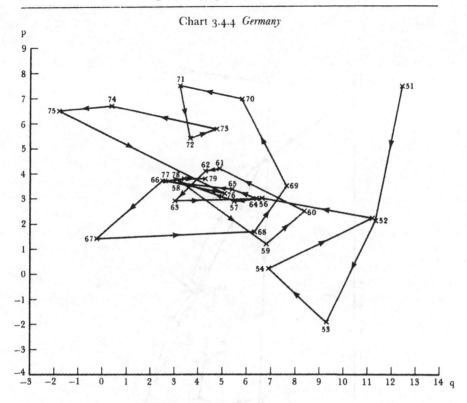

THE COURSES OF *q* AND *p*

The first observation is that no country in the sample shows a very close approach to a constant, or smoothly-varying, growth rate. National coefficients of variation lie between 0.5 and 0.9. Every one except France experienced decrease of output in at least one year; the range between largest and smallest annual growth (as percentage of GDP) between 1953 and 1979 inclusive, varies from 7.4 per cent for France to 14.1 per cent for Japan. The average change in growth rate between one annual interval and the next, similarly expressed, is 1.5 per cent for the former country and 2.8 per cent for the latter. It is true that, in every one of the countries except Germany, the range of inflation rates is greater than that of growth rates. In most instances, however, any tendency for growth rate to be more stable than inflation rate is a long-term rather than a short-term one. In the United States, Canada, the United Kingdon, Italy and Sweden, in particular, inflation seemed to have moved onto a quasi-permanently higher level in the 1970s, but the majority of year-to-year movements

Chart 3.4.5 *France*

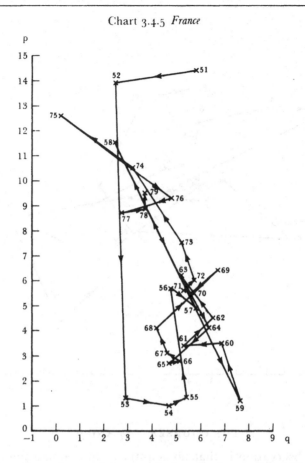

(especially after the early 1950s) involved considerably greater changes in growth rate than in inflation. France and Australia are the countries in which this generalisation about shorter-term movements most clearly fails to apply.

To see what economic relationships the incremental quantity–price diagrams do suggest, however, we must look at them individually. They show strongly individual characters. There is some family resemblance between the Netherlands and Denmark and rather less between both of them and West Germany. Apart from this, no two countries' patterns have much in common, superficially, though the United States and Canada (of which the latter shows much the greater price variability) can be seen on closer inspection to share some important features.

Every country in the sample, except the United Kingdom and France, where it comes in the following year, and Italy and Japan,

Chart 3.4.6 *Italy*

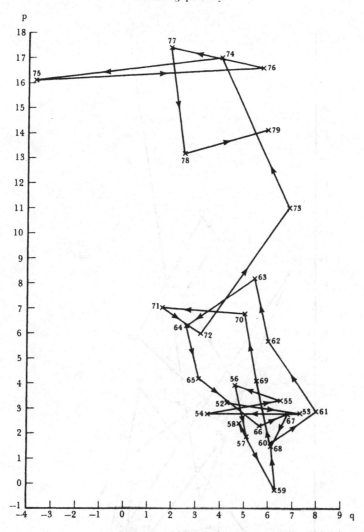

where these data start only later, shows a very big fall in price
inflation in 1952; but whereas in the United States, Germany,
Sweden, the Netherlands and Australia it goes with a fall in growth,
the opposite is true of Canada and Denmark. In France there is a fall
of growth in 1952 with little change in price inflation, followed next
year by a big fall in price inflation with a very slight increase in
growth; in the United Kingdom the pattern is rather similar, except
that there is an actual increase in inflation in 1951–2, and the increase

Chart 3.4.7 *Australia*

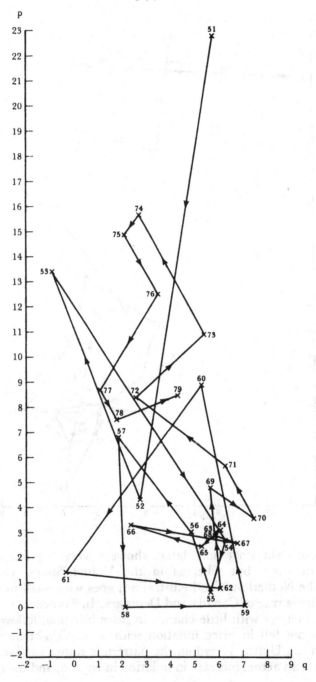

Chart 3.4.8 *Canada*

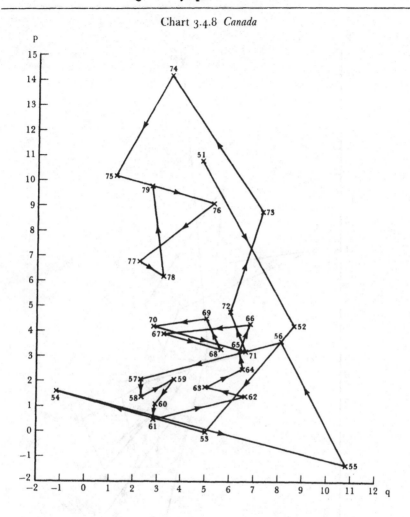

of growth in 1953, when inflation falls drastically, is bigger. Although events in the world market impinged heavily on all countries, their reactions were by no means all the same.

From about 1953, in most countries, there begins a period of cyclical fluctuation in which price and quantity variations repeatedly traverse much the same ground, but the international differences are substantial. The United States shows sometimes wide variations of growth rate with a slight upward tilt (inflation slightly greater when growth is high than when it is low) until 1965; the points describe flat loops, in an anti-clockwise direction, suggesting regular fluctuations with *q* leading *p* by less than a year. The chief deviations from this

Chart 3.4.9 *Sweden*

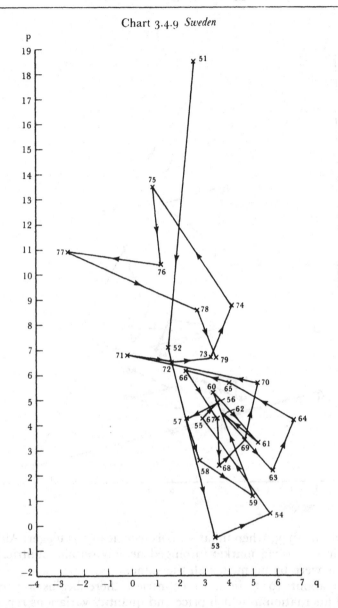

well-beaten path of variation are the high level of the 1956 and 1957 points and the lowness of that for 1961.

No other country shows this degree of regularity, nor is the generally slightly upward slope of the paths traced out by United States quantity–price variations easy to find elsewhere. Japan, after a period (1954–9) when biggish fluctuations in price inflation show little

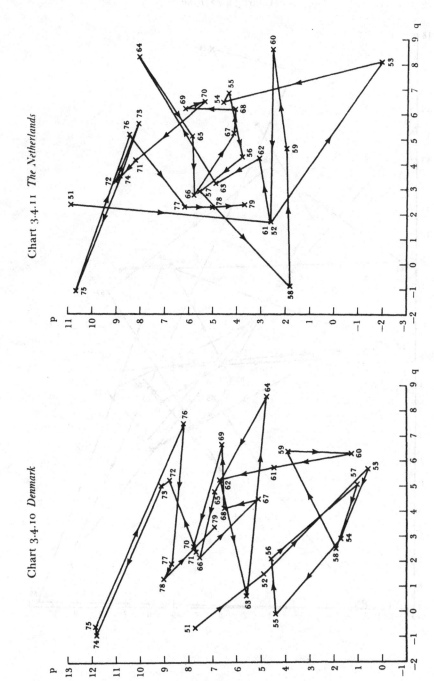

Chart 3.4.11 *The Netherlands*

Chart 3.4.10 *Denmark*

Chart 3.4.12 *India*

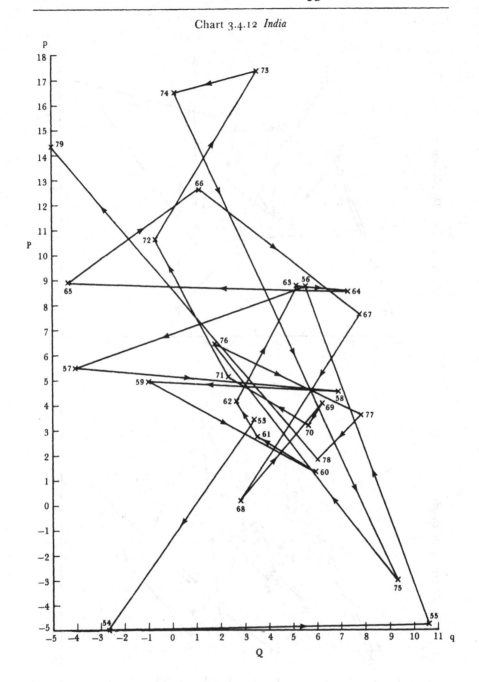

Chart 3.4.13 *Brazil*

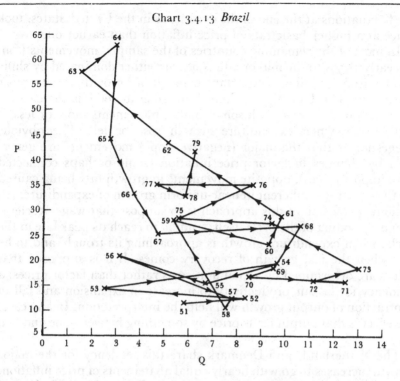

clear relation to the smaller variations of the high growth rate, enters one upward-tilted anti-clockwise cycle (1960–3) with large growth rate amplitude and smaller inflation amplitude, followed by a couple more (1964–6 and 1967–9) in which the general trend is horizontal or slightly downward with little sign of lag. The suggestion is that *q* leads *p* by a varying interval or even that *p* leads *q* a little, but price inflation became nearly constant in the 1960s. Germany, from 1955 to 1969, displays repeated anti-clockwise cycles of various amplitudes, more deeply looped than those of the United States and Japan, and mostly about a roughly horizontal longer axis, though that of 1959–62 has a negative tilt. Output seems thus to lead price by varying amounts, averaging roughly a year, and price inflation shows considerable cyclical change. For this, variation of factor price inflation may be responsible. Canada, from 1954, shows, like the United States, a cycle of very wide growth amplitude, with price inflation in 1956 and 1957 fairly high, but the big expansion at the beginning, unlike that of the United States, goes with a fall of price inflation (actually to a negative figure), and this is so with the expansion phases of some later Canadian cycles, though not all. There were accelerations of inflation bearing little obvious relation to output growth in the mid-1960s, and the fluctuations at the end of the decade, as in the United States, took place at a higher basic rate of price inflation than earlier ones.

In most of the remaining countries of the sample, movements from the early 1950s to the mid or late 1960s are either dominated by shifts not far from 45° lines of constant expenditure growth, or are more disorderly. The United Kingdom, from 1952 to 1969, is the clearest case of near-45° shifts, with some smaller movements more or less at right-angles when expenditure growth rose or fell. The obvious suggestion is that the major (negative slope) movements are generated by changes in factor price inflation (some perhaps connected with import prices), opposite movements in growth rate being caused by the constraint inherent in near-uniform growth of expenditure. An optional extension of this approach is to suppose that wage acceleration is a product of the cycle itself, tending to reach its peak late in the cycle, when expenditure growth is approaching its trough, and to be low when the fast growth of recovery comes. If it is supposed that prices are determined by actual unit costs rather than factor prices, a tendency for labour productivity to increase in expansion and fall in contraction of output growth will help the interpretation. In any case, the effect is that output leads price by something between one and two years.

The Netherlands and Denmark share this tendency for the major growth increases to go with nearly equal abatements of price inflation, with occasional striking exceptions (1964 in the Netherlands, an expansion of both rates of growth; the same year in Denmark, a major growth increase with only slight fall of inflation).

France is remarkable for the change in price inflation nearly always being greater than (and opposite to) the concomitant change in growth rate. In particular, from 1956 to 1964 the points move up and down a long track with inflation changes about a third bigger than growth changes, with only that for 1961 seriously out of line. The growth rate, indeed, is remarkably steady; the immediate suggestion is that quite wide fluctuations in increase of money costs were very largely, though not completely, accommodated by monetary and budgetary policy. In 1965, however, there was a sharp curtailment of both nominal and real income growth, and for four years the economy moved up a line of lower expenditure growth, or rather, up a rather steeper line than that would imply, until the sharp reflation (of both price rise and growth rates) in 1969.

Sweden shows a similar tendency for recoveries of growth rate to go with larger declines of price inflation, though in her case this is often followed by increase of both ordinates together, as part of a narrow triangular loop with a very steep negative tilt. An immediate suggestion is that wage inflation tends to accelerate about half way through the upswing and continues to grow after output expansion has slowed down. The direction of movement round these loops does not accord well with a suggestion that exogenous variations in price induce corresponding movements in output with a short lag; rather activity leads price by over a year.

In relation to the interpretations we have been trying to arrive at, Australia and Italy are the most disorderly of our subjects. Australia shows little tendency for either positively or negatively sloping transitions to predominate, or to follow each other in a regular way. Shocks from both supply and demand are suggested, and the nature of the economy makes the suggestion plausible. Italy is a little more susceptible to discussion in our terms. From 1952 to 1956, movements are mainly in output growth, with little change in the moderate level of price inflation. From then until 1960 the reverse is the case – there is movement up and down a steep, negatively-sloped line, as in France. Then begins the first of a number of very large closed anti-clockwise loops (this one of six years' duration) which, together with upward shifts, dominate the rest of the story.

So far we have been concerned only with experience up to the mid or late 1960s. From then, most countries show marked changes in their general levels of inflation, and some in their patterns of behaviour. The clearest cases of jumps to higher sustained levels of inflation are provided by the United States (from around $2\frac{1}{2}$ per cent a year to around $4\frac{1}{2}$ per cent in 1968), the United Kingdom (4 per cent to 8 per cent, most notably in 1970–1), Germany ($3\frac{1}{2}$ per cent to $6\frac{1}{2}$ per cent, also in 1970) and Italy (from 2–8 per cent to 6–14 per cent in the same year). France retained for a couple of further years rather more than half the extra $2\frac{1}{2}$ per cent of annual inflation that had been manifested in 1969, though this only brought her back to rates reached before in 1956 and 1963, and greatly surpassed in 1958. Australia shows a jump from around 3 per cent to about 5 per cent in 1968, Canada had changed level earlier, in 1964–5, Sweden drifted more gradually upwards during the 1960s and the Netherlands showed a vertical jump in 1969. Only Japan seems to have experienced no marked upward shift of the average level of inflation in the 1960s, though Denmark showed only a small one.

At this first transitional stage, changes in quantity–price behaviour are not very great. The United States from 1968 to 1972 shows once again the nearly route-retracing cycle that seems to be her speciality, though this time with a downward tilt. In view of the preceding jump of the inflation rate in 1968, it seems likely that incomplete accommodation of factor price inflation was of some importance here, though the alternative explanation of q and p positively connected, with a roughly two-year lag remains in principle open. In the United Kingdom the years 1970–3 have their growth concentrated heavily in the last one, when price inflation relaxed less than in most growth spurts of the previous two decades, perhaps because more of the accelerated increase of productivity was offset by wage inflation (before the wage freeze became effective), or by earlier impact of pressure of demand. Something may have been due to the fact that this was by far the country's largest annual increase of output in our period. In Germany, the (peak-to-peak) cycle 1969–73 displayed an unusually wide range of year-to-year inflation rates (with a considerable reduction in 1972), even apart from the general upward shift. The remarkable feature in France was the large expansion of nominal GDP growth rate in 1969, with roughly equal increase of price and output growth (an unusual feature in French experience during our period), partially reversed in the following year. Italian experience of 1969–72 was partly repetition of that of 1960–5, the easiest superficial interpretation of which is that price change was negatively associated with growth change, which it led by about one year – a case of price increase being incompletely accommodated.

For most countries, however, it was from 1972 or 1973 onwards that the most striking changes, both in average inflation rate and in the shape of the quantity–price relation manifested themselves. The outstanding exception is Germany, where inflation was lower in 1975 than in 1971.

The great oscillations of 1972–6 (which, incidentally, do not everywhere reach their peak in the same year) are all negatively inclined in our diagrams; some (those of the United States, France, the Netherlands, Denmark, and perhaps Germany) take the form of lines rather than loops, so that in terms of our chart 3.3 they conform to case A. This gives us a choice between an unlagged negative connection of inflation with growth, and a positive connection with q leading p (or p leading q) by a half-period – about two years. In others, of which Japan is the most spectacular, there is something broadly resembling the downward-tilted anti-clockwise loop of chart 3.3(B), consistent with either inflation negatively associated with output growth of something less than a year later, or growth positively connected with the inflation of between one and two years later.

Where the cycle in question is of much greater amplitude than previous ones, so that it looks as if some special factor has suddenly come into play, it seems reasonable to look for the variable that has first given an abnormally large kick, and to choose the interpretation consistent with that variable having the priority. Thus, in Japan, the great loop starts with the surge of the inflation rate from 4½ per cent a year to over 18 per cent a year in 1973–4. This can hardly be accounted for by the course of growth rate of one to two years earlier – a period in which substantial fall in growth was succeeded by a smaller recovery. But if we start with a (from our present point of view) exogenous price inflation in 1973–4, the succeeding course of growth rate is entirely consistent with a consequential squeeze on output growth operating with something less than a year's lag.

In Canada, also, the great acceleration of price inflation from 1972 to 1974 was on a scale not easily related, in the light of such regularities as can be detected in the cycles from 1964 to 1970, to the course of growth in the preceding couple of years. In Italy, abnormal increase of inflation set in from 1972, after only a very modest recovery of growth rate from a very low level, and events then proceeded as one might expect from a rather slow-acting inflation-generated constraint, as far as the output fall of 1975; there, however, the previous large inflation increases of 1961–3 and 1968–70 had already established something of a pattern of what look like initially, but in the end incompletely accommodated upward shifts of the aggregate supply curve. In Sweden, the chief difference from previous times was that inflation hardly abated in the recovery of 1971–3, so that the succeeding cycle, to 1976, was traversed at higher levels of inflation than previous ones – a fact perhaps not unconnected with the restrained levels of growth rate. The recovery of 1978–9 brought a return to the pattern of reduced inflation, so that the suggestion of unusual circumstances operating on prices in 1971–3 stands.

As we have already noted, the United Kingdom, after the upward shift of 1969–71, shows a proportionally smaller remission of inflation in the very large expansion of 1973 than had gone with some earlier expansions, perhaps in part because of the great amplitude of the swing, though the rise in import prices must also have had its effect. Thereafter, the superficial appearance is an unusual one, involving a clockwise loop between 1974 and 1977. It seems more useful, however, to think of this as due to the great upward displacement of the single point for 1975, through the perverse operation, then collapse, of the prices and incomes policy gearing wages to world prices by means of 'threshold payments'. Allowing for this, and perhaps some effect in 1976 of depreciation of sterling, the whole range of points from 1973 to 1979 might be regarded as lying near to a line of constant nominal expenditure growth.

This brings the United Kingdom into the same group as those other countries, already mentioned, where negatively-sloping, linear fluctuations prevailed in the 1970s – the United States, France, the

Netherlands, Denmark, and, with qualifications, Germany. In the United Kingdom, United States and, rather less markedly, France, the surge of price inflation from 1973 was sharply in advance of those in the preceding cycles, and was accompanied by collapses of growth rate no less out of keeping with preceding experience. It is *prima facie* reasonable to connect the two, and suggest a direct causal connection – growth falling as the aggregate supply curve shifts upwards, because the rate of growth of aggregate expenditure is under constraint.

In the Netherlands and Denmark, the rise in price inflation was less unusual, but the fall of growth rate was equally prompt and proportionally more severe – growth of aggregate nominal income fell sharply. The suggestion of expenditure constraint in the face of shifting aggregate supply curves is strong, especially as inflation was already at a relatively high level, likely to discourage policies of accommodation. In the years after 1976, the rise of the aggregate supply curves seems to have decreased. In Germany it can be argued that this had begun already after the big surge of inflation in 1969–70.

Finally, among the relations between p and q, we may glance at the experience of India and Brazil. Their diagrams show a certain family resemblance in that they are dominated, at first sight, by steep negative slopes. In a closed economy, where agriculture was important, one might expect that variations in crop yields would give rise to variations in the same direction in total output, and to variations in the opposite direction in the price level, thus giving a generally negative slope. On the other hand, in so far as the country in question is linked to the world market for agricultural products, without dominating it, poor crops will directly and indirectly reduce total real GDP, with an effect on the price level which will depend on circumstances – substitution of imports for home production will usually involve some rise in cost, but not necessarily a very large one, while loss of export income may have monetary effects which tend to depress prices as well as income. In an open economy, also, exogenous changes in the price of commodities exported will tend to move both price level and real income in the same direction.

In India, some years of absolute fall in GDP – 1954, 1957, 1959, 1965 and 1972 – were years of poor agricultural performance. 1954 and 1965 were years of poor manufacturing performance also, which no doubt depressed the real (and money) demand for the produce of agriculture, and in any case cheap imported supplies were available to fill the gaps, so that on the occasions mentioned agricultural shortfall was not accompanied by an important increase, sometimes even by a decrease, of inflation. In 1972 and 1979, poor agricultural performance (though accompanied by a fall in total real demand) went with rising prices in world markets, so that reduced growth and higher inflation were combined. That the good agricultural output of 1973 went with rising inflation must be attributed in part to the accompanying industrial boom and in part to the effects of import price inflation. Nevertheless, the general orientation of quantity–price relations remains more negative than positive.

Some of these considerations no doubt applied in Brazil, also, but there the dominant one seems to have been the rather longer-term variation in the rate of growth of nominal expenditure – the shift of the expenditure line in our diagram – associated with different rates of credit creation undertaken in connection with public and private capital formation, and accompanied by price–wage spirals of varying vigour. The high levels of real growth achieved in 1958 and 1961 were followed by major accelerations of inflation, which persisted (in the later case for several years) even though real growth rate fell. Relatively low growth rates and high levels of unemployment from 1965 to 1967 were accompanied by a fall of inflation to its 1960 level, and still more rapid growth from 1968 to 1973 went with a further fall, but from then to the end of our period inflation accelerated again in spite of irregularly diminishing growth rates. There has thus been a rather long cycle of inflation and growth in which policy has played a central part, swinging between higher and lower levels of inflation-financed growth.

INFLATION AND THE DEVIATION OF OUTPUT FROM TREND

We noted earlier in this chapter, however, that instead of examining the relation between the first differences of the (greatly trend-ridden) statistics of output and price, one may look at that between the first differences of price (the inflation rate) and the deviations of (the logarithms of) output from a linear trend. The latter variable may be regarded as a rough measure of the pressure of productive activity on the resources available to support it. With some obvious qualifications it may be expected to bear a reasonably close relation to the unemployment rate, measured inversely.

This being so, the relation between price inflation and deviations of output from trend is of the same family as the Phillips curve – the relation between *wage* inflation and unemployment – to which we shall be returning in a later chapter; and before we look at the relation in question we may note an investigation covering part of our period (1954–68) in which the relation between price inflation and unemployment is investigated in such a way as to make the nature of the family connection clear. Maynard and van Ryckeghem start with a wage equation embodying a version of the Phillips curve (wage inflation related to unemployment and expected price inflation), a price equation (price inflation related to wage inflation, import price inflation, and indirect tax changes) and a price expectations equation (expected inflation, a variable compromise between actual current inflation and the inflation expected in the previous period). In the simplest case, where expectations are dominated by the current inflation rate, these equations boil down to a reduced form in which price inflation is related simply to unemployment, import price inflation and indirect tax changes. Where previous expectations matter, a given unemployment rate, with import prices and indirect taxation stationary, will make the rate of price inflation gradually converge to a 'long-term' level.

Maynard and van Ryckeghem find reasonably good fits to this model in a number of countries, including Germany and the United States; in some others there are suspicious circumstances such as negative signs on the coefficients of indirect taxation or lagged inflation rate. But the point of immediate relevance is that the unemployment coefficient is significant and, indeed, has the largest standardised ('*beta*') value of any coefficient, in the United States, United Kingdom, Germany, France, Canada, Belgium and Denmark. In Norway, Sweden, the Netherlands, Ireland, and Japan, import prices seem to take pride of place. We shall see in a later chapter that other studies, taking in later years, have found rather less clear evidence of the influence of the unemployment or related variables than emerges from this investigation of the period in which comparatively regular trade cycles prevailed in most countries.

Let us come now to our own examination of the relation between price inflation and deviations of total activity from trend. It will suffice if we confine our attention here to the 'Big Six' economies (see charts 3.5.1–3.5.6). For this purpose, the trend we have used is a linear one fitted to the logarithms of output over the period 1950–79. Since the deviations of actual growth from this refer to calendar years, and since the inflation rates are annual first differences (of GDP deflators), the two do not exactly match; the nearest we can manage is, broadly, a half-year's lag of one series in relation to the other. It will, in fact, be useful to consider both of these possibilities, the deviation of (for instance) 1951 related to the inflation rates of both 1950–1 and 1951–2. The Pearsonian correlation coefficients between the variables for the whole period and for sub-periods defined by dividing it in two, first in 1968 and then in 1973, are shown in table 1. Charts 3.5.1–3.5.6, however, relate to the case where deviation leads.

If we take the former relation – inflation slightly leading deviation –

Chart 3.5 *Price inflation and the deviation of output from trend, 1952–79*

Chart 3.5.1 *United States*

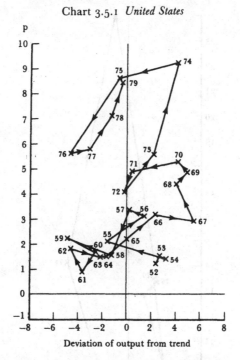

Deviation of output from trend

for the Big Six, the immediate impression is that there is less indication of meaningful relation than we have been finding in our incremental quantity–price diagrams. The general slope of year-to-year movements is, if anything, negative for the United Kingdom over the period as a whole, and more definitely in the 1970s, which would be consistent with deflationary pressure on output following accelerations of price inflation. For the United States there is a positive relation up to the late 1960s, followed by a negative one, but the prevalence of anti-clockwise loops suggests that a change in lag would give a more markedly linear relation. For Germany there is a rather stronger suggestion of two separate positive relations in the sub-periods 1953–69 and 1970–9 respectively, with a break between. For France, Italy, and Japan the picture is more chaotic. The French relation is predominantly negative, but weak; the Japanese positive but weak; the Italian shows signs of changing from positive to negative.

With deviation slightly leading inflation (see charts 3.5.1.–3.5.6), things are little altered for the United States in the earlier period; the relation is still positive, although there are some erratic movements

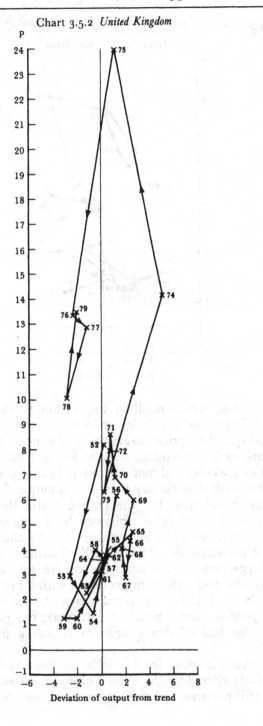

Chart 3.5.2 *United Kingdom*

Chart 3.5.3 *Japan*

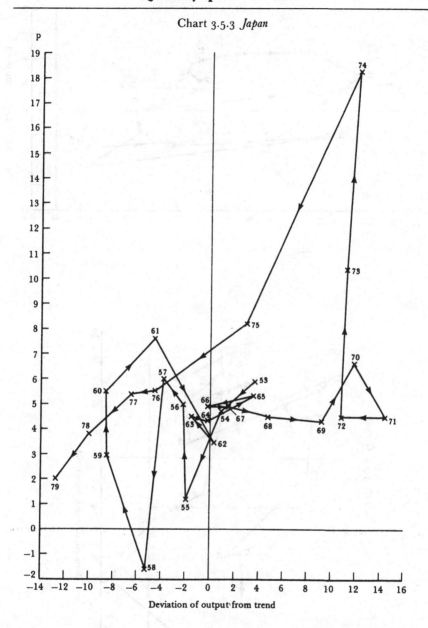

Deviation of output from trend

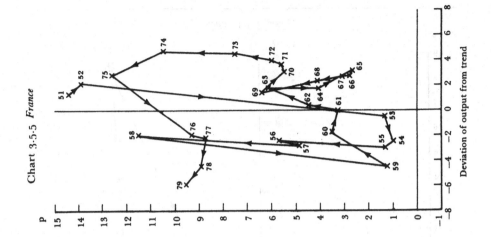

Chart 3.5.5 *France*

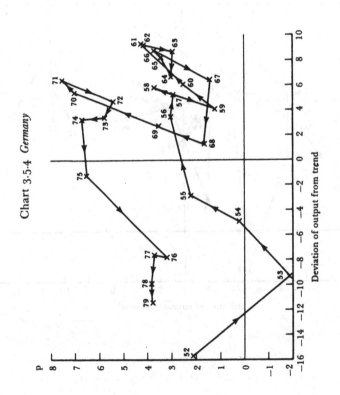

Chart 3.5.4 *Germany*

Chart 3.5.6 *Italy*

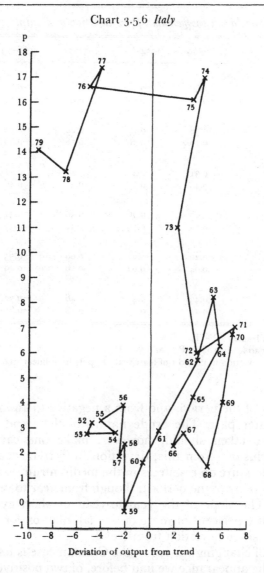

Deviation of output from trend

(1952 and 1953 low, 1956 and 1957 high). There is then an upward shift to another, roughly parallel positive relation, 1970–3, followed by a bigger one to a steeper and well-defined line for 1974 (or 1975) to 1979. The change of slope is quite marked – from something like $\frac{1}{3}$ per cent of inflation for each 1 per cent of deviation from trend in the earlier period, $\frac{1}{2}$ to $\frac{3}{4}$ per cent for each 1 per cent after 1973.

For the United Kingdom, the effect of altering the lag is to change the general relation from a weakly to a more strongly positive one in

Table 3.1　*Correlation coefficients: price inflation and output gap 1954–79*

	1954–79	1954–68	1954–73	1968–79	1973–9
US					
A	0.60	0.74	0.66	−0.63	−0.37
B	0.27	0.63	0.65	−0.10	0.55
UK					
A	−0.38	0.27	0.28	−0.63	−0.51
B	0.10	0.76	0.56	−0.08	0.28
Japan					
A	0.31	0.40	0.48	0.21	0.75
B	0.48	0.15	0.36	0.46	0.91
Germany					
A	−0.06	0.76	0.30	0.34	0.66
B	0.13	0.75	0.41	0.57	0.89
France					
A	−0.29	−0.25	0.09	−0.55	−0.10
B	0.04	0.02	0.26	−0.29	0.22
Italy					
A	−0.43	0.40	0.46	−0.72	−0.16
B	−0.21	0.57	0.56	−0.61	0.10

Note: A: Inflation leading $(P_t - P_{t-1}$ and $G_t)$
　　　B: Output gap leading $(P_t - P_{t-1}$ and $G_{t-1})$
[Output gap G_t = deviation in period t of log (Real Output) from linear trend, 1954–79].

the early part of the period, and from a negative to an indeterminate one in the later part. The crude nature of the trend from which deviations are taken should, however, make one cautious about drawing conclusions from this; deviation from trend may be a poor indicator of pressure on resources in the medium run (exaggerating it in the middle years of the period), though from year to year it is more meaningful. The slope of the year-to-year, or short cyclical movements is high; 2 per cent or more of annual inflation for each extra 1 per cent of positive deviation from trend.

The effect of changing the lag in the German case is less marked; it emphasises the appearance we had before, of two positive relations in different sub-periods, though, once again, caution is required because the true trend is probably far from linear. The short-term relation between about 1957 and 1973 may well have been ½ per cent rising to 1 per cent of inflation per extra 1 per cent of deviation above trend, though the appearance over each half of the whole period is of a lower sensitivity. The big shifts upwards (or to the right) seem to have been in 1968 and after 1973 or 1974.

Neither Japan nor France shows a consistently better relation between inflation and slightly lagged deviation from trend than was evident with the lag in the opposite direction. All that can be said is that, in Japan, inflation comes down dramatically as deviation falls and becomes negative from 1974 to 1979; otherwise, and for France throughout the period, the picture is much more like one of exogenous shocks to the rate of inflation than of any systematic relation to deviation from the growth trend, even over short sub-periods. Italy, however, does (with deviation lagged) show what looks like a rather steep positive relation, drifting gradually to the right, from 1959 to 1970 or 1971, with inflation on the high side in 1963 and 1970. Before and after, there is no apparent relation, though inflation shows a slow general downward tendency as deviation becomes rapidly negative after 1974, having in the two preceding years shot up to great heights without any appreciable change in deviation from the output trend.

In thinking of our two approaches to quantity–price relations, one comparing the first differences of the quantity and price series, the other comparing the first difference of price with the absolute deviation of quantity from a linear trend, we should bear in mind the way in which they are necessarily related, and not independent of one another. Suppose, once more, that we are dealing with sinusoidal fluctuations in both series. Then, if we find the first differences of quantity and price negatively related, we may take it that the (integral) variables themselves are similarly related, apart from any linear trends they may have, and that de-trended quantity will be perfectly uncorrelated with the first derivative of price (they will differ in phase by a quarter of a period). The annual first difference of price which we are using, however, is not precisely in phase with the first derivative, but, as we have already noted, either leads it or lags behind it by about half a year, according to whether it is calculated as a forward-looking or a backward-looking difference. The forward-looking difference will thus, with fluctuations of the kind of period we find (typically, about four years) be positively correlated with quantity, though in general not perfectly so – the correlation would be perfect only with a period of two years. Similarly, the backward-looking first difference of price will be negatively correlated with (de-trended) quantity.

Very broadly, our data for the United States, up to about 1968, are consistent with quantity leading price by about a year in a four-year cycle, which implies that it moves more or less simultaneously with the rate of change of price. In the United Kingdom the lead of quantity over price is about a year and a half, so that its lead over rate of change of price is perhaps half a year – though, of course, since the fluctuation is nowhere precisely a regular sinusoidal one, these implications are not precise, either. Germany presents an appearance somewhere between those of the British and American cases. These relations are consistent with some kind of 'Phillips' effect of demand pressure on rate of inflation (with, especially in the British case, a short time lag), but they are equally consistent with some mechanism whereby price inflation causes the brake to be put on output growth (with a short time lag in, at least, the United Kingdom case). There is no obvious reason why these two types of mechanism should not coexist.

In the late 1960s and early 1970s, shifts are superimposed on, and disturb, cyclical changes. The general impression is that in the United States the lag of price behind quantity is lengthened, or in other words that something nearer a simultaneous and opposite fluctuation of the two is established, a change which could also be read as a lengthening of the lag by which price inflation follows pressure on capacity, and something of the same sort, in a milder degree, seems to be true of Germany. (In the United Kingdom, the non-cyclical shifts make this kind of interpretation harder.) The more obvious interpretation, however, is that rising price inflation causes a brake to be put on growth with more nearly immediate effect than hitherto. The general upshot is that the cyclical movements we observe are subject to alternative causal interpretations of the price–quantity relations embedded in them, not necessarily mutually exclusive. The hypothesis of perfectly-clearing markets in which capacity remains fully occupied is not well supported. Another that seems to be rarely supported so far is the one that posits stationary, upward-sloping supply curves and bodily fluctuating demand curves.

DEVIATION FROM TREND AND THE OUTPUT ELASTICITY OF PRICE

In this connection, it is perhaps worth asking a question of a different form from those we have hitherto discussed about the relations between output growth, inflation and capacity utilisation (roughly represented by deviation of output from trend). We have already noted that experience in our period gives us little or no help in discovering whether p/q (that is to say $\Delta \log P / \Delta \log Q$), approximately the elasticity of price with respect to output, has different values according to whether nominal income is falling or rising – because it has been rising all the time. What one might reasonably expect is that with expenditure continually increasing, the existence of spare capacity is crucial; so long as there is spare capacity, increased nominal expenditure will raise output more than it raises price, but that, as spare capacity becomes short, the value of p/q will rise.

Chart 3.6 *Price–Quantity elasticity and deviation of output from trend*

Chart 3.6.1 *United States*

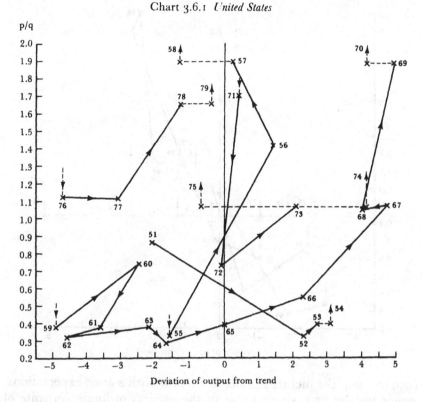

Deviation of output from trend

Chart 3.6.1 shows the result of plotting p/q against the deviation (of a year earlier) of real output from trend for the United States. The chart shows only the lower values of this elasticity (up to 2.0); from time to time it shoots up to much higher values, which we have treated here as if they were infinite; we have also treated as infinite, or as 'going off the scale', negative values which arise when p is positive in spite of q being negative.

It is obvious that there is no constant relation over time. What we have is a series of episodes, some of them represented here by a J-shaped track, some by a rising one. For instance, p/q comes down from 1951 to 1952 as capacity utilisation increases, then starts to rise and finally shoots off the scale in 1954. It reappears (drops from the sky, so to speak) in the following year, when capacity utilisation has fallen, rises rapidly with a fairly modest increase of output in relation to trend until 1957 and goes off the scale in 1958 in spite of capacity utilisation having fallen again. Less erratic behaviour follows. From

Chart 3.6.2 *United Kingdom*

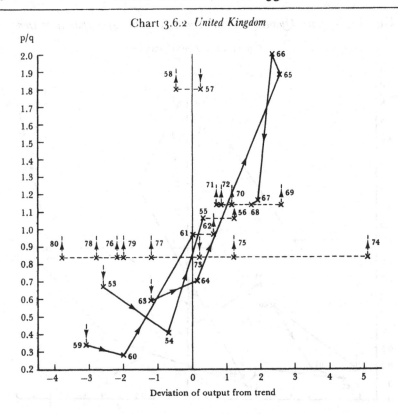

Deviation of output from trend

1959 to 1969, the picture is more in keeping with *a priori* expectations, except for the high single value of the vertical ordinate (in spite of apparently quite low capacity utilisation) in 1960. With this exception, there is a gradually accelerating rise as capacity utilisation is increased until the point flies off the scale again in 1970. It comes to a minimum value again in 1972, rises with increasing use of capacity, and flies off again in 1974 and the following year, the latter despite a very large fall in capacity utilisation. A similar episode is enacted from 1976 to 1981, albeit at an apparently much lower level of pressure on capacity.

These separate episodes, leaving either J-shaped or simply rising tracks, are broadly in accordance with our expectation that the extent to which increased expenditure goes into price inflation, as opposed to real expansion, depends on how little capacity there is available for the latter. But there is no obvious regularity about the degree of capacity utilisation at which p/q flies off the scale. It does it three times in years when activity is above trend, and five times in years when it is below. There is, moreover, a tendency for the minimum

Chart 3.6.3 *Japan*

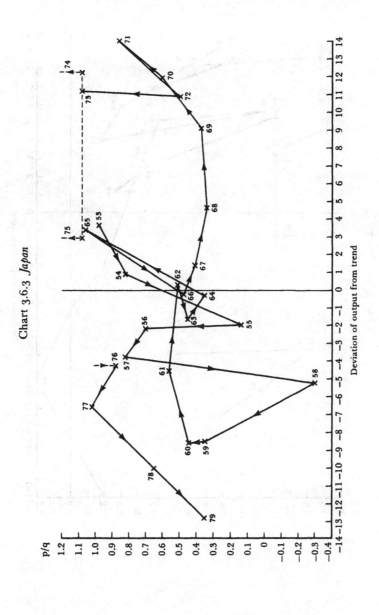

Deviation of output from trend

Chart 3.6.4 *Germany*

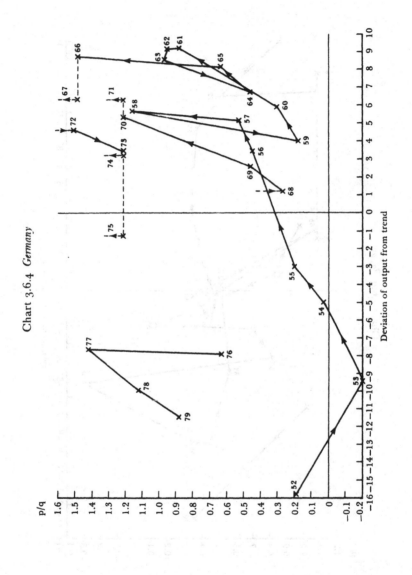

p/q

Deviation of output from trend

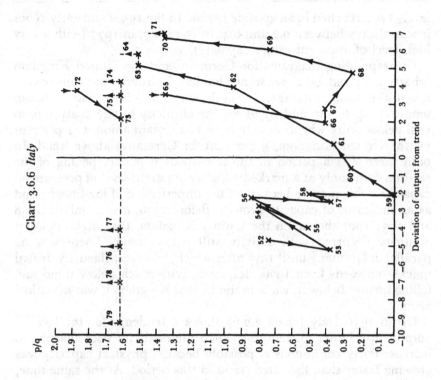

Chart 3.6.6 Italy

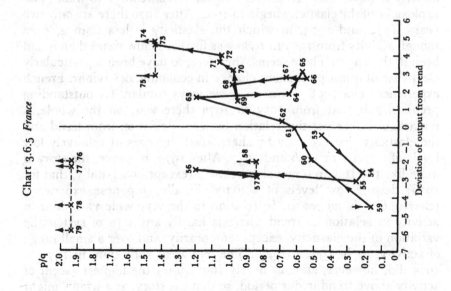

Chart 3.6.5 France

level of p/q reached in an episode to rise. In the 1950s and early 1960s it was always between 0.2 and 0.4; in 1972, 0.7; in 1977 (with a very high level of apparent excess capacity), 1.1.

Corresponding diagrams for Germany and the United Kingdom (charts 3.6.4 and 3.6.2) are somewhat less disorderly, but convey very much the same message. In both countries there was a broad tendency up to the mid-1970s for the elasticity to rise sharply from well below unity whenever activity was a certain amount (1 per cent for the United Kingdom, 5 per cent for Germany) above trend. In both there was a period in the mid-1960s when steepening of the relation came only at a markedly higher apparent level of pressure on capacity – this may be because of the imperfection of log-linear trend as an indicator of capacity growth. Before 1976, it was only in 1958 and 1951 (not shown) in the United Kingdom, that high apparent elasticity occurred with activity still below trend. There was no parallel in Germany until 1975 after which, however, elasticity drifted quickly upwards from 1976, despite activity much below trend and falling further below it, while in the United Kingdom it was never low again.

Up to 1970 Italy (chart 3.6.6) shows a tendency for the level of output, in relation to trend, at which the elasticity rises sharply, to increase fairly continuously, possibly because physical capacity was growing faster than the fitted trend in this period. At the same time, activity is pushed to successively higher levels relative to trend, and explosions of the elasticity begin in 1964. After 1970 there are only two years, 1972 and 1973, in which the elasticity is less than 2, even though activity from 1977 to 1980 was further below trend than it had been in the 1950s. There seems, therefore, to have been a particularly clear case of quasi-permanent change in economic behaviour. French experience (chart 3.6.5) was in some ways similar. Its outstanding peculiarity is that from 1953 to 1973 there was, on the whole, a remarkably clear positive relation between deviation from trend and the elasticity, marred only by sharp elasticity rises at relatively low levels of activity in 1956 and 1957. After 1973, however, the story is more like the Italian – no value below 2 (except, marginally, that for 1976) despite low levels of activity. Finally, Japanese experience (chart 3.6.3) is *sui generis*. In relation to the very wide variations in activity in relation to trend, there is hardly any sign of systematic variation in the elasticity, except temporarily, and over a small range of activity, as in 1962 to 1966. The one great explosion, in 1973 to 1975 did, however, start at nearly (not quite) the highest ascent of activity above trend in our period, so that the story, as a whole, might be told as one of the elasticity varying around 0.5, more or less irrespectively of the level of activity, until the latter is more than 10 per cent above trend, and then, though only after two or three years of this high pressure, taking off into an ascent which, however, proved to be wholly reversible. If this seems like a textbook discontinuity, encountered on reaching truly full use of capacity, it must be admitted that the development of results from the encounter was rather sluggish.

This approach shows differences between different countries, and between different sub-periods, at least as drastic as those revealed by our other two explorations of the relations between quantity and price. It is clear that there is some connection between pressure of activity and the partition of additional expenditure between output increase and price increase, but it is nowhere a regular and unchanging connection. Changes in factor prices, which either come from outside the economy in question, or are produced within it in loose or irregular relation to the general pressure of demand on its resources, are perhaps the most obvious (though not the only) potential agents of confusion. We return to this subject in the next chapter.

'BASIC' AND 'CYCLICAL' COMPONENTS OF INFLATION

This brings us to the important point that the process of inflation is only partly explained by short-term cyclical events, to which a large part of our attention in this chapter has been given. The positive average level of inflation over our whole period, and the rise (in most countries) of its average level from one sub-period to the next, are due only partly to repeated cyclical rises above some 'basic' level to which the rate relapsed; they are attributable also to what, within our period, appear as once-for-all rises in the 'basic' level typical of cyclical inflation minima. A simple sorting-out of the total inflation between these two modes of increase – the regularly reversed and the unreversed up to 1979 – will be in order (see table 3.2).

In none of our countries has there been fluctuation for any considerable time about a zero average inflation level; it is only in a few isolated years and in some countries that the GDP deflator has actually been lower than in the year before. The 'basic' level of inflation, below which, in the 1950s and 1960s, only a few years fell, varies from country to country in our sample; it could be stated, rather impressionistically, as varying from about 1 per cent in Germany, Canada, and Australia to perhaps 2.4 per cent in Japan and France.

If one calculates the annual average inflation rate from 1953 (when things had settled down from the Korean disturbances) until the date

Table 3.2 *'Basic' and 'cyclical' inflation*

per cent

	Average rate, pa. 1953–79	First period	Average rate, first period	Basic inflation, first period	Cyclic inflation
United States	4.0	1953–67	2.2	1.4	0.8
United Kingdom	6.7	1953–69	3.5	2.0	1.5
Germany	4.1	1953–69	3.3	1.0	2.3
Japan	4.5	1953–72	3.3	2.4	0.9
France	5.8	1953–72	5.2	2.4	2.8
Italy	7.2	1953–61	2.3	2.0	0.3
Canada	4.4	1953–72	3.5	1.0	2.5
Sweden	5.5	1953–69	3.7	2.0	1.7
Netherlands	5.5	1953–68	4.2	2.0	2.2
Denmark	6.3	1953–61	2.9	1.4	1.5
Australia	5.5	1953–67	2.8	1.0	1.8

	Second period	Average rate, second period	Basic inflation, second period	Cyclic inflation
United States	1968–79	6.4	4.1	2.3
United Kingdom	1970–9	11.8	6.4	5.4
Germany	1970–9	5.3	3.2	2.1
Japan	1973–9	7.7	2.4	5.3
France	1973–9	9.6	8.8	0.8
Italy	1962–79	9.4	6.0	3.4
Canada	1973–9	9.3	6.2	3.1
Sweden	1970–9	8.5	6.5	2.0
Netherlands	1969–79	7.3	3.7	3.6
Denmark	1962–79	7.8	4.8	3.0
Australia	1968–79	8.7	3.6	5.1

preceding the first non-cyclical upward shift we have identified (dates varying from 1961 in Italy and Denmark to 1972 in France and Japan), the amounts by which these averages exceed the 'basic' rates vary from less than 1 per cent per annum in the United States to about 2.8 per cent in France. This may be regarded as a rough measure of the average annual inflation generated by the cyclical process in this period; it is broadly of the same magnitude as the 'basic' rate which persisted in all but the three or four least inflationary years, exceeding it in France, Germany, Canada, the Netherlands, Australia, and probably Denmark, and falling below it in the United States, the United Kingdom, Italy and probably Sweden (see table 3.2). In this simple sense, we may say that the inflation from the end of the Korean war until some date in the 1960s (or in a couple of cases the early 1970s) was mainly a cyclical phenomenon in rather more than half our sample countries, though a basic, non-cyclical component was probably nearly as important in the sample as a whole.

Since the first upward shift, things have been less neat. It seems reasonable for a start to regard the 'basic' rate of inflation as having moved up to whatever is the lowest annual level subsequently reached up to 1979. If we do this, the balance between basic and cyclical inflation for the post-shift period emerges as considerably different from that before the shift; there are only three countries (Japan, Italy, and Australia) in which the cyclical component exceeds the basic. Japan is the only country in which the basic element was no greater after than before – in which inflation came down (in 1979 in her case) to virtually the level taken as our pre-shift basic one. The results for Italy and Australia are deceptive, because there (as also in the United States) the shift in question was followed eventually by a further one, by which a still higher basic rate, within the terms of our definition, was established. What emerges, therefore, is that for the period of generally more rapid inflation, after whatever we have taken as the first upward shift in the cyclic pattern of growth and inflation movements, it is the basic rate, rather than the cyclical peaks, spectacular though some of the latter are, that accounts for most of the aggregate (or annual average) inflation.

The moral is that, in looking more closely at the various national records, with the help of additional data, we should pay particular attention to the non-cyclical upward shifts in the growth–inflation relationship, and to the reasons why these shifts have not been reversed. Meanwhile, however, it is worth looking at the main shifts in the general relation between growth and inflation in consideration of two questions which we have already had before us in a more general connection; do abnormal (and quasi-permanent) rises in the inflation rate go with abnormal growth rates (in other words, are they simply consequences of non-linearity not otherwise apparent in the growth–inflation relation), and do they go with abnormally high levels of activity in relation to trend?

To the first of these questions, the answer seems to be predominantly negative. It is true that the upward jump of price inflation in 1973 in the United Kingdom, Italy and the United States was associated with high peaks of growth rate (though in the last-mentioned country not so high as those of the mid-1960s). The jumps of 1973 (or neighbouring years) in other countries were mostly associated with only moderate growth rates, not high peaks; this was so, for instance, in Japan, where the rise of inflation was especially spectacular, and in France. The earlier points of transition to higher inflation are no more closely connected with peak growth rates. Italy and Denmark in 1962 show such a connection, and so, if one forbears from comparison with years before 1961, does Germany in 1970; but in the United States in 1968, United Kingdom in 1970 and Italy in 1969, growth was not outstandingly high, while Sweden, the Netherlands and Australia in their transitions of the late 1960s seem to have enjoyed successive years of moderately high growth rather than one outstanding one.

This last point is clearly consistent with what, on the whole, we find on asking the second of the above questions, namely a closer association with high activity (in relation to trend) than with currently abnormal rate of growth. There are some exceptions – the United Kingdom did not show especially high activity in 1970, nor Italy in 1962, nor the Netherlands in 1973, but otherwise the association with cyclically high activity (and high summits) is fairly general.

This is, of course, in line with a 'Phillips' type of relation between high *pressure* of activity and high *rate* of inflation, for which we have already found some limited general evidence. The large, transitional, leaps of inflation are exceptional in their magnitude, but less so in their timing.

THE VARIABILITIES OF GROWTH RATE AND OF INFLATION

One final aspect of the relation between quantity and price changes invites inspection. Table 3.3 shows the standard deviations of annual rates of output growth and price inflation for our OECD sample countries over the period 1953–79 as a whole (the earlier years being excluded to avoid the disturbances of the Korean war), and also for the earlier and later parts of that period, the dividing date being fixed at two different years, corresponding to the chief times at which the quantity–price relations appear to have shifted.

In the fairly long run (1953–79), and over our sample countries as a whole, inflation is substantially more variable than output growth, but before 1967 the two variabilities were about equal. They were both higher after 1967, that of price inflation having shown the greater rise. The differences that appear if one divides the whole period at 1973–4 are in the same direction, but markedly smaller.

It is sometimes suggested that there is some degree of trade-off between the two kinds of variability. A country where wages and prices (or wages alone) are institutionally rigid may be expected to find that fluctuations in the rate of growth of aggregate money demand will result in relatively wide fluctuations in growth rate of output, while variability in the rate of inflation will presumably be low. A country with flexible and market-responsive wages and prices may come nearer to the classical ideal of full employment and smooth

Table 3.3 *Standard deviation of per cent rates of annual inflation and real output growth*

| | 1953–79 | | 1953–67 | | 1968–79 | | 1953–73 | | 1974–9 | |
	p	*q*	*p*	*q*	*p*	*q*	*p*	*q*	*p*	*q*
United States	2.4	2.4	0.8	2.3	1.7	2.5	1.5	2.2	1.5	2.9
United Kingdom	5.2	1.9	1.3	1.4	5.4	2.3	2.1	1.6	4.8	2.0
Japan	3.5	3.6	2.3	2.8	4.3	4.1	2.4	2.7	5.8	2.7
Germany	2.1	2.8	1.6	2.9	1.8	2.6	2.2	2.5	1.5	2.6
France	3.3	1.6	2.7	1.3	2.5	1.7	2.5	1.2	1.5	1.6
Italy	5.5	2.4	2.1	1.5	5.6	2.9	2.7	1.6	1.7	3.4
Sweden	3.1	1.9	1.9	1.3	3.0	2.2	2.0	1.6	2.3	2.4
Australia	4.5	2.3	3.5	2.5	4.0	2.0	3.6	2.4	3.5	1.2
Canada	3.5	2.4	1.5	2.8	3.2	1.8	2.1	2.6	2.9	1.4
Denmark	3.0	2.5	2.2	2.3	1.7	2.5	2.6	2.2	2.0	3.1
Netherlands	2.7	2.4	2.2	2.6	2.1	2.1	2.6	2.3	2.6	2.1
Average	3.5	2.4	2.0	2.1	3.2	2.4	2.4	2.1	2.7	2.3

growth at the cost of a price level (or its first difference) which fluctuates widely in response to variations in the growth of nominal demand. Similarly, if there are autonomous fluctuations in the rate of rise of the aggregate supply curve (because, say, of irregular pushing up of money wages which are not entirely market-flexible) then the country which follows an accommodative monetary policy may achieve smooth growth at the cost of varying (and probably high) wage and price inflation, while one which maintains steady growth of the money supply, or, *a fortiori*, one which squeezes money growth in response to accelerating inflation, may be expected to reduce the variability (as well as the average rate) of inflation at the cost of wide variations in rate of growth of activity. Do our sample countries manifest such differences of policy and/or institutional character in the balances which they achieve between the variabilities of the first differences of output and of price?

It is plain that, over the period as a whole, there is only the ghost of a negative relation. Six of our countries show very nearly equal dispersions of growth rate, with those of their inflation rates varying over a wide range, from Italy at the top to the United States at the bottom. The two countries with more variable growth rate, Japan and Germany, are at the lower end of the range of inflation variability, but then so are two (France and Sweden) out of the three with low growth variance; only the fact that the third, the United Kingdom, is towards the upper end makes the correlation slightly negative.

Nor can it be said that the corresponding correlations for either of the sub-periods (on either of their two definitions) are more promising. In the absence of a clear overall relation, it is perhaps best to start with the characteristics of our sample countries, assessed from their rankings in regard to the two kinds of variability in question. How far is a given country consistent, as between sub-periods? Such consistency is not common. Japan has high variabilities of both growth rate and inflation throughout. Australia would have a similar record but that variability of growth becomes low after 1973. The United States shows low variability of price throughout and middling variability of growth rate rising to high after 1973. France starts with high variability of inflation falling later to a middling rank, while the variability of her growth rate is low throughout. The United Kingdom starts with both variabilities ranking low, but growth variability rises to a medium and inflation variability to a high rank; and so on.

If one looks simply at the ratio of the two standard deviations, inflation to growth, and compares it with the unweighted average for all the countries, there is still only limited consistency. One can say firmly that the United States and Germany show low ratios throughout (so would Denmark but for a period of relatively high inflation variability in the middle), and that for Australia the ratio is high throughout. But the United Kingdom, Japan, Canada and the Netherlands start on the low side and finish on the high; France, Italy and Sweden go the other way.

Of course, these last-mentioned instances of clear change in a country's ratio of inflation variability to growth variability might suggest a trade-off between the two through, for instance, a change from more to less accommodating monetary policy (or *vice versa*) in the face of irregular cost inflation. If, however, one turns back to the simple plots of one variability against the other for sub-periods, one finds that, in moving from the first sub-period to the second, about as many countries show changes of the same sign in both variabilities as show the opposite signs, which would suggest that some kind of trade-off may have occurred. (The results vary with the definition of sub-periods; the count is 6 to 5 against trade-off if one divides at 1967–8, 6 to 4 in favour with one neutral if one divides at 1973–4). It does not seem that any clear and simple empirical results on this question can be got from inspection of our data.

CONCLUSION

Subject to further inspection, taking other variables into account, what can we say about the relations of prices and quantities, or rather of price inflation and growth of output? We have just noted that their variabilities, in general, increase from the late 1960s, that of inflation rate especially, and that the extent to which one can characterise countries by reference to these variabilities, or the relation between them, in a way that holds good over both halves of our period, is very limited; and there is little sign of trade-off between the two. More generally, perhaps the most noteworthy point to emerge from our attempt to interpret price–quantity relations is the limited applicability of a reading which a simple Keynesian scheme might suggest – that the picture is dominated by short-term variations in the rate of movement of the aggregate demand curve, or in the advance of total nominal expenditure, with an upward-sloping, or steepening, aggregate supply curve playing a relatively passive part. The United States does, indeed, provide a basis for such an interpretation (with a barely sloping supply curve) through several cycles from the mid-1950s to late in the 1960s; though with the implication that the supply curve was rising bodily at a roughly uniform rate. Some other countries – Germany, Japan, Italy – give a hint of this nearly horizontal curve for a cycle or two, and there is an occasional upward-sloping line or loop. But for most of the time in most countries changes seem to owe at least as much to shifts of the aggregate supply function as to shifts of the expenditure line. This is so especially in the 1970s, but for the United Kingdom and France, for instance, it is so throughout. In particular, the major quasi-permanent shifts of inflation to higher levels seem to have been associated with shifts of the aggregate supply curve, sometimes accommodated by shifts of expenditure, sometimes not fully accommodated. With some exceptions, they occurred when activity was high in relation to trend, but not systematically in coincidence with large increases of activity.

In the cyclical movements of the earlier part of our period, appearances in several countries (including United States, United Kingdom and Germany) support the suggestion that high activity, in relation to trend, goes with, or is shortly followed by increase of inflation; they are equally consistent with increased rate of inflation being shortly followed by a reduction of the rate of increase of nominal expenditure.

After about 1968, the connection between high inflation and reduced activity becomes stronger and more nearly simultaneous in the United States, United Kingdom, France and Italy, and change in level of activity is no longer closely followed by change of the rate of inflation in the same direction. Japan and Germany alone establish, or re-establish, the positive, short-lagged or simultaneous activity-inflation connection after 1973. In the former four countries, the aggregate supply curve apparently became more dominant and independent from the late 1960s; in the latter two its movements apparently began in the mid-1970s (or, in Germany, began again) to follow those of the expenditure line fairly closely.

4

INFLATIONARY AND DISINFLATIONARY IMPULSES

INFLATIONARY AND DISINFLATIONARY EPISODES

One way of looking for the nature of the forces behind specific changes in the rate of price inflation is to define the main kinds of inflationary and disinflationary impulse to which they might be attributable, to consider whether these kinds of impulse are likely to have particular symptoms in the data, and then to search for such symptoms. For this purpose we propose to examine the eleven OECD countries previously considered; data (especially those relating to profit share) are not available for Brazil or India on a sufficiently comparable basis, and we shall therefore make what observations we can about those two countries separately.

This is an episodic approach; each acceleration and each deceleration of inflation is treated as a separate episode. The periods of rising inflation are shown by horizontal straight lines in table 4.1. We may begin with some remarks about the number and duration of these episodes in aggregate and in the different countries.

In the eleven OECD countries, over our 29 annual intervals, we have 76 episodes of rising inflation rate. Twenty-nine of them are single-year affairs (including a number in the first and last years of the period, which may not be complete), 28 extend over two years, fourteen over three, four over four years and one (the gentle acceleration of inflation in Canada, 1962–6), over five. If we exclude the end-years, 1951 and 1979, two or three years is the most common duration of an inflationary episode. Their distribution in time is interesting. There is only one year, 1967, when price inflation was not accelerating in any of the eleven countries and only in two years, 1951 and 1974, was it doing so in all of them. Judged simply by the number out of this small sample of countries in which such acceleration was taking place, there were five well-marked peaks of inflationary experience; 1956 (nine countries), 1962 (seven), 1969 (ten), and the summits of 1951 and 1974 already mentioned. The final year, 1979, turned out to be leading to another eleven-country peak in 1980. But the general impression is of very considerable variety of experience between countries.

Collectively, our OECD Eleven experienced accelerating inflation for about 46 per cent of the time. Given this, if their episodes had been perfectly synchronised, there would have been thirteen or fourteen years out of our 29 in which they all had this experience and fifteen or sixteen in which none had it. In fact, the most frequent number of countries having it was six (in six years). In over half the years, the number of countries with accelerating inflation was three, four, five or six out of our eleven. This reinforces or amplifies the impression given by the inter-country correlations in chapter 2. To judge from this sample the temporal pattern of worldwide inflation is far from being common to all countries, but also some way from random international variation.

India and Brazil both start the period with biases towards one-year inflationary episodes but both lose it later; indeed, Brazil reverses it with only two episodes of increasing inflation (totalling five years together) in the last fifteen years of our period – a surprising record for by far the most inflationary member of our extended group.

We also mark in table 4.1 (by dots) the periods of accelerating real output growth. It is clear that they do not correspond with the periods of rising inflation. A χ^2 test shows that the coincidences of the two kinds of period are less frequent than would be expected if the years of rising inflation were randomly distributed, the deficiency being significant at the 10 per cent level. If, however, we count the number of occasions on which a year of rising growth is followed by one of rising inflation, we get a number in excess of random expectation, though not quite at the 10 per cent level of significance.

It will be adequate to assume for present purposes that in any year when the inflation rate in a country is not rising, it is falling. The number of cases of constancy, within the limits of our measurement, is small. This gives us 70 disinflationary (or, at least, non-inflationary) episodes in the eleven-country sample, against 76 inflationary ones. Since the former occupy a nearly equal (in fact, slightly longer) total time, they are, on average, appreciably longer than the inflationary episodes. They include far fewer one-year episodes (18 against 29) and more of four or more years' duration (sixteen against five). Perhaps this reflects the greater acceptability of falling than of rising inflation and a smaller tendency, in our period, to seek its early reversal by measures of policy.

INFLATIONARY IMPULSES

We shall try to distinguish four kinds of inflationary impulse; wage-push, expenditure-pull, cost-push from non-labour inputs and

Table 4.1 *Inflationary and disinflationary impulses*

	1951	1952	1953	1954	1955	1956	1957	1958	1959	1960	1961	1962	1963
United States		W			W		M		E		M	E	M
		NI, NE	NM		NM	NE			NM		NI, A		
United Kingdom	E, I		E, M	M, I	W, I		M	M	M, I	E			E, M
		NE, NI	NW, NI		NM	NM	A	A, NI		NM	NM	NE, NM	
Japan	I			I		M, W	E		I	E, M	E, M		
		NI		NW	NE		NM, NW	NI, NE	NM			NE	
Germany	I			I, W	E	W	M	M	I	I, W		W	
	NM	NI, NW	NE		NM	NE		NI	NM	NM	NI, NE	NE	A
France	I			I, W		W		E	M	M, E	M, W		
		NI, NE	NI, NW			NM	NM, NW	NM		NW	NE		NM
Italy	I		M, E	W		W		M	M	W	W	M, W	W
		NI	NW	NM, NE	NM		NE	NI	NW				NM
Sweden	I			E	W	I, A	M		I, M, E	W	W	M	M
		NI, NE	NI, NE		NM		NW	NI, NE		NM	NM, NE	NE	NE
Australia	I, W		E	M	I		M		E	W		E	M, E
		NI, NW	NM, NW	NE	NM, NE			NW			NE	NW	
Canada	I	M	I	M		A	W	M	A		M	E	M
		NI	NE	NE	NW	NM	NE		NM	NM	NW		NW
Denmark	I		M	I	I		M	M	I, E	I	W	M, E	I, M
		NI, NW	NI	NM, NE	NM, NE			NI, NE		NM, NE	NM		NE
Netherlands	I	M	E	I, W	I, M	I		M	E	E		W	M
		NI, NE	NI, NM	NM	NW	NM, NE	NM	NI		NM	NE	NM	

the accelerated injection of money, running ahead of any increase of demand. For a start we take any of these impulses to be exogenous events; remarks on how they, in turn, are to be explained should be regarded as, in the main, preliminary to later consideration. We shall also recognise that any of them may impinge upon an economy without in fact causing an increase in the rate of price inflation: a wage-push may be wholly absorbed by compression of profits; increased expenditure whether resulting from money injection or not, may result in increase in physical output rather than increase in price, and so on. We may therefore take note of such impulses in some instances when we cannot connect them directly with faster increase of price.

This approach does not presuppose that the influence of money supply on inflation is limited to those occasions on which we diagnose money injection. Accommodating increases in money supply, in response to demands generated by wage-push or expenditure-pull, may be essential to the effectiveness of those impulses in accelerating

1964	1965	1966	1967	1968	1969	1970	1971	1972	1973	1974	1975	1976	1977	1978	1979
A NM	E	A NM	M NE	A	NM	M NE	M, E	E	NM	I, W NE	NI, NM	E NM, NW	M	M	I NE, NM
M, A NE	W NE, NM	NE, NM	M NW	W, I	NI, NM	W	E, M	M	I, M	W, I NE, NM	E NI, NM	I NE	M NW, NI	M NI	M, W, I
E NM	NE		E NM	E NM	M		M NE		I, W NM	I, W NE, NM	NI	E NW	NE, NM	NI, NW	I
E	M	NE	M NW	E	W NM	W NI, NM	I, M NE	M NE	I, W NM	I NE	M NI, NE	E NM, NW	NE	NI	E, I NM
NM	NW		M	W	I, E NM	M	M NI	M	I, W NM	I, W NM	M NI, NE	I NM		NM, NI	I NM
NE	M NW	M, E NW	NM		W NM	W	M NE	M A	I, E	I, E NM	M, W NI, NE	I, E NW	W NI	M NI, NW	I, E NM
E NM		M NE	M, A A	M NM	E NM	I, E NM	M NI, NE	M, W	I, E NW	I, E NM	W NI, NM	W NM, NE	I NE	M, E	I, M
M, W NM, NE						W NM	M NM	W NW	W	I, W NM	M NI, NW	M NI, NW	I NM	M NI, NM, NW	I
M, A NM	W NM	W NM	M NE	M, E NM	A NE		E	M, E	I, E	I, E W	NI, NE	NI	I NE	NM, NW	E
E NE	W NE	M NE		I, E		I NI	W NM	M, E NM	I, M NI, NW	I, W NE	M NI, NW	I, E NW	I NM, NE	NI, NM	I, M
M, A A	W NE	M NM	M, E NI	I, E NM, NW	I NM, NE	M, W NI	M NI		I, E	I, M	NI.	E NW	NI, NE	NI, NE, NM	I NE

inflation and absence of such accommodation may be effective in reducing the inflation rate – a subject which we shall have to examine separately later. For the time being, we are concerned only to identify the leading inflationary impulses of particular years and, of these impulses, the injection of money ahead of demand for it is only one. Whether the non-monetary impulses always accompany or follow, and appear to be consequences of, previous money injections is one of the questions on which we hope to throw some light.

How then do we diagnose our four kinds of impulse? The easiest, on the face of it, is *money injection*, but there are two sources of possible ambiguity connected with it; the definition of the money stock and the criterion of change in demand for it. There are also two possible bases for assessing whether supply has run ahead of demand; interest and velocity of circulation. Market-determined interest rates presumably fall, other things being equal, if the supply of money rises more than the demand for it; the money supply, in this context, being M1, which mostly does not bear interest. But if it happened that expectations of increased inflation arose at the same time, then interest rates might well fail to fall, or might actually rise, while the perceived real rate of interest (which is relevant to decisions to spend) was still reduced. Interest changes as indicators of greater monetary ease have therefore to be looked at with discretion. The alternative indicator is the velocity of circulation, though this, of course, gives information only about how money stock is changing in relation to *transactions* demand, not total demand. In calculating it for this purpose it would seem at least as appropriate to use M2 (or M3) as M1; while the latter constitutes the means of payment, the former come nearer to measuring the stock of liquid assets which might be expected to influence decisions to spend.

We shall return to these ambiguities in chapter 6. For the present purpose of making a list of *prima facie* impulses, we propose to take the 'broad money' (money *plus* quasi-money) from *International Financial Statistics*, which approximates to M2 or M3, and to use velocity rather than interest as our criterion of the relative movements of monetary supply and demand.

Our criterion of *expenditure–pull* operating as an inflationary impulse is an increase in the rate of growth of money GDP and, at the same time, a rise in the share of gross profits in value-added. The reason for the latter condition is that increased expenditure on the country's output (either at home or abroad) is likely, in the first instance, either to raise the degree of utilisation of productive capacity or to raise output prices, or both. If the wage and salary bill does not rise to match the increased revenue of enterprises at once, then the gross profit share will be expanded. This is not, of course, an inevitable consequence of increased expenditure; it is possible in principle that the overhead elements in labour costs are unimportant, that prices are rigid and that wages respond quickly to increased demand. In that case, events will conform to some of the signs of wage–push, to be discussed below. However, increased growth of nominal GDP and a shift to profits, if they occur, seem likely to indicate an expansionary impulse from the demand side, even though such an impulse might sometimes produce other symptoms. The presumption is that the percentage rate of increase of the wage and salary bill will adjust itself to equality with any steady rate of growth of total nominal income, but that if the latter is raised from the demand side the share of wages and salaries in value added is likely to dip, that of gross profits to rise.

The data on the share of profits in value-added which we have used are mainly those calculated by T. P. Hill (1979) (updated in OECD (1984)) for manufacturing industry. The restriction of the test to that sector of the economy is less than ideal, but it makes possible a matching of profit-share data with wage data which is desirable. Professor Hill's data do not cover our whole period, nor are they available for France. To fill the gaps they have been supplemented by estimates from the McCracken Report and by calculations of our own based not on the manufacturing sector but on national accounting data for the whole economy. Some caution is therefore called for in interpreting these calculations.

It will be obvious that money injection, discussed above, may result in an increase in domestic demand, leading to expenditure–pull, with the symptoms we have just noted. The expenditure–pull symptoms may occur in the same period as those of money injection, or they may be delayed until a later one. In the former case, therefore, we have increased growth of GDP, increased share of profits, increased growth of (broad) money stock and reduced growth of velocity of circulation. If, on the other hand, increase of expenditure growth is currently running ahead of that of the money supply, velocity of circulation grows faster. We may think of this as a pure increase in expenditure growth, without prejudice to the question whether it is the consequence of money injection in an earlier period – the point is that money supply is not wholly (though it may be partly) accommodating it as it occurs.

Wage–push clearly implies an increase in the rate of increase of wages. To distinguish this from the case where wage inflation is pulled up by increased growth of expenditure on products, we also stipulate that the profit share of value-added should at least temporarily be reduced. The argument is the inverse of the one we used in formulating the symptoms of expenditure–pull – an acceleration of increase in the wage bill is unlikely to be matched simultaneously by an equal acceleration of the growth of the nominal income of enterprises. Either unit prices will fall behind unit labour costs for a time, or growth of real sales will be adversely affected, or both. Once more, it is possible that these consequences may be avoided; foresight and monetary accommodation to the wage acceleration may be perfect, but that is a limiting case of which actuality is likely mostly to fall short. For our purpose, hourly earnings provide the best measure of wages since they represent the prices actually paid for labour, inclusive of any effects of wage drift and, one hopes, also of any black wages in excess of the published wage rates included in wage rate indices.

Non-wage cost–push, for a national economy, can be most conveniently interpreted as coming mainly from import prices and we accordingly treat it as synonymous with import price–push. Since the national price indices we have chosen are the GDP deflators, they are not directly and necessarily affected by import prices; if an increase (say) in cost of imports is fully and exactly passed on into prices of final products, the GDP deflator is unaffected. Domestic purchasers of goods and services, with unchanged money incomes and higher prices to pay, will suffer a fall in real income, but how the profit share of value-added is affected will depend on the relative speeds with which enterprises raise their prices by *more* than the absolute amount of the rise in import costs in order to maintain real profits, and employees manage to bid up their wages and salaries in efforts to maintain the real purchasing power of their pay. Both price and wage raising are likely to follow a rise of import prices, unless shortage of final demand forbids, so that import price–push may be regarded as a probable inflationary influence. The effect on the factor distribution of incomes, however, is not sufficiently certain to be used as a test of whether cost–push rather than demand–pull is the main process at work, as we do with wage–push. Indeed, there is usually no comparable need for such a test. Most countries are sufficiently small parts of the world economy for rises in import prices to be regarded as mainly exogenous – influenced in only a minor degree by their own levels of demand. (The United States will have to be treated with caution as a possible exception.) Changes due to foreign exchange depreciation are in a different case, but depreciations are directly observable and their price effects can be assessed. Our criterion for import price–push can therefore be simply a rise in import prices, or rather, in their rate of increase. For simplicity we have limited our diagnosis of this kind of inflationary impulse to cases where increase in the percentage rate of annual import price inflation, multiplied by the ratio of imports to GDP, exceeds 1 per cent.

Changes in net indirect taxation affect the GDP deflator directly, as well as indirectly (since we are dealing with aggregates at market prices). They will have to be borne in mind.

Our *prima facie* tests for the four kinds of inflationary impulse are therefore as follows:

Money–injection (M) – rate of increase of broad money rises and rate of increase of the corresponding velocity (V_2) falls.

Expenditure–pull (E) – rate of increase of money GDP rises; profit share of value-added in manufacture rises.

Wage–push (W) – rate of increase of hourly earnings rises and profit share of value-added in manufacture falls.

Import price cost–push (I) – rate of change of import price weighted by import share of GDP rises by more than 1 per cent.

It will be seen that money-injection and non-wage cost-push can go together, or with any of the other two kinds of impulse, but that wage-push is by definition incompatible with expenditure-pull.

DISINFLATIONARY IMPULSES

These four types of impulse have counterparts which may be presumed to exercise disinflationary effects. It will be simplest to think of them as simply negative versions of our four inflationary impulses, and to symbolise them accordingly as NM, NE, NW and NI. Their symptoms thus are:

NM – a fall in the rate of growth of the money stock coupled with a rise in that of V_2.

NE – a fall in the rate of growth of money GDP coupled with a fall in the profit share of value-added (normally in manufacturing),

NW – a fall in the rate of wage inflation coupled with a rise in the profit share of value-added (normally in manufacturing), and

NI – a fall of 1 per cent or more in a year in the weighted rate of increase (or corresponding rise in the rate of decrease) of inflation of import prices. The impulses are, of course, incompatible with their inflationary opposite numbers but not with other inflationary impulses nor with each other, save that NE and NW are mutually incompatible (as are E and W), because of opposite requirements in regard to movements of the profit share.

AMBIGUOUS CASES

There are, however, some cases in which the rates of growth of both nominal expenditure and hourly earnings increase without any definite change in the profit share. These can be thought of as involving the forces of both expenditure-pull and wage-push working simultaneously or, at least, too close together for the differences in their times of operation to be visible in annual data. They need further scrutiny, however, at least because of the complications which changes in the rate of growth of productivity may introduce.

Accelerated growth of expenditure may fail to raise the profit share, even though wage inflation has not changed, if growth of labour productivity has declined. Cases of this are, however, rare in our data. Productivity growth declined while expenditure growth rose in the United States in 1966, but wage inflation rose too and even though the profit share did not change appreciably it seems appropriate to class this as essentially a case of simultaneous wage-push and expenditure-pull, or accommodated wage-push. There are a number of cases like this, except that they do not involve the rather rare event of expenditure growth and productivity growth moving in opposite directions (for example, United States 1968, United Kingdom 1964); also of the negative counterpart – remissions of both demand pressure and wage inflation (for example, United Kingdom 1958). We denote all these by the symbol A (for accommodation), with a further indication of whether they are positive or negative.

A case of a different and unusual kind arose in Japan in 1969, when expenditure growth fell and wage inflation rose, but there was a big surge of productivity growth and the profit share remained constant. We do not attempt to classify this event. Nor do we classify several other occurrences in which the data we are using on the directions of change in growth of wages, productivity, prices and factor shares are in some way mutually inconsistent. It has to be remembered that the data (apart from their inherent imperfections) do not all relate to the same concept – the prices relate to the whole economy, the rest to the manufacturing sector.

NUMBERS OF IMPULSES

The results of searching for these symptoms are shown in tables 4.1, 4.2 and 4.3. In table 4.1 the top line for each country is reserved for the indicators of inflation and growth rates, the second line for symbols of positive impulses and the bottom line for symbols of negative ones. Tables 4.2 and 4.3 show the numbers of different kinds of impulse classified by year and by country respectively – also (table 4.3) according to whether they occur in or out of periods of rising inflation.

We have diagnosed 588 impulses in our eleven countries, 312 of them inflationary and 276 disinflationary. The numbers of occurrences of each of the four kinds, positive and negative, are graphed year by year in chart 4.1; the numbers of negative impulses (dashed lines) are measured downwards from the same base lines from which their positive counterparts (continuous lines) are measured upwards. (The positive and negative A impulses are ignored in this chart.)

The (inversely-measured) negative impulse series show generally quite good correlations with their positive counterparts, though there are times when the correlation breaks down – for the two wage-push series from about 1957 to 1966, for instance. The general characteristics of the pairs of series for each kind of impulse are not without interest. The money impulses show a well-marked cyclical tendency with a period of four (sometimes five) years. A similar, not quite so well marked, tendency is visible in the expenditure-pull series, perhaps more clearly in the negative one, but its phases do not coincide with those of the monetary impulses. There is a noticeable tendency for the expenditure series to lag a year behind the monetary ones, for example in the peaks of 1958 and 1959, 1963 and 1964, 1967 and 1968, 1972 and 1973, 1975 and 1976. The relation is lacking

Table 4.2 *Impulses: kind and year*

Year	M	E	W	I	NM	NE	NW	NI	A+	A−
1951	—	1	1	10	1	—	—	—	—	—
1952	2	—	—	—	—	5	3	11	—	—
1953	3	4	1	1	3	3	4	5	—	—
1954	3	1	4	6	3	4	1	—	—	—
1955	1	1	2	4	7	3	2	—	—	—
1956	1	—	5	2	4	2	—	—	2	—
1957	5	1	1	—	3	2	3	—	—	1
1958	7	1	—	—	1	3	1	7	—	1
1959	4	5	—	5	4	—	1	—	1	—
1960	2	4	4	2	6	1	1	—	—	—
1961	4	1	4	—	3	5	1	2	—	1
1962	3	4	3	—	2	4	1	—	—	—
1963	7	2	1	1	2	2	—	—	—	1
1964	4	4	1	—	4	1	—	—	4	—
1965	2	1	3	—	2	4	1	—	—	1
1966	3	1	2	—	3	5	1	—	1	—
1967	7	1	—	—	3	2	2	—	1	—
1968	3	5	2	2	1	—	—	1	1	1
1969	1	3	2	2	8	—	1	2	1	—
1970	2	1	3	3	5	3	—	1	—	—
1971	8	3	3	1	2	4	2	3	—	—
1972	9	3	1	—	—	1	2	2	—	1
1973	2	4	4	9	4	—	1	—	—	—
1974	1	3	6	11	6	5	—	—	—	—
1975	5	1	3	—	3	3	2	11	—	—
1976	1	6	1	4	4	2	7	2	—	—
1977	2	—	1	4	3	6	1	3	—	—
1978	4	1	—	—	5	1	4	8	—	—
1979	3	3	1	10	4	2	—	—	—	—
Total	99	65	59	77	96	74	42	58	11	7

before 1958; the data are, however, less complete and reliable for the first half of the 1950s than subsequently.

The wage-push series show a cyclical tendency also, especially the positive one. In some cases its peaks fall a year behind those in instances of expenditure-pull, for example in 1953 and 1954, 1959 and 1960, 1964 and 1965 (if we ignore the 'A's) and in 1973 and 1974; but at other times there is little relation between them. The import-push series differ in general shape from the others in being mountainous at both ends and flat in the middle – only one impulse of either sign in the six years 1962–7 inclusive. The positive series shows a close correspondence in its movements with those of the wage-push series between 1967 and 1975 and one is tempted to suggest that the little spate of import price impulses in the mid-1950s may have helped to produce the wage-push impulses of that time. We must, however, not put too much weight on these rather fragile series of numbers of

Table 4.3 *Impulses: kind and country, 1951–79*

Country	M	E	W	I	NM	NE	NW	NI	A+	A−	Total +	Total −
United States	8	6	3	2	10	6	1	3	3	1	22	21
United Kingdom	14	6	6	9	9	6	3	7	1	2	36	27
Japan	5	7	3	6	8	7	4	4	—	1	21	23
Germany	7	5	7	8	9	10	3	6	—	—	27	29
France	8	3	6	7	11	3	4	5	—	1	24	23
Italy	10	6	10	5	7	4	6	5	—	1	31	23
Sweden	11	8	6	8	9	10	2	5	2	1	35	27
Australia	7	4	6	5	8	4	8	4	—	—	22	24
Canada	9	7	4	5	7	7	4	3	4	—	29	21
Denmark	10	6	4	13	8	9	4	7	—	—	33	28
Netherlands	10	7	4	9	10	8	3	9	1	1	31	31
Total	99	65	59	77	96	74	42	58	11	7	312	275
Out[a]	70	29	13	28	34	50	33	42	3	7	143	166
In[b]	29	36	46	49	62	24	9	16	8	0	168	111

[a][b] Occurrences In or Out of periods of rising inflation

ME Series of impulses, 11 countries

Chart 4.1 *Time series of impulses, eleven countries*

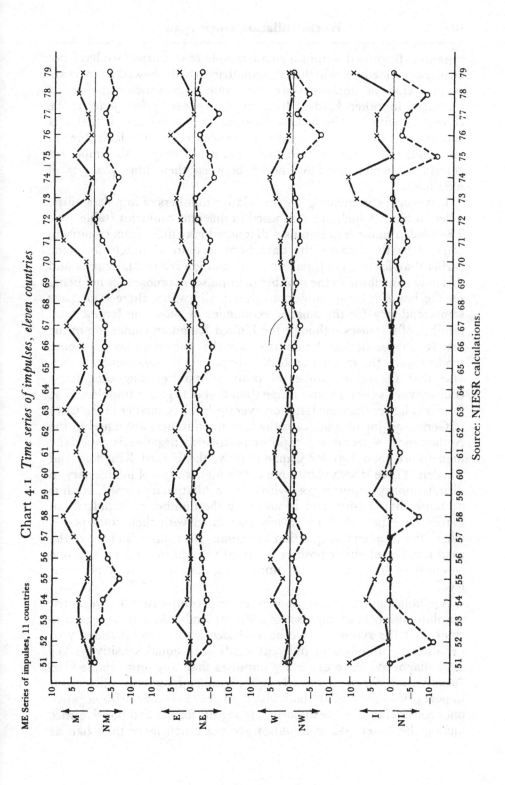

Source: NIESR calculations.

impulses diagnosed within a small sample of countries; we have not even ascertained yet whether the countries which showed an increase in one kind of impulse were the same ones which experienced increases in other kinds which might appear, *prima facie*, to be connected with it. The firmest observation that emerges is that of a considerable degree of cyclicality in the occurrence of at least three of our kinds of impulse within these countries, despite the imperfect correlation which we have noted between their time patterns of inflation.

It is worth commenting on the relative numbers of impulses of the different kinds which are diagnosed in different countries (table 4.3). The *absolute* number of impulses diagnosed may differ from country to country partly because the data become more complete for some earlier than for others (Japan, in particular is a relative latecomer and this may contribute to the number of impulses diagnosed for her being on the low side) but, subject to this qualification, there is perhaps some tendency for the smaller economies to show the largest total number of impulses – though the United Kingdom comes top of the list. It may be nearer the point to say that the *more open* economies tend to show the larger numbers of impulses. It is, however, noticeable that the total number of positive impulses diagnosed for a country varies over a wider range than that of negative impulses. The former is larger than the latter on average but it is smaller in the cases of Germany, Japan and Australia and the numbers are equal in the Netherlands; whereas the ratio of positive to negative is especially high (more than 1.3) for Canada, Italy, the United Kingdom and Sweden. There is some hint here that a higher ratio of inflationary to disinflationary impulses goes with a more inflationary record, but it is no more than a hint, and in any case the number of impulses can hardly be expected to be closely correlated with their total power where the numbers in question are small. No country's share of the total number of either positive or negative impulses differs from one eleventh of the total by an amount significant at the 5 per cent level.

A similar qualification applies to any comparison between the absolute numbers of impulses of different kinds; there is no reason to think that the symptoms we have chosen lead us to inflationary or deflationary impulses of different kinds with equal sensitivity. We have diagnosed more monetary impulses than any other single kind (positive and negative in nearly equal numbers); our expenditure and import price impulses are both about 30 per cent fewer, with negative ones considerably in the majority among the former and positive ones among the latter. Wage impulses are not much more than half as numerous as monetary impulses, with positive ones very much in the majority.

The balance between positive and negative impulses of the same kind is perhaps more meaningful. The nearly equal numbers of positive and negative monetary impulses is in keeping with their having a predominantly cyclical character. The preponderance of positive impulses from import prices and wages, while not inconsistent with a good deal of cyclicality in their occurrence, carries some suggestion of their part in producing the upward trend in inflation rates over our period. The preponderance of negative expenditure impulses could mean that the positive ones are more powerful, on average, than the negative, but it perhaps more plausibly suggests that accelerations of expenditure growth were accompanied by cost accelerations, which prevented the profit share from increasing, more often than decelerations were accompanied by correspondingly effective cost decelerations.

Different countries in our sample vary considerably in the relative numbers of particular kinds of impulse which we have diagnosed in them. The United Kingdom, Italy, Sweden, Denmark, the Netherlands and Canada are above average in the numbers of positive monetary impulses which they show, but only the United Kingdom's excess is significant at the 5 per cent point. The United States, France and the Netherlands are slightly above average in negative monetary impulses. Japan shows few monetary impulses in either sense, but rather more than her share of expenditure impulses; the Netherlands also shows large numbers of positive and negative expenditure impulses, whereas France and Australia show relatively few, but the discrepancies are not significant. Italy, however, shows a significant excess over her expected number of positive wage impulses, with the United Kingdom, Germany, France, Sweden and Australia also (though not significantly) above average. The United States, Canada, Denmark and the Netherlands are below. Australia presents a significantly large number of negative impulses of this kind. The highest scores in import price impulses go, naturally enough, to the most open economies – Denmark, the Netherlands, Sweden, the United Kingdom, and by far the fewest to the United States. The Danish and American discrepancies are significant.

THE TIMING OF IMPULSES IN RELATION TO INFLATION

The timing of the impulses with regard to periods of accelerating inflation in the country in question is shown in the simplest way (according to whether they fall in or outside such periods) in table 4.3.

In aggregate, positive monetary impulses fall nearly two-thirds outside inflationary periods, the other kinds of positive impulse mostly inside, especially positive wage impulses, though the departure of expenditure impulses from a random distribution between the two kinds of period is not significant. Correspondingly, negative monetary impulses occur mostly inside inflationary periods and the other kinds of disinflationary impulse mainly outside (all to significant extents). National experiences do not all correspond to these generalisations, however. The only exception to those about monetary impulses is provided by Japan, three out of whose five positive impulses were during inflationary periods, but there is much less regularity in the occurrence of expenditure impulses; Germany and the Netherlands had most of their positive impulses outside inflationary periods (with the United States, United Kingdom and Australia breaking even) and the United States, United Kingdom and Denmark had most of their negative impulses of this kind within bursts of accelerating inflation. Wage impulses provide fewer exceptions; only Germany had most of her positive impulses outside (though Sweden and Canada broke even) and none of our sample countries was a clear exception to the generalisation that negative wage impulses are mostly outside, though France broke even. Denmark provides the only exception to the general experience of import price impulses; four out of her seven negative impulses occurred inside inflationary periods. The general tendency seems to have been, therefore, for monetary impulses to work against the current tide of inflation and the other impulses to swim with it, but the tendency is least clear-cut in the case of expenditure impulses, with Germany, in particular, against the rising tide on balance and the United States and United Kingdom neutral with respect to both the ebb and the flow.

SEQUENCES AND COINCIDENCES OF IMPULSES

In looking at the time series of numbers of impulses of different kinds in our sample countries collectively, we remarked that there seemed to be some tendency for peaks in M to be followed by peaks in E in the succeeding year and perhaps a weaker tendency for these in turn to be followed at a year's distance by peaks in W. Can such a sequence be traced frequently within individual countries? It is, of course, a sequence which appears *a priori* not improbable, being consistent with, for instance, the theory of the trade cycle associated mainly with the name of Hawtrey – perhaps especially as expounded along with related theories, by Haberler.

Let us look first at the occurrences of M and E. We may usefully count the occurrences of M followed by E in the immediately succeeding year and the cases where they occur in the same year. For completeness, and because it is possible that expenditure-pull may sometimes lead in the following year to a money-injection which is essentially accommodating, but is sufficient to lower the velocity of circulation (which may have been driven up by the expenditure impulse), we may as well also count the occurrences of E followed immediately by M. Where the two impulses occur in the same year, we cannot, of course, distinguish from our data the cases in which M caused E from those in which, by eliciting an accommodation of the sort just described, E caused M. If, however, we consider first the cases where there is a year's lag in one direction or the other, we find that in aggregate those where M leads predominate, in the ratio of about 3:2 (26 cases to 18 if we exclude the A impulses, 32 to 20 if we include them). This predominance does not extend to all countries; in Australia and France it is reversed and the same is true of the United Kingdom if one does not include the two cases in which A immediately follows M. The tendency for M to lead rather than follow is, however, particularly strong in the United States, Germany, Italy and the Netherlands.

Taking occurrences of M as given, however, one can readily calculate the numbers of cases in which they might be expected to be preceded, accompanied and followed by E, if the actual number of Es were randomly distributed. The actual number of cases in which M leads E turns out to be appreciably greater than expectation, though not quite to the 10 per cent level of significance; the actual cases of E leading M and of coincidence, do not differ from random expectation significantly. In individual countries, the tendency of M to lead E seems to be significant only for the United States and the Netherlands.

On looking at the corresponding negative impulses, we find that the differences between their numbers are in the same directions as with the positive ones, and that the number of cases where NM leads NE is significant at the 10 per cent level. None of the other numbers differ significantly from what might have been expected from a random distribution.

There is thus some (though not very strong) evidence of a tendency for E to follow M; is there also one for W to follow E? The number of cases does not, in fact, exceed random expectation significantly; nor does the number of positive As, which can be regarded as coincidences of E and W, obliterating the distinguishing marks of both, differ significantly from the number of coincidences that might be expected between the two kinds of impulse if they were independent of

Table 4.4 *Cases of coincidence and sequence*

	Expected	Observed	χ^2
Rising inflation with rising growth*	59.5	50	2.8
Rising growth → rising inflation (next year)*	57.2	66	2.5
M with rising inflation	45.6	29	11.1
M → rising inflation (next year)	44.2	42	0.2
M → rising inflation (in 2 years)	42.4	51	3.2
M with rising growth	42.5	36	1.8
M → rising growth (next year)	41.1	47	1.2
M → rising growth (in 2 years)	37.5	39	0.1
E with rising inflation	30.0	36	2.2
E → rising inflation (next year)	28.6	29	0.0
E with rising growth	28.0	53	39.2
E → rising growth (next year)	26.7	19	3.9
M → E (next year)	19.6	26	2.6
M with E	20.2	17	0.7
E → M (next year)	19.2	18	0.1
M with W	18.3	8	7.1
M → W (next year)	17.8	16	0.2
M → W (in 2 years)	17.0	19	0.3
M with I	23.9	9	12.3
M → I (next year)	23.2	21	0.3
M → I (in 2 years)	22.2	29	2.8
NM → NE (next year)	21.1	26	1.5
NM with NE	22.0	18	1.0
NE → NM (next year)	21.4	20	0.1
E → W (next year)	14.4	12	0.5
E with NM	19.4	23	1.0
NE with M	23.0	19	1.0
W with rising inflation*	26.6	45	23.6
W with I	14.2	17	0.7
I → W (next year)	12.4	14	0.3
I with rising inflation	35.4	49	9.7
NM with rising inflation	43.8	61	12.5
NM with rising growth	39.1	45	1.5
NM with W *or* I	40.5	58	13.2
NE with rising inflation	34.0	24	5.4
NW with rising inflation	19.3	9	10.2
NI with rising inflation	26.7	16	7.9

* From 1953 inclusive. *Significance points of* χ^2: 10% 2.7, 5% 3.8, 1% 6.6, 0.1% 10.7.

each other. Similarly negative conclusions follow from an examination of the NEs and NWs. The suggestion that there might be a significant MEW sequence, or its negative counterpart, thus runs into the sand.

Is there then any evidence for M being accompanied or followed by W, for a monetary impulse to tend to generate a wage impulse without the intervention of an impulse of expenditure? The number of coincidences of M and W (8) turns out to be significantly (well above the 1 per cent level) *below* chance expectation, which may be taken as meaning that positive monetary impulses are to a significant extent avoided when wage-push is in progress. The numbers of cases of W immediately succeeding M, and following it after two years, do not differ significantly from what one would expect from the given number of Ms and a random distribution of Ws.

Results rather like these last two follow from an inspection of coincidences between M and I and of the sequence M–I. The number of the former is *below* expectation by an amount significant at the 1 per cent level; there is a strong tendency to avoid positive monetary impulses when there is import price-push. The number of instances of the one-year sequence again does not differ significantly from random expectation but I follows M after *two* years more often; the significance level is above 10 per cent. If one regards the Is as exogenous for each particular country, there is no theoretical presumption that M should lead to I after some interval. This rather weak empirical tendency may, in that case, be regarded as the result of the international cycle, which we detected in chart 4.1, underlying the diversities of national experience. Alternatively, or in addition, there may be cases where I is *not* exogenous, but results from currency devaluation following as a consequence of earlier national expansion.

One might well look for some evidence that I tends to be either accompanied or followed by W. The numbers of instances of these associations are, indeed, both above random expectation, though not significantly so in aggregate; but for the United Kingdom, which exhibits four coincidences of these two impulses, the conjunction approaches significance. For all our countries together, broadly similar results are obtained for negative import price and wage impulses.

Besides their relations with each other, the relations of the impulses with price and output acceleration are worth a further glance. We have, indeed, already looked at their coincidences with periods of accelerating inflation; we saw that positive monetary impulses are dissociated from such periods (highly significantly, in fact) and negative ones associated with them, and that all the other kinds of positive impulse are associated with rising inflation and of negative impulse dissociated from it, except that positive expenditure impulses do not show a significant relation.

Do positive monetary impulses show a systematic connection with accelerating inflation in the *following* year? They do not. The number of instances of the sequence is slightly below random expectation, but the association of positive monetary impulses with rising inflation *two* years ahead falls not far short of significance at the 5 per cent level. Do positive expenditure impulses show any more sign of association with accelerating inflation in the following year than in the current one?

Again, the answer is negative. On the other hand, it will be recalled that the association of positive *wage* impulses with currently accelerating inflation is very close (in fact, much above the 0.1 per cent level).

The association of positive monetary impulses with currently accelerating *output* growth is negative, but not significantly so. Their association with accelerating growth in the *following* year becomes positive, but falls short of the 10 per cent point of significance. Positive expenditure impulses, on the other hand, show an association with currently accelerating output growth which, unlike that with current or immediate future inflation, is very close indeed – nearly five-sixths of them coincide with rising growth rates. Their association with the rising growth rate in the *following* year, however, is just significantly negative at the 5 per cent point.

The prevalence of offsetting impulses is another matter of interest. Neither E nor NE is accompanied by countervailing monetary impulses (NM and M respectively) to an extent that differs appreciably from a random distribution of the latter taking the data as a whole, nor do the records of separate countries differ significantly from the general experience, except that the United Kingdom stands out to some extent in showing no positive monetary impulses coinciding with negative expenditure ones, and that Canada and Denmark do so by showing no combinations of E and NM.

There is, however, more sign of a general tendency for W and I to be opposed by other impulses. If we take these two kinds of inflationary impulse together and see how far negative expenditure and monetary impulses (also taken together) coincide with them, we find the excess over what a random distribution would lead one to expect is significant at the 10 per cent level. The United States, where all five occurrences of W or I are thus opposed and Germany, where twelve out of fifteen are, stand out significantly from random expectation; the United Kingdom and Italy (both six out of fifteen) stand out in the opposite direction, but not quite to the 10 per cent significance level.

Of the two kinds of negative impulse, it is NM that is by far the more closely associated with W and I. If one omits the years before 1953, for which monetary data are less complete, the association is significant at the 0.1 per cent level.

MAJOR MOVEMENTS

It is a limitation of the method of diagnosis used in this chapter that no account is taken of the relative strengths of particular impulses nor of the relative severities of different inflationary episodes. Many of the movements on which it depends are cyclical and we saw in chapter 3 that most of the inflation of our period is attributable to increases in the inflation rate which were not reversed by 1979. We need to identify these main non-cyclical (or, at least, not reversed) increases and to enquire to what kinds of impulse they seem to have been due. (We may usefully do the same for non-cyclical decreases as well.)

There are, to start with, certain years when major increases or decreases in the rate of inflation were common to all, or nearly all our countries; 1951 and 1973–4 for increases, 1952 and 1975–6 for decreases. In most cases, these years are associated with shifts on the diagrams of quantity and price, and of output gap and price, which stand out from the more repetitive cyclical movements of the period. In terms of the impulses we have identified, what are their characteristics?

Data for 1951 are not so complete as for later years, but it is clear that all the countries except the United States (with a little doubt about Japan and Germany) received import price-pushes. Apart from a wage impulse in Australia and expenditure-pull in the United Kingdom, other impulses are not recorded partly, though probably not wholly, for lack of data. At all events, it is fairly clear that the largely speculative rise in prices of primary commodities and metals due to the Korean war was the main driving force. The fact that average consumer prices in the industrial countries and the dollar export prices of manufactures, primary products, and non-ferrous metals rose by 10 per cent, 18 per cent, 25 per cent and 34 per cent respectively supports this interpretation. (Import prices rose more than export prices because of insurance and freight increases.)

For the fall of inflation rates in 1952, we have correspondingly negative import price impulses in all our countries, along with negative expenditure impulses in five and negative wage impulses in three of them (there were also two positive monetary impulses) and in the following year, when the inflation rate was still falling in most countries, import price and wage impulses were the most numerous kinds on the negative side. The Korean episode, in both its upward and its downward phases, seems to have affected our sample countries mainly through the rise and fall of inflation in the traded goods markets, reinforced in some cases by positive or negative wage-push. The United States differs from the others mainly in that the impact of world prices came more through internal channels (or exports) rather than imports.

The great upsurge of inflation in 1973–4 shows some similarities with that of 1951. In these two years, our eleven countries between them show twenty occurrences of I and ten of W. Cases of E and NE are not far from equal (7:5) and NM has a large (10:3) majority over M. This has to be viewed in conjunction with the record of the preceding two years, 1971–2, in which M had a 17:2 majority over NM, other kinds of impulse showing rough balance between their positive and negative manifestations, except that NI exceeded I (5:1). If one takes the four years together, however, it is import prices and wages that provide the most striking upward asymmetry in aggregate, though there were more Ms than NMs. Similarly, in 1975–6, when large falls in the rate of inflation were registered in most countries, it is the thirteen occurrences of NI and the nine of NW (against four of W) that seem to provide the downward bias, positives and negatives among both expenditure and (this time) monetary impulses being near to balance.

Apart from these episodes which turn on major disturbances in world markets, one has to look at individual countries for clues to their main accelerations and decelerations of inflation. There was a sharp jump in the rate in France in 1956, which is associated with W (and NM). The considerable falls in the United States, Japan, Australia and the Netherlands in 1958 may be regarded as connected with a world market recession – Japan and the Netherlands show NI – but the former also shows NE and Australia NW. The bounce-back in 1959, especially noticeable outside the usual cyclical pattern in Japan and Denmark, is marked by I in both.

At various times in the 1960s most countries showed upward movements from their previous cyclical tracks, though Italy, for instance, can be regarded as moving into a new, longer, cycle with a bigger inflation rate amplitude. The Italian upsurge of inflation in 1960–3 is marked by four occurrences of W, one of M and one of NM, the Netherlands upward creep of 1962–4 by a W, a positive A, and two Ms; the two United States jumps of 1966 and 1968 by positive As, the gradual Canadian ascent of 1964–6 by two Ws a positive A, an M and two NMs, the major German inflation peak of 1969–70 by two Ws (as well as an NI and two NMs), the corresponding Italian ascent (the 'hot autumn') also by two Ws (and an NM), the French jump of 1969 by an I (the result of devaluation), an E and an NM, following a W in 1968. And so on. The point of this catalogue, which could be extended, is that in movements that are unusually large or shifts of the cyclical pattern, or both, the two cost-push variables, W and I, seem to have played a disproportionately large part. At the end of our period, in 1979, I seems to have been associated with incipient quickenings of inflation in the United States, United Kingdom (assisted by W), and in Sweden, France, Germany, Italy and Australia, though in Japan, Denmark and the Netherlands it did not overcome the downward momentum and in Canada inflation quickened without the aid of any diagnosed impulse.

In assessing the roles of these impulses and of W and NW in particular, it must be remembered that we are not speaking simply of changes in the rate of wage inflation. To say that wage inflation generally goes up and down with unusually marked changes in price inflation would be little more than trivial. The accompanying change in factor shares, suggesting a leading part, not a passive part, for wage changes, should be borne in mind.

To some extent, this question of the major shifts (for our present purpose, upward shifts) of the rate of inflation can be related to our investigation, in chapter 3, of the behaviour of the elasticity of price with regard to output, p/q. We found there that, in the Big Six, there were a number of occasions when the annual value of this elasticity assumed a high or even a negative value (in the latter case price rising although output fell), which we described as 'going off the scale'. In considerable measure, these occasions correspond with the major upward shifts of inflation; at all events they were occasions when inflation was high in relation to real growth.

There were 39 such occasions in the Big Six between 1953 and 1979 inclusive (we omit 1951 and 1952 because of data difficulties in some countries). The number of these occurring when real income was above trend was 22, which does not differ significantly from half the total. Nor does the number accompanied by a positive wage-push impulse differ appreciably from what one would expect if those impulses were randomly distributed. The number immediately *preceded* by a wage-push impulse, however, is fifteen, which is above expectation at the 1 per cent level of significance. The number accompanied by an import price-push impulse, twelve, is significant at better than the 10 per cent level, but the number preceded by such an impulse (sixteen) is significantly above expectation at almost the 0.1 per cent level. As for other types of impulse, the association of these cases with simultaneous positive monetary impulses is very close to random expectations, that with preceding ones significantly below, and that with *negative* monetary impulses, both preceding and simultaneous, significantly above. There is also a significant association with simultaneous negative expenditure impulses.

The strong associations of these cases of inflation without much real growth, therefore, are not with high demand in the sense of high activity in relation to trend, but with immediately preceding wage-push, and, still more, import price-push. Acceleration of inflation seems to come from the factor markets, and its effect on the GDP deflator is postponed until the monetary and expenditure impulses have gone into reverse gear, with adverse effects on growth rate. This is true of the major cases of off-the-scale p/q, 1974–5 (in all the Big Six) and 1979 (in most of them), as well as of some other, mainly cyclical cases, though, as we noted in the last chapter, the major jumps (in terms of inflation rate) mostly occurred while activity was still above its trend.

CONCLUSIONS

The strongest association we have observed in this investigation (significant at much better than the 0.1 per cent level) is the positive one of expenditure-pull with simultaneously rising real growth rate, closely followed in degree of significance by the positive association of wage-push with simultaneously rising inflation rate (see table 4.4). Next come three connected with monetary impulses – the positive association of *negative* monetary impulses with either of the cost-push impulses (W or I) and the *negative* associations of positive monetary impulses with simultaneously rising inflation rates and with simultaneous import price-push. They are accompanied by the positive associations of I and of NM, and the negative association of NW, with rising current inflation. These associations are all significant at better than the 0.2 per cent level.

The only others that we have found to be significant at better than the 5 per cent level are the negative association of M with W (in line with the three indications of negative association of monetary impulses with inflation which we have just mentioned), negative associations of NE and NI with rising inflation and, rather surprisingly, a negative association of expenditure-pull with rising growth rate in the *following* year – though this is perhaps less surprising if one puts it in the form that when expenditure-pull stops, growth stops accelerating. Just below the 5 per cent point of significance, however, we have the association of M with rising inflation rate in the *next year but one* and, around the 10 per cent point, its association with expenditure-pull in the year following it; two relations whose link with each other is not visible directly, since the relation of E with rising inflation in the following year is almost purely neutral. Negative monetary impulses are similarly associated with negative expenditure impulses a year later.

Round about the 10 per cent significance point also, we have the *negative* association between rising growth and currently rising inflation, its *positive* association with rising inflation in the following year and that of M with I two years later. Not much below come the coincidence of E with rising inflation, and the association of rising growth with rising inflation in the following year. Associations less unlikely to arise from random dispositions of the impulses and episodes in time are hardly worth taking as evidence of systematic connection.

The emphasis of these findings is on the counter-inflationary incidence (not necessarily effect) of money-injection, the pro-inflationary incidence of wage and import price-push, and the very strong association of expenditure-pull with accelerating output growth – much stronger than its association with rising inflation. Time-lagged associations emerge in much more shadowy forms. We get a rather blurred picture of a cycle in which E has some, not a very strong, tendency to occur in the year after M (with a corresponding relation between their negative counterparts), and rising growth rate has a weaker tendency to do so, while import price-push and rising inflation have not very strong tendencies to occur two years after M, in spite of rising inflation having no tendency to follow a year after E in general. The cycle, such as it is, is, of course, a composite one, made up of the experiences of different countries whose cyclical patterns are visibly different in important respects. And the cycle does not necessarily have much to do with the major inflationary leaps and the general trend to higher inflation in our period. We have seen reasons to believe that the leaps, at least, are largely connected with import prices in most of the sample countries, that is to say, with prices in the world markets for traded goods, primary products especially, strongly assisted by wage-push.

THE COURSE OF EXPECTATIONS

It is clear that inflationary processes generally cannot be understood without regard to the expectations that are entertained about the future course of prices. In looking more closely at the kinds of inflationary impulse that we have distinguished, especially in seeking to use changes of interest rate as confirmatory evidence of monetary impulses, and in examining the relation between wage inflation and the state of the labour market, or between inflation of commodity prices and the state of the commodity markets, the possibility of changes in expectations about the future of the relevant prices has to be taken into account, and any empirical evidence of the actual course of expectations will be of great value. In this chapter, we seek for such evidence, but for a start it may be useful to call to mind the general framework within which these expectations necessarily operate.

SOME THEORETICAL CONSIDERATIONS

Imagine an economy in which all prices are market-flexible, and in which an expectation becomes generally entertained that prices, say a year hence, will be 20 per cent higher than at present. Sellers of durable goods will be unwilling to part with them at prices which fall below those anticipated for a year hence by more than the interest and storage costs of holding them until that time arrives. Buyers, whom we assume to share the sellers' expectations, would be willing to make purchases now, ahead of normal requirement, at any prices which fall below the anticipated one by more than these interest and storage costs. Thus, prices of all durable goods will at once come to stand below any generally expected higher future level by not more than the interest and storage costs of holding them until the date to which the expectation refers.

But what will have happened to the interest rate? The universal expectation of price increase will, at first sight, have raised both the supply and the demand schedules for loanable funds by precisely the expected annual rate of inflation. This being so, it will not pay buyers and sellers of durable goods to do anything about their holdings of them that they would not do under an expectation of constant prices. There will be no immediate changes in prices, only in the rate of interest, which will jump 20 percentage points upwards. Prices may well rise by 20 per cent in the course of the year, as expected, but so far as our argument has gone, the change in interest will have prevented this from affecting business behaviour, including any shift between durable and non-durable goods.

The qualification that has to be made to this, on second thoughts, arises from the fact that it obviously will pay to shift away from holdings of money, which is now expected to depreciate in value in relation to goods and services. There will thus be an immediate increase in spending on goods and services in general, producing an immediate rise in prices, which, it is sometimes claimed, will proceed to the point where the fixed stock of money bears a sufficiently reduced ratio to the raised nominal value of income and non-monetary assets to achieve the necessary adjustment.

This, in turn, is still too simple. First, in a modern monetary economy any desire to reduce money holdings is likely to be satisfied to a considerable extent by the repayment of debt to banks. Second, in so far as there *is* an immediate increase in price, it may well cause an upward revision of the original expectation of inflation; the dynamic possibilities flowing from this are numerous. Leaving them aside, one has to consider whether, apart from any initial price rise financed by increase in velocity of circulation, the expectations of continuing increase are likely to be disappointed for lack of finance. If the banks are not constrained, and share in the general expectations, each one will presumably think it both safe and prudent to increase loans sufficiently to support the anticipated 20 per cent increase in turnover – safe because they have reason to suppose that their competitors will keep in line, prudent because they would otherwise fail to keep their share of the business. If they are constrained through limitations on the expansion of high-powered money, there is some presumption that interest rates will rise further, increasing the margin by which current prices can find equilibrium below the expected future level. But, again, there may be revision of that level, this time downwards.

Institutional rigidities of prices and of interest rates are also likely to complicate the working of actual economies under the influence of inflationary expectations, and it is no doubt possible, for a time, for expected prices to exceed actual ones *plus* interest and storage costs. Indeed, where inflationary expectations are gradually raised by a succession of new pieces of information, there seems no reason why prices and interest should not lag behind those which would be in equilibrium with current expectations for a considerable period.

Finally, among the general considerations to be borne in mind, it is obvious that uniform expectations by everyone in a market or an economy are highly unlikely, and that any measure of expected inflation that can be deduced from empirical data is bound to be some kind of average of various expectations held by different people. Indeed, the whole notion of specific expectations requires careful handling. The conventional treatment of an individual person's expectations, under uncertainty, is to represent them as a distribution of possible outcomes to each of which the person attached a weight representing its probability. This is a strange way of dealing with situations in which relevant information to serve as the basis for the probabilities in question is generally more absent than present; a much more realistic scheme is that developed by Shackle from 1939 onwards, in which finite, possibly large ranges of possible outcomes are characterised as ranges of 'zero potential surprise' for the forecaster, and rising potential surprise attaches to outcomes as they move outward from either end of this range. The character of ignorance about the future, which includes ignorance of what evidence is relevant to it, should be remembered, not least when looking at forecasts collected by survey methods.

It would not be appropriate at this point to pursue this subject further. Our immediate concern is with the empirical evidence for the existence of such expectations among economic decision makers generally, and with the magnitude of the changes expected. It will be useful to consider four sources of such evidence; direct surveys of opinion, the relation between actual inflation and the accompanying (or slightly later) interest level, the relation between the yields of bonds and of equities, and, finally, that between long and short-term rates of interest.

SURVEY DATA

Evidence from opinion surveys exists for the United States and the United Kingdom, and in a different form for several continental European countries. For the United States, one series was collected by Joseph Livingston from 1947 onwards, by periodically asking a panel of economists to predict the levels of the consumers' price index and the wholesale price index six months ahead (effectively, eight months ahead from the dates of the latest official figures available to them). Predictions for the levels twelve and eighteen months ahead were also collected. The other long series for the United States and one for the United Kingdom rest on a different basis, since they consist in their original form not of cardinal estimates of price changes, but of the proportions of respondents who thought, respectively, that prices would rise, stay about the same, and fall. Mean expectations of change have been calculated from these ordinal data on the basis of assumptions about the frequency distributions of cardinal expectations and the width of the band of changes which respondents should be regarded as including in the category 'remaining about the same'; the latter is crucial for the amplitude of movement of the deduced cardinal estimates, but not for their general pattern over time.

The Livingston series have been tabulated, up to 1975, in the form of mean expected annual rates of inflation, and discussed by J. A. Carlson (1977). They are perhaps chiefly notable for their general tendency to underestimate rates of actual inflation, and, even more, the amplitudes of their short-term fluctuations. The forecasts are fairly accurate about the trough levels of inflation rates, but grossly underestimate the peaks (except the minor ones between 1958 and 1964, when inflation was low) and have some tendency to miss – to be late in predicting – the major turning-points. The forecasts constitute a much smoother series than the actuality. They provide on the whole a fair estimate of medium-term changes in what, in chapter 3, we referred to as the 'basic' rates of inflation. From the later 1950s there are no mean predictions of an actual fall in either index, and forecast rates rise from about 1964, and again, more steeply, from about 1972.

The ordinal data collected by the Survey Research Centre have been translated into cardinal terms by Wachtel (1977) following, broadly, a procedure first developed by Shuford (1970). They yield results not very different from the Livingston series; in particular, although the forecasts of consumer price inflation deduced from them ran above actuality in the low inflation period 1958–66, they greatly underestimated the 1968 peak, and totally failed to indicate the great rise of inflation in 1971–4.

Carlson and Parkin (1975) analyse a monthly United Kingdom series, calculated in the Shuford manner from ordinal Gallup survey data, for the years 1961–72. It divides, as they show, into two dissimilar halves. Up to late 1967, the deduced forecasts show a much lower amplitude of variation than actual inflation rates, and it is demonstrated that forecasts seem to depend significantly only on what was said in the previous month and, possibly, a constant term; there was no detectable influence of current inflationary experience. From late 1967 to 1973, the constant term is larger and significant, and so is the coefficient of the last month's forecast, but there is also some appearance of forecasts being high when actual inflation is rising, and low when it is decreasing. Forecasts vary with a wide amplitude, but this is due mainly to two very high peaks; one at the end of 1967, presumably due to the November devaluation of sterling (the actual price effects of which were much later and more gradual) and another at the end of 1970, less easily associated with any notable event, though a wage explosion had been proceeding for some time. The increase of inflation in 1972–3 did not bring a comparable peak, however, and inflation during 1971–3 was almost continuously under-anticipated, so the effect of the rising inflation rate on the level of forecasts can hardly be regarded as dependable.

There is another compilation of United Kingdom evidence, not strictly from survey data, but from the forecasts issued by the Cambridge Economic Policy Group, the London Business School, HM Treasury, the OECD and the National Institute of Economic and Social Research (NIESR): made from 1968 onwards by Holden and Peel (1983), and later updated by the Bank of England (1983). This average of estimates also underpredicts inflation for most of the time, especially in the peaks of 1975 and 1979–80. The NIESR forecasts, which are among its constituents, and have a good record in predicting the general shape of variations in the rate of CPI inflation for periods lying on average about six months ahead (see *National Institute Economic Review*, February 1984), nevertheless, between 1964 and 1979, never overpredicted an annual rate, and on average underpredicted the actual rates by about a quarter. They did, however, subsequently overpredict in 1980 and 1982.

In Europe, the EEC Commission has collected data from Belgium, France, Germany and Italy which have been analysed over the period 1965–77 by Batchelor (1982). These are rather different from the data on expectations about movements in general price indices, which we have just discussed; they result from asking firms, monthly, for three-month forward estimates of prices (and outputs also) in their own trades, and combining these estimates into more general indices. They are thus syntheses of short-term predictions by specialists rather than averages of longer forecasts made by respondents about the average movements of very wide ranges of prices. The series for France and Germany nevertheless show some similarity with the Livingston data for the United States; they greatly underestimate the peak of the early 1970s, and are in general much smoother than the course of realised inflation. The Italian series likewise underestimates the 1973 peak, but it greatly overestimates the inflation of 1970 and slightly overestimates that of 1976, perhaps through exaggeration of the weight to be attached to the sharp wage inflations preceding those two years. The Belgian series shows a very close prediction of the rise of the rate of inflation in 1968–9, but overestimates the reduction of it in 1970–1.

THE FISHER EFFECT

The second approach to expectations of inflation which we have mentioned is that through the 'Fisher Effect' of anticipated inflation on interest rates. If inflation at (say) 5 per cent a year, for the duration of the loans in question, comes to be generally expected, then 5 per cent is likely to be added to the asking rate of lenders, and borrowers are likely to become correspondingly willing to pay more. If, therefore, what looks like a systematic effect of actual inflation on simultaneous or slightly later market rates of interest can be discerned, its coefficient (the derivative of interest with respect to inflation rate) is a measure of the extent to which inflation at the rate of that currently or recently experienced is expected to persist for the duration of the loans to which the interest rate in question refers.

The situation is, however, complex. Not only may interest have an effect on inflation (the timing of which might serve to distinguish it from that of inflation on interest) but interest is influenced also by profitability, which may show a systematic connection with inflation, and by monetary velocity, of which the same may be true, and by changes in the supply of money. The empirical relation between interest and inflation over the trade cycle, in particular, requires very careful interpretation. In general, at least for the United States, the United Kingdom and Germany, there seems to be a more or less simultaneous positive relation between the two, but it would be rash to accept its coefficient (which varies between about $\frac{1}{4}$ and $\frac{3}{4}$) as an indicator of the extent to which expectations are a projection into the near future of current cyclical inflationary experience. It is perhaps a little better to look to expectations of inflation as the main possible causes of upward shifts in the schedule of interest rates expressed as a function of monetary velocity. For both the United States and the United Kingdom, plots of Treasury Bill rate against V2 (see charts 5.1.1 and 5.1.2) suggest upward shifts of perhaps $1\frac{1}{2}$ per cent in the former and $2\frac{1}{2}$ per cent in the latter during the later 1960s, and further upward shifts of some 2 per cent during the 1970s. For both countries, these shifts, together, amount to a little less than half the increase in the average rate of inflation of the CPI between the early 1960s and the later 1970s, which suggests that cumulative inflationary experience has been substantially, but still very incompletely, built into expectations.

Chart 5.1 *V2 and the Treasury Bill rate*
Chart 5.1.1 *United States*

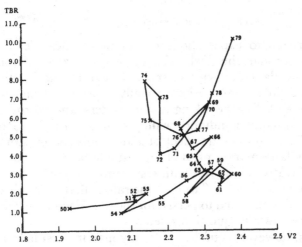

Source: *International Financial Statistics* and NIESR calculations

Chart 5.1.2 *United Kingdom*

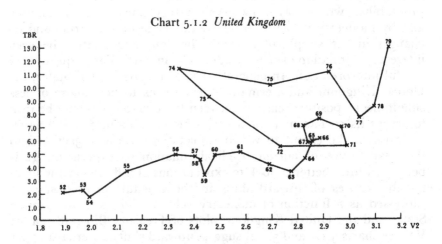

BONDS AND EQUITIES

Our third avenue of approach is through the relation between the
yields of bonds and of equities. If expectations of inflation rise, then
bonds, which pay fixed nominal interest, become less attractive to
hold in relation to equities which, *ceteris paribus*, pay dividends based
on unchanged real rates of return – that is to say, dividends which, in
money terms, are expected to go up with inflation. The yield of

irredeemable or very long-term bonds, calculated as their annual interest divided by their price, is the nominal long-term interest rate. If equities were expected with certainty to go on paying a dividend equal in real terms to the current one, their yield (current dividend divided by current price) would be the *ex ante* real rate of interest – nominal rate minus expected rate of inflation.

In practice, comparisons are, of course, complicated by other factors. Prospective real earnings of equities vary over time, and so does the proportion of earnings distributed as dividend, a fact made troublesome by the consideration that undistributed profits are still relevant to equity prices, but seem to carry less weight with investors than distributed profits. Nevertheless, the 'yield gap' between the two is useful evidence for our purpose.

Traditionally, in the English-speaking countries at least, the dividend yield of equities of (say) the highest grade has been above that of bonds of comparable quality, a fact usually ascribed to the greater uncertainty of future equity dividends. Reversal of this state of affairs, a positive bond–equity gap, has, until the last generation, been rare; it appeared, for instance, briefly at the height of the New York 'bull market' of 1929, when hopes of future rise in equities were extravagant. In the early 1950s, the gap (using government rather than industrial bond yields) was, as had been usual, negative, averaging about $-2\frac{1}{2}$ per cent in the United Kingdom and -3 per cent in the United States. In the latter it was already narrowing, and in both countries did so in the later 1950s, becoming positive in the United States in 1959, and in the United Kingdom (on an annual average basis) in the following year. In both countries, this was more a matter of equity yield falling than of nominal interest rate (bond yield) rising. Thereafter, the gap remained positive. It stayed not very far from 1 per cent until 1966, and then expanded rapidly to 3 per cent (United States) and 4 per cent (United Kingom) by 1969 – an expansion due more to rise in bond yield than to fall in equity yield. In the United States, the width of the gap fluctuated, mostly between 3 and 4 per cent, until 1979; in the United Kingdom it broadened again after 1972 to about 7 per cent, around which it remained for the rest of the decade.

For other major countries the necessary yield figures are available only for shorter postwar periods. From the times when they became available for Germany (1956), France and Italy (1960) and Japan (1966) the bond–yield gap is already positive. In Germany it fluctuates around 3 per cent until about 1968, with a peak of 4.4 per cent in 1960, then rises to 6 per cent in 1974, before falling to its old average of 3 per cent in 1977–9. Japan's gap also stood at about 3 per cent in the later 1960s, then rose to a maximum of 7 per cent in 1974 and, like price inflation, fell back thereafter. The French gap is remarkable for showing no general trend over the period for which it is available, fluctuating with peaks of 3½ per cent or a little higher in 1961–2, 1970 and 1974, and a trough as low as 1.1 per cent in 1967. The Italian gap fluctuates around 2½ per cent, with no trend, until 1968, then embarks on a fluctuating upward course leading to 10 per cent by 1977.

SHORT AND LONG INTEREST RATES

Finally, we may hope to extract something from the gap between short and long rates of interest. What we may hope to get this time, however, is not relevant to the expected *level* of inflation, since anticipation of a particular rate of price increase extending indefinitely into the future should affect long and short rates alike; it is on expectation of *change* in the inflation rate that some light should be thrown. If it is accepted that market rates of interest are positively correlated with the rate of inflation that is being experienced, an expectation of *rising* inflation rate should carry with it expectation that interest rates will rise. Given this, borrowers will be keen to borrow long, before rates go up, and lenders will prefer to lend (if at all) for short periods, so as to be able to re-lend at the anticipated higher rates without undue loss of time. Such expectations should, therefore, tend to raise long rates in relation to short. Expectations of a falling rate of inflation should do the opposite.

Chart 5.2 shows the excess of long-term Government bond yield over Treasury Bill rate in the United States plotted against recent rate of inflation (backward-looking first differences of CPI). It is clear from this that there is a short-term, cyclical negative relation between the two, suggesting that when inflation is at a cyclical high point it is expected to decrease, and when at a low point it is expected to go up; but that the 'normal' rate of inflation with regard to which these expectations are formed has increased from time to time – sometimes from cycle to cycle. It seems to have been between 1 per cent and 3 per cent a year from 1952 to 1967, then to have shifted to about 5 per cent for the first four years of the 1970s, then to some 9 per cent for 1974–9.

If the excess of long over short rate is plotted against the backward looking *second* difference of CPI – virtually the rate of change of inflation over a three year period to the third of which the interest data refer – as in chart 5.3.1, quite a good negative correlation is obtained for the period as a whole. This appears to fit in with the suggestion that, on a scale geared to the ascending and descending phases of the trade cycle, inflationary expectations are stable. When

Chart 5.2 *Excess of long-term Government Bond yield over Treasury Bill rate and CPI Inflation rate*

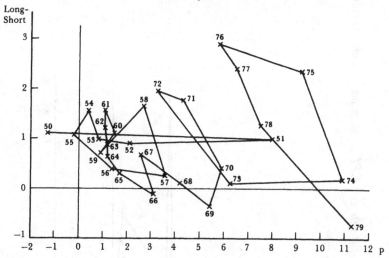

inflation has been getting faster for two or three years, it is expected to slow down, and vice versa. From 1953 to 1973 the cycles all overlap; there is not much evidence of shift, non-accelerating inflation being apparently consistent with a long-rate premium of somewhere around 1 per cent. From 1973 to 1977 it looks as if the premium is rising to, and beyond, 2 per cent, which presumably means that with a given experience of acceleration (or deceleration) of inflation, the tendency to expect acceleration is stronger than before. But there is also a hint that in the following years, 1977–9, there was a return to an interpretation of experience with regard to *acceleration* of inflation more like that of pre-1973. This is not, of course, in conflict with our previous deduction that ideas about the normal *level* of inflation had changed.

The corresponding picture for the United Kingdom (chart 5.3.2) is somewhat more disorderly. Here again, the 1950s and 1960s present evidence for a negative relation between recent acceleration of inflation and the size of the long-rate premium, the non-accelerating inflation value of which rises a little (from about 1 per cent to nearly $1\frac{1}{2}$ per cent) between the two decades, but after that there seems to be a larger premium for the period 1970–3, with an exceptionally high premium in 1971. Even more exceptionally high premia, in relation to the general run of experience, occur in 1974, 1975 and 1977. These are all occasions on which recent acceleration (in 1977 reduced deceleration) of inflation seems to have led, not to the stable expectation of its

Chart 5.3 *Excess of long-term Government Bond yield over Treasury Bill rate and CPI Acceleration of Inflation rate*

Chart 5.3.1 *United States 1950–79*

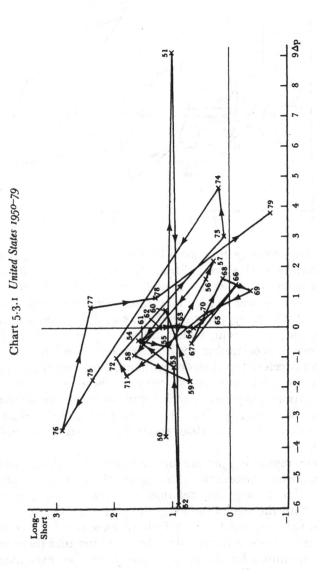

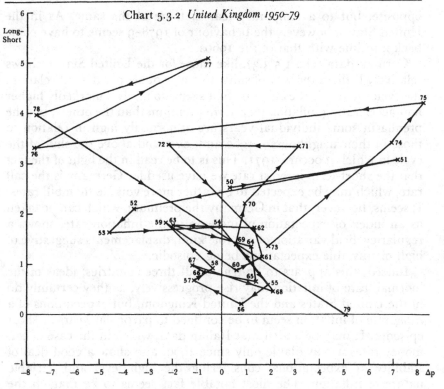

Chart 5.3.2 *United Kingdom 1950–79*

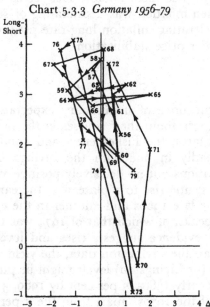

Chart 5.3.3 *Germany 1956–79*

opposite, but to a temporary fear of more of the same. As in the United States, however, the behaviour of 1978–9 seems to have come back into line with that of the 1960s.

German data (chart 5.3.3), like those for the United States, shows relatively little in the way of shifts to a new quasi-permanent relation; the cycle 1970–3 is the only one that seems to imply a markedly higher non-accelerating inflation long-term premium than the others, but the premia in some individual years are abnormally high in relation to those in their neighbours – 1962 and, over and above the shift of the cycle in which it occurs, 1971. This is to be read in the light of the fact that the short-term interest rate we have used for Germany is the call rate, which may be expected to be rather more volatile than bill rates. It seems, however, that in Germany the premium, which can be taken as an index of expectation of increase in the inflation rate, shows a regular cyclical variation of a stable kind, displacements suggestive of high or unstable expectations being episodic.

Indeed, this appears to be true of all three countries; ideas of the 'normal' rate of inflation may rise progressively, as they certainly do in the United States and the United Kingdom, but expectations of a *rising* rate of inflation seem to be confined to particular years or short episodes. It may be added that Italian data, which in the case of call money rates are available only since 1969, also show a good deal of stability of expectations, considering the high level and variable nature of inflation. The most notable fact seems to be that, in the years 1975–8, when inflation was decelerating or steady, an implied negative non-accelerating inflation long-rate premium suggested expectations of further price stabilisation.

CONCLUSION

Taking these indications of inflationary expectations all together, what do they suggest about their courses in the principal countries? For the United States, the Fisher effect and bond–equity evidence seems to be broadly in line with the Livingston CPI forecasts; short-term fluctuations but no decisively positive average level until the mid 1950s; a gentle rise to a plateau in the early 1960s, a more marked one in the late 1960s and another in the early 1970s, apart from temporary peaks, of which that of 1974 was the most striking. The Fisher effect evidence suggests rises and levels of expectation rather smaller than the Livingston data, the yield gap rather larger ones; the average (or Livingston) levels might be put at around 1 per cent a year in the early 1960s, 3 per cent by 1969, 5 per cent by 1972 and for the rest of the 1970s, apart from the 7 per cent 1974 peak.

According to the long-rate premium data, expectation of *change* in the rate of inflation is a regular short-term cyclical affair, the years 1974–7 being the only ones in which markets were abnormally sensitive to current rates of change.

The United Kingdom survey data (which are from consumers rather than professional economists) show a pattern not unlike the United States (Livingston) one, but with higher values. Yield data suggest a rise to an expectation of 2 or 3 per cent inflation in the 1950s, before survey data start; there is a general concurrence on a further 3 per cent rise in the late 1960s and, with some variations on the precise timing, another of 2 or 3 per cent around the mid-1970s. This is all apart from two sharp temporary peaks shown by the survey data; the devaluation peak of late 1967 and the council workers' and miners' strike peak of late 1970. Long-rate premium data suggest short-lived accelerating-inflation scares in 1951, 1971, 1974–5, and 1977, apart from normal cyclical fluctuations.

For Germany and Japan, the yield gap evidence suggests some expectation of inflation from at least the 1960s, but it is hard to quantify; German survey data (again not comparable with those from the United States or United Kingdom surveys) indicate something not unlike current experience, with the peaks reduced. For both countries the yield data suggest that expected inflation, like that actually experienced, came down again after the peak of 1974, and German long-term premium values suggest that the cycle 1970–3 was the only one in which fears of accelerating inflation were unusually sensitive to experience. Italian data generally suggest modest expectations until about 1968, then an irregular advance to a level of about 10 per cent per annum in the later 1970s. The course of French expectations remains a mystery, apart from the business survey data, which, as we have noted, give a planed-down version of actual experience.

These indications, such as they are, of the actual levels and courses of expectations about inflation, are what most concern us. It is, however, worth pausing to reflect on the extent to which they were correct, or to which they provide evidence bearing on the extent to which expectations in the general goods and services markets concerned were rational and the markets efficient in the technical senses that have come to be attached to those two adjectives. 'Efficiency' means that prices responded in a full, market-clearing way to supply and demand forces, including the actions based on the expectations of the participants, and that these expectations were based on all the available knowledge. That the expectations were rational would mean that the participants had not only used all the relevant knowledge (or as much of it as was worth the cost of collection), but had used it in the most efficient way for planning (see Batchelor, 1980). Thus, if the price levels in question have been subject to systematic fluctuation, participants in the markets should have found this out by analysing past prices; their speculative actions should then, in principle, iron out the systematic fluctuation in question, leaving only random price variations due to unpredictable events.

It is fairly plain that these conditions are a long way from holding in the macro-markets which we have been considering. It is, for instance, obvious that some of these markets do not clear, and fail to clear to extents which vary widely from time to time – a matter to which we shall return in considering labour markets in chapter 8. Secondly, we have already had occasion to note that rates of inflation (along with other macroeconomic magnitudes) have varied far from randomly over time. Third, and more to the immediate point of this chapter, expectations of inflation, so far as they are known, have shown a strong tendency to be in error in a non-random way. Carlson notes that the CPI series based on the Livingston survey had overestimated the following six (or eight) months' inflation in only ten of the 58 surveys covered by his study, and while the correctness of this survey as an unbiased indicator of effective market opinion has been challenged (on the ground, apparently, that expectations *must* have been rational), we have not found such United States non-survey evidence as we have adduced to be in conflict with it in this respect; our evidence suggests a downward bias of expectations in other countries also, during most if not the whole of our period. To some extent, one might account for this by characterising the formation of expectations as adaptive, rather than rational, in a period when the trend of actual inflation rates was upward, but that does not provide an adequate description of events. Carlson found that the mean Livingston forecasts were generally better than those which could be produced by linear combinations of the previous dozen six-monthly inflation rates, using coefficients obtained by regression from all previous data. It was not that the series of inflation rates contained some inner logic which forecasters (or the market generally) failed to discern; rather that they failed to foresee the course of the Vietnam War, the wage explosions and the oil shocks which gave the second half of our period a different character from the first – in fact, like other mortals, they could not foresee the future of the world.

6

MONETARY IMPULSES

We can now return to the instances we identified in chapter 4 in which change in the money supply seemed to lead the dance in one direction or the other; in which its growth showed signs of either accelerating ahead of growth in transactions demand, or decelerating ahead of the fall of that demand. First, we must face some difficulties, previously mentioned but passed over, in the practical definition of the money stock. Then we must look at the mechanisms by which money is created. So prepared, we take a closer look at our previous criterion of monetary impulse and consider the consequences of amending it, for the Big Six, by adding a condition related to interest. Some attention can then be given to the differing amounts of monetary expansion that occurred in different countries to the accompaniment of the apparent application of a monetary accelerator, or a monetary brake, or neither. Finally, we come to an examination of the sources of change in monetary expansion (especially in the case of impulses); first the immediate processes by which banks' liabilities were increased, then the sources – and the significance – of growth in the stock of reserve money which, in varying degrees, permitted or encouraged total monetary growth. The varying extents to which acquisitions of potential reserves were sterilised in the early 1970s require special attention, so do the part of public authorities' borrowing in monetary expansion, and experience of attempts to constrain monetary growth to a 'target' rate.

MONEY AND DEBT

Total private sector expenditure presumably depends first on the sector's disposable income (with some modification to discount elements not thought of as permanent), on the prospects seen for investment and on the size and distribution of the sector's net wealth, which is, at first sight, the value of its physical assets and its net holding of public sector and foreign debt. There is some controversy about inclusion of public sector debt on the ground that taxpayers are ultimately responsible for servicing it but the possession of government liabilities, acceptable in the market, seems likely, nevertheless, to increase the private sector's willingness and ability to spend.

All good debt with a redemption date can be turned into known and certain amounts of money simply by waiting. Short-term debt can thus be transmuted within a short time. On the assumption that the government does not default on its debts, therefore, the whole body of short-term government debt held by the private sector could, in principle, be turned into demand deposits (or even into notes and coin for that matter) within a few months, simply by virtue of the holders' wish to have it in that form. In the process, interest rates might be raised and the values of long-term debt and physical assets reduced, but the price of remaining short-term debt would be little affected.

Long-term public sector debt differs from short-term in that it can be turned into money at fairly short notice only by persuading someone else to buy it at a market price which falls with any shift of sentiment in favour of realisation, to the point where that sentiment is checked by the lowness of the price and expectation of its later improvement. Such a fall reduces the private sector's net wealth, encourages saving and discourages capital formation, and is thus likely to dampen its spending intentions. A move towards increasing private expenditure by drawing on holdings of long-term public debt is self-limiting, unless the authorities intervene to maintain the value of their bonds as, not infrequently, they have done. It is a means of drawing money into the hands of those who want to spend it, by tempting existing holders with cheaper long-term assets. In the same way, any general move towards financing an increase of expenditure by sales of real assets (or titles to them, in the form of equities) is self-limiting through a fall in prices (and thus in private sector net wealth) and a rise in yields. Nevertheless, high prices of government bonds or of private sector real assets are likely to encourage expenditure; not only can they increase the scope for financing additional expenditure by some holders who, at the cost of a fall in prices, sell to others, who in turn are attracted by newly-raised yields or hopes of price recovery, but they make holders feel richer and may thus dispose them to reduce their rate of saving or to realise their liquid, short-term assets for extra spending.

Debts of people and institutions within the non-bank private sector held by others within it do not, of course, contribute directly to the sector's net wealth; they are offset by liabilities. Nevertheless, it is doubtful whether all is completely symmetrical in this connection. A high price level of bonds (a low interest rate) is perhaps more likely to stimulate expenditure by holders of those bonds than it is to depress spending by their issuers, though it does, of course, diminish the latter's power to pay off their debt by buying them back. With short-term debt within the sector the symmetry is rather clearer; the creditor's liquidity is the debtor's illiquidity. Short-term private debt is by no means so certainly convertible into money as is its public counterpart, since the possibility of default when the private sector wants to become more liquid and is unwilling to re-lend is higher. But the monetary authorities are unlikely to be completely unresponsive to cries for help in such a crisis. A good deal of the short-term private debt held within the private sector is in practice convertible into money, even when one takes the sector as a whole.

In short then, if we ask on what expenditure by the private sector is likely to depend, given its disposable income and the prospects of income from new capital formation, one part of the answer concerns the sector's net wealth, the other concerns its total liquid assets. If the former is large (or large in relation to income) it may provide a stimulus to higher expenditure. Liquid assets supply the means of increasing expenditure, in that they can be turned into additional supplies of actual means of payment – money – though some increase of expenditure is usually possible without additional money, by raising the velocity of circulation of the money already in existence.

DEMAND AND TIME DEPOSITS

If it is granted that liquid assets of the private sector can fairly readily be turned into money (by simply waiting until the debts of which it consists are paid), what is the significance of the existing money supply? The question can, of course, be asked about money supply on any of the several usual (or any of the indefinite number of possible) definitions. Monetary theory has most commonly been concerned with money as an asset on the holdings of which interest is not paid and which is available for purposes of payment without delay. This corresponds broadly to M_1; notes and coin in the hands of the public plus current accounts (or sight or demand deposits) in commercial banks. One fundamental fact, however, is that the distribution of money on any of the broader definitions (M_2 or M_3) between M_1 and the rest (mainly time deposits or deposit accounts, usually bearing interest, and mostly not transferable in unlimited amounts without delay) is entirely at the discretion of the holders, subject (in the case of transfers to current account) to formal notice; there is complete freedom to transform the one kind of account into the other.

It seems reasonable to suppose that, if there were no interest on time deposits, virtually all bank money would be kept in the form of sight or current accounts, for the sake of the extra liquidity which they provide. If, at the other extreme, the rate of interest on time deposits (which for the moment we may assume to move with the hierarchy of interest rates generally) were to be very high, there would still be some amount of money held in the form of sight or current accounts for immediate transactions purposes – it would presumably be related to the money value of the GDP. We can imagine some limiting minimum level of transactions money being approached as interest rises higher and higher. On these suppositions the equilibrium holding of M_1 is positively related to money income and negatively to the general level of interest rates, but may well also have some positive relation to the level of M_2, since more M_2 in relation to the level of transactions means more money available for division between liquid demand deposits additional to the bare minimum and interest-bearing time deposits.

Perhaps we should look at experience in this connection in two or three countries, beginning with the United States. The best instrument for doing this empirically is 'Cambridge k', the ratio of money holdings to GDP. This can be calculated for M_1, for time or deposit money (M_2-M_1), and for the total, M_2; the ratios may be called k_1, k_t (t for time) and k_2 respectively, and all three k's can be plotted against what seems an appropriate measure of the general level of interest rates at the short end of the market – Treasury Bill rate, say. If this is done (chart 6.1) we get a picture which, with some qualifications, seems in broad accordance with our expectations. The current account (sight) ratio k_1 is negatively, the deposit account (time) ratio, k_t, positively related to interest rate. Their sum – k_2 – is negatively related to interest at the lower rates which prevailed until about 1965; after that there is no consistent relation. The ratio then varies little with interest, though it is not constant, being somewhat higher throughout the wide interest variations of 1972–5 than either immediately before or afterwards.

The respective correlations of k_1 and k_t with interest are largely due to their trends over the period as a whole. In the 1950s, and after about 1967, when interest fluctuated widely from year to year, k_1 in particular went on falling with only few and relatively small reversals – we shall return to it shortly. k_t changed very little during the 1950s, then began an increase which lasted (interrupted only briefly in 1968–70) until 1974. For the rest of the period it remained stable, despite wide interest variations. One might suppose that it took some years in the 1950s to shake expectations of a return to the low short-term interest rates of the later 1930s and the 1940s, but that, once they were shaken, a relative growth of time deposits set in, encouraged by the steadily rising interest rates of 1961–6, and

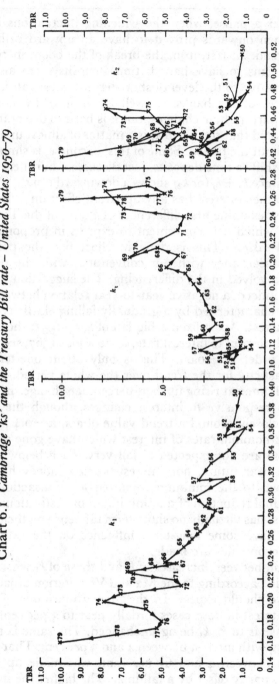

Chart 6.1 Cambridge 'ks' and the Treasury Bill rate – United States 1950–79

resumed, after a pause, when the widening fluctuations in interest rates from then onwards proved to have an upward rather than a downward trend. At last, from the break of the boom in 1973–4, the trend in k_t seems to have halted: time deposits seem also to have become insensitive to the level of short-term interest rates. No doubt the preferences of the banks, as well as those of their depositors, played some part in these changes, but it is hard to disentangle them.

We have noted that the fall in k_1 is a matter of almost uninterrupted trend throughout the period. Some of this, of course, is simply another aspect of the shift to time deposits, just discussed, but there is more to it than that, since $k_1 + k_t$ (or k_2) shows a downward trend.

To see whether interest has any apparent effect on k_1 in the short term, we must examine first differences of k_1 and of the Treasury Bill rate, both of which it is convenient to express in proportional form $(\Delta k_1/k_1)$ and $(\Delta i/i)$. This is done in chart 6.2, the points being labelled, in accordance with our convention, with the date of the second year involved in the differencing. The suggestion from this is that there is, indeed, a negative year-to-year relation between the two, but that it is characterised by a gradually falling elasticity of k_1 with respect to interest. Apart from a big fall of k_1 in 1951, the short-term elasticity with respect to interest rate, up to about 1967, seems to have been of the order of -0.06. This is only about one-tenth of the long-term elasticity for the trend over the whole period. After 1967, however, with interest rising further, percentage changes in k_1 become less and less responsive to interest changes, though they fluctuate increasingly closely around a trend value of about -0.4 per cent. It looks as if, at nominal rates of interest which have gone above 5 per cent or so and are not expected to fall very much below some such figure in the near future, non-interest-bearing money holdings are squeezed down to the minimum required for transactions, subject only to a gradual reduction of that minimum by institutional changes, so that interest has virtually no short-term influence on them – though it may well have some long-term influence on the rate at which institutional economies are made.

The relation between increases of k_t and those of k_1 when there is a money injection according to the M2 and V2 criterion broadly follows the course we should expect. In the money injections of 1958 and 1961, with interest in both cases initially near to 3 per cent, virtually all the increase is in k_t, k_1 being unchanged. The same is true of the 1967 injection, with interest between 4 and 5 per cent. That of 1971–2, with interest between 4 and 6½ per cent, was made up of a large increase in k_t, partly offset by a fall in k_1. The higher the interest, the greater the tendency of time deposits to constitute most – or even

Chart 6.2 *k_1 and Treasury Bill rate, proportional rates of change, United States 1951–79*

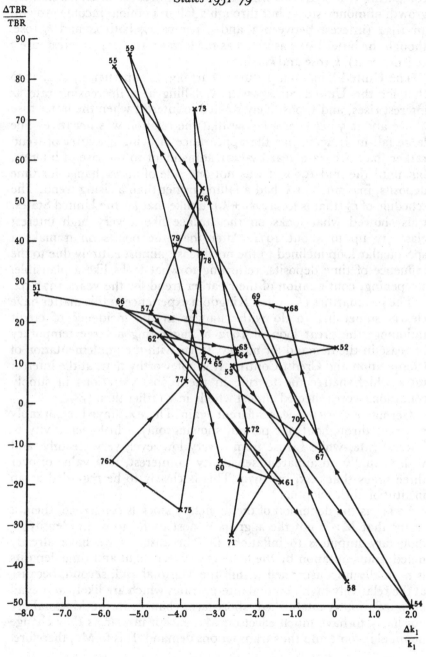

more than all – of the extra liquidity. The same can be seen by comparing two occasions when k_2 rose, not because of an accelerated growth of money stock, but through a fall in nominal income growth. In 1954 (interest between 1 and 2 per cent), both k_1 and k_t rose, though the latter twice as much as the former. In 1974 (interest rate 7 to 8 per cent), k_t rose and k_1 fell.

The United Kingdom picture (chart 6.3) is superficially similar to that for the United States, with k_1 falling at a decreasing rate as interest rises, and k_t positively related to interest when the latter rose above about 5 per cent – below that the relation was negative. The large fall in k_1 again has the appearance of being a matter of trend rather than accurate year-by-year adjustment to the rise of interest, but until the mid-1960s it was not one side of an exchange for time deposits, inasmuch as k_t had a falling rather than a rising trend. The schedule of k_2 (that is to say, $k_1 + k_t$), unlike that for the United States, thus showed what looks on the surface like a very high interest elasticity up to about 1971. After that, the points on it make a spectacular loop inclined to the north-east, almost entirely due to the influence of time deposits, returning to what looks like a plausible, steepening, continuation of their earlier trend for the years 1977–9.

The peculiarities of United Kingdom experience in this matter have clearly something to do with changes in the incidence of credit rationing; the great loop of 1972–6, suggesting a large temporary increase in the demand for money, starts with the implementation of Competition and Credit Control. It is noteworthy that, at the interest rates which had come to rule in the 1970s, variations in supply conditions were reflected almost wholly in k_t rather than k_1.

German experience was different again. There k_1 stayed remarkably constant throughout our period, showing only a little sensitivity to interest rate, while k_t rose from a very low level, very steadily, and with virtually no apparent sensitivity to interest, to a value of over three times that of k_1 by 1979. This is clearly to be regarded as an institutional development.

So far as the definition of the monetary stock is concerned, then, it seems that M1 is not the aggregate most useful to us in identifying monetary impulses to inflation, first because, as we have already noted, transmutation by the holders between sight and time deposits is normally unconstrained within the M2 total and, second, because at the relatively high nominal interest rates which are likely to prevail once inflation is established, short-term changes in the M2 total are not likely to have much effect on M1, except insofar as they change nominal income and thus transactions demand. It is to M2, therefore,

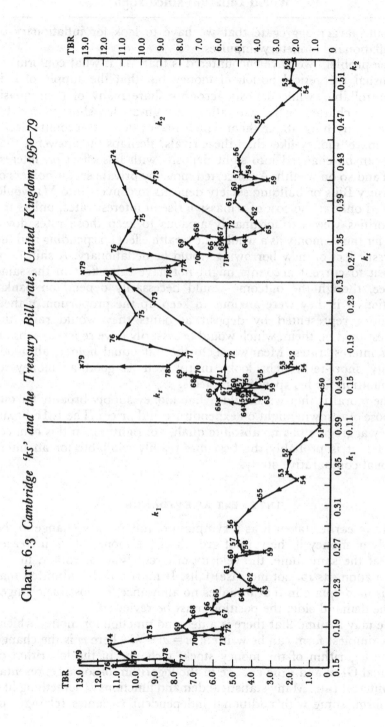

Chart 6.3 Cambridge 'ks' and the Treasury Bill rate, United Kingdom 1950–79

or some larger aggregate that we have to look for inflationary or disinflationary monetary impulses.

The problem we have encountered is that M1 is what conforms to the usual theoretical notion of money but that the supply of it is uncontrollable, while deposit accounts share many of their quasi-monetary characteristics with all other high-quality short-term debt. Is there anything about them which makes deposit accounts decisively more 'money-like' than these rivals? Perhaps the answer is that they can be changed into sight deposits with less effect on interest rates and so on wealth. A concerted move by private sector holders of Treasury Bills or building society deposits to convert into M1 would succeed only at the cost of a massive rise in interest rates, unless the authorities were extraordinarily anxious to keep those rates down and, for the economy as a whole, the wealth effect on spending and the interest effect on new borrowing would be deflationary. A shift from deposit to current accounts might not have this effect in the same degree, though the outcome would necessarily depend on banks' reactions – if they were anxious to keep up the proportion of their liabilities represented by deposit accounts they would raise the interest paid on them, which would necessarily have repercussions on other interest rates. Meanwhile, to the individual holder, all good-quality short-term debt looks pretty well as good as money as ammunition for his spending projects.

The moral is that we should define money supply broadly for our purpose of throwing light on expenditure and prices. The IMF broad money aggregate has no absolute quality of rightness in this connection but it is probably the best one readily available for an international comparative study.

INTEREST AS EVIDENCE

We have earlier taken it as a symptom of inflationary change in the supply of money if the rate of growth of the money stock increases and, at the same time, the velocity of circulation (or rather, in our formulation, its rate of increase) falls. It must now be admitted that this is inadequate in that it makes no allowance for possible changes on the demand side; the position must be reviewed.

We may assume that there is a demand function for money which, in its simplest form can be written: $m = ay - bi$ where m is the change in the logarithm of the money stock, y change in the logarithm of nominal GDP and i the change in the logarithm of some representative interest rate. Many statistical demand functions of something like this form, some with additional independent variables (changes in stocks of various non-monetary assets, changes in the rate of inflation, and so on) have been fitted for a number of countries.

The game may be said to have started as long ago as 1939 with an attempt by Brown (1939) to derive a demand function for *idle* money (the sum of current accounts in excess of those required to finance total debits at an estimated standard velocity, and of deposit accounts) for the United Kingdom. The implied average interest elasticity of demand for total money holdings was about -0.4.

An OECD investigation of demand functions for money in seven of our sample countries (the Big Six plus Canada) for the years 1960–77 by Broughton (1979) met with incomplete success; no satisfactory equation could be fitted to the Italian data, for instance; but where the fitted equations were satisfactory and the values of a and b (the income and interest elasticities of demand for money) statistically significant, those values were, respectively, round about unity and within the range 0.1 to 0.5.

The imperfect success of these attempts raises the possibility that the functions, as specified, have shifted. This is a question which has been extensively discussed. In the United Kingdom until the early 1970s there was some evidence that the short-run demand for money was stably related to income and interest rates. Goodhart and Crockett (1970), for example, found a long-run income elasticity for $M1$ of around unity for the period 1955(2) to 1969(2) and a slightly higher one, about 1.5, for $M3$ over a shorter period, 1963(2) to 1969(3). (Some variation is found in other studies, for example Price (1972) found an income elasticity for $M3$ of over 2.0.) They also found an implied long-run interest elasticity of around minus unity for $M1$ and between -0.2 and -0.5 for $M3$. Perhaps these results were distorted by the gradual shift from current to deposit accounts, which we have discussed.

Following the reform of credit control in 1971, however, these demand relations appeared to break down, especially for $M3$. The evidence for the stability of United Kingdom $M1$ demand functions is mixed; neither Hacche (1974) nor Coghlan (1978) find instability in the early 1970s, whereas Artis and Lewis (1976) do. Broughton (1979) finds that although demand for $M1$ appears to have been stable in more recent years, there may have been a significant shift in 1971. Extending Coghlan's equation beyond 1976, Artis and Lewis (1981) find similar long-run coefficients to those of Coghlan (an income elasticity of about unity and interest rate elasticities of around -0.3), but note that sharp changes in the rate of growth of $M1$ are not picked up. They conclude that people may now react to interest rate changes more forcefully than in the past and that estimated interest rate elasticities may be too low. The major problem with studies of M3 demand functions is that the coefficient on the lagged dependent variable (the adjustment term) is found to be very high, unity or above, so that it is impossible to evaluate the steady state properties of the equations.

At least two reasons, other than instability, have been put forward to explain why these equations broke down in the early 1970s. First, Artis and Lewis (1976) argued that it was not the demand function which shifted but rather that independent variations in supply conditions gave rise to a marked disequilibrium to which it took time to adjust. However, although their empirical work finds some support for the early 1970s, their equations do not predict well after 1974. A second approach started from the view that the usual M3 demand functions were badly misspecified, because they omitted an own-rate on money as well as some of the more important interest differentials, particularly the margin between bank lending rates and deposit rates. Both sets of variables were important in the new competitive environment. The own-rate related to the process of 'reintermediation' whereby banks, by offering more competitive interest rates, attracted deposits that would previously have been lost to to the parallel money markets. The interest differential variables were designed to explain, among other things, the extent of 'round-tripping', the practice of borrowing in order to hold money on deposit account. However, although equations estimated along these lines get quite good fits for the period 1971–3, it has not been possible to find the same sort of result for the 1960s.

In the United States a shift in the money demand function seemed to occur in the mid-1970s. Goldfeld (1973 and 1976), using quarterly data from 1952–72, found a stable relationship between real money balances (in terms of M1), income and interest rates, with a point estimate of the long-run income elasticity of about 0.7 and long-run interest elasticities on the commercial paper rate and the time deposit rate of 0.07 and 0.16 respectively. On adding 1973 data to the original equation the results were generally consistent with the original ones although the income elasticity fell to 0.55. However, when the equation was used to forecast outside the sample period, it consistently and widely overpredicted actual money demand and when it was re-estimated to include post-1973 data, the coefficient on the lagged dependent variable became very large, implying implausibly long adjustment lags.

Judd and Scadding (1982), in their survey of the post-1973 literature on United States money demand functions, conclude that the most likely cause of observed instability in the demand for money after 1973 is innovation in financial arrangements which allowed the public to economise on its holding of transactions balances. These innovations appear to have been, in part, induced by the high inflation rates and corresponding interest rates. An alternative hypothesis is put forward by Hamburger (1977) who has argued that the original equation was misspecified because it did not include real assets as substitutes for money. He measured the yield on real assets by the ratio of dividends to equity prices (as a proxy for the rate of return on equities and thus on physical capital). He found a significant, negative coefficient on this variable and obtained post-sample predictions for 1974–6 which were considerably more accurate than those found using conventionally specified equations.

This was done at the cost of restricting the real income elasticity of demand for money to be unity. The general weight of evidence and the *a priori* probabilities, however, do seem to suggest that the short-run income elasticity is not far from unity, though in the long run parallel trends in income and in monetary habits and institutions may give a different impression.

If the income elasticity is indeed unity, our simple money demand function turns into: $y - m = bi$ which means that changes in velocity of circulation and in interest are directly related – so long as the function remains stable. If money stock rises in relation to the community's desire to hold it, interest rate falls, because people move to invest some of the extra money in securities, thus reducing their yields, and the fall in yield reconciles them to holding the extra money. Since we are dealing with annual changes in money, income, and the rest, we can amend our criterion for an inflationary monetary impulse – such an impulse has been given if rate of increase of the money stock has increased, rate of increase of velocity has fallen and rate of increase of a representative interest rate has fallen also.

The interest condition would, of course, be redundant if we could assume that the demand function does not shift. We have, implicitly, made this assumption in taking a fall in velocity of circulation (or rather, its first difference) as evidence that the monetary situation has become easier. It is perfectly possible for the community to wish to increase the ratio of its money holdings to nominal GDP without creating a presumption that an acceleration of spending is on the way – people may want more money to hold, not more money to spend. Hence the interest condition must be added. A fall in the first difference of interest, going with a fall in that of velocity, does not guarantee that the demand for money has not shifted, but it is, at all events, a simple minimal indication that it has not done so sufficiently to offset the credit-easing effects of a positive shift in the supply curve.

In applying our modified criterion of a positive monetary impulse – faster growth of money, slower growth of velocity, slower growth of interest – we may usefully, in practice, keep an eye also on the *level* of interest, besides its first difference. The difference between the two, as symptoms, is a matter of timing. Fall of interest rate will, in important easings of credit, follow fall of its rate of change. If the series is roughly sinusoidal, the lag is a quarter of a period. In practice, it seems to be frequently somewhat under a year and with our annual data the two quite often coincide.

There is one further important qualification to our criterion. The rate of interest that matters for the purpose of effecting expansion of expenditure growth is that corrected for the expected rate of price inflation. If, from expecting no inflation, everyone concerned suddenly comes to expect a more or less indefinite inflation at 5 per cent a year, that fact alone will raise the market rate of interest by about 5 percentage points and this may swamp any fall in interest which. would otherwise have been caused by a money injection. Expectations of inflation are important in another way, since they affect demand for money as opposed to goods and we need not be surprised, therefore, if the simple demand function specified above shifts with these expectations; but what we are concerned with at the moment is something different – the *ex ante* real rate of interest as an influence on expenditure.

We need, in principle, to know what were seen, *ex ante*, as real rates of interest. We must not forget the evidence on this matter that we have reviewed in chapter 5; nevertheless, in view of its imperfect conclusiveness and coverage, it will be useful also to employ some rules of thumb derived from the hard data of nominal interest rates and their *ex post* real counterparts.

Expectations may operate in many 'gears'. Most conservatively, any change in price level may be treated as temporary, its early reversal being expected (zero elasticity of expectations of price *level*). Less conservatively, any new price formed may be expected to continue indefinitely, every experienced change being treated as permanent (*unit* elasticity of expectations of price level or zero elasticity of expectations with regard to the inflation rate) and third, any newly-established rate of inflation may be expected to continue indefinitely (unit elasticity with regard to inflation). One could, of course, proceed to higher gears, relating to the rate of change of inflation, but our survey of the evidence suggests that they are not very important for our main sample countries in our period – they belong to the dynamics of hyperinflation. It looks as if the second and third of these gears set the useful limits to the interpretations we should assume in estimating *ex ante* real interest in our period; at one end of the scale we accept change in the nominal interest rate as measuring also the change in the perceived *ex ante* real rate, at the other end we assume that recent change in the rate of inflation is fully taken into account and that any year-to-year change in the *ex post* real rate is taken as applying also to the *ex ante*, expected, rate for the immediate future.

Perhaps the best way of using interest rate data to test whether the perceived monetary situation has been eased or tightened is to take account of directions of movement of both nominal and *ex post* real rates and their first differences, using both short- and long-term rates for this purpose. We can then be guided by the predominant direction of change of these indicators and by the strength of the predominance.

IMPULSES AND THE INTEREST INDICATORS

Table 6.1 summarises these interest data, along with those on velocity and money stock, for each of the Big Six. The first two columns show the directions of change of M2 and V2; the second pair give corresponding information about M1 and V1. It will be seen at once that the growth rates of the two money aggregates usually change in the same direction and so do their respective velocities, but there are exceptions, some of them notable. The fifth and sixth columns of the table summarise the evidence from interest rates by giving the numbers of indicators which point respectively towards expectations of higher real rates (positive) and lower ones (negative). Mostly, we have eight indicators altogether for each annual interval: the direction of change in *level* and in *rate of increase* of long and short nominal interest rates and the directions of change of the four corresponding *ex post* real magnitudes, calculated from the nominal rates *minus* the year's percentage increase in the CPI. In some cases, the number of indicators divided between the two columns is less than eight, either because some interest data are lacking or because one of the indicators shows no change over the year. How the (usually eight) indicators divide between positive and negative provides a useful general assessment of the direction and strength of market tendencies, though in subsequent discussion it may sometimes be necessary to go into detail.

The last three columns of the table show the general verdict as to whether there has been a positive or a negative monetary impulse, first as already adumbrated from the directions of movement of M2 and V2, then as judged from M2 and the general direction of the interest indicators and finally on a consideration of both these criteria.

Table 6.1 Money, velocity and interest indicators; six countries

	United States									United Kingdom								
					Interest indicators		Diagnosis from							Interest indicators		Diagnosis from		
	ΔM_2	ΔV_2	ΔM_1	ΔV_1	+	−	$\Delta M_2,\Delta V_2$	Interest	Confirmed	ΔM_2	ΔV_2	ΔM_1	ΔV_1	+	−	$\Delta M_2,\Delta V_2$	Interest	Confirmed
1951	−	−	−	−	4	2		NM					+	4	0			
1952	−	−	−	−	5	3		NM		−	−	−	−	7	1	(M)		
1953	+	+	+	+	6	2	NM	NM	NM	+	+	−	−	3	5	M	M	M
1954	−	−	−	−	0	7		NM		−	−	−	−	0	8	NM	M	M
1955	+	+	+	+	7	0	NM	NM	NM	+	+	+	+	7	1	NM	NM	NM
1956	−	−	−	−	4	4				+	+	+	+	5	3	M	NM	NM
1957	0	0	+	+	3	5	M	M	M	−	−	−	−	2	5	M		
1958	+	+	+	+	3	5	NM	NM	NM	+	+	−	−	4	4	M	M	M
1959	−	−	−	−	8	0	M	M	M	+	+	+	+	5	2	NM	NM	NM
1960	+	+	−	−	0	8				+	+	+	+	2	6	NM		
1961	+	+	+	+	3	5	M	M	M	−	−	−	−	0	8	NM		
1962	+	+	+	+	7	1				+	+	+	+	5	3	M		
1963	+	+	+	+	8	5	M	M	M	+	+	+	+	4	4	M	NM	
1964	+	+	+	+	3	0	NM	NM	NM	+	+	+	+	5	3	NM	NM	
1965	+	+	−	−	4	5	NM	M	M	+	+	+	+	6	2	M		
1966	+	+	+	+	4	4	M	M	M	+	+	+	+	4	4	NM	NM	NM
1967	−	−	+	+	4	4				+	+	+	+	5	3	M	M	
1968	+	+	+	+	7	1	NM	NM	NM	+	+	+	+	5	3	NM	NM	NM
1969	+	+	−	−	3	5	M	M	M	−	−	−	−	1	7	M	M	M
1970	+	+	−	−	3	5	M	M	M	−	−	−	−	1	7	M	M	
1971	+	+	+	+	6	2				+	+	+	+	7	1	M		
1972	−	−	+	+	4	4	NM	NM	NM	−	−	−	−	6	2	NM		
1973	−	−	−	−	2	6				+	+	+	+	3	5	NM		
1974	−	−	−	−	4	4	NM	NM	NM	−	−	−	−	0	8	NM	NM	
1975	−	−	−	−	5	3	M	M	M	−	−	−	−	4	4	M		
1976	+	+	+	+	3	5	M	M		−	−	−	−	8	0	M	NM	
1977	+	+	+	+	7	1	M	M		+	+	−	−	0	8	M	M	M
1978	−	−	+	+	4	4	NM			+	+	+	+	6	2	M		
1979				+	4	4				−	−	−	−	4	4			

Table 6.1 (cont.)

	Japan									Germany								
	ΔM_2	ΔV_2	ΔM_1	ΔV_1	Interest indicators +	Interest indicators −	Diagnosis from ΔM_2, ΔV_2	Diagnosis from Interest	Confirmed	ΔM_2	ΔV_2	ΔM_1	ΔV_1	Interest indicators +	Interest indicators −	Diagnosis from ΔM_2, ΔV_2	Diagnosis from Interest	Confirmed
1951					1	1								2	2			
1952	+	+	+	−	4	0								1	3			
1953	−	−	−	+	0	3								1	3			
1954	−	−	−	−	2	1				+	+	+	+	3	1		(M)	
1955	+	+	+	+	2	2	M	M	M	−	−	−	−	4	0	NM	NM	NM
1956	+	+	+	−	1	3	NM	NM	NM	+	+	+	−	4	4		NM	
1957	−	−	−	−	2	2	NM			+	+	+	−	0	8	M	M	M
1958	−	−	−	+	4	0	M			−	−	−	−	6	2	M	NM	NM
1959	+	+	+	−	0	4	M			−	−	−	+	6	2	NM	NM	M
1960	−	+	−	−	0	4				−	−	−	+	0	8	NM	NM	NM
1961	+	+	+	+	4	0				0	0	0	−	4	4			
1962	−	+	−	−	0	4				+	+	+	+	8	0	M	NM	
1963	+	+	+	+	4	0	NM	M	NM	+	+	+	+	6	1			
1964	−	−	o	−	0	4	NM	NM	NM	+	+	+	−	4	4	M		
1965	+	+	+	+	3	1				+	+	+	+	8	0	M	M	M
1966	−	−	−	+	6	0				+	+	+	+	2	6	NM	NM	NM
1967	−	−	−	+	5	3	NM	NM	NM	−	−	−	+	8	6	NM	M	NM
1968	+	+	+	+	3	5	NM	NM	NM	+	+	+	+	6	0	M	NM	M
1969	+	+	+	−	4	4	M	M	M	+	−	−	−	0	1	NM	NM	M
1970	+	+	+	+	4	4				+	+	+	+	0	8	NM	M	NM
1971	+	+	+	−	4	4	M			+	+	+	−	3	5	M	M	M
1972	−	−	−	+	4	4	NM			+	+	+	−	8	0	M	M	M
1973	−	−	−	−	4	4	NM			−	−	−	+	3	5	NM	NM	NM
1974	−	+	−	−	4	4				+	+	+	−	1	7			
1975	+	+	+	+	4	4				+	+	+	+	6	2	M	M	M
1976	−	−	−	+	1	7	NM	M		−	−	−	−	3	5	NM	NM	NM
1977	−	+	−	−	3	5								4	4			
1978	0	−	+	+	4	4				+	+	+	+	7	1	NM	NM	NM
1979	−	−	−	+	6	2			NM									

Table 6.1 (cont.)

	France				Interest indicators		Diagnosis from			Italy				Interest indicators		Diagnosis from		
	ΔM_2	ΔV_2	ΔM_1	ΔV_1	+	−	$\Delta M_2, \Delta V_2$	In-terest	Confirmed	ΔM_2	ΔV_2	ΔM_1	ΔV_1	+	−	$\Delta M_2, \Delta V_2$	In-terest	Confirmed
1951	−	−	−	−	1	2												
1952	−	−	−	−	6	2	NM	NM		+	+	+	+	2	2			
1953	+	+	+	+	6	2	NM	NM		−	−	−	−	3	1	M		
1954	+	+	+	+	1	7	M	M	NM	+	+	−	+	0	3	NM	NM	NM
1955	+	+	+	+	3	5	NM	M		+	+	−	−	4	0	NM		
1956	−	−	−	−	4	4	NM			0	−	−	−	2	2			
1957	−	−	−	−	8	0	NM	NM	NM	+	−	−	+	3	1	M	NM	
1958	+	+	+	+	1	7	M			+	+	+	−	0	3	M	M	M
1959	+	+	+	+	4	4	M	M		0	+	+	−	2	2			
1960	+	+	+	+	5	3	M	M	M	−	−	−	−	1	3			
1961	+	+	+	+	3	5				+	+	+	+	4	0			
1962	+	+	+	+	2	6	NM	NM		+	+	+	+	2	2	M		M
1963	−	−	−	−	5	3	NM	NM	NM	−	−	−	−	1	3	NM	NM	
1964	−	−	−	−	8	0	NM	NM	NM	+	+	+	−	4	0	M	M	
1965	+	+	+	+	3	5				+	+	+	−	1	3	M		
1966	+	+	+	+	6	2	M	M		+	+	+	−	3	1	NM		
1967	+	+	+	+	5	3				+	+	+	+	2	2	NM		
1968	+	+	+	+	4	4	NM	NM	NM	−	−	−	−	4	0		NM	NM
1969	+	+	+	+	8	0	M	NM		+	+	+	+	4	2	NM	NM	
1970	+	−	+	+	4	4	M	M		+	+	+	+	4	1			
1971	+	−	+	+	0	8	M	M	M	+	+	+	−	0	8	M	M	M
1972	+	−	+	+	2	6	M	M	M	+	+	+	+	2	6	M	M	M
1973	−	−	−	−	7	1	NM	NM	NM	−	−	−	+	2	5		M	
1974	+	+	+	+	3	5	M	M	M	+	+	+	+	5	3	NM	NM	NM
1975	−	−	−	−	2	6	M	M	M	+	+	+	−	3	5	M	M	M
1976	−	−	+	+	6	2	NM	NM	NM	+	+	+	+	5	2		M	
1977	−	−	+	−	6	2	NM	NM		−	−	−	−	2	6			
1978	−	−	+	+	0	8	NM	NM		−	−	−	−	4	4	M		
1979	−	+	+	+	5	3	NM	NM	NM	+	+	+	+	4	4	NM		

Looking at the year-to-year evidence for the six countries, we can further summarise it for each of them (and for all together) as in table 6.2. We start with the numbers of M (and NM) impulses as already given in chapter 4 from the M2, V2 criterion. We then give the number of cases in which the balance of the interest indicators confirms this first diagnosis and the number in which it contradicts it; this is simply a matter of whether the interest indicators are, on balance, of the same sign as the change in the growth rate of V2, or of the opposite sign. Finally, we give the numbers of extra impulses, not diagnosed from M2 and V2, which can be diagnosed in a corresponding way from M2 and the predominant sign of the interest indicators.

The interest evidence confirms that of velocity in about three-fifths of all cases, 60 out of the 105 *prima facie* M and NM impulses added together. The confirmation is rather fuller for the negative impulses than for the positive ones. There is contradiction in about a third as many cases (twenty) and in 25 cases the interest evidence may be judged broadly neutral. There are 23 cases in which the interest rate evidence suggests an impulse which that from velocity change would not suggest. Taking the six countries together, therefore, the extent to which velocity and interest indicators are in agreement is substantial, but a good way from complete.

The degree of confirmation or conflict in the different countries varies. The outstanding feature is the high degree of conflict in the United Kingdom, where nine of the 23 *prima facie* monetary impulses (positive and negative together) are contradicted by the predominant evidence of the interest indicators – in particular, five of the fourteen positive impulses are thus contradicted. Interpretation of this is not perfectly straightforward, because of the composite nature of our battery of interest indicators, but broadly the suggestion is that in some of these cases where M2 accelerates more than Y, the demand curve for money has also risen (or rather risen faster), so that the tendency of interest has been upward instead of downward. Although the United Kingdom showed an outstandingly large number (fourteen) of *prima facie* positive monetary impulses in our period, the number in which the indications of velocity and interest march together is only five – about the average for the Big Six. No country has all its velocity indications of positive impulses confirmed by the interest indicators, but Germany has none of them actually contradicted.

The picture is very similar for negative impulses; broadly the same countries have high or low proportions of them confirmed by interest data as with the positive impulses. Germany has all eight of hers confirmed and the United States has none actually contradicted but

Table 6.2 *Summary of evidence on monetary impulses from velocity and interest indicators*

	M					NM				
	From V_2	Con-firmed	Contra-dicted	Not contra-dicted	From i only	From V_2	Con-firmed	Contra-dicted	Not contra-dicted	From i only
United States	8	6	1	7	1	10	6	0	10	2
United Kingdom	14	5	5	9	1	9	5	4	5	2
Japan	5	2	1	4	2	8	4	2	6	1
Germany	7	5	0	7	1	8ᵃ	8	0	8	3
France	8	4	2	6	3	11	7	1	10	3
Italy	10	5	2	8	1	7	3	2	5	3
Total	52	27	11	41	9	53	33	9	44	14

ᵃ Excluding the impulse of 1951, for which the data are not compatible with the main series.

the United Kingdom has four contradicted, suggesting that in those cases the demand schedule for money had fallen.

If we accept the evidence from interest changes as modifying our initial diagnosis of monetary impulses, what difference does the modification make to the relations which we investigated in chapter 4? To answer this question fully would be wearisome, since there are various ways in which amendments from the evidence of interest rates could be incorporated. We should at least have to cut out the diagnoses from velocity changes which were contradicted, but we might or might not eliminate those where interest evidence is roughly neutral and we might or might not insert the new cases suggested by interest but not by velocity.

It is easy to look first at this small number of new interest-based diagnoses by themselves. On the positive side, there are nine of them and one can quickly see whether they show any particular tendency to coincide with or immediately to precede positive expenditure impulses. The numbers of cases in which they do so are not significantly greater than chance; with the caution due in such cases where the numbers are very small one may express some doubt of their having quite the same claim to be correct as the original, velocity-based identifications. (They are, of course, instances in which velocity growth did not fall as money growth accelerated, though interest change, in some sense, did, with a suggestion that the demand schedule for money fell.)

If our revised list of positive impulses is the most comprehensive one, from which only the definitely contradicted velocity-based diagnoses are removed and to which these new interest-based diagnoses are added, we find (for the Big Six taken together) that coincidences of M and E are *fewer* than on the pure velocity criterion; in fact less than expectation with random distribution, though to an extent significant only at about the 20 per cent level; but M is immediately followed by E more often – significantly above random expectation at better than the 5 per cent level. The tendency of M to be followed by accelerating inflation after two years, however, which approaches significance for the Big Six on the pure velocity criterion, virtually disappears on the revised criterion.

At the other extreme, we can retain only those diagnoses of M in which the velocity and interest criteria positively agree. We are then reduced to 27 impulses for the Big Six, but their relations to other kinds of impulse show signs of becoming more clear-cut. Coincidence with E is below expectation, though not significantly; the connection of M with accelerating inflation two years later is significant at about the 10 per cent level (rather less than with the more inclusive revised definition), but the connection with E in the immediately following year is much closer – significant at better than the $\frac{1}{2}$ per cent level. Another strong connection of the confirmed Ms is that with accelerating real growth in the immediately following year (significant at the $2\frac{1}{2}$ per cent level). This is much closer than the connection with rising inflation two years ahead, while that with rising inflation one year ahead (that is, in the immediately following year), like that shown by the original, velocity-based, Ms is negative but non-significant.

THE 'CONFIRMED' IMPULSES

Broadly, then, restricting the diagnosed positive monetary impulses by admitting only those for which the velocity and the interest criteria agree gives us a stronger connection with expenditure-pull and with real growth, both in the immediately following year, and somewhat reduces the, in any case feebler, connection with rising inflation two years ahead (making that with rising inflation one year ahead rather more negative, but still short of a reasonable level of significance). On the face of it, the United States, Germany and Italy are the countries that show the strongest associations of the redefined Ms with accelerating real growth in the following year, the United States and Italy those with the closest association of Ms with immediately following expenditure impulses; the absence of Germany from this second group is consistent with the evidence we shall see later that a relatively high proportion of its Es originated abroad.

It is noticeable that a third of these confirmed Ms for the Big Six fall in two years, four (United States, United Kingdom, Germany, Italy) in 1958, five (for all our Six except Japan) in 1971. Germany, France and Italy all show confirmed impulses in 1972 and 1975 but otherwise the scatter is wide.

On any criterion of diagnosis, positive monetary impulses have been, at least at first sight, mainly counter-cyclical in their timing. We saw in chapter 4 that on the velocity criterion they occurred for our present sample of eleven countries mostly when inflation and growth rate were falling, the connection with inflation being much closer than that with growth. For the Big Six, and for confirmed positive impulses only, the association with falling inflation is significant at the $\frac{1}{2}$ per cent level, that with falling growth at somewhat better than the 10 per cent level. Seventeen of the 27 impulses occurred when both inflation and growth were falling in the country concerned, against four when inflation was rising, five when growth was, one when both were. All the Big Six showed at least one impulse that was pro-cyclical in one of these senses; Germany, Japan and (more surprisingly) Italy showed only one each, whereas France showed three and the United States and United Kingdom two.

Another, perhaps a better, way of assessing the timeliness or untimeliness of the impulses is to see where they came in relation to deviations of real output from trend, which we discussed in another connection in chapter 3. Eleven of them (out of 27) occurred in a trough year which, remembering our convention that growth rates and impulses are identified by the second of the two years with respect to which they are defined, means that they were slightly ahead of the trough. This was true of the four impulses of 1958, already referred to, and of the United States impulses dated 1961 and 1971, that in the United Kingdom in 1977, those in Germany in 1967 and 1975 and in Italy in 1965 and 1972. Eight more occurred on the way down from a peak to a trough; those of 1970 in the United States, of 1971 in the United Kingdom, of 1956 in Japan, 1971 and 1972 in Germany, 1975 in France, 1971 and 1975 in Italy. The remaining eight (United States, 1963, 1977; United Kingdom, 1953, 1954; Japan, 1969; France, 1961, 1971, 1972) came during an upswing.

Is this a record of an inflationary or a disinflationary distribution of monetary impulses? Presumably the time distribution is inflationary if the impulses become effective in raising expenditure at times when activity is already high in relation to capacity or in relation to trend, which we are using to represent the course of capacity; disinflationary, by comparison, if they become effective at times when capacity is to the greatest extent unused. Or, since our inflationary impulses are defined with reference to *rates of increase* of money and expenditure, it is better to say that positive monetary impulses are least inflationary if they become most effective in raising expenditure at times when output is *falling* fastest in relation to capacity. In any case, to answer the question we need to know what interval elapses between a monetary impulse and the associated change in the rate of growth of expenditure. We shall see in a future chapter that this will depend on circumstances; in some (when there is a surge of export demand or of public expenditure financed by the banks) the symptoms of M and E may be expected to appear simultaneously; in others easier money may take a year or two to induce a surge of expenditure. The only empirical indicator we have so far is the significant (though very far from invariable) association between M and E in the following year. This, by itself, would suggest that positive monetary impulses are least productive of inflation (and most stabilising of activity) if they occur about a year before the mid-point of the downswing of activity (measured from trend), which is likely to be near to the trough of the cycle of growth rates. The phase of the cycle at which the impulse ought to come to satisfy this condition obviously depends on the cycle length. With four-year cycles which correspond roughly with experience during much of our period, the implication is that impulses should coincide with the cyclical peak of activity or the mid-point of the downswing of the rate of growth. The tendency of impulses to occur when real growth rate was declining is thus consistent with their predominantly counter-cyclical influence as far as it goes and assuming four-year cycles and a one-year lag between M and E. (The way in which we label impulses means that, on these assumptions, the mid-point of the year to which they are assigned should be six months after the actual peak of activity rather than coincident with it; but annual data blur these fine distinctions.)

Of course, in practice we are not dealing with regular cycles and the lag between M and the corresponding E may be expected to be a distributed one; but we have nevertheless some basis for comment on the timing of the actual confirmed impulses. The impulses of 1958 were, on the above reckoning, too late, because they coincided with the trough of activity (measured from trend), but it is not obvious that they all did great inflationary harm. It was only in the United States that this impulse was followed by an E and there, too, the E (in 1959) coincided with a cyclical peak; but the peak was a minor one with appreciable spare capacity and the acceleration of inflation was small and temporary. The immediate apparent effect was mainly on output growth. The same was broadly true of the United Kingdom, where inflation went on falling in 1960 and also of Germany, where it rose only a little, despite a high peak of activity. Only in Italy, of the four countries with a confirmed impulse in 1958, did inflation in the following year set off on a serious increase, accompanied not by expenditure-pull but by four successive years of wage-push impulses.

Other trough-timed monetary impulses also had varying aftermaths. The Italian impulse of 1965 (though the trough was a shallow one) was followed by two years of rising growth rate, inflation not accelerating until 1969. The German one of 1975, with substantial excess capacity, was followed by an acceleration of growth but none of inflation within our period. The Italian impulse of 1972 (the year before a peak of activity) was not so fortunate, nor was the United States impulse of 1971 (following on one of the previous year), though in that case the peak did not arrive for two years.

Did the downswing-timed impulses, on the face of it, do better? They too are a mixed bunch. Japan exhibits one in 1956 in the middle of a long apparent easing of pressure on capacity, but accompanied by wage-push and both accompanied and followed by rising inflation, with no increase of growth until 1959. Germany was in the first half of a downswing in 1971–2, when two impulses occurred; growth rate improved for two years and there was little increase in the already relatively high inflation rate, despite I impulses in 1973 and 1974. France experienced one in 1975, the second year of a downswing that lasted until the end of our period, with some revival of growth rate in the following year and no rise of inflation until 1978. Italy also shows one in 1975, still in the first half of a downswing lasting until 1978; it was followed by a sharp recovery of growth rate, which had been negative in 1975, and there was no considerable change in the already very high inflation rate; there were W impulses in 1975 and 1977 and an I in 1976. The United States impulse of 1970, already referred to, occurred during a downswing, but its effects are no doubt mixed up with those of the one already mentioned which happened in the following, trough, year. All things considered, perhaps experience connected with downswing-timed monetary impulses is not very inflationary, especially if one takes I and (more cautiously) W impulses as having been independent of them.

Are upswing-timed impulses more inflationary in practice? That in the United States in 1963 was a small one, so it is perhaps not surprising that the rise in inflation rates after it was also small, not bigger than that of the already high growth rate. The United Kingdom impulses of 1953 and 1954, however, were followed by a considerable rise of inflation rate (for which two Is may be partly to blame) and a downward trend of growth rate. The Japanese impulse of 1969 was also small; there was some acceleration of inflation, not of growth, to the following peak year, after which both declined. France shows three examples of the upswing-timed impulse, in 1961, 1971 and 1972. After the first, inflation rate continued a moderate upward trend and growth, already high, a downward one on balance. The substantial impulses of 1971–2, however, were followed by drastic rises in the rate of inflation (assisted by both I and W) and an almost equally drastic fall in growth rate. The same is broadly true of the smaller United States impulse of 1977 – the I of 1979 no doubt contributed. So far as the relative performances of inflation and growth after them are concerned, the upswing-based impulses do seem to have had a poor record on the whole but the variation is considerable and, once more, the occurrence or non-occurrence of import price or wage-push impulses was clearly important.

The relation (or lack of it) between the national records on the timing of impulses and on inflation makes it clear that the former did not dominate the latter. Germany and Italy, at the bottom and the top respectively of the range of inflations among the Big Six, have identical records on timing; three impulses in troughs, two on the downswing, none on the upswing. France stands at the opposite extreme, with her three on the upswing and one on the downswing but, as we saw in chapter 3, with the least variable growth rate of all our sample countries, despite this *prima facie* destabilising monetary record. Timing is only one factor among many.

The negative impulses can perhaps be more shortly dealt with. The 33 members of that class confirmed by the interest evidence, as well as that on velocity, are significantly biased towards years of rising inflation and years of rising growth in the records of the Big Six, but in contrast with the purely velocity-based diagnoses for the eleven OECD countries, the association with rising growth is in this case the closer. (The number of coincidences is the same with rising growth as with rising inflation – 21 – but random distribution would yield a higher expected number of coincidences with the more numerous years of rising inflation; the inflation association is significant at about the 7 per cent level, the growth one almost at the 1 per cent level.) The United Kingdom, France and Italy, taken together, show a bias (significant at better than the 10 per cent level) towards association of their negative monetary impulses with rising inflation, no significant bias towards association with rising growth. With the United States, Japan and Germany together, it is the other way about; association with rising *growth* is significant at better than the 5 per cent level. It may be added that United Kingdom negative impulses coincide with rising growth less often than a random distribution would lead one to expect, but not significantly less.

For more light on the contribution of monetary impulses to inflation in our period as a whole, however, it will be necessary to look more particularly at the major jumps in the inflation rate to which we gave some attention in relation to impulses in general in chapter 4. The leaps of 1951 will have to be passed over, since we do not have sufficient evidence from the monetary series we have used about the years preceding it. The largest number of major leaps occurs, of course, in 1973–4 and, so far as the Big Six are concerned, the confirmed positive monetary impulses that look as if they have something to do with it are those of 1970 and 1971 in the United States, that of 1971 in the United Kingdom, possibly that of 1969 in Japan and those of 1971 and 1972 in Germany, France and Italy.

First, how strong do they appear to have been? The United States impulse of 1971 was very strong, even apart from being a continuation of a smaller one begun in the previous year. The growth rate of M1 did not start to rise as soon as that of M2 did and, in 1971, unlike that of M2, was below the growth rate of nominal income. There was apparently some shift of demand towards time deposits. Nominal interest rates, however, moved generally downwards and so, in 1970 as well as 1971, did the *ex post* real short rate. The long one, which had fallen in the previous two years, did not fall, but its first difference did. The interest indicators are thus not unanimously for the easing of monetary conditions at this important time but they give a majority verdict in that sense.

The United Kingdom impulse of 1971 was also substantial in terms of monetary expansion (though not the largest of our period as its United States counterpart was) and its substantiality is confirmed by a fall of all the interest indicators except the first difference of the Treasury Bill rate, which had fallen in the previous year. It was, moreover, followed by two further years of expansion, of which that in the first was very large indeed. During that year (1972), short rate continued to fall, but at a decreased speed, while the long rate and all the *ex post* real rate indicators rose. In 1973, both nominal rates rose and only the *ex post* long rate and its first difference suggested any easing. In view of our evidence about expectations reviewed in the last chapter, it seems likely that the *ex ante* real rates rose. This combination of money injection with the absence of most of the interest effects one would normally expect to accompany it suggests a positive shift of the demand schedule for money. It can hardly be denied that there was a powerful positive monetary impulse in the United Kingdom in the early 1970s, but it seems to have been a good deal less powerful than the movements of the broad money aggregate and its corresponding velocity would lead one to think. Consideration of chart 6.3, along with the evidence about expectations in chapter 5, suggests that the increase in demand for money in these years was mostly a matter of deposit accounts; there may have been a shift of demand away from current accounts, but probably little more than a continuation of the trend in that direction which we discussed earlier.

The Japanese monetary impulse of 1971 was substantial in terms of money expansion, but failed to receive unambiguous confirmation from the interest indicators (even by a marginal majority such as its considerably smaller predecessor of 1969 had received). The *rates of change* of the *ex post* real long and short rates, however, which increased, had fallen in the previous year (as the *levels* did in 1971), so that one should perhaps not deny some sort of confirmation of a positive impulse, though there is a suggestion of a rise in demand for money there too. In Germany, the confirmed impulses of 1971 and 1972 were also major ones, though not larger than those of 1957–8 – nor, for that matter, was the German inflation of 1973–5 the dominating feature of the landscape that it was in most other countries. Similarly, the French and Italian impulses of those years, confirmed by the interest indicators in both cases, were large but not much (if any) larger than others experienced in those countries, notably the French impulse of 1959–61 and the Italian of 1958–9 and 1965–6, all of which, however, were only partially confirmed by the interest indicators. In contrast with these, the 1971–2 impulses, in both countries, were rather fully confirmed; for 1971, completely. While the impulses of the early 1970s in these countries were less remarkable, in terms of money stock and velocity changes, than those in the United States and (more especially) the United Kingdom, there is no suggestion in the data that they were partially offset by changes in the demand for money.

The extraordinary increases in the inflation rates in the Big Six (except Germany) in 1973–4 thus had as their precursors monetary impulses with some title to be regarded as unusually strong, though for various reasons (ambiguity of interest indicators in United States, United Kingdom, Japan, less than dominating magnitude of the money injection in France and Italy) the easings of the monetary situation seem to have been less remarkable than the following inflations. We come back to the fact that other kinds of impulses were also involved on this occasion; in chapter 4 we noted the great concentration of import price- and wage-push in these years.

The other occasions on which inflation shifted decisively upwards include 1968 in the United States, 1962–3 in Italy, 1969–70 in Germany and the United Kingdom. The first of these is preceded only by the small positive monetary impulse of 1967 and failed to be reversed by the much stronger, and strongly confirmed, negative impulse of 1969. The great rise of the inflation rate in Italy in the early 1960s was preceded by the sizeable impulses of 1958–9 (the first of them confirmed) and was pushed along by a small unconfirmed impulse in 1962 but, as we have noted in another connection, the occurrence of four successive wage pushes seems to make it clear that, whatever the importance of money injection in maintaining this rise of inflation, it was not led by demand-pull in the goods market. The important rise of inflation in Germany in 1969–70 was preceded only by the very small (in terms of money injection) impulse of 1967, and took place against a background of sharply accelerating velocity and rising interest indicators. But, once more, there were two wage-pushes. In the British case, the impulse of 1967 was rather bigger than the German one, but the interest indicators were entirely ambiguous and again, in 1969, there was a major and on balance confirmed negative impulse – but an import price-push following the 1967 devaluation, and a wage-push impulse had occurred in 1968. Both monetary and cost impulses have to be taken into account in these, as in other, cases and the two do not go hand in hand.

Table 6.3 *Proportions of (logarithmic) growth of broad money stock taking place in years of confirmed M and NM impulses, and in other years; 1952–79 (per cent)*

	M	NM	Rest
United States	21.1	16.4	62.5
United Kingdom	16.6	8.1	75.3
Japan[a]	9.0	17.0	74.0
Germany	19.4	28.9	51.7
France	19.0	23.6	57.4
Italy	18.0	10.0	72.0

[a] 1954–79.

THE CONFIRMED IMPULSES AND TOTAL MONEY GROWTH

Having somewhat refined our diagnoses of positive and negative monetary impulses for our six main sample countries, we can answer at all events one question about them. How large do these periods of confirmed active monetary influence, when money was apparently 'leading the dance', bulk in the whole story of the growth in monetary stock in our period? If one sums the (logarithmic) increases in M2 for the annual intervals which we have classified as carrying positive monetary impulses (see table 6.3), they generally account for round about a fifth or a sixth of the total increase from 1952 (or whenever M2 statistics first become available) to 1979. The odd country is Japan, where it is only an eleventh. For negative impulses the proportion varies from a twelfth to more than a quarter, the United Kingdom and Italy standing at the bottom of this range, Germany and France at the top.

The broad impression from this is that monetary expansion was more prominent than monetary restriction in the United States, United Kingdom and Italy and the reverse was true in Japan and Germany and to a smaller extent in France. There remains about three-quarters of the total monetary expansion in the United Kingdom, Japan and Italy and more than half in the other three countries which took place in the absence of any overt sign that the money supply was either pushing the momentum of the economy forward or resisting it. The suggestion is that, at the times in question, and for something like the indicated proportions of the total expansion, the role of the money supply was essentially an accommodating one. For the United Kingdom, Japan, Italy and less conspicuously the United States, this role seems to have been predominant.

THE DETERMINANTS OF THE MONEY SUPPLY

The money supply is, of course, not far from being the same thing as the net aggregate liabilities of the banking system. That being so, it is clear that it is increased by bank lending, subject to leakage abroad of the proceeds of that lending, and by the depositing with the banks of receipts from abroad. Lending by the central bank can usually be assumed to be a matter of policy, discretion, or sometimes necessity – at all events, not to be commercially motivated. That of the commercial banks is normally so motivated and is limited either by the amount of demand from creditworthy borrowers at rates of interest that make the lending worthwhile, or by necessity, imposed either by the central monetary authorities or by generally accepted convention, of keeping their liabilities below certain maximum multiples of liquid assets of specified kinds which rank as reserves – notably, claims on the central bank. It is also, in some countries and at some times, limited by direct instructions or exhortations of the authorities.

The authorities thus have three types of operation at their command for controlling the monetary stock. They can give instructions of various kinds to the banks, limiting the extent or destinations of their lending, as in the United Kingdom and in France for much of the time since the second world war. They can use their influence to raise rates of interest, so that the demand for loans from the banks is restricted by the cost of obtaining them. This is usually done by fixing at a high level the rate at which the central bank is willing to act as lender of last resort directly or indirectly to the commercial banks and at the same time creating a reserve shortage by open market operations – in this case by selling securities. This is an important method in the United Kingdom, Japan, France, Italy, Australia and Denmark. The third method is to operate on the supply of bank lending by insisting on minimum required ratios of reserves to liabilities, while altering the required values of those ratios from time to time and/or working through open market operations on the available supply of the assets which count as reserves. This is the predominant method of the Federal Reserve System in the United States, also broadly that of the German and Canadian authorities.

Distinctions between these lines of action, however, are far from clear-cut; in particular, sales of securities by the authorities, even if primarily intended to make a higher borrowing rate from the Central Bank effective, also raise the long-term rate directly and, at the same time, directly reduce the reserve base of the commercial banks. Methods of credit control by the central bank can never be quantitatively precise; control of the money stock is somewhat blurred by the central bank's obligation to act as a lender of last resort (without which the confidence on which modern credit systems depend would be insecure); control by way of interest rates presupposes some knowledge and some stability of demand functions for money, both of which are, as we have seen, in practice imperfect.

In inquiring where our monetary impulses came from, therefore, we have two questions to ask: was the expansion of bank liabilities in question generated by extra lending to the public authorities, or to the private sector, or by net inflow of funds from abroad and, if by extra bank lending, how was that permitted – in particular was it permitted by concomitant growth of reserves, and if so, what generated those extra reserves? We shall also ask how far the authorities have succeeded in achieving their target rates of growth of money supply in the recent years in which several countries have published target rates in advance.

SOURCES OF MONETARY EXPANSION AND CONTRACTION

In the United States, all the cases of inflationary monetary impulse that we have identified seem to have been associated with accelerations in growth of the monetary stock which came, immediately, from increased banking system loans to the public authorities, with growth of loans to the private sector either constant or decreasing. The quantitative contribution of increase in the banking system's foreign assets was mostly small; in the great expansion of 1969–71, however, though secondary to growth of government debt, it was considerable. The cases of negative monetary impulse, moreover, mostly correspond to reduced growth of governmental indebtedness and increased growth of private indebtedness to the banking system, the exception being the rather doubtful case of 1966, where the growth of both these forms of indebtedness fell. Changes in private indebtedness are, in general, both larger and more variable than those in public sector indebtedness, but they tend to be associated with periods when growth of transactions is increasing or decreasing with, or ahead of, the money supply, whereas changes in public indebtedness to the banking system tend to run ahead of transactions. Fluctuations in public indebtedness tend to lead those in private by a year or more.

In the United Kingdom, the most obvious variations in government indebtedness to the banking system are those connected with off-setting changes in net foreign assets. Apart from these, generalisations about the sources of monetary impulses are less easy to make than for the United States. The monetary impulse of 1958, the doubtful one of

1967, and the major one of 1971 show some sign of having been primed by increased growth of public debt holdings, but these primings were soon swamped by the accelerated growth of lending to the private sector. In the unconfirmed case of 1963–4, the private element seems to have predominated from the start, growth of public debt holdings being roughly parallel, but smaller. With negative monetary impulses, the role of public debt holdings does not seem to have been very different. Only in 1955 and 1969 does reduced growth of them appear to have been dominant, and on all the occasions we have identified, growth of loans to the private sector declined at virtually the same time, on most of them much more drastically. Net foreign asset changes were, as we have already implied, mostly offset by official action, but the offsetting of inflows was apparently incomplete in late 1970 and 1971, when the contribution from this source to the monetary impulse of that time was substantial. Over the whole period 1954–80, the correlation between changes in M2 and in bank lending to the private sector is remarkably close.

Japanese bank holdings of public liabilities have been so small in comparison with those of private debt that they play little direct part in the story, until after 1974. Nor are net foreign asset changes considerable until 1971, when their increase (or the major part of it, not offset by reduction of public debt holdings) was perhaps half as important as increase of private debt in the positive monetary impulse of that year. In 1972–4 a larger fall in net foreign assets, slightly supplemented rather than offset by the course of public debt holdings, played a considerable part in the substantial but unconfirmed negative monetary impulse of the time, though the fall in growth of private debt was very much larger.

In Germany, holdings of public debt have played a rather larger part in direct monetary creation. Increase in them was apparently important in the unconfirmed positive impulse of 1957 and their lower increase in the confirmed negative one of 1959–60; they were again important in the positive impulse of 1967 and in 1975–6 also public liabilities were the main source of an acceleration and then a decline of money growth which we have associated with positive and negative impulses respectively. Between 1968 and 1974, however, rate of growth of net foreign assets was the most active source of changes in monetary expansion – the negative impulse of 1970 and the positive one of 1971 especially, with reduced growth of lending to the private sector the chief element in the negative impulse of 1973. Holdings of public liabilities were of minor importance in this middle period.

French data suggest an important role for net foreign assets in the unconfirmed positive impulses of 1960 and 1970 and the confirmed one of 1975 and the negative ones of 1956 and 1969 especially, though other elements were also of importance – private sector loans in 1961 and, particularly, the main (later) part of the great expansion of 1971–2, while public liabilities, though generally less prominent, played some part in the negative impulse of 1963–4 and in amplifying the great positive one of 1975.

Italy, despite her record of high and variable inflation (in the later part of our period, at least) shows a markedly less irregular growth of the money stock in relation to GDP than do the other members of the Big Six. Loans to the private sector predominate absolutely in the monetary increase of the early 1970s but cyclical fluctuations such as the accelerations of 1958 and 1965, the rather doubtful negative impulse of 1966–7 and the more definite ones of 1969 and 1974, owe a good deal to net foreign trade.

It is plain that most creation of money in all the Big Six (and, for that matter, in other countries, including Canada and the Netherlands) comes from bank loans to the private sector. There is, however, a difference between countries and between times in the extent to which this lending is the leading element in those crucial monetary expansions and contractions which we have identified as impulses, when change in the rate of money runs ahead of corresponding changes in demand, instead of accompanying or following them. In the United States, loans to the public sector seem to have almost a monopoly of these pioneering changes in rates of growth, though they are fairly regularly followed by larger changes, in the same sense, in the rate of lending to the private sector. In the United Kingdom, the pioneering role of loans to the public sector is less prominent: and, at least in the important case of 1971, uncompensated inflow of foreign funds had a significant, though subsidiary, part. In Germany public borrowing from the banking system has a significant pioneering role at the two ends of our period, with foreign funds taking its place in the middle; in France and Italy foreign funds play a considerable part in cyclical impulses.

RESERVE MONEY

We come now to our second question: what permitted the growth of loans to the private sector which, whether or not they played a pioneering part in monetary impulses, at all events accounted for the great bulk of monetary expansion in, probably, all advanced market economies? Some part of the answer, of course, relates to changes in official reserve requirements, and to direct restraints on lending, in particular countries, but the main part of it concerns growth of reserve

Table 6.4 *Correlations between Δlog reserve money and Δlog M1, Δlog M2*

		ΔRM and ΔM1	ΔRM and ΔM2
United States	1953–81	0.85	0.74
	1953–79	0.85	0.82
United Kingdom	1953–81	0.41	0.54
	1953–79	0.47	0.77
Japan	1955–81	0.67	0.39
	1955–79	0.60	0.30
West Germany	1953–81	0.57	0.55
	1953–79	0.36	0.30
France	1953–81	0.42	0.33
	1953–79	0.43	0.37
Italy	1957–81	0.12	0.55
	1957–79	0.12	0.55

money; currency in circulation and bankers' deposits at the central banks.

How closely is the growth of the total money supply linked to that of reserve money? Departure from strict proportionality arises from three sources: variations in official or customary reserve requirements of the commercial banks, variations in their holdings of reserves in excess of these requirements, and variations in the amount of currency in circulation which is held by the public. Table 6.4 shows the correlation coefficients for the Big Six over the periods 1953–79 and 1953–81, using both M1 and M2 as the money stock variable. The connection is closer with M2 in the United Kingdom and Italy, with M1 in the United States, Japan and France and about the same for both in Germany.

The striking fact, however, is that only in the United States, the country where monetary control is pre-eminently through reserve ratios, is it really close at all (a similar result for M2 in the United Kingdom over 1953–79 deteriorates sharply when the two following years are added). Even in the United States, it is plain from a scatter diagram (chart 6.4) that if one takes, for instance, the periods 1953–61 and 1962–81, there is virtually no correlation between the two (first difference) variables within either of them. The absence of general year-to-year relationships between changes in reserve money and in total money stock is, on inspection of the corresponding diagrams, found to be equally striking in the United Kingdom and Germany.

Nevertheless, if one is interested in particular instances of monetary expansion, such as are associated with our positive monetary impulses, it is still relevant to ask whether they go with notable expansions of the reserve money base. Of the *prima facie* positive

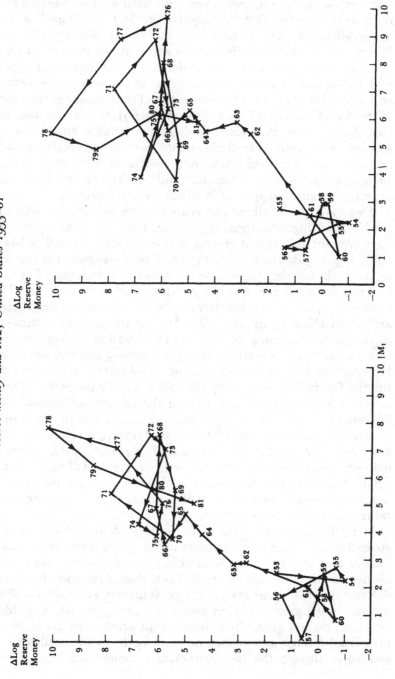

Chart 6.4 First differences of the logarithms of reserve money and M1 and reserve money and M2, United States 1953–81

impulses identified for the United States, those of 1961, 1967, 1970–1 and 1977–8 do, in fact, seem to be associated with accelerated growth of reserve money, though only in the last mentioned was that acceleration very large in relation to that of M2 (NB: according to the IFS new series of M2 statistics, this and that of 1970 are not positive monetary impulses, growth of M2 declines). The impulse of 1958 goes with falling reserve growth. Of the negative impulses, three seem to go with accelerated growth of reserves and of the remainder the sharpest in terms of decreased M2 growth (1969) is one in which the curtailment of reserve growth is disproportionately small. The great increase in the general level of annual growth of both reserves and M2 between 1961 and 1965 was not associated with money growth running ahead of transactions demand – it even included one year of negative impulse, in spite of increasing reserve growth.

If we look specifically at our years of *prima facie* money injection in the United Kingdom, 1954, 1957, 1964, 1972, 1973 and 1979 seem to have brought accelerated growth of reserve money as well as M2, but 1958, 1959, 1963, 1967, 1971, 1977 and 1978 – slightly the majority – to have shown decreased rate of growth of reserves. There is a tendency for acceleration of M2 growth to lead that of reserves. This is so in 1963–5 (M2 starts accelerating before reserves in 1963, reserves are still catching up in 1965, after M2 has started decelerating) and, in the huge expansion of 1971–3. Deceleration of M2, moreover, seems to lead that of reserves in 1955–6, 1960–3 and 1965–6. It might be argued on the other hand that the fall of reserve growth in 1966–9 led the fall in M2 growth in the last year of that period, that the reserve acceleration of 1970 primed the money acceleration of the following year, when reserve growth had fallen again (it can hardly be thought responsible for all of it) and that reserve acceleration in 1976 had something to do with the modest M2 acceleration of the two following years, when reserve growth was again falling off. On the whole, however, the impression is that there was a two-way relationship between M2 and reserves but that reserves adjusted to M2 rather more often than *vice versa*.

As for the changes in the reserves, it is plain that claims on the government change to offset most of the fluctuations in net foreign liabilities of the monetary authorities; the two series nearly always change in opposite directions in both their first and their second differences. This is true even of the great incompletely offset shift from net loss to net gain of foreign assets between 1968 and 1971. Money injections do not generally coincide with accelerated acquisitions of net official foreign assets; they do so in 1978–9 and possibly in 1954 and 1959, though the last-mentioned occasion was one on which growth of total reserve money fell. Of our cases of NM, those of 1956 and 1961–2 go with falls in the first differences of net foreign assets – in the former case more than offset, in the latter not quite offset, by claims on the government – while later negative impulses go with increased growth (or reduced diminution) of the foreign item. Internal, rather than external, events seem on the whole to have dominated United Kingdom money supply.

In Japan, despite the poor overall correlation between changes in reserves and in M2, there is some tendency for money injection to be associated with rise in reserve growth; this happens in 1956, the doubtful case of 1960–1, and 1969, but not in 1971 or the honorary (no velocity fall) case of 1976. Central bank assets have not been dominated by a foreign component and the huge influx of 1972 was more than offset by falls in claims on government and private quarters. The big bulge in growth of reserve money in 1972–3 was mainly ascribable to claims on the deposit money banks; it was the means by which rise in transactions demand was accommodated, but the peak of expansion in money stock preceded that of reserves.

In Germany, of the years of money injection, by our velocity criteria, 1957 and 1958, 1971 and 1972 were peak or near peak years of growth in reserves as well as of money stock and the same can be said, rather less emphatically, about 1965; but not of 1967 or 1975, which were the two years of lowest reserve growth in our whole period. There is no visible tendency for negative monetary impulse to go with low reserve growth.

Germany, unlike the United States, the United Kingdom and Japan, shows very plainly the influence of net foreign assets on the monetary authorities' total reserve holdings. From 1954 onwards they constituted the greater part of the total, and when money injection went with acceleration of the growth of reserves, in 1957–8 and 1971–2, the main responsibility lay with foreign assets, the accelerated growth of which was only partially offset by reductions in government and private items (in 1972 private items made a net contribution to the general increase).

In the French money injection of 1958–61, changes in reserves and in M2 show a common rising tendency, though reserves start a year behind M2 and in 1970–2 they do the same. But in 1975, the rate of change of reserve money becomes negative while the rate of increase of M2 is rising. In the changes of asset holdings by the French monetary authorities, obligations of the government have played only a small part; it is to private obligations that one has mainly to look for offsetting (or failure to offset) fluctuations in net foreign assets. There was a good deal of offsetting in the earlier years and the large fall in

foreign assets in 1969 was mostly offset, but the rise in 1971–2 was
increasingly not countered. From then on, changes in private obligations were predominant; they rose greatly in 1974, only partly offset
by change from gain to loss on the foreign side and the very large
gains of foreign assets in 1975 were much more than offset by falls on
the private side, so that total reserve money decreased – though, as we
have already noted, that did not prevent a remarkable surge in growth
of M2.

The *prima facie* monetary impulses we identified in Italy are
associated with increasing rises in reserve money in four cases (1958,
1962, 1975 and 1978), though in the second and third of these, the
peak of reserve growth came a year later. The impulse of 1965, on the
contrary, is associated with a trough of reserve growth and the
important one of 1971–2 with a modest rise in the first year followed
by a falling back. The part played by net foreign assets in total reserve
changes is limited. There was much offsetting of fluctuations in them
before 1969, but they were important in the spurt of 1971 (claims on
the Government had principally started the rise in the previous year)
and they were partly responsible for the falling off in 1972. The great
acceleration from then to 1976 was in its first part a matter of
government obligations compensating, or over-compensating, a fall in
foreign assets and then the two rising together.

In contrast with these casual empirical observations, much systematic study has been focused on the relation between expansion of
foreign assets and expansion of high-powered money, or to put it
otherwise, on the extent to which acquisitions of foreign assets were
sterilised. Their main purpose has been to estimate the inflationary
effects of the great increase in dollar reserves of countries other than
the United States in the years 1970–2 – official holdings of United
States liabilities nearly quadrupled in the world as a whole in those
years and world liquidity more than doubled. The reason for this
great expansion was twofold. First, the United States ran considerable
current account deficits in the years 1971 and 1972. Second – and
more important – decline of confidence in the international value of
the dollar in 1970 and 1971 caused very large privately held dollar
balances, the proceeds of previous American lending, as well as of net
United States imports, to be dumped into the laps of non-United
States monetary authorities (see Corden, 1977).

How far were these official acquisitions of foreign assets sterilised?
For individual countries the question is complicated by the fact that,
so long as there is any international mobility of capital, an autonomous change in money supply will be partially offset by induced
capital movements. Indeed, with *perfect* mobility of capital, changes in

interest rates would have been induced by incipient monetary expansion which would have been sufficient to reconcile non-United States private investors to the retention of their existing American liabilities and the acquisition of the additional ones required to finance the United States current deficit and strangle the reserve changes at birth (see Victor Argy, 1981, pp. 150–6). Most of the investigators, however, have taken account of the offsetting of autonomous changes in money supply by induced capital flows – in fact there is evidence that it does not make much difference to estimates of propensity to sterilise official foreign exchange acquisitions, because induced capital flows are comparatively sluggish.

The investigations in question, notably Argy and Kouri (1974), Hickman and Schleicher (1978), Laney (1979), Miller (1976) and Darby and Stockman (1980), have been surveyed by Laney and Willett (1982). Their main object is to estimate the sterilisation coefficient, the systematic relation between changes in the domestic and foreign components of the money base, after allowing for other influences which affect the former component. Estimates vary a good deal from country to country, as one would expect in view of the very different abilities which different money authorities have to sterilise – open economies with weakly-developed capital markets have obviously less ability to cope with international flows by means of open market operations than have less open economies with heavy trading in gilt-edged securities. Average of estimates, however, for some countries (Canada, France, Sweden, United Kingdom) suggest that their sterilisation has been virtually complete, that for Australia, Germany, Italy, Japan and the Netherlands it was more than three-quarters complete, for Belgium about two-thirds, and only for Switzerland, of the countries studied, at a much lower level (about a quarter).

Laney and Willett proceed to estimate the proportions of the growth rate of the money stock (both M1 and M2 or M3) that can be attributed to foreign reserve inflows in the years 1970–2. For the countries to which complete sterilisation is attributed, the proportion is, of course, zero. For Germany, it works out (using the average of estimates of the sterilisation coefficient) at somewhat under half, for Japan about a quarter, for Italy a negligible proportion, but for Switzerland virtually the whole. For the total money stock of their eleven sample countries, they derive an estimate that about a fifth of the growth in the money stock was attributable to reserve inflows.

This, as they themselves point out, may underestimate the total effects of the great creation of international liquidity at that time. Monetary authorities and governments which thought it best to sterilise the whole, or nearly the whole, of the inflow of foreign liabilities may nevertheless have been encouraged by the healthy state of their (sterilised) holdings to accommodate, or to initiate, increases in the growth of nominal expenditure which they would have resisted, or refrained from initiating, if their international reserves had been lower. All one can say is that by far the greater part of the monetary expansion of the early 1970s seems to have taken place with the consent, or at the instance, of governments and monetary authorities; it may have been regarded as a more or less unwelcome means of preventing damage to real income and employment, but it was not, for the most part, imposed upon national economies as an automatic consequence of the growth of international liquidity.

In short, it is hard to generalise about the expansion of high-powered money, just as it is about that of total money. There are some cases in which it can be linked to accumulation of foreign assets, but mostly monetary authorities seemed to find it possible to offset the effects of this, if they wanted to. In some cases in which it was not completely offset, as in Germany during certain periods of high export earnings, the high foreign demand which produced those earnings of foreign exchange also created high domestic activity and an internal demand for accelerated growth of money supply, which part of the faster growth of reserves conveniently accommodated. On a year-to-year basis, as we have already noted, the linkage of total money supply to reserves is very loose, but in general reserves would appear to have been tailored (by central bank lending) to fit approved monetary expansion at least as much as money supply expanded to fit with available reserves. It is perhaps significant that instances of negative monetary impulse going with decelerations of reserve growth are considerably harder to find than those of positive impulses going with accelerations of reserves.

There is, however, one further question about money supply at which we should look – namely how far it has been shaped by variations in public sector borrowing requirements (PSBR). Public borrowings from the banking system which, along with private borrowing from it and net receipts from abroad, makes up the increase in money supply, can obviously be viewed as the difference between *total* public sector borrowing and that part of it which is from the non-bank private sector. Moreover, it can be argued that, insofar as the public authorities borrow (or try to borrow) from the non-bank private sector, they deprive private borrowers of funds which they would otherwise be able to obtain, and drive them to borrow, or try to borrow, from the banks. In one extreme case (bank lending to the private sector perfectly elastic), this crowding out of private borrowers from the non-bank loan market would mean that any increase in total net public sector borrowing would make an equal contribution to monetary expansion. More generally, more public borrowing in the market will mean higher interest rates, some curtailment of private borrowing and some diversion of it to the banks; but also, if the start is from a Keynesian under-employment equilibrium position, generation of more real income and more saving, so that total increase in investment is greater than the increased creation of credit.

The effects of increased public borrowing requirement are thus complex. How complex, how dependent upon institutional arrangements and policy reactions, is suggested by a simulation, conducted by the OECD (1982), with models of the financial sectors of the United Kingdom and German economies. Sustained 15 per cent increases in public sector borrowing requirements were assumed, and the reactions of the authorities to the results were supposed to be those deducible from their past behaviour. In the United Kingdom model, money supply increased to take the first shock, bank lending to the private sector rose, the external position deteriorated sharply, and public bond sales to the private sector slowly increased in the face of raised interest rates. In Germany, with a supposedly tighter control on bank credit, money supply stayed nearly constant, as did the external balance, bank lending to the private sector fell sharply, interest rates and public bond sales to the public sector rose fast.

If one looks at the statistical record, the relation between the public deficit and expansion of the money supply appears weak. For the United Kingdom, over our period as a whole, it is positive but considerably short of 5 per cent significance. From 1973 onwards, it is strongly negative, with the peak of PSBR in 1975 coinciding with a trough of monetary expansion. A similar pattern prevails in Japan. In the United States, the relation, using the Federal borrowing requirement, is positive until 1971 (but with the amplitude of monetary expansion very much the wider), and then, as in the United Kingdom after 1973, becomes sharply negative. In Germany, from the mid-1960s, the relation is poor – negative if anything. In France, where the public borrowing requirement has been small, there is no obvious relation. Of our Big Six, it is only in Italy where the borrowing requirement is large, and mainly financed by bank credit, that the relation between public borrowing requirement and monetary expansion seems to be fairly consistently positive.

As for the crowding out of private borrowing in the market by public borrowing, the purely observational evidence is even vaguer than that concerning the relation between public borrowing and monetary expansion. It has to be borne in mind also that there is another possible relation between the variables concerned; PSBR is likely to vary inversely with private borrowing because it varies inversely with prosperity. This is probaby what is observed in several countries in 1975. The more general problem of crowding out is one to which we shall have to return when we discuss the sources of positive and negative expenditure-pull impulses.

MONETARY TARGETING

At the beginning of our period, in the United States, the United Kingdom and in varying degrees in other OECD countries, the quantity of money and its rate of increase were not matters of primary concern to governments or central banks. Macroeconomic policy aimed generally at maintaining high and stable levels of employment without running into manifest general shortages of labour, which would have been recognised as inflationary, in the faith, or the hope, that this state of affairs would be compatible with a reasonable degree of price stability and, given only infrequent and agreed adjustments of foreign exchange rates, with equilibrium in the balance of external payments. Monetary policy, along with adjustments to fiscal policy, was seen as an instrument for correcting short-term internal or external imbalances, as they arose; not as an instrument of medium or long-term strategy. Experience in the 1950s did not shake this view too rudely. Some countries, notably the United Kingdom, experienced an upward drift of their labour costs in relation to their competitors, but it seemed likely that adjustments of the exchange rate once in a decade or two would accommodate this without too much difficulty or, after the invention of the Phillips curve, that a modest increase in the level of unemployment tolerated would serve to stop the drift – if some form of incomes policy could not be devised to do so.

The acceleration of inflation in the late 1960s and the early 1970s made it clear that avoidance of manifest labour shortage in national markets was not enough. It also coincided with the wide diffusion of the first wave of monetarist doctrine, including the view that a managed, steady increase in the supply of money at a rate approximating to the equilibrium real growth rate of the economy was both a prescription for long-term steadiness of the price level and superior to the established counter-cyclical use of monetary policy as a scheme of short-term management. After the inflationary shock of 1973–4, this view, or elements of it, began to be applied in the leading OECD countries. The United Kingdom monetary authorities began unpublished annual targeting of the rate of growth of the money stock from

1973, and published targets (or target ranges) from 1976. Germany was the first country to publish targets, from 1974. France did so from 1977. The United States, where unpublished targets had been formulated for some years, imposed the legal obligation on the Federal Reserve to submit such targets to Congress by the Full Employment and Balanced Growth Act of 1978 (amending the Employment Act of 1946). Targeting, with or without publication, became the practice in many other countries. The problems and experiences have been discussed, *inter alia*, in Meek (ed) (1982).

The obligation to achieve a stated, cardinal, rate of change in the money stock, as opposed to changing it simply in one direction or the other, in an attack on a perceived but as yet imperfectly quantified diversion of expenditure from its desired path, put the instruments of monetary regulation to a severe test. To be seen to achieve something like the forecast rate of increase was thought important – the establishment of a conviction that the target would continue to be hit was believed in some quarters to be a means of forming the expectations and thus moulding the price and wage determining behaviour of the community. At the same time, it was seen that demand for money is subject to very considerable, largely unpredictable, short-run variations, the non-accommodation of which would cause market interest rates to become more volatile, with a corresponding loss of confidence. Some sacrifice of short-term rigidity was thus required, without loss of the medium-term precision needed to establish credibility – by no means an easy compromise to strike.

The initial degrees of success in achieving the targets were various. In the United Kingdom, the first seven targets announced (between December, 1976 and March, 1980) were annual rates of growth gradually declining from 9–13 per cent to 7–11 per cent. Only two of these were achieved; the first was undershot but the tendency was to overshoot and the series of outcomes had a sharply upward trend instead of a declining one. In the United States, also, the tendency was to overshoot, apparently because of delay in deciding on the increases of interest rates that were necessary. In both France and Germany also, up to 1979, there was overshooting, but in neither case by very serious amounts. After 1979, results were rather different. The German rate of growth was in the target range in that year, and below in the following two; the United States achieved closer control under a new procedure which strictly regulated non-borrowed bank reserves, and allowed market forces to drive the rate for borrowing to supplement them very high. The British degree of overshooting, however (as already noted) increased, and so did the French; this was, of course, the period of the second oil shock.

The resort to monetary targeting naturally raised the question (related to the one with which we started this chapter), what money aggregate is the appropriate one for observation and control? The German authorities seem to have concentrated mainly on Central Bank money (bankers' deposits), with which M3 has moved in harmony over the period of control, but M2 and M1 much less so. While this narrow aggregate might seem a more manageable projectile than the wider ones, it has to be remembered that the commercial banks are normally in debt to the Bundesbank, so that the extent of their deposits with it depends in part on their keenness to borrow. The Canadians, who have also been seriously involved in targeting, have been faithful to M1, despite its variability, only partly in response to interest, as a proportion of the wider aggregates. The French have concerned themselves mainly with M2, and the British, despite recurring doubts, with M3, until 1982, when a wider range of variables was brought into consideration. In the United States, consideration has not been confined to one aggregate.

The final questions in this connection, of course, are whether targeting has had any discernible effect, and whether, if so, it has been the 'right' effect, first in relation to the suppression of inflation and, further, in relation to other policy objectives. One simple test is to see whether, among the Big Six, the numbers of confirmed M and NM impulses during, say, 1974–9 were different from what one would have been led to expect from the earlier experience in our period. The answer to this, from our analysis, is a clear 'no'. For the Six together, the average numbers of both kinds of impulse per year were slightly, but only slightly, smaller after 1974 than before. But, clearly, the NMs may have been more powerful and/or the Ms less powerful since targeting began. That the proportion of years in which anti-inflationary policy was felt to be called for was lower after 1974 is hardly likely, since the average rate of inflation was higher in most countries and awareness of it as a problem was certainly greater. It may be relevant that the same was true of unemployment.

In this period when targeting was becoming widespread, the course of annual changes in money stock was mostly less variable in the Big Six than it had been in the previous twenty years – whether one judges from M1 or M2, and whether by the standard deviations of annual percentage increases or by their coefficients of variation (standard deviations divided by means). M1 in Germany and Italy provides at least partial exceptions to this statement; on the other hand it is especially true of Japan, the United States and France. Without exception, the annual percentage real growth rates of GDP were *more* variable after 1974 than before, both absolutely and, still more, in relation to their means, as well as being everywhere absolutely lower, but how far this was because the non-monetary weather was stormier, and how far from greater sins of omission or commission on the part of monetary policy it would be hard to judge. Inflation ran higher in all of the Big Six; average rates of monetary expansion were higher everywhere except in Japan and, for M2, Germany. Variability of inflation, however, changed less simply – in annual percentage terms it was lower in France, Germany and Italy, higher in the United States, United Kingdom and Japan; in relation to its (increased) mean, it was reduced in all of the Six except Japan.

Targeting, in spite of the less than sparkling success in actually hitting the stated targets, may perhaps be provisionally credited with some reduction in the variability of monetary expansion. Whether it smoothed the course of the other macroeconomic variables concerned, especially the real variables, is more doubtful. And, as we have just noted, the greater attention paid to money supply went with reduction of its rate of growth below the 1953–73 level only in Japan and Germany, both countries in which the reduction in growth of real output was especially severe. If monetary targeting is the key to reasonably smooth and inflation-free growth, experience up to 1979 suggests that it needs a much longer time, or calmer economic weather, to prove it. And after 1979, the weather did not become calmer.

CONCLUSION

We started this chapter with some consideration of the complexities arising from the absence of an unique definition of the money stock – from the existence of a spectrum of assets with gradually decreasing endowments of the quality of pure liquidity which constitutes the essence of money. In the three countries which we examine in this connection, the relation between holdings of what are generally recognised as money and quasi-money seemed to have changed over our period – a gradual, institutional change rather than a prompt response to any identifiable stimulus. We then re-examined, for the Big Six sample countries, the *prima facie* cases of monetary impulse identified in chapter 4, eliminating the considerable number of cases in which it could be judged that the demand schedule for money, rather than the supply function, had shifted, as indicated by perverse behaviour of indicators which we took to represent the course of *expected* real interest. The shorter list of confirmed monetary impulses which emerged appeared to be rather more closely related to expenditure impulses than the *prima facie* list. It seems that a major, but variable, part of monetary expansion has taken place in conditions which can be described as accommodating.

So far as the immediate creation of money is concerned, it seemed that bank lending to the private sector has been the main agent in major variations of the growth of the money stock everywhere, but that in the United States positive impulses had all been primed by lending to the public sector and this was true of some impulses in the United Kingdom and Germany – two countries in which (as also in Italy) acquisition of foreign assets by the banking system played some part. The short-term relation between reserve money and M2 is weak – less so in the United States than elsewhere – but some positive impulses go with, or follow, accelerated reserve growth; others are followed by it. Italy is the only one of the Big Six in which the pattern of monetary growth shows signs of having been consistently dominated by that of public sector deficits. Systematic studies of the relation of high-powered money to foreign exchange reserves seem to have shown that, in the major countries outside the United States, changes in holdings of foreign exchange were mostly sterilised and that the multiplication of official dollar holdings cannot *directly* account for the great monetary expansion of the early 1970s, even though it may have affected official attitudes to that expansion.

Thus, outside the United States and Japan, at least, external monetary influences played some part, but the vicissitudes of monetary growth are, in general, more home-made than imported and the greater part of growth in all our main sample countries seems to have taken place as either a full or a partial response to demand rather than with supply running ahead. To treat the money supply as exogenous to the private sector would be very wide of the mark.

This is true even after the adoption of monetary targeting in the late 1970s. Targeting was associated with reduced variation in the rate of growth of money stocks, though, except in Japan and Germany, with higher average rates of growth of those stocks than before; it was also associated with slower and more variable real income growth and with higher and in some senses less variable inflation. Its effects are hard to judge.

7

EXPENDITURE-PULL

In our terms, expenditure-pull is a rise in the rate of increase of nominal expenditure, accompanied by a rise in the profit share. We take these as symptoms of acceleration of monetary demand for final goods and services, to be distinguished from an acceleration of expenditure growth which happens because factor prices have gone up (or gone up faster). There is, of course, a borderline case, where factor prices go up nearly in line with expenditure, so that factor shares do not change or, at least, cannot be seen from our annual data to change appreciably. On the whole, however, we have seen that it is usually possible to distinguish those cases where final expenditure is in the lead and factor prices, if they respond, do so with an appreciable lag, so that the profit share rises, from those in which factor prices accelerate and final goods prices respond only with a lag, so that the profit share at least temporarily falls.

There are two obvious questions to be asked about cases of expenditure-pull, which will turn out not to be entirely independent of each other. The first is what section of expenditure (if any) has taken the lead in the acceleration in question? The second is what is the relation of the expenditure-pull episode to monetary conditions? Is it preceded or accompanied by a positive monetary impulse (reduced rate of growth of velocity and interest), or does it go with rises in the first differences of velocity and interest rate (expenditure pressing harder on the money supply), or does the money supply apparently accommodate to the raised expenditure growth?

THE CROWDING-OUT PROBLEM

As we have just noted, these questions are not without interconnections. One of them is manifested in the crowding-out problem. The rise of any section of expenditure, if not accompanied by a corresponding increase in the money stock, may be expected to have the effect of restricting or 'crowding out' other sections, by raising the rate of interest against them. In its extreme form, this argument is sometimes used to suggest that increase in, for instance, public capital formation, unless financed by new money, cannot raise total expenditure, because equal amounts of private expenditure (probably capital formation, in the main) will be crowded out.

This extreme form of the argument would hold, of course, if velocity of circulation of money, or at least its first difference, were constant, and we have seen in chapter 2 that, in the short run at all events, this is far from being the case. The first difference of velocity is, in nearly half our countries (Japan, Germany, France, Sweden, the Netherlands and India) more variable than that of money stock, and is in all the sample countries negatively correlated with it. Velocity varies to help in accommodating changes in expenditure, and in the countries just mentioned does more in this direction from year to year than money supply does.

Complete crowding out, however, does not require constant velocity (or its adherence to a constant trend). It requires only that expenditure should be a *function* of money supply (not necessarily a constant multiple of it) and of nothing else. It is therefore worth glancing at the formal conditions and limits of crowding out in terms of the simplest of Keynesian models. Suppose that a change in total nominal expenditure, ΔY, in a closed economy can be expressed as: $\Delta A + a\Delta Y - b\Delta r$, where A is an autonomous element, r is a representative rate of interest, and a and b are constants. Also take the demand schedule for money to be (in its differential form): $\Delta M = k\Delta Y - l\Delta r$. It follows that the multiplier equation showing the equilibrium change in income following a change in autonomous expenditure can be written as either:

$$\Delta Y = \frac{\Delta A - b\Delta r}{1 - a} \qquad (1)$$

or

$$\Delta Y = \frac{l\Delta A + b\Delta M}{l(1 - a) + bk} \qquad (2)$$

If interest is held constant (perfectly elastic supply of money) it follows from (1) that the multiplier, $\Delta Y/\Delta A, = 1/(1 - a)$, a result familiar from the case where consumption is the part of expenditure taken to be dependent upon income and the coefficient corresponding to a is the marginal propensity to consume. With interest constant, income expands to the extent necessary to provide extra saving equal to ΔA; the rest of the expenditure is not compressed.

If, on the other hand, the money supply is held constant ($\Delta M = 0$), (2) gives the multiplier, $\Delta Y/\Delta A, = 1/(1 - a + bk/l)$. This approaches the 'constant interest' multiplier if bk/l is small, that is to say, if spending is insensitive to interest and demand for money is insensitive to absolute change in nominal income, but sensitive to interest. If these conditions are reversed, the multiplier will be small; it becomes zero if demand for money is totally insensitive to interest while its sensitivity to nominal income is still finite, and expenditure also is not wholly insensitive to interest. Crowding out is then complete.

This all relates to crowding out of nominal expenditure. Increases in any section of real expenditure are, of course, bound to crowd out other sections if the extra demand does not increase real output. We have already given some attention to this under the heading of incremental relations between quantity and price in chapter 3. In an open economy, real crowding out may occur through additional expenditure worsening the balance of current payments, lowering the external value of the currency and so squeezing the real value of elements of nominal expenditure which have not been increased. (This mechanism is apparently important in the National Institute econometric model of the United Kingdom.) For the moment, however, it is with *nominal* crowding out, or its absence, that we are mainly concerned.

How this works out in quantitative simulations, or in the real world, is obviously a more complex matter. An OECD investigation (1982) has tried two approaches. First, a small model of nine equations, including a foreign exchange sector, was solved analytically and the solutions quantified by insertion of coefficients estimated or collected from a variety of sources. The response of private expenditure to a unit increase in government expenditure was calculated under various assumptions; first that exchange rates were fixed, then that they were flexible (with the rather extreme supposition that, given constant interest rates, this would prevent any change in the current external balance) and, for the latter case, both with accommodating monetary policy (interest rates fixed) and with money supply fixed. With accommodating monetary policy, all calculations show private expenditure as increasing; by two or even three units under flexible exchange rates and from 0.6 to 1.4 units under a fixed rate regime. With non-accommodating monetary policy, the calculations for four countries (the United States, Germany, Italy and Canada) show some crowding out; private expenditure falls, though only by 0.1 to 0.4 of a unit. For the other three countries (Japan, France and the United Kingdom), it still shows a modest rise. A considerable contributor to the difference between the accommodating and non-accommodating cases is the fact that, in the latter, interest rate changes generate capital movements which prevent the exchange rate from moving far enough to maintain current account balance.

The other OECD approach to the crowding-out problem consisted in estimating the nominal and real government expenditure multipliers under accommodating and non-accommodating monetary policy by the use of the main large econometric models in operation in the United States, United Kingdom, Canada, Japan and France (eight models in all). Under accommodating policy, the models show the nominal multiplier, in response to a single, permanent, unit increase in government expenditure, as building up, over three or four years, to various values between 2.2 and 6. (The real multipliers, which are not our immediate concern in this chapter, frequently rise to a maximum within two years or so and then fall, as inflation accelerates, but only in the most pessimistic estimates do they fall below unity.) Under fixed money supplies, the odd model out is that of the Federal Reserve Bank of St Louis, in which no interest elasticity of demand for money is incorporated and which, therefore, predicts only a transient multiplier with complete crowding out. The other models yield nominal multipliers building up to between $1\frac{1}{2}$ and 3 over two years, some rising further thereafter, some falling slightly. Except for the St Louis model, therefore, there is little suggestion of crowding out here. The broad conclusion (not out of line with that of the OECD study) seems to be that, while the effect of an increase in public expenditure must depend critically on various features of financial behaviour and while the majority of the large models may make too little allowance for these, anything like a complete crowding out of private by public expenditure is unlikely, even under the extreme assumption of zero monetary accommodation. In seeking relations between monetary and expenditure impulses, we are not merely looking at an identity obscured by measurement errors.

MONETARY IMPULSES AND EXPENDITURE

The mechanisms of monetary impulses are, as we have seen, not all alike, and one would expect some of the differences to be relevant to the connection which is to be found with expenditure impulses. In the first place, some augmentations of the growth of the money supply are the direct consequences of bursts of expenditure on goods and services, which are likely in themselves to produce the symptoms of E. This is the case where there is a surge of demand for the country's exports, which both accelerates the growth of its nominal GDP, probably with a rise in the profit share, and also produces faster growth of the supply of high-powered money. Even if there is vigorous action to sterilise the additional reserves and prevent a secondary expansion of credit, money supply rises. The *immediate* effect, nevertheless, will be a rise in velocity, because income is assumed to jump with the sudden rise of exports, whereas money stock merely increases its rate of growth. More generally, without leakages, the build-up of money stock would lag behind the build-up of income level, being related to its integral.

In the slightly longer run, still assuming a jump in the level of export earnings, income builds up further through the Keynesian multiplier and money stock also builds up until it reaches the level at which additional leakages from it equal the additional rate of inflow from exports. It can be shown[1] that, other things being equal, the velocity of circulation when both money stock and income are in equilibrium will be greater or less than the original (pre-export boom) velocity, according to whether the ratio r/s is greater or less than that original velocity, where r is the proportional rate of leakage of the additional money into repayment of bank loans and s is the marginal propensity to save. The case more in accord with our analysis, however, is that in which the impulse comes, not from a jump in the level of export earnings, but from a jump in their rate of increase. This means that the equilibrium levels of both income and money stock will gradually rise, with the *actual* levels lagging somewhat behind them, so that matters become rather more complicated. Velocity, and its first difference, may either rise or fall. *If* the velocity is lowered, the presumption is that interest rates fall and domestic expenditure may be encouraged. If the additions to foreign exchange holdings are not completely sterilised, further secondary extensions of bank credit become possible.

The same may be said of a surge of government expenditure which is to a substantial extent financed by the banks. Here, too, accelerating GDP and increased profit share may, after a short interval of increased velocity of circulation, go with an easing of monetary conditions, though this is by no means certain; the courses of velocity and interest rates will depend, *inter alia*, on the relation between the propensity to save and the extent to which new money penetrates to those who use it to repay debt to banks.

---

[1] If, from a situation of steady income flow, constant money stock and balance of payments equilibrium, there is a once for all rise, ΔX, in the annual value of exports, there will at once be a rise of ΔX in income, but no corresponding jump in money stock (though money will start to flow in at a rate ΔX). Income will build up further, approaching a new equilibrium position where the total increase $\Delta \bar{Y}$ is $\Delta X/(s + m + t)$, s being marginal propensity to save, m marginal propensity to import and t the marginal tax rate (all taxation assumed to be direct, and public expenditure unchanged). The newly acquired money from abroad leaks out of private balances at a rate $(m + t)\Delta Y + r\Delta M$, so additional private holdings build up to the point where this rate of leakage equals ΔX. Substituting for ΔY its equilibrium value $\Delta X/(s + m + t)$ gives the result $\Delta \bar{M} = \Delta \bar{Y}.s/r$, where $\Delta \bar{M}$ is the equilibrium rise in money stock. Velocity falls, of course, if $\Delta \bar{Y}/\Delta \bar{M}$ is less than the original velocity, Y/M.

At the other end of the scale, a monetary impulse which has its origin simply in an easing of lending conditions by the banks does not go with any primary surge of expenditure; its expenditure effects are secondary. It will probably lead to some extra borrowing for speculative purposes, a rise in money stocks, and a fall in long-term rates but, in conditions of low confidence, effects on expenditure may be slow to manifest themselves. Where the monetary authorities ease the situation by open market operations, the effect on long-term rates and the wealth and liquidity of asset holders is more direct, but appearances are still likely to be different from those in cases where expenditure leads the way, accompanied by a more than accommodating increase in the money supply. It is, of course, also possible that some expenditure impulses arise from within the private sector, unaccompanied by any features (foreign exchange earnings or government borrowing from the banks) which tend, in themselves, to ease monetary conditions. Banks may well accommodate such impulses to varying extents, but velocity of circulation and interest are unlikely to be lowered, so that monetary impulses, according to our criteria, will probably not be registered.

Insofar as association between monetary and expenditure impulses depends on the effect of the former on the latter through reduced interest rates, the very substantial amount of systematic investigation, ever since the inquiries of the Oxford Economists' Research Group (Meade and Andrews, 1938) has left its strength and reliability doubtful. The OECD (*op. cit.*) has surveyed the evidence, mainly covering the 1960s, from various national econometric models. Only in the United States out of the seven countries included have significant interest rate effects been identified on all four of the categories of expenditure distinguished; private non-residential investment, residential investment, stockbuilding, and expenditure on consumers' durables. Nowhere else is the evidence concerning stockbuilding unambiguously positive and Canada is the only other country in which it is so for consumer durables. At the other extreme, the evidence relating to residential investment is nowhere wholly negative and in five countries wholly positive. Private non-residential fixed investment comes in between; significant in four out of the seven countries, and definitely not significant in only two, the United Kingdom and Italy. From the earliest empirical considerations of the question it has, of course, been recognised that interest effects may be expected to strengthen rapidly with the length of the pay-off period of the expenditure in question; hence the long presumed, and largely confirmed, sensitivity of residential building.

The contingent nature of the connection between monetary impulses and expenditure impulses which this mainly theoretical discussion suggests, seems to be consistent with the definite, but rather weak associations between M and E (or NM and NE) which we found in chapter 4.

We come now to the first of the questions posed at the beginning of this chapter; from what sections of expenditure do the surges associated with our expenditure-pull impulses apparently come? Is the leading section of expenditure in a particular case internal or external? If internal, is it public or private? If private, is it on consumption or capital formation? So far as external expenditure, private internal capital formation and private internal consumption are concerned, we shall apply, in the first instance, the very crude test of seeing whether one or more of these sections of expenditure has increased appreciably in relation to total GDP. Public expenditure raises more complex questions, because the extent to which it is offset by taxation comes into the picture, and it may be useful to pursue those questions briefly.

The relevant relation emerges especially clearly if we consider a closed economy, or one in which imports and exports are somehow kept constant while taxation and public expenditure change. It is simplest to suppose that private capital formation stays constant also, while private consumption varies in some fixed proportion to the change in private disposable income. We then have:

$$\Delta Y = (1 - s)(\Delta Y + \Delta G_t - \Delta T_d) + \Delta G_{gs} - \Delta T_i$$

where Y is national income at factor cost, s is the marginal propensity to save out of disposable private income, G_t is public transfer expenditure (assumed all to go to households), G_{gs} is public expenditure on goods and services, and T_d and T_i are direct and indirect taxation respectively. This statement (that the increase in national income at factor cost is the sum of the increases in consumption and public expenditure on goods and services, *minus* any increase in indirect taxation) can be rearranged to give:

$$\Delta Y = \frac{\Delta G_t + \Delta G_{gs} - \Delta T_i - \Delta T_d}{s} + \Delta T_d - \Delta G_t$$

That is to say, the increase in national income at factor cost is the increase in budget deficit, multiplied by the inverse of the propensity to save, but *plus* any increase in direct taxation and *minus* any increase in transfer expenditure. This accords with the well known proposition

(Peacock, 1956) that a unit increase in public expenditure on goods and services financed by an equal increase in direct taxation ($\Delta T_d = 1$, $\Delta G_t = 0$) will produce a unit increase in national income; the balanced budget multiplier in these circumstances is unity. It is equally clear that the balanced budget multiplier can be zero if an increase in direct taxation is used to finance an equal increase in transfer expenditure ($\Delta T_d = \Delta G_t$), or if an increase in indirect taxation is used to finance an equal increase in expenditure on goods and services ($\Delta T_d = \Delta G_t = 0$). It can also be minus one if an increase in indirect taxation finances an equal increase in transfers.

In an open economy, where imports vary with income, the multiplier to which any change in the budget deficit is subjected will, of course, be smaller, because the leakage of purchasing power is greater; the effects of changes in direct taxation and public transers will also be toned down, but the total effect can still be viewed as the sum of three parts, one depending on the change in budget surplus (or deficit), one on the change in direct tax revenue and one (negatively) on the change in transfer expenditure.

All this refers to the effect, other things being equal, on national income at factor cost, the factor incomes of the economy. If one is interested in change in national income at market prices, the change in indirect tax revenue has to be added, so that the change in income still consists of three parts; the multiplied change in budget deficit plus (in the closed economy case) the change in total tax revenue and, negatively, the change in transfer expenditure.

The increase in the national income at factor cost may, if factor supplies of all kinds are elastic, express itself mainly or even wholly in increase of real output, not increase of price. There is, however, a strong presumption that any change in indirect taxation which is added to convert the result into terms of market prices will act on prices rather than quantities. An increase in income (or expenditure) at factor cost is inflationary to the extent that factor prices are sensitive to the pressure of demand, and that decreasing physical returns prevail. An increase in indirect taxation is inflationary in the more direct sense that it tends to raise prices of goods and services immediately. Any increase in prices of final goods and services may also, of course, give rise to further inflation through demands from factor owners for the maintenance of the real value of their rewards.

THE PERIOD AS A WHOLE

Before looking at these matters on a year-to-year basis, we may perhaps usefully take a longer view. What sectors of expenditure seem to have been abnormally large or expansionary in our period and the major sub-divisions of it in comparison with earlier times? Long series of the relevant data are not available for all our sample countries but on the United States and the United Kingdom it is possible to say something without having to dig too deeply.

Concerning the United Kingdom economy, a great deal of deep digging has already been done by Matthews *et al.* (1982). In the first place, they show that gross domestic fixed capital formation and public sector consumption were the components that increased most in relation to GNP between earlier periods and the postwar years; the former averaged 18.7 per cent of GNP in 1951–73 compared with 10 per cent betweeen the wars and about 9 per cent before 1914, and the figures for the latter are broadly similar. *During* the period 1951–73, gross fixed capital formation was also the component with the fastest proportionate rate of growth, as it had been between the wars, and in contrast with pre-1914, when it had been the slowest. Public sector consumption, which had shown the fastest proportionate rate of growth of any major component before 1914, and had run fixed capital formation close between the wars, was the slowest grower during 1951–73, mostly because it was stationary in real terms between 1955 and 1960, when military expenditure was decreasing fastest, though even in the rest of the period it grew more slowly than GDP. From 1973 to 1979 there was a modest reversal of these trends; the share of fixed capital fell and that of public consumption rose somewhat. Exports, however, which had fallen between the wars, increased nearly as fast, proportionately, as fixed capital formation from 1951 to 1973, and absolutely they formed a bigger part of demand. Their growth is estimated to have made the biggest contribution to total GDP growth in the second half of that period, though two-thirds of the contribution was offset by the rise in the average propensity to import. Their proportionate rise continued up to 1979. The general suggestion, therefore, is that domestic capital formation and public consumption were the components of demand which were proportionately *high* in the postwar period, as compared with earlier times, whilst domestic capital formation (again) and exports were the components most responsible for high growth rate.

These estimates do not directly answer the question whether the whole current account operation of the public sector (expenditure and taxation) can be held responsible for high and rapidly rising demand since the war. Matthews *et al.* suggest that it cannot, since budget surpluses were more in evidence between 1951 and 1973 than in previous periods. The issue is, however, not quite so simple as that, as we have seen. The work of Maynard and van Ryckeghem (1976) includes an attempt to estimate the net total multiplier impact of all taxation and public expenditure, as compared with the situation if the ratio of tax revenue to expenditure was 'neutral', for a number of countries. For the United Kingdom, they deduce a net expansionary impact of about 18 per cent of GDP, with some upward trend, over the years 1950–68, but this includes the effect of public expenditure on capital account. Whether with or without the inclusion of public capital expenditure, the United Kingdom revenue–expenditure ratio was higher in the 1950s and 1960s than in the 1930s, though it fell somewhat after 1972. The only respect in which the postwar budgets of the public sector were more expansionary than those between the wars is that after 1950 higher proportions of taxation were direct and lower proportions of expenditure consisted of transfers, features which would tend to raise the 'balanced budget multiplier'; it seems unlikely, however, that this was sufficient to outweigh the fact that budget surpluses were larger (or deficits smaller if capital account is included).

In the United States also, public expenditure on goods and services has been the outstandingly fast growing component in the longer run, from 8 per cent of GDP in 1929 and 13 per cent in 1937 to more than 20 per cent in the postwar years, during which it has shown little trend. Private capital formation in the last-mentioned period was a high proportion of GDP in comparison with the 1930s, though not with the 1920s. Changes in the export proportion have not been big enough to suggest great importance; within the postwar period and in the period as a whole in comparison with the 1930s, it seems to have been a mildly expansionary influence. A great deal turns, however, on the balance between revenue and expenditure in the public sector. Maynard and van Ryckeghem suggest, for the first half of the postwar period, an average budget multiplier impact about equal to that which they estimate for the United Kingdom, some 19 per cent of GDP. From 1952 onwards (to 1968) there is little sign of trend in this impact. It is hard to compare it at all precisely with that of prewar periods, but it is clear that postwar public sector deficits have, on average, been substantially smaller (in relation to GDP) than those of the 1930s, larger than those of the 1920s. Against this, the proportion of tax revenue which is direct has greatly increased, with a smaller shift of expenditure towards transfers, so that the balanced budget multiplier has increased, as in the United Kingdom. So has the relative size of the budget. It seems likely, on balance, that the public sector in the United States has increased its expansionary impact in the postwar period as compared with the inter-war period as a whole, though whether it has done so in comparison with the 1930s and whether there has been an increasing trend *within* the period 1950–81 as a whole, are more open questions.

For a number of other countries also we have Maynard and van Ryckeghem estimates of the inflationary impact of the public sector over the period 1950–68. For Italy, Denmark and Canada, as for the United States and the United Kingdom, the influence seems, from this calculation, to have been inflationary for all or most of that time. For the Netherlands it became so from 1953 onwards and for Japan it was so from the first availability of the required data in 1960. For Germany it is negative in the 1950s, positive in the 1960s; for France the other way round. The authors emphasise that these results are to be treated with caution. A hypothetical economy with a neutral public sector makes a nebulous basis of reference and relations which appear more or less linear over the range of recent experience might be very different over a much wider one.

YEAR-TO-YEAR BUDGETARY CHANGES

We may hope that we are on less speculative ground when we come to year-to-year changes in expenditure, or its rate of growth. So far as the impact of the public sector is concerned, we can draw on existing studies, primarily the OECD calculations of fiscal impact contained in the McCracken Report and subsequently refined and extended (OECD, 1978), and the work of Maynard and van Ryckeghem, to which we have already referred. The OECD calculations are already on a year-to-year basis; they use annual changes in the main classes of tax revenue and in public investment and consumption to calculate primary (first-round) impacts on GDP, using marginal tax and consumption propensities which are estimated for each country over the period of study (1965–76) and assumed to remain constant. From 1977 onwards we can use the related, but not identical, estimates of changes in general government financial balances calculated by Price and Chouraqui (1983).

We have already mentioned that Maynard and van Ryckeghem provide estimates of the total impacts of the public sector transactions in a number of OECD countries. Using the first-round versions of these estimates, we may take first differences, which should provide results comparable with those in the OECD (1978) article. The two series overlap in the four years 1965–8, revealing considerable discrepancies, but perhaps not so many or so bad as to forbid our use of the combined outcome as a rough general guide to the public sector's responsibility for assisting, or moderating, the expenditure

Table 7.1 *Primary impacts of budget changes (per cent of GDP) with positive (E) and negative (N) expenditure impulses*

	United States a	b	c	United Kingdom a	b	c	Japan a	b	c
1951	0			E 5					
1952	N 3			N 2					
1953	1			E 1					
1954	1			−2					
1955	−4			−2			N		
1956	N 0			1					
1957	1			−1			E		
1958	4			0			N		
1959	E −2			1					
1960	−2			E 1			E		
1961	2			0			E −1		
1962	E 0			N −1			N 1		
1963	−1			E 3			0		
1964	0			−2			E 1		
1965	E 0	−0.1	1.3	N 1	1.0	−0.1	N 0	1.0	1.3
1966	0	1.3	2.7	−2	−0.8	0.3	1	0.9	1.5
1967	N 3	3.0	3.0	2	1.4	1.7	E −1	−0.5	1.0
1968	−2	−0.3	1.3	0	−0.2	−0.1	E 0	0	1.4
1969		−1.5	−0.6		0	−1.5		−0.7	0.4
1970	N	1.4	0.5		−2.2	0.3		−0.3	0.9
1971	E 0.7	0.3	0.7	E 1.5	1.2	1.3	N 0.5	1.2	1.7
1972	E −1.4	−1.4	0.5	N 2.7	2.9	2.5	1.0	1.1	1.5
1973	−0.8	−0.3	0.5	1.5	1.3	1.7	−0.1	−0.5	0.7
1974	N 0.7	0.3	0	N 1.1	0.6	1.1	N 0.1	0.9	0.7
1975	4.0	2.7	1.2	E 0.8	−0.4	−0.4	3.1	3.5	1.9
1976	E −2.1	−1.9	0.3	N 0.3	0.1	−1.0	E 1.0	0.6	0.8
1977	−1.2		−0.2	−1.7		−1.3	N 0.1		0.3
1978	−0.9		−0.2	1.0		2.3	1.7		1.9
1979	N −0.6		−0.4	−1.0		−0.9	−0.7		−0.5
1980	1.9		0.6	0.1		−1.7	−0.3		−0.5
1981	−0.3		−1.0	−0.8		−2.8	−0.5		−0.6
1982	2.8		1.1	−0.5		−1.8.	0.1		0.1

impulses we have identified. The results (along with expenditure impulses up to 1979) appear in table 7.1, columns a and b.

These figures, expressed as percentages of the preceding year's GDP, are intended to represent the first-round impact of the actual, realised, changes in public revenue and expenditure. Such an impact includes not only the effect of any change in tax rates, or rates of unemployment benefit, or expenditure on defence, which may have been provided for in the budget in line with changes in government policy or perceptions, calculated on the assumption (for instance) that the real GDP will continue to grow in parallel with the growth of capacity. It includes also the effects on revenue, and on income-sensitive items of expenditure, such as unemployment benefit, of any

	Germany			France			Italy	
a	b	c	a	b	c	a	b	c
−1			−1					
−1			N 3			1		
N −1			0			E −1		
0			−2			N 0		
E −1			0			0		
N 0			2			−1		
2			−1			0		
2			E −3			0		
−1			−1			0		
−1			E 0			−1		
N 1			N 0			0		
N 1			1			−1		
2			0			1		
E −1			0			N 0		
2	1.4	2.1	0	0.3	0.7	3	2.3	1.2
N 0	0.2	0.4	0	−1.0	−0.5	E 0	0.6	1.0
2	0.9	0.4	1	0.7	1.5	−2	−0.4	0.1
E −1	−0.2	0.9	1	0.9	1.6	1	0.9	1.1
	−0.8	0.3	E	−0.5	0.6		0.5	0.8
	0.9	1.8		−0.1	1.1		0	0.3
N 0.4	0.7	1.1	0.2	0.5	0.9	N 2.1	1.6	1.1
N 0.3	0.5	0.9	−0.1	0.2	0.9	2.1	1.7	1.4
−1.7	−0.7	0.5	−0.1	0	1.0	E −0.7	1.3	1.2
N 2.5	2.0	1.4	0.3	0.6	2.6	E −0.4	0	0.7
N 4.4	2.5	1.4	N 2.8	1.9	0.3	N 3.6	3.4	1.2
E −2.3	−1.2	0.3	−1.7	0.1	1.7	E −2.7	−0.7	−0.1
N −1.0		−0.9	0.3		−0.2	−1.0		−1.3
0.1		0.2	1.1		1.0		1.7	1.4
E 0.2		0.7	−1.2		−1.3	E −0.2		0.2
0.5		0.2	−1.0		−2.0	−1.5		−1.1
0.8		−0.2	2.2		1.1	3.7		2.4
−0.1		−1.5	0.7		−0.2	0.3		−1.2

[a] Indicators of first-round budgetary impact (year-to-year changes): 1951–68 Maynard and van Ryckeghem (1976), table 6.5. 1971–9 Price and Chouraqui (1983), table 5: change in actual budget balance, signs reversed.
[b] As a: 1965–76 OECD (Dudler et al.) 1978, table 1.
[c] Impacts of discretionary elements in changes, 1965–76, OECD, 1978, loc. cit., 1977–82, Price and Chouraqui, loc. cit. (signs reversed).

departure of GDP from this steady growth course, whether caused by the budget changes in question or by some quite different influence; an export slump or a collapse of domestic capital formation, for instance. A positive expenditure impulse, in our sense, is rather likely to carry with it some increase in public sector revenue and reduction of expenditure which would not have been anticipated in a budget forecast based on the assumption of steady equilibrium growth. In the absence of any budget change calculated on this assumption to alter the public surplus or deficit (as a percentage of GDP), it is likely to bring about an increase in the surplus, or reduction in the deficit, in the actual outcome. In other words, an exogenous acceleration of expenditure is likely to improve the budget surplus and thereby, through the operation of the built-in stabiliser, to have its effects on the economy toned down. An upward departure from the steady growth path due to a budget change will, likewise, tend to be moderated by the built-in stabiliser of progressive tax rates and negatively income-sensitive expenditure items.

Sorting out from changes in the actual budget balance, or its first-round effects on GDP, how much is due to changes announced in the budget (the budget 'stance'), is not easy. The best available series, from the OECD (1978; also Price and Chouraqui, 1983), give 'discretionary' changes in budget balance (or impact) based on estimates of what tax-yields and income-sensitive expenditures would have been, given growth of real income in line with productive capacity. The difference between these changes and those observed (or calculated from observed outcomes) is the 'built-in stabiliser' effect. The estimated 'discretionary' changes are shown in column c of table 7.1.

How far are positive expenditure impulses (as we have diagnosed them) associated with positive budgetary impacts, either actual or estimated discretionary? If they are associated with discretionary budget impacts, then the presumption is that those impacts contributed to them. If they are associated with observed positive budgetary impacts (reductions in surplus or increases in deficit), the presumption that they are at least reinforced by a discretionary impact is still greater, because, of themselvs, they tend to go with an opposite, built-in stabiliser, effect. Corresponding statements apply, of course, to negative expenditure impulses.

On examination, we find that, for the United States, Japan, Germany, France and Italy, the E impulses in our period are, on average, associated with negative (in Japan zero) budgetary impacts and the NEs with positive ones. This is what we should expect if discretionary budget changes were absent, or neutral; the impulses (from non-budgetary sources) would generate opposing, built-in stabiliser effects. A similar result applies to the sub-period 1965–79, for which we also have OECD estimates of 'discretionary' budget impacts, and there we can observe that the positive and negative expenditure impulses do not seem to go systematically with discretionary budget impacts of the opposite sense – the two kinds both go, on average, with positive ones, of not very dissimilar average sizes, except that in Italy and Japan there is a slight tendency for E to go with low impacts, NE with higher ones. Discretionary budget impacts in these countries do not seem to have systematically opposed variations in expenditure impulses (except perhaps in Italy and Japan), nor did they systematically reinforce or cause them – so long, at least, as we look only at occurrences of impulses and budgetary impacts in the same year. The most important single occurrence of an E along wth a positive budgetary impact in these countries was probably that in the United States in 1971 – no doubt connected with the Vietnam war.

We have omitted the United Kingdom from this list. There we have an unusual association of all the Es with positive budgetary impulses, and the NEs with positive impulses too (except in 1962), but with on average considerably weaker ones. This positive association of budgetary impact with expenditure-pull is largely due to two episodes – 1951, when the Korean war presumably caused public expenditure to take the lead in promoting expansion, and the famous 'dash for growth' of 1963. Even without these episodes, however, the United Kingdom still fails to show the evidence of built-in stabilisers opposing expenditure impulses which we find in the other members of the Big Six. Within the sub-period 1965–79, for which we have estimates of 'discretionary' budget changes, there is, however, a very slight tendency of less expansionary ones to go with Es than with NEs – and the same is true in an even more marginal degree of actual budget changes.

One may ask, of any of the sample countries, whether there are signs either that expenditure impulses *followed* discretionary budget impacts in the same sense (say with a year's lag), suggesting that they may have caused or reinforced them, though with some delay, or that discretionary budget changes followed expenditure impulses of the opposite sense, suggesting perhaps a stabilising intention, marred by delay. The short answer is that only Italy and Japan, of the Big Six, show either of these associations to an extent worth noting. Both of them show both tendencies.

We can now look more closely at the expenditure impulses, budgetary and other, in our main sample countries.

The United States
The United States shows six *prima facie* cases of positive expenditure impulse in our period (1955, 1959, 1962, 1965, 1971–2 and 1976) and seven cases of negative impulse (1951–2, 1956, 1958, 1967, 1970, 1974 and 1979). The obvious questions to ask about them are: are the relevant accelerations or decelerations of nominal income growth

composed mostly of changes in real growth or in inflation? What part of expenditure (especially among those which can be treated as exogenous in the first instance) appears to be mainly responsible? How are they financed and what is the connection, if any, with monetary impulses, as we have defined them?

As to the first question, we have already seen in chapter 2 that the course of money income is much more closely related to that of real income than of price over either of the sub-divisions of our period. In all the positive impulses but one (1965, where honours are about equal) real income is the main constituent; indeed, in 1971–2 and 1976 price change goes the other way. In the negative impulses, price is the senior partner in 1952 and about equal with output in 1958 (both years of major fall of inflation in world primary product prices), but in the other five cases real income is mainly or wholly responsible; indeed, in four of them inflation rises, not surprisingly in view of the negative correlation between inflation and growth in the later part of our period and over the period as a whole.

Where did the impulses come from? Not, apparently, from public finance; we have seen that the actual operation of budgetary impacts was in general against our expenditure impulses, and the estimated 'discretionary' element in them broadly neutral – the only important exception was the positive impulse of 1971.

When we look at the main components of the nominal GDP, it becomes clear that most of the expenditure impulses are connected with changes in gross private capital formation, which rose as a percentage of GDP in every year of positive impulse and fell in every year of negative impulse. The other chief candidate (the chief one with a truly exogenous status), exports of goods and services, is in any case smaller than private capital formation and in general its variations are smaller too, but it also moves (as a percentage of GDP) in the opposite direction from capital formation in ten out of our thirteen impulse years. It assists capital formation only in the recessions of 1952 and 1958, and in the positive impulse of 1972. Change in import prices, the other exogenous factor, is likely to have mitigated the negative expenditure impulse of 1952 and reinforced those of 1974 and 1979. Private consumption does not seem to have played a leading part in any of our expenditure impulses.

It seems then that, as one might expect, the expenditure impulses affecting the United States are all mainly home grown, which suggests that the domestic monetary situation, including monetary impulses, is likely to have been relevant to them. In fact, of our thirteen impulses, five were financed by changes in velocity growth, with changes in money stock going the other way (the positive impulses of 1955, 1959,

1976 and the negative ones of 1958 and 1970); three negative ones (1952, 1956 and 1974) mainly by velocity change, with money stock as the junior partner, one positive impulse (1965) by M and V about equally. Money change alone, with velocity going the other way, accounts for the large positive impulse of 1971-2 (if it is broken up, the first year is wholly M, with V going the other way, the second year the reverse); also for the negative impulse of 1979. This leaves one positive and one negative impulse (1962 and 1967) in which money stock was the senior partner and velocity the junior.

Thus only two of our expenditure impulses (one positive, 1971, and one (unconfirmed) negative, 1979, though the positive one is the largest of all) coincide with monetary impulses of the same sign. There is also a case (1967) of an unconfirmed positive money impulse going with a negative expenditure impulse; what seems to have happened in this case is that, as we noted in the last chapter, money injection came when a recession of growth was strongly established, so that the fall in velocity growth was greater than the rise in that of money stock. There was in the next year a rise in income growth with which costs kept pace (a positive 'A' impulse). In 1961, when another positive money impulse came during an established recession, it had been followed by a positive expenditure impulse in the succeeding year.

The tendency for money impulses to be immediately followed, rather than accompanied, by expenditure impulses of the same sign is more clearly evident on the negative side, where this is the case with the negative monetary impulses (not all confirmed) of 1966, 1969 and 1973. There is one instance of the reverse order – negative expenditure impulse followed by negative money impulse – namely 1952. The fall in money growth, after the Korean war boom, continued into 1953 and caused a monetary tightening, since the growth rates of both price and output stabilised for the year; but in the year following, growth of money income plunged to zero for the only time in our period, though a fall in wage inflation prevented negative expenditure-pull from being registered.

In the United States, therefore, there is a reasonable indication that the monetary situation, as characterised by our impulses, had a substantial, though by no means exclusive, short-term influence on demand variations, as characterised, again imperfectly of course, by our expenditure impulses. Indeed, the respectable evidence we have quoted that interest in that country has, uniquely, an influence on all the main branches of private domestic expenditure, coupled with the subsidiary position of foreign demand, and the counter-cyclical working of public finance, should go far to guarantee such a result. Is it the same elsewhere?

The United Kingdom
The United Kingdom is the most open of the larger economies in our
sample and one in which exports of goods and services have,
throughout our period, been greater than gross domestic capital
formation. One therefore looks to see how far the positive and
negative impulses in expenditure have come from abroad. Fluctuation
in the volume of exports has, indeed, been quite closely correlated
with that in real GDP, though less so between 1963 and 1970 than
before or after. It is, however, important to note that the external
balance on current account has been negatively correlated with both;
imports of goods and services vary positively in money value with
value of exports and to a greater extent. In the 1950s and early 1960s,
the *volume* of imports clearly varied more than that of exports and in
the same direction. In the 1970s both the greater amplitude and the
correlation were less evident, but changes in the relative prices of
imports made for the broadly counter-cyclical movement in the
current balance which we have mentioned, the great exception to this
being the heavy deterioration of the balance and the recession of
activity and trade volume which both followed the oil shock of 1973–4.

But though domestic capital formation is, as already noted, smaller
in value than exports, its year-to-year variations are greater. Something like half of this year-to-year variation up to the later 1960s and a
greater proportion of it thereafter, was due to inventory investment;
fixed capital formation pursued a course not much less staid than that
of the total GDP. It seems that inventory investment was particularly
import-intensive, especially in the first half of the period, variations in
it being almost equal and opposite to those in the current balance.
From the boom of 1963–4 (mainly in fixed investment) this simple
correspondence decayed and the phenomenal deterioration of the
external balance in 1973–4 came a year *after* the equally striking peak
of stockbuilding; though a reasonably close relation between imports
and stockbuilding has persisted, apart from changes in the *amplitude* of
the latter – reduced from about 1965, greatly increased from 1972.

Fixed investment, which became bigger and more variable from
1963 onwards, shows a weaker correspondence with export fluctuations, moderately close up to 1963, poor from then on, except for
coincidences of troughs in 1971–2 and peaks in the following year.

There can be no doubt that external impulses had much to do with
British cycles, but the connection is not altogether simple. In 1953,
1959 and 1973, the surge of exports coincided with domestic fixed
investment booms; these were worldwide increases of demand. In
1964, the home investment boom, associated with an expansionary
budget, was not accompanied by faster growth of export demand and

for that reason the fast growth of demand for imports, which as in other booms accompanied this acceleration in growth of GDP, brought an unusually severe balance of payments crisis. On the other hand, the export boom of 1968, associated partly with devaluation and partly with demand expansion in other countries, including the United States, Japan and Germany, was accompanied by restrictions of domestic expansion and thus by a smaller increase of import growth and, indeed, by the beginning of a strong improvement in the current balance. Something of the same kind might be said of the export expansion of 1976, but the relation between restocking and imports may on that occasion have been made a lower geared one by the existence of more excess capacity in the economy than had existed earlier in our period.

If we look at the specific cases of expenditure impulses, according to our criteria, the positive one of 1951 seems to have been mainly a matter of domestic investment, though strongly supported by export values, with the rise of import prices pulling the other way, but the budgetary impact was also strongly positive. The negative impulse of the following year was overwhelmingly due to domestic investment, assisted to some extent by exports and consumption, but partly buffered by public finance. The 1958 negative 'A' impulse, on the other hand, was on the face of it more exports than home investment, though the fall in import expenditure in fact improved the current foreign balance; the budget change was neutral. The positive impulse of 1960 came from home investment. The negative one of 1962 came mostly from investment, with some help from exports, against a positive public finance offset; the positive one of the following year had investment only slightly ahead of the rest of GDP but with strong budgetary assistance. The continuing rise of expenditure growth in 1964, which qualifies as an A rather than an E under our rules, was very much an investment boom, as we have already noted. It was investment that led the way down again in 1966, though consumption and the realised budget impact helped. The 1971 positive impulse seems to have come, though not very strongly, from exports and the budget, with investment lagging, but investment was to shoot ahead in the next two years. The substantial rise of exports as a proportion of GDP in 1973 was more than offset by the rise of import prices but there is not the evidence of rising profit share in this boom that would make it a clear positive expenditure impulse. The negative impulse of 1974 was probably more a matter of rise in import prices than anything else, though investment fell slightly as a proportion of GDP; it crashed in the following year, as did consumption.

The important, though by no means exclusive, part that domestic capital formation seems to have played in expenditure impulses in the United Kingdom invites inquiry into the influence that monetary conditions exerted on it. There is some correspondence between monetary and expenditure impulses. Positive impulses of the two kinds coincide in 1953, 1963 (the M unconfirmed) and 1971, and negative ones in 1966 and (the M unconfirmed) 1974; though there are conjunctions of opposites of sorts, in 1957, 1958 and 1960. The positive expenditure impulse of 1960, however, follows three years of money injection; the negative one of 1962 follows two years of negative monetary impulse.

In assessing this evidence one has to admit that in two of the coincidences of like impulses (1971 and 1974) the main cause of the expenditure impulse in question does not seem to have been an internal one, easily identifiable with the accompanying monetary impulse. On the other hand, the fact that the negative A impulse of 1958 coincided with a positive monetary one can be overlooked in view of its predominantly external origin.

Altogether, there is some balance of evidence of a tendency for monetary impulses to produce expenditure impulses of the same sign in the same or the following year, but it is hardly a strong balance. One has to remember that expenditure impulses, in our sense, can be frustrated by changes in cost. The great boom of 1973, for instance, in the last of three years of money injection, fails to qualify as an expenditure impulse because of import price-push and wage inflation which prevented the profit share from increasing.

Japan
In general, expenditure impulses in Japan are dominated by variations in growth of the enormous private capital formation – two or three times as great as export income. In 1968 and 1977, however (the former a positive impulse, the latter a negative one), export changes were important junior partners. Public finance seems to have helped in the positive impulse of 1964 and the negative one of the following year, but it has generally been counter-cyclical and thus against net positive and negative impulses. But the great negative impulse of 1974 seems to have been due to the suddenly increased leakage of expenditure into paying for imports.

There was a fairly clear case of a positive monetary impulse being followed by a positive expenditure impulse in 1956–7, though a negative monetary impulse had set in by the time the profit share improved. This 1957 impulse was followed by a negative expenditure impulse, and the rather doubtful negative monetary impulse of 1977 was accompanied by one which, however, as we have just noted, seems to have been due partly to exports. There is thus *prima facie* evidence of some effectiveness of monetary impulses on expenditure in Japan, though there are several occasions when this association between the two kinds of impulse is not observed. The most obvious conjunction of opposites, positive expenditure impulse with negative money impulse in 1967–8, can perhaps be blamed on export demand.

Germany

In West Germany, there is a strong tendency for the expenditure impulses to be the joint product of domestic investment and exports. The latter feature on all occasions except the negative impulse of 1966 and the positive one of 1979 were particularly important in 1973, when capital formation fell as a proportion of GDP, and in 1976. Public finance, with its built-in stabiliser effect, seems to have been mostly counter-cyclical and opposed to our positive and negative impulses, the exceptions being some reductions of expansionary influence in the growth recessions of 1966 and 1971, both apparently rooted in discretionary budget changes. Consumption changes do not seem to have played a leading part in expenditure impulses.

There are some cases in which positive monetary impulses in Germany were followed by positive expenditure impulses; this happened in 1967–8 and 1975–6. The monetary impulses of 1957–8 and 1971–2, however, were not so followed; the first was, indeed, followed by a rise in nominal income growth (attributable largely to recovery of export markets), but also by import price-push; the second was frustrated by severe import price-push. We noted in the last chapter that these frustrated monetary impulses seem to have been connected with increases in the net foreign reserves of the monetary authorities. More generally, the importance of foreign demand in assisting German expenditure impulses directly tended to be supplemented by its monetary effects in enabling the domestic part of them to be financed.

France

The available statistics of profit share in France make the diagnosis of expenditure impulses, on a comparable basis with our other sample countries, difficult. The apparent scarcity of clear cases, however, may to some extent reflect reality, since the course of real growth in France is the least variable in our sample. Domestic capital formation seems, nevertheless, to have been part cause of all the positive and negative impulses, with help from exports in the positive ones of 1960 and 1969 and the negative ones of 1961 and 1975. Consumption played some part in the negative impulse of 1952. The budgetary impact was in all

these cases negligible or against the impulse in question. The built-in
stabiliser effects in 1951 and 1975 were very substantial.

With due allowance for some extra doubt about the identification of
expenditure impulses, the evidence of their association with monetary
impulses seems extraordinarily weak. Only the positive expenditure
impulse of 1960 and the negative one of 1975 show such an
association; the former both follows and coincides with positive
monetary impulses, the latter follows two negative ones, but coincides
with a positive one. The positive expenditure impulse of 1958 follows
two negative monetary ones; the negative expenditure impulses of
1961 and 1971 both coincide with and follow positive monetary ones.
Expectations, possibly affected by indicative planning, seem to have
transcended monetary influences more often than they took their cue
from them.

Italy
In Italy, too, expenditure impulses, on our definition, are rarer than in
some countries, in this case because expansions and contractions of
the growth rate of nominal income often go with changes of wage
inflation which, respectively, lower or raise the profit share; in other
words changes in the growth rate of nominal income derive mainly
from the substantial, but not complete, accommodation of changes in
wage inflation. Fluctuations in the growth of private domestic capital
formation seem to have played the main part in producing positive
expenditure impulses; consumption may have had an important part
in negative ones in 1954, 1957 and 1964. Export fluctuations, as a
proportion of GDP, are considerable and tend to go with the cycle,
but the current external balance is on the whole counter-cyclical. The
great deterioration in the terms of trade in 1974, as in many other
countries, was a strong deflationary impulse. Budgetary impulses
have mostly been counter-cyclical, most notably (through built-in
stabiliser effects with some discretionary help) in 1975–6.

Monetary impulses, though, as we saw in the last chapter, their
diagnosis if often doubtful (velocity and interest symptoms failing to
march together), show interesting conjunctions with expenditure
impulses on a number of occasions. The positive expenditure impulses
of 1966, 1976 and 1979 were preceded by positive monetary impulses
(the last one not fully confirmed), and negative impulses occurred in
the right order in 1974 and 1975. There are, however, more anomalous combinations in 1958–9 and 1971, and a number of rather
doubtful negative monetary impulses have no visible effect on expenditure. On balance, monetary influences seem to be of importance, but
far from exclusive importance, in regard to expenditure impulses.

Other OECD countries

Apart from Australia, the remaining OECD countries in our sample have more open economies, as measured by the ratio of exports to GDP, than the United Kingdom, which is the most open of the Big Six; the Netherlands, in particular, has a very much more open one. One is therefore tempted to ask whether their expenditure impulses coincide with those of their larger trading partners.

As we saw in chapter 2, however, national patterns of nominal income growth are not very similar; with 23 pairs of countries (in our whole sample) showing correlations significant at the 1 per cent level over the whole period, out of a possible 78, they fall between price increases, which are relatively well co-ordinated with 43 pairs significant and real growth rates with only fourteen. It is especially noticeable that Germany, an important trading partner of Sweden, Denmark and the Netherlands in particular, shows no significant positive correlation of nominal income growth rates with these countries, or any others in the sample, either over our whole period or over either of the two sub-periods 1953–67 or 1968–79. She does show significant correlation of price increases with all three of them (as with all the sample countries except Japan, Australia, Brazil and India) over the whole period, but on dividing the time into the sub-periods just mentioned, all correlations significant at the 1 per cent point vanish, except one with Sweden in the earlier interval. Between real growth series, the Netherlands is the only one of these three countries to show good correlation with Germany over the whole period (United Kingdom, France and Italy do also), but no country does so over the first sub-period, though Denmark and the Netherlands (along with Japan, France and Italy) do over the second. Fragmentary similarities of pattern in price increase and in real growth therefore fail to add up into any considerable similarities, as measured by correlation coefficients, between patterns of nominal income growth.

It may be more fruitful to look at the positive and negative expenditure impulses which we have identified in chapter 4. There are occasions when a number of the smaller OECD economies share similar impulses with some of the Big Six. The recovery of 1959 is one, shared by the Netherlands, Denmark, Australia and Sweden (and Canada, with a positive A) with the United States. So are 1962 (Denmark, Canada and Australia with the United States, though with Sweden agreeing with the United Kingdom, Japan and Germany in the negative direction), 1968 (the Netherlands, Denmark and Canada with Germany and Japan), 1972 (Denmark and Canada with the United States), 1973 (the Netherlands, Canada and Sweden with Italy), and 1976 (the Netherlands and Denmark with the United States, Japan, Germany and Italy, but with the United Kingdom and Sweden on the opposite tack). On the negative side, other than the instances already mentioned, there are 1961 (the Netherlands, Australia and Sweden with Germany and France), 1965 and 1966, when the Netherlands, Denmark, Australia and Sweden all share negative impulses in one or both years with one or more of the United Kingdom, Japan and Germany, 1970, when Canada, Denmark and the Netherlands go with the United States and 1977 (the Netherlands, Denmark, Canada and Sweden with Japan). One cannot help noticing that, like some of the pairs of countries which show closely correlated patterns of inflation, growth, or nominal income increase, a number of these combinations of smaller countries with larger ones have the air of owing something to the long arm of coincidence.

In part, the absence of a greater degree of international coordination of impulses must be put down to the fact that surges of demand, either stimulating a country's trading partners or stimulated by them, can easily fail to register as instances of expenditure-pull, because costs are quick to adjust. The poor correlations that we have noted between patterns of nominal income growth make it plain, however, that even the smaller and more open economies both receive different impresses from abroad, because their trading partners and their trade goods differ, and also modify those impresses by important contributions of their own.

Canada and the United States form the pair of countries most closely connected according to the correlation coefficients of chapter 2. The extent to which the similarity was produced by the drag of the United States market, acting through trade channels seems, however, to be limited. The Canadian expansion of 1968 was export-induced, with domestic capital formation playing little part; exports played a considerable part (along with domestic capital formation) in 1961–4 and seem to have operated to moderate the recession of 1970. Otherwise, expansion seems to go with deterioration of the foreign balance, recession with improvement in it, as one would expect if variations in internal rather than external demand were the prime movers. To a large extent, therefore, the resemblance to United States growth patterns must derive from common impulses to internal expenditure, especially on capital formation. Differences between the compositions of United States and Canadian imports and exports became important in the early 1970s, when Canada's status as a net exporter of primary products introduced a stronger and more sustained element of demand-pull than the United States experienced.

A strong rise in export prices (roughly in parallel with those of imports) was a feature of the Swedish economy also in 1973–4. Exports had also played an important, though hardly predominant part in the previous expenditure impulse of 1969–70; in the two earlier ones of 1954 and 1959 internal expenditure seems to have been the predominant element. The Swedish economy is certainly far from being merely carried along on the currents of international trade and the importance of wood products in its exports introduces a special and volatile element into those currents, as they affect it, in any case.

Australia is, on the face of it, in a somewhat similar position; though now not a very open economy, she sells largely primary exports in highly volatile markets. Of her positive expenditure impulses, that of 1953 was largely due to recovery of exports (volume as well as price), domestic capital formation falling; that of 1959, however, was mainly a matter of internal expenditure, as was that of 1962–3 and after that there is a remarkable lack of expenditure impulses, either positive or negative. Foreign trade prices fluctuated greatly in the 1970s, but wage inflation, sometimes not unconnected with foreign trade prices, emerged as the dominant variable. The great accelerations of nominal income growth in 1973 and 1975 and its great deceleration in 1977 were more than matched, proportionately, by changes in growth of factor prices.

India
Of the more variable portions of expenditure in India, that on fixed capital formation is about twice as big as public consumption expenditure, and two or three times larger than export receipts. It surged forward notably, in relation to expenditure as a whole, between 1953 and 1957, in 1963, 1965, 1970–2, 1975–6 and, in a smaller way, in 1978. It thus contributed to the cyclical GDP peaks of 1956 and 1978 and the manufacturing growth peaks of 1957, 1963, 1976 and 1978, but other components of output (notably agriculture) moved largely independently. Public consumption made its biggest relative advance between 1961 and 1963, the period which includes the brief 1962 war with China. To judge by the government deficits, public finance has not played a consistently stabilising role; it was broadly pro-cyclical during 1953–7, counter-cyclical for the next ten years, and about a year late in its counter-cyclical influence from then onward.

There are, however, as we have just implied, other factors to be taken into account in an economy such as the Indian in which fluctuation of agricultural yields and the impacts of world agricultural (and other primary) prices are important. The course of year-to-year change in Indian real output is dominated during most of our period by variations in agricultural and related production. Inflation, as we saw in chapter 3, is negatively correlated with output growth, but until the more active world price movements of the 1970s (and even then, in the peak of 1977, for instance) the main peaks and troughs of nominal expenditure growth corresponded with those of the physical increase of agricultural output. This was true of peaks in 1958, 1960, 1964 and 1967 (as well as that of 1977, just mentioned) and of troughs in 1957, 1959, 1965 and 1968. There are a number of cases in which a peak of growth in agricultural output and total expenditure is followed in the next year by a surge of manufacturing output, though whether this has the makings of a systematic relationship is not clear.

At all events, it is clear that, in a country where agriculture and trade in agricultural products account for nearly half the gross domestic product, the generation of positive and negative expenditure impulses is very different from its counterpart in the industrial countries. Exogenous variations in output generate their own inflationary and disinflationary impulses. It is worth recalling in this connection, from chapter 2 (chart 2.1.12), that the course of growth in the money stock in India was relatively smooth, about an upward trend. The large fluctuations in the growth rate of nominal income were carried mainly by changes in the growth of velocity.

Brazil
Apart from fluctuations in the early and middle 1950s associated mainly with agricultural vicissitudes, the course of variation in growth of Brazilian nominal income is dominated by long sweeps rather than year-to-year impulses. The first of these is the great expansion from 1958 to 1964, interrupted only for a year in 1960. It is followed by a corresponding downsweep from 1964 to 1970, interrupted for a year in 1968. What follows, up to the end of our period (indeed, up to 1981) is more irregular, but is dominated by a trend in which declining rate of physical growth is combined with a more than offsetting rise of the rate of inflation.

If one judges where the pressure for expansion mainly came from by the changes in shares of total expenditure between its principal divisions, it seems that capital formation has been the active agent. Its share of GDP rose sharply in 1959, as the Kubitschek regime's expansionary policy got into its stride. Consumption and the trade balance temporarily made way for it, but both regained their 1958 position as shares of GDP in the following year, in which there was a very large growth of output. Although real growth fell heavily during the Quadros and Goulart regimes (1961–4), the extent to which capital formation fell in relation to GDP was fairly modest; the share of public consumption also fell somewhat and that of private consumption rose. During the whole period 1958–64 there was a rapid rise in the rate of domestic credit expansion, rather less than half of it in favour of the government, rather more than half for the private sector.

From the *coup d'état* of 1964, the share of public authorities' consumption fell and so (for two years) did the budget deficit, but that of capital formation started on a new upward trend that lasted for a decade. Private consumption, on the whole (with some fluctuations), made way for it as, to some extent, government consumption continued to do and, from about 1970, as did the external goods and services account.

Much of the capital formation has been public. It is, primarily, the public authorities' zeal for development at a rate which could not be sustained by domestic voluntary saving plus the (very large) feasible borrowing from abroad that has caused high inflation in Brazil during our period, the variations in its rate being traceable to a combination of the pressure for capital expenditure and the extent to which government consumption was restrained or financed from taxation. So far as the forces behind expenditure are concerned, the story resembles that of many war economies.

CONCLUSIONS

At the beginning of this chapter, we posed the questions, what sections of expenditure were responsible for the various expenditure-pull impulses, and how were these impulses related to monetary conditions? We first looked at the 'crowding-out problem', which is related to both of these questions, and were satisfied with the evidence that a surge forward in one section of expenditure is not likely to displace anything approaching an equal amount of expenditure under other heads, even in the absence of any monetary expansion. In looking at our period as a whole, in relation to some earlier times, we found indications that public finance probably contributed to its more expansionary character in the United States, but not in the United Kingdom, and noted evidence that capital formation and (for the United Kingdom) exports had been the most expansionary sections of total expenditure. We then found, not surprisingly, that the sections of accelerated expenditure growth which take the lead in the impulses we have identified are various. In general, however, domestic capital formation – fixed capital or inventory-accumulation, or both – seems to have provided most of the variation in question in the Big Six, with export surges also of consequence on several occasions in each of the more open economies, Germany and the United Kingdom especially. The current external balance, however, did not always vary procyclically (it did not in Italy, for instance), and in 1974 especially, in most of these countries, the drain of purchasing power due to the sharp rise in import prices produced a powerful negative impulse. In most of the Big Six, the built-in stabiliser effects of public sector transactions seem to have been quite powerful in moderating our identified impulses. From 1965 to 1979, at least, discretionary budget changes in years of positive expenditure impulse had about the same average impact as those in years of negative impulse, though there may have been some delayed effects (in both directions) between these budget changes and our E and NE impulses. In the United Kingdom, the effects of the built-in stabiliser are harder to find, and some important positive expenditure impulses (1951, 1963) seem to have owed a good deal to discretionary budget changes. (The same may be true of the impulse of 1971 in the United States).

The extents to which impulses in the smaller, more open, economies are in line with those in particular major countries are sometimes significant but always limited, and parallelism sometimes seems to owe more to a coincidence of internal investment impulses than to the transmission of demand through international trade channels. India and Brazil both display different patterns from the more developed economies; in India year-to-year variations in agricultural output are a major source of short-term variations in aggregate expenditure; in Brazil the medium-term variations in governmental enthusiasm for development have taken precedence over shorter-term fluctuations in the growth rate of nominal expenditure.

We have found the relations between monetary conditions and the expenditure impulses complex. The simplest general statement is perhaps that these conditions, as represented by the monetary impulses discussed in chapter 6 rather than by mere change in the growth rate of the money stock, seem to be among a number of circumstances on which acceleration (or the reverse) of expenditure growth depends. The significant but loose statistical relations mentioned in chapters 4 and 6 probably convey a fair impression of the strength, or weakness, of the causal connection.

8

WAGES AND THE LABOUR MARKET

INTRODUCTION

Explanations of the relation between effective demand and inflation turn on nothing so much as the nature and behaviour of the labour market. We have ourselves made use of the concept of wage-push, which we have characterised as involving acceleration of wage inflation together with a reduction of the profit share, and to be distinguished from expenditure-pull, in which growth of aggregate expenditure accelerates and the profit share rises. But if the growth of effective demand increases, why should that affect value of final output more than it affects the wage bill? And how can wage inflation speed up without a rise in the growth rate of effective demand which one might expect to affect the value of final output to something like the same extent? The answers given to these questions (perhaps more especially to the second) turn mainly on differences between the markets for labour and for final output, which it is perhaps most convenient to examine by way of the differences between each of these markets, respectively, and the flexible-price markets of classical economic theory, to which the markets for some primary products approximate.

In this chapter, therefore, we begin by briefly examining the labour market, with some reference to the different forms it assumes in our sample countries, and to the difference made to its working by collective bargaining, but with special reference to its propensity, or its reluctance, to clear. We then examine the relations which appear in each of the sample countries between wages (or their rate of inflation) and unemployment, notably the existence or non-existence of stable Phillips relations. Insofar as such relations fail to appear, we then enquire how far this can be accounted for by the unreliability of unemployment as a measure of excess supply of labour – how far changes in unemployment are traceable to changes in the degree of imperfection of the labour market, for instance – how far by the influence of expectations of price inflation, and how far by miscellaneous other causes.

We then turn to a brief survey of the main systematic, econometric, investigations which have been made of wage-formation in a number of the principal countries, including the light thrown by them, and by more specific investigations, on the effectiveness or non-effectiveness of incomes policies. Finally, we look at the evidence concerning the effect of wage-push on the profit share of value-added in a longer run than the year-to-year movements with respect to which we have defined wage-push, and we seek to pull the conclusions of this chapter together.

The basic disagreement in economic theory about the labour market is between those who think the market clears quickly, and is therefore usually at or near to equilibrium, and those who think it is mostly out of equilibrium, and moving only slowly, if at all, towards it. In the latter case one is left with the task of explaining why so many bargains which, *prima facie*, are mutually advantageous, do not take place, and to this we shall have in due course to come. At the outset, however, we must note that the labour market is one with very special characteristics, which may be expected to vary with the institutional differences between one country and another.

THE ATOMISTIC LABOUR MARKET

It is possible to imagine an economy in which something like atomistic competition operates, with employees bargaining individually with employers, of whom there are many, competing with each other for labour, and with contracts holding for short periods only. In such an economy, one would expect that any excess of person-hours on offer at current rates over person-hours demanded at those rates would bring the rates down; and deficiency would put them up. These adjustments of rates would seem likely to reduce excesses and deficiencies of supply in relation to demand.

Would there be unemployment in such an economy? There would certainly be unemployment of the kind generally described as 'frictional', which has more recently come to be considered in terms of the time taken by the unemployed and new entrants to find a job-offer which they consider worthy of acceptance. The level of such unemployment will depend on the frequency of quits (voluntary or involuntary leaving of jobs, other than into retirement), plus first entries into the labour market, and on the length of the average 'period of search'. Quits may be divided into the voluntary and the involuntary. The former are, almost certainly, mostly not actions taken in order to search full-time for a better job, but parts of a shift to a supposedly better job already found; that is to say, they are associated with a zero search time, if by that term *full-time* search, or at least, search by the unemployed is meant. It is certain that, in reasonably prosperous times, the great majority of the nine million or so employees engaged each year in the United Kingdom jump straight from one job to another without a period of registered unemployment. There will be some quits-to-search, largely among the young, however, and one would expect their number to rise with the pressure of demand for labour – with the knowledge that there are plenty of jobs to be had.

Involuntary quits will consist of dismissals for inadequacy or misconduct and of redundancies, of which one would expect the latter to be the more variable in number, varying with the rate of change in the specific skill requirements of firms and the rate of turnover of jobs in establishments (frequency of job-extinguishments by closures or employment-reductions, even if these are balanced by expansions or new starts elsewhere).

What will govern the time taken to find an acceptable job? The most obvious answer is that it will depend on the balance between the total number unemployed and the total number of vacancies, with the degree of occupational and geographical mismatch between the compositions of the two totals as a further factor. The assumption that the market clears, however, means that, in every occupational category (and every travel-to-work area if labour is immobile) an excess, say, of vacancies over acceptable applicants will raise wages, choking off the demand and encouraging the supply, so that the numbers become equal. Neither unemployment nor vacancies will disappear; people out of a job will still take a finite time to find what looks worth applying for, to be considered for a vacancy where they win an offer, and perhaps, beyond that, to find an offer good enough to convince them that it is not worth looking further – though the amount of standing out for the best possible offer will in many cases be reduced by the consideration that one can take a reasonably acceptable job with the intention of keeping an eye open for a better one, especially within local labour markets where acceptance and subsequent change do not involve house moving. What market-flexible wages should mean is simply that acceptable applicants and vacancies become equal within each labour market. Acceptable applicants, of course, may not all be from among the unemployed; for many kinds of job they very rarely will. But appointments from among the already employed create further vacancies, and for the economy *as a whole* a balance between unemployed and unfilled vacancies would be likely to result, if wages were market-flexible, and both the unemployment and the unfilled vacancies would be attributable to search for acceptable jobs and search for acceptable candidates. The time taken in these searches would depend on judgements about the probability of improvement from looking further and on the financial sacrifice involved in doing so. For applicants, the sacrifice would be inversely related to the level of family income available without taking a job, and to the size of accumulated reserves of purchasing power. For firms, it would be positively related to estimates of profits foregone by leaving posts empty.

This 'search' theory of frictional unemployment gives no reason for expecting that there will be more of it when demand for labour is low than when it is high, except through the suggestion, most notably by Friedman (1968) and Phelps (1967) that the job-seekers rely on out-of-date information, and thus delay acceptance of the lower wages appropriate to a less favourable market. This would make unemployment vary inversely with the rate of change of demand, not with its level; it could not explain prolonged heavy unemployment extending beyond the falling phase of the trade cycle.

Apart from frictional unemployment, however, would the kind of atomistic labour market we are imagining guarantee that there would be no continuing aggregate deficiency of demand for labour? The answer depends, immediately, on two considerations: the relative movements of the prices of labour and of output in the event of such a deficiency and how elastic is the demand for labour in terms of real-product wages. If prices came down as much as wages, then the real-product wage would be unchanged and questions involving the real-wage elasticity of demand for labour would not arise. There would be no increase in employment – provided, at least, that the reduced price-level proved to be an equilibrium one.

If, however, prices came down less than wages, then the real wage would be reduced, though less than the money wage, and the outcome would depend on the real-wage elasticity of demand for labour. Pigou (1933), who approached the problem in roughly this way, but very thoroughly, argued that this elasticity is numerically high, not less than -3 and perhaps greater than -4, and that the *money*-wage elasticity of demand is unlikely to be numerically less than -1.5. However, Solow, in his 1979 Presidential Address to the American Economic Association (Solow, 1980), quotes recent econometric estimates of even the *real*-wage elasticity lying between -0.15 and -0.5. It does, indeed, seem likely that the high elasticities deducible from production functions (-3 or -4 if one assumes a two-factor Cobb-Douglas function to hold, with the coefficients usually attributed thereto) are relevant to the longer run in which a substantial degree of re-equipment is possible. The short-term elasticity is probably much smaller.

The fundamental difficulty in considering the money-wage elasticity of demand for labour arises from the fact that lower wages mean lower expenditure, as well as cheaper labour. Aggregate supply and demand analysis should enable this difficulty to be dealt with (see, for instance, Weintraub, 1958). We start with the aggregate supply function corresponding to a particular money-wage level, which shows the employment that will be offered in response to each hypothetical level of expected total revenue, and the aggregate demand function showing the total expenditure which is to be expected at each hypothetical level of employment, and we then consider how each of these functions will be affected by altering the wage level – for a closed economy, to start with.

It is reasonable to suppose that the aggregate supply function will be lowered in the same proportion as wage levels, and if the same were true of the aggregate demand function, employment and output would be unchanged. Increase of employment depends on the demand schedule falling less than in proportion to the wage level and this, in a closed economy, depends on three considerations: (1) the level of investment, which depends on the rate of interest (assuming that the prices of capital goods and those of their products are similarly affected by the wage reduction), (2) the effects on expenditure of a shift of real income towards rentiers, and (3) the wealth effects of the rise in the real value of money, and of stocks of government and net external securities held by residents.

It seems likely that the net effect of these considerations will be to support the aggregate demand function, so that it does not fall as much as the wage level and the aggregate supply function. Interest is likely to have been lowered unless special measures were taken to bring down the money stock in line with wages, and the wealth effects on the private sector of the net increase in the value of its government and foreign debt holdings are likely to be expansionary. The expenditure effects of distributional changes are more problematic, but unlikely to be overwhelming.

In addition, there are the demand-switching effects of wage and price reduction which have to be taken into account once we abandon the assumption that the economy is closed. With fixed, or sticky, exchange rates, these may be decisive in making reduction of money wages an expansionary influence on domestic employment, as domestic goods become more competitive with foreign ones. Under flexible exchange rates this effect of net foreign demand on home activity would be diluted, as wage and price reduction would tend to make the external value of the currency rise.

It seems, then, that the balance of probability is in favour of money-wage changes, due to excess supply or demand in the labour market, operating to reduce those excesses; but that this is not to be completely relied upon in all circumstances, and that the macroeconomic reactions of general wage changes on demand may well in any case render the achievement of full employment equilibrium by this means a rather messy business. It was for reasons similar to these that Keynes, in the famous chapter 19 of the *General Theory*, concluded that they were likely to affect activity little.

It is interesting to ask what the larger macroeconomic models make of this issue. Wren-Lewis (1983) explains that the National Institute model of the United Kingdom economy, in common with those of the Treasury and the Bank of England, does not include a direct effect of real wages on employment, but makes the latter depend on lagged employment and on current and lagged output. Reduction in money wages therefore affects employment first adversely, through expenditure and current output, then favourably through increased profits, increased investment, and improved competitiveness with foreign goods. A National Institute simulation (*National Institute Economic Review*, November 1983), in which the wage equation is altered in such a way as to make the consumer price level after five years some 9 per cent lower than it would otherwise have been, yields by that time a reduction of unemployment, below what the model would otherwise have given, of only about one-fifth of 1 per cent of the labour force. This seems to be a result, largely, of the fact that the relevant estimated foreign trade elasticities are low. Subject to its limitations, this supports the Keynesian conclusion.

So much for the sensitivity of employment to money wages. How sensitive are money wages to excess supply of or demand for labour? We shall come to the empirical evidence on this matter later, but it is appropriate to point out here that, even in labour markets that approximate to the atomistic, with little unionisation of workers and with many competing employers, there are obstacles to the wage flexibility which would be necessary for complete market clearing. They have been well analysed by Okun (1981).

The costs to the firm of recruiting, selecting, and training employees are substantial; it therefore pays it, when demand for its product slackens, to hold on to its established employees, and to reduce or suspend recruitment, rather than to promote a higher quit rate (either immediately or when demand picks up again) by lowering wages below the course that employees have come to expect. Career employees, in particular, as opposed to casual workers, are willing to accept lower starting pay – in effect to bear part of the cost of their own selection and training – in return for some prospect of stability once they are established, and firms would destroy this prospect by lowering wages below their generally expected course in order to take advantage of a temporary weakness of the labour market. Akerlof (1979) has argued that, if texts on personnel management bear any resemblance to what is practiced, 'remuneration policies of corporations are . . . merely parts of elaborate codes of behaviour regarding the reciprocal relations between firms and their workers . . . Firms will, by and large, conform to such codes of 'standard practice' for much the same reasons that individuals will, almost always, conform to prevailing social custom in their societies'.

The force of this argument is clearly greater in connection with salaried staff than with wage-earners; it is probably least powerful in relation to part-time employees, who make up an increasing proportion of, at least, the United Kingdom workforce. It has, however, some general cogency. It is probable, too, that slower recruitment brings recruits of higher average quality and faster recruitment causes the quality to be lowered, so that the appropriate wage offer does not vary with rate of recruitment as much as it would in a homogeneous labour market. Moreover, in the short run, demand for labour does not vary as widely as that for products (a fact embodied in 'Okun's Law'); not only do firms have the reason just mentioned for holding on to established employees (even at the cost of some under-use of them) in recessions which they believe to be temporary, but, as Bowers, Deaton and Turk (1982) have argued, the division of labour and indivisibilities make it hard to reduce employment in proportion to output, short of closing down whole establishments. Even wage-setting employers, operating in the absence of trade unions, may therefore find a fairly steady course of wage rates optimal in the face of fluctuating demand for output.

COLLECTIVE BARGAINING

To extents which we shall discuss shortly, however, the normal method of wage determination in our sample countries is not unilateral action by competing employers, it is some form of negotiation between employers (either singly or in combination) and trade unions. Where this happens, the situation is one of bilateral monopoly, in which the outcome is not determined by the demand curve for the product and the supply curve of unorganised labour, as under perfect competition or unilateral monopoly on the part of the firms, but lies within limits (possibly wide limits) which these functions set. Whereabouts it lies within these limits depends on the perceptions of the two parties to the bargaining and the amounts of pressure they can put upon each other – which turns mainly on the relative amounts they stand to lose from temporary cessation of production or the temporary withdrawal of various kinds of cooperation in the productive process; that is to say, from strikes, lockouts, 'going slow', refusing to work overtime, and 'working-to-rule'. The theory of this kind of bilateral bargaining, generally incorporating the assumption that employers can take on whatever numbers of employees they find optimal at the wage rates finally agreed, has been elaborated in the models of Hicks (1932), Shackle (1964), Hieser (1970) and Johnston (1972).

In some cases, however, the profit calculations of the employer are not the relevant thing on the non-employee side. In parts of the public sector where the output is not marketed, and in some public utility (and, indeed, some other) industries where it is, but where production is, or may be, subsidised from the public purse, the employees' claim may, essentially, be upon public funds, and thus ultimately on the taxpayer. A further complication arises (not only in these public or publicly-subsidised areas) from the fact that the volume of employment may be a subject of collective bargaining; employees may strike against redundancy plans. In the extreme case, the employees' organisation may be in a bargaining position rather like that of a monopolistic state trading organisation, which can specify a particular level of supply at a particular price as an alternative to no supply at all (for the time being, at least). In principle, failing countervailing bargaining power on the other side, the specification can be such as to reduce the community's consumer surplus from the good or service in question to near zero. In an economy in which particular inputs are essential, in the short-, and indeed, medium-run, for the production of a wide range of outputs, the size of the consumer surplus which depends upon supply or non-supply of a particular input can clearly be large. Moreover, where more than one input is essential, the same consumer surplus can be used as a bargaining counter repeatedly, by the suppliers of those different inputs. Since the bargaining is for money income, and the fact that one group of suppliers can be given more of the economy's real output only at the expense of other groups is implicit rather than explicit, the possibility becomes strong of a 'price-price spiral', in which the different input suppliers, in turn, receive, temporarily, real incomes which, together, would add up to more than the value to consumers of the total final output to which the inputs contribute.

This is, as we have said, the extreme case. In practice, what the suppliers of an input can threaten is a temporary rather than a permanent denial of it, its duration and effectiveness depending on their ability to provide strike-pay or to achieve disruption without overt strike action, on the accumulated resources and social security entitlements of strikers' families, and on the striking organisation's ability to prevent, and to secure the cooperation of other employees' organisations in preventing, access to alternative supplies of labour or of the input in question. But this limitation applies much less strongly to various kinds of disruptive action short of total stoppage, to which we have already referred – overtime bans and working to rule. Employers are highly vulnerable to the concerted withdrawal of various forms of working adaptability and goodwill, which have relatively little direct cost to the employees.

There is, of course, to be taken into account the countervailing power, against employees' organisations, of employers (either separately or through joint bargaining organisations) and of the state. The monopsony power of employers against unorganised employees is generally given as the reason and justification on equity and welfare grounds, for the formation of employees' organisations in the first place, and it is plain that monopolistic or oligopolistic enterprises which are also not in active and uninhibited competition with each other for labour, could divert very large proportions of income to profits, especially (though by no means only) if they used the monopsonist's power to beat each employee down to his individual opportunity cost, rather than specifying a 'rate for the job'. In a world of organised employees, however, the countervailing power of employers is mainly that of the lock-out, or, in the extreme case, of closing down permanently; at the cost of stopping production they can throw their employees onto the labour market. It may be an effective reply to disruptive practices intended to stay short of complete work stoppage; otherwise it is simply an active, as opposed to a passive, use of the employers' superior power to endure stoppage – if it is superior.

As for the state, what action it can and will take, or threaten, in reply to collective employee action directed against either itself, as an employer, or other employers, or consumers, is a complex matter, involving all the elements that enter into 'the art of the possible' – what political support the government of the day stands to receive for various kinds of intervention, and its further gain or loss of support according to their probable results, not to mention the fixed ideas and commitments of those in power. This must vary very widely not only between different countries but between times and administrations within each country, and both governmental decisions and their outcomes will generally be hard to predict.

Perhaps the first effect of collective bargaining is either to introduce or to reinforce the concept of the 'rate for the job', at least within an individual establishment, if not more widely. (Within a local labour market in the United Kingdom, rates of earnings-inflation in a given occupation can vary very substantially between firms; see for instance Nolan and Brown, 1983). The picture of unemployed workers calling on firms with offers of their services at lower wages than are paid to existing employees, already atypical of most non-unionised labour markets, becomes altogether irrelevant – most decisively so where the 'closed shop' prevails. The mechanism which is essential to the simple automatic clearing of the atomistic labour market thus vanishes. Processes by which the existence of unemployment can influence the outcome of bargaining in a unionised world are much more shadowy. In the United Kingdom, at least, it is only in a small number of craft unions and professional associations that the unemployed have votes in union affairs. Even where they have them, so long as the great majority of union members are in work, it is only that majority's concern for their unemployed brethren, or perception of the risk of becoming unemployed themselves, that is likely to bring pressure on the leaders to take unemployment into account in formulating wage demands. And they will still not be eager to do so if they do not accept the theoretical view (not always notably popular in trade union circles) that excessively high wages are a cause of unemployment. Robbins' suggestion (1934) that wage demands had been more responsive to unemployment when the cost of unemployment relief fell largely on union funds may have some force. In practice, the sensitivity of wage demands and wage settlements to the level of unemployment is hard to separate from their sensitivity to other influences which go (or have gone) with it – low profits and, for much of economic history, low or falling consumer prices. Under collective bargaining, the link between wage settlements and the state of the labour market itself is certainly greatly weakened.

Another effect of collective bargaining, with its highlighting of 'the rate for the job', is to encourage comparisons between the rates for different jobs. In a static world, a hierarchy of such rates might become generally accepted; as it is, changing market situations and changing fortunes at the bargaining table are constantly modifying the existing hierarchy, and those groups which see themselves as falling behind are frequently motivated to stronger exertions of bargaining power in an effort to restore what seems to them the proper order. Since effectiveness in bargaining is a function of motivation, *inter alia*, the result can be an episode of 'leapfrogging', accompanied by at least a temporary growth of rivalry and aggressiveness between a number of unions – a 'wage-wage spiral'. 'Leapfrogging' seems both to increase, and to be stimulated by, the dispersion of occupational or

industrial average earnings and the more democratic union consti-
tutions are, the less restraint there is on it.

There is little doubt that the organisation of labour and the
institution of collective bargaining enable a larger wage increase to be
prised out of the employers in an industry, on any given occasion,
than would be forthcoming in the absence of organisation, simply
because the union can put pressure on employers, by the threat of
collective action, which unorganised workers could not produce. It is
often held that this makes simply for a once-for-all rise in at least the
nominal wages of unionised industries in relation to what they would
have been without unionisation (even though this bonus to the
workers may be realised over some years rather than suddenly). It
can, however, be argued that this is incorrect; that unionisation opens
the possibility of a continuing higher *rate of increase* of nominal wages
than would be forthcoming without unionisation. Okun (1981) makes
the points that each wage settlement is built on the foundation of
expectations (on both sides) left by the last one, and that on each
occasion organisation enables the 'strike-avoidance premium' to be
extracted. This does not necessarily mean, however, that the wages of
unionised industries in a country rise continuously in relation to those
of the non-unionised – indeed, they are not in general seen to do so.
The reason is probably that the wages of the two classes of industry
interact; the further ahead those in unionised industry get, the greater
is the pressure on employers in the non-unionised to avoid falling
further behind, both through the usual labour supply channels and
through the urge to forestall union development. Similarly, the further
ahead the unionised industries get, the higher is their real wage, and
their wage level in relation to that in non-unionised industry, the
weaker, *ceteris paribus*, is their motivation for getting further ahead,
and the greater, for reasons varying from the waning of public
sympathy and the attraction of the attention of anti-inflationary
governments to the rise of various forms of market pressure, is the
difficulty they are likely to encounter in doing so. The wage gap
between the two classes of industry fluctuates rather than increasing
continuously, but it seems likely that the existence of a significant
unionised sector raises the rate of increase of money wages both in
itself and among the non-unionised.

This probability is given further colour by a formulation due to
Scitovsky (1983). He points out that what happens to prices (and to
the demand for purchasing power) depends largely on whether the
price makers in the various markets in which they exist have an
interest in raising or in lowering prices. Manufacturers and the
suppliers of many final services mostly dominate the markets in which

they sell and are, on the whole, price makers who can raise their product prices to compensate for any rises in cost. Some of their inputs are bought in near-perfect markets, not dominated by either side; some (for example, petroleum) are sold to them by other price makers. Even if labour was bought and sold in a near-perfect market, there would probably be some inflationary bias in the economy, because the agents with power to manipulate prices would be mainly in a position to exercise it as sellers rather than as buyers. Monopsonistic employers facing unorganised workers might redress the balance by exercising their power to depress the price of labour, but every shift towards a situation in which the sellers of labour are price makers rather than price takers tips the balance more strongly towards inflation – towards a situation in which the agents who are in a position to manipulate prices fight for shares of the final product by competitively pushing prices upwards rather than downwards, as (on a more restricted stage) in the traditional model of the price–wage spiral. It is, of course, true that power to force prices up without reducing quantities bought is contingent on an elastic supply of purchasing power; but the supply of purchasing power seems always to have shown some elasticity.

In the light of these general considerations, let us look very briefly at the forms of the labour markets in our sample countries.

MARKET FORMS

In fact, the markets of our sample countries display a considerable variety of organisational forms (Dean, 1980; Bain and Price, 1980). The *United States* has one of the lower incidences of union membership – in 1979 about 25 per cent of the total labour force – with a very high degree of fragmentation, and little power of control residing in the central body (the AFL-CIO) to which about three-quarters of the whole (reckoned by membership) are affiliated. In private manual employment, however, over 50 per cent of the labour force is unionised; it is in private white collar employment and in the public sector that the percentage is low (Clegg, 1976). The wages of unionised workers are higher than those of the apparently comparable non-unionised by appreciable margins, which vary on the whole anti-cyclically, as well as in other ways. Unionisation is strong in some of the more cycle-prone industries (70 per cent in building and construction). It seems to have the effect of making wages less sensitive to the level of activity and more sensitive to consumer prices than in the non-unionised sector and there is evidence that wage levels in the two sectors interact in the ways that have been described above.

Collective bargaining, whether by the large unions or by small ones (not infrequently company unions operating in closed 'company' or 'agency shops') certainly exerts an important influence on the general course of wages, and the fact that the course shows less short-term variability than is seen in most other countries certainly owes much to the practice of making long-term contracts with escalator clauses. It has been punctuated by four episodes of wages policy; the Wage Stabilisation Board, 1950–3; the 'guideposts' in the years following 1962; President Nixon's wage-price controls of 1971–4, and President Carter's pay and price standards, 1978–80.

At the other extreme, in one sense, stands the *United Kingdom* with a union membership of nearly half the labour force – more than half the total of employees – a ratio which until the end of the 1970s was increasing; and with the pay of over three-quarters of all employees fixed by some kind of collective agreement. The degree of unionisation is particularly high in the public sector (85 per cent), relatively low (27 per cent) in private white collar employment and about 50 per cent (as in the United States) in the private manual category (Clegg). The scale and scope of bargains have changed greatly (Brown, 1980). In the first part of our period, up to the late 1960s, the old emphasis on multi-employer, often industry-wide, settlements was breaking down through the rise of wage drift, caused by local, generally single workshop, negotiation of payment-by-results bonuses, overtime and other supplements. Since then, especially among manual workers in manufacturing industry, there has been a strong move to the overt fixing of effective rates of pay by single employer (sometimes single plant) bargaining, with industry-wide agreements relegated to the role of providing safety nets, affecting the pay of only the least well paid fraction of the industry's employees. The role of combinations of employers has thus diminished. The power of the TUC over individual unions is greater than that of the AFL-CIO in the United States, but weaker than that of the corresponding bodies in several continental European countries. Official pay policy has, in various forms, been a recurring feature of the story. The United Kingdom is thus a country in which collective bargaining in various forms, with occasional interference by Government, is the norm in wage determination.

Germany displays an intermediate degree of unionisation; by 1978 about 38 per cent of her employees were members of a trade union, with the distribution between different sectors of the economy rather similar to that in the United Kingdom – very strong among government employees, medium in manual and weaker in white-collar occupations in the private sector. There is much stronger central control within the employees' and employers' organisations than the

United States or the United Kingdom can show, and the government has intervened in the process of wage formation only to the extent, since the mid-1960s, of promoting meetings with the two sides of industry and other relevant bodies to discuss the general macroeconomic framework within which impending wage bargains should be made. The bargaining itself is decentralised, but the general tone appears to be set by one or two large settlements, and though the year-to-year changes in degree of restraint have been considerable, the system has survived.

Smaller European countries in our sample show some resemblance to the German system in that they tend to possess strong central institutions on the two sides of industry, but operate centralised systems of bargaining, though with varying success, and varying degrees of government participation. *The Netherlands*, which has about the same degree of unionisation as Germany, worked, from 1950, with a bipartite Foundation of Labour and a consultative Social Economic Council including government representatives, but from the 1960s the latter body became less effective, agreement in the Foundation of Labour became more difficult, and direct government intervention with price control or wage freezes more frequent. *Sweden* has 87 per cent of her labour force in unions, and strong employers' and employees' central organisations. In 1952 a system of central bargaining, in the light of an assessment of the macroeconomic situation but without government participation, was instituted. It has continued to work, but did not avoid quite large amounts of wage drift (indeed, may have caused some by attempting to compress wage differentials), and since the large world price movements of the 1970s has encountered increasing difficulties, with the government – while refraining from direct intervention – attempting to influence outcomes by strategic social and fiscal measures. *Denmark*, nearly three-quarters of whose labour force is unionised, presents a history combining features reminiscent of those of the Netherlands and Sweden.

The trade union movements of both *France* and *Italy* differ from those we have so far mentioned in that they have no single central bodies, their structure being divided on both political and religious lines. In France, only about 25 per cent of the workforce is unionised, and the greater part of the union system does not regard collective bargaining as a major part of its function; its aim is political. In Italy the figure has been uncertain, but higher – by 1978 it was as high as 60 per cent. Legislative measures (minimum wage legislation in France, indexation in Italy) have supported union aspirations, and at critical times the unions' combination of economic and political power has proved to be considerable. Italy did not attempt a wages policy within our period; France did so in 1964–5, and also made considerable use of price control.

Japan's labour market is entirely unlike that of any other country. Within the rapidly expanding area of large-scale enterprises, especially, a paternalistic system of lifetime employment with age-related pay is widespead. Nevertheless, about a third of all employees are unionised, mostly in enterprise unions, connected to central bodies by a system of affiliation; employers' organisations have a single tight organisation for labour matters, and (with an Industry and Labour Round Table which includes governmental and independent experts) there is some resemblance to the German system. As there, negotiations in one or two key industries set the pace; others follow, many at enterprise level, with local variations. It is widely remarked that lifetime employment and the prevailing system of bonuses, which prevail in the large organisations (about a quarter of the total by employment) promote a higher degree of identification of the employee with his enterprise than is found elsewhere. As in Germany, the banks are believed to exercise considerable influence over employers' attitudes to wage bargaining.

Australia, where union membership was about 54 per cent of the labour force in the mid-1970s, shows an entirely different set of unique features (Brown, 1979). Traditionally, from early in this century, a quasi-judicial system of wage determination has operated, both federally and in four of the States, along with indexation since 1921; though (indeed, in part because) trade unions have been strong and active. Our period was marked by a decay of this system, with the abandonment of indexation in 1952, and the increasing prevalence of over-award wages and 'leapfrogging', until its partial re-establishment in 1975, but though its mode of operation has varied, collective determination of wages with the active participation of the unions has prevailed throughout.

The *Indian* trade union movement is small in relation to the whole economy (about 4½ million members), but not inconsiderable in relation to the non-agricultural sector. About 40 per cent of employees in manufacturing industry were union members in the mid-1960s. The movement consists of a large number of separate unions affiliated to national bodies which are divided on political party lines. It operates, however, in conjunction with active government-sponsored conciliation and adjudication services and with non-statutory tripartite wage boards. One view (Sinha, 1975) is that the Indian machinery for the resolution of industrial conflict is over-protective, and has inhibited the development of collective bargaining. Whether one thinks this is a good or a bad thing, it seems to imply that the system is also a very long way from leaving wage determination to the forces of an atomistic market.

Finally, the *Brazilian* labour market, in the urban sector of the economy, began our period with trade union organisations set up by the Vargas regime in the 1930s, which acted to some extent as instruments of official wage regulation in the 1950s, and also in the later 1960s, but from time to time have shown themselves capable of exercising pressure on their own account, more especially when the government of the day was sympathetic to them. Outcomes have thus depended greatly on government and union attitudes.

In this range of widely differing wage-fixing institutions, in our sample countries, perhaps the nearest to an atomistic labour market is the non-unionised sector in the United States, but even there, as we have seen, there has been an important influence from the sector in which collective bargaining prevails, apart from that arising from the mutual interest in stability of the employer–employee relationship and from occasional more direct government interventions. Elsewhere, forces ranging from statutory regulation in response to political pressure to the ability of unions to prevent the unemployed from undercutting established wage levels have removed the reality of labour markets far from the model of atomistic competition in which the market automatically clears.

CHANGES IN WAGES AND IN UNEMPLOYMENT

If the labour market cleared instantaneously, by the operation of flexible wage rates, there would be no unemployment except that due to frictional or 'search' influences which, as we have seen, might be expected to show cyclical variations of some kind, but probably not very big ones, and rather uncertain as to phase. If wage changes were quickly responsive to the direction of demand changes, but not responsive enough to keep employment constant, we should presumably have wages and unemployment moving in opposite directions, and their rates of change doing so too; there would be counter-cyclically varying amounts of involuntary unemployment. If wages were *slowly* responsive to the tightness of the market, then we should expect something like the Phillips relation – rate of change of wages varying inversely with the *level* of unemployment. Before looking at the well-known Phillips relation, let us briefly examine, for the Big Six, the relation between rates of change of unemployment and rates of change of wages (in our case, of hourly compensation, including employers' insurance contributions).

When we examine year-to-year changes in unemployment and in

wage level for our main sample countries (charts 8.1.1–8.1.6), we find a considerable variety of apparent relations, or lack of them. In the United States from 1951–64, and again (at a higher level of wage inflation) from 1968–73, and in Italy from 1953–68, there were quite wide fluctuations of unemployment change with relatively little change in the rate of wage inflation; in the former case wages appeared slightly sensitive, negatively, to unemployment, in the latter (Italy) the relation was, if anything, positive. In some instances – Germany and Japan, 1970–3, France 1959–65, and, with greater irregularity, Italy 1966–71 – the relation is negative, higher unemployment growth going with lower wage inflation with little sign of a lag from, at least, our annual data. In others – the United Kingdom 1955–69, France 1953–9, perhaps Germany 1958–69 and Japan 1959–61 – there seems to be a negative relation with wages lagging behind unemployment, which can be interpreted as a delayed response to labour market conditions. In yet others – the United States 1972–81, France 1972–6 – there is an indication of the opposite, namely a positive relation in which unemployment lags behind wages, the interpretation of which may well be that wage changes, not traceable to simultaneous or immediate unemployment changes, are incompletely accommodated by expenditure, so that opposite changes in activity (same-sign changes in unemployment) follow. Finally, there are several intriguing instances in which the evidence can be interpreted as suggesting either a negative relation with wages lagging by about a year, or a positive one with unemployment similarly lagging since we are dealing with fluctuations within a period of about four years. There is, of course, no reason why such instances should be inconsistent with two-way causal links, increased unemployment causing, with a year's delay, lower wages which, in turn, produce lower unemployment after a further year. Experience in the United Kingdom 1970–81, Germany and Japan 1973–5 or 1972–6, and Italy 1974–7 and perhaps 1979–81, lends itself to this interpretation, that either higher unemployment causes lower wages, or lower wages cause lower unemployment (both with about a year's lag) or that both these statements are true.

Besides these instances of relations which preserve some semblance of regularity over a few years, there are, of course, cases of wage change not obviously connected with alterations in the unemployment rate. Apart from the fall that occurred in several countries in 1952, there were what appear to be shocks to the wage rate in the United States 1965–8 (one down and two upwards), and upwards in 1973, and the upward shocks in Germany and the United Kingdom in 1970, Japan 1959 and 1968–9, France 1967–8 and 1979–81, and Italy 1962

Chart 8.1 *Wage inflation and the rate of change of unemployment, 1951–81*

Chart 8.1.1 *United States*

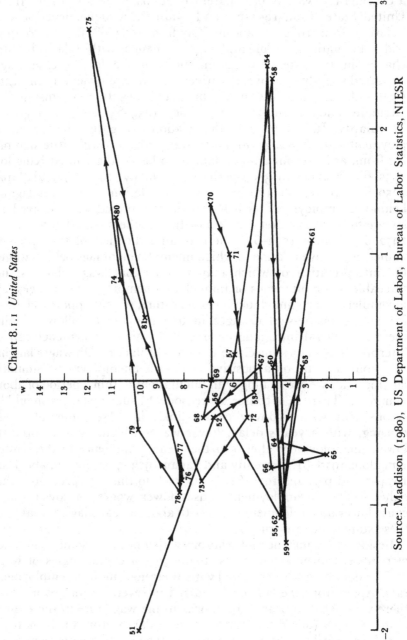

Source: Maddison (1980), US Department of Labor, Bureau of Labor Statistics, NIESR

Chart 8.1.2 *United Kingdom*

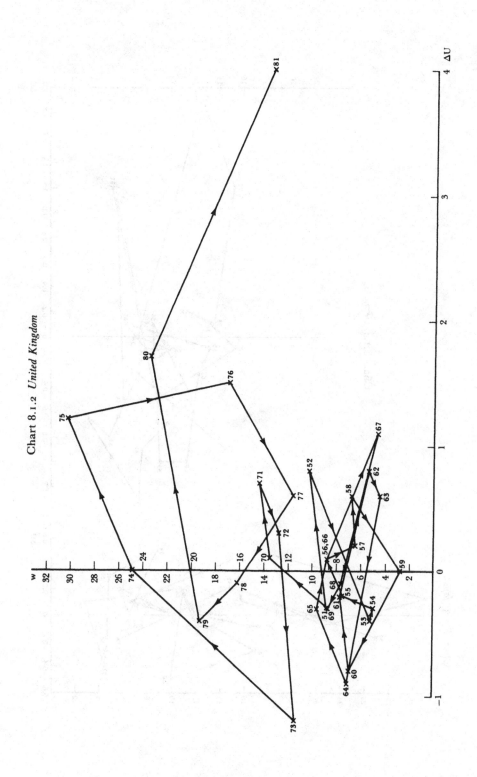

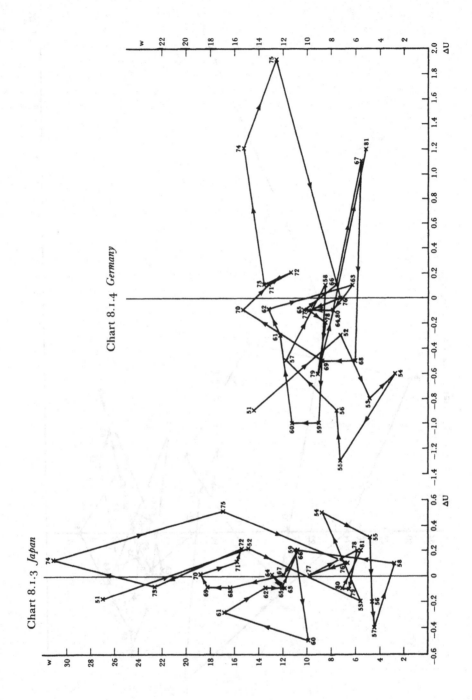

Chart 8.1.3 *Japan*

Chart 8.1.4 *Germany*

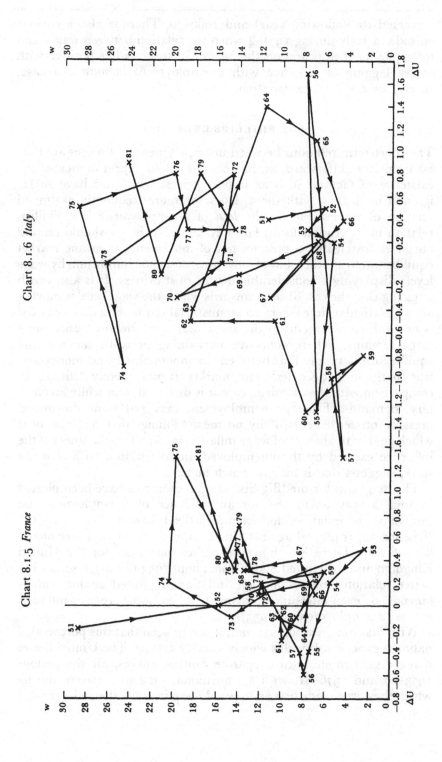

Chart 8.1.6 *Italy*

Chart 8.1.5 *France*

(reversed the following year) and 1969–70. There is also a curious episode in Italy during 1971–4 when the relation between wages and unemployment appears, on the face of it, to be either positive with wages lagging or negative with unemployment lagging – a case, surely, for a special explanation.

THE PHILLIPS RELATION

The short-term relations between unemployment and wages are thus far from straightforward, as, indeed, one might expect in view of the existence of factors, such as import prices, which we have so far ignored in dealing with them. Does the more frequently examined relation of wage *change* to the *level* of unemployment (the Phillips relation in its crudest form) fare any better? It is, we should remind ourselves, ostensibly a product not of movements from one market equilibrium to another, but of movements *towards* equilibrium by wage levels displaying a considerable degree of stickiness. It is also worth stressing that the equilibrium towards which the wage level is moving at any particular time where an atomistic labour market does not exist is not 'full employment' in the sense that only frictional unemployment remains. Where collective bargaining prevails, the notional equilibrium is simply that between the monopolistic and monopsonistic bargaining agencies. The market is not merely 'sticky'; in comparison with the atomistic case it is distorted, and while involuntary, demand-deficiency unemployment may put some downward pressure on settlements, it by no means follows that the level of it which goes with absence of wage inflation is zero. The slightness of the influence exerted by the unemployed, in comparison with those in work, suggests that it may be much higher.

The diagrams for the 'Big Six' sample countries have been plotted in such a way as to test for an influence of unemployment on rate of wage inflation, for example, the inflation rate of 1951–2 (labelled 52) is plotted against the unemployment of 1951 (see charts 8.2.1–8.2.6). There are, however, indications that, for the United Kingdom and the United States from about 1953 to 1967, a somewhat better relation emerges if wage inflation is plotted against simultaneous, or even later unemployment (for example, 1954–5 inflation against unemployment of 1955).

With that qualification in mind, it can be seen that this portrayal of national experiences yields widely varying results. The United States may be said to show two separate Phillips curves, for the periods 1953–67 and 1976–81, with a transitional time in between, during which the curve made first an upward jump in 1968, then a larger and

Chart 8.2 *Wage inflation and the level of unemployment*
Chart 8.2.1 *United States*

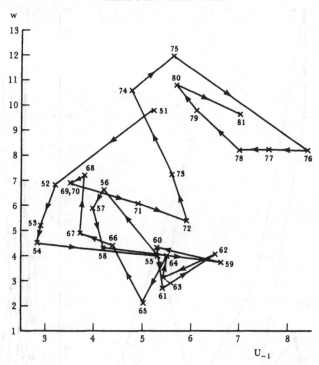

more prolonged upward shift from 1973–5. The curve of the first of these periods was very flat (although perceptibly downward-sloping), the second somewhat steeper, but still gentle, by international standards. By contrast, any curve drawn for Japan is extremely steep – steeper by a factor of perhaps twenty or forty. The different methods of measuring unemployment in the two countries may make some contribution to this (though the figures adjusted by Angus Maddison (1980) to give the greatest possible measure of international comparability have been used); nevertheless a sharp contrast certainly remains. The Japanese curve shows no permanent shift, though there are temporary wanderings, some of them plausibly relatable at least partly to import price shocks (1951, 1974, perhaps 1980 upwards, 1958 downwards).

Germany is the other country whose curve shows no permanent shifts. If the early years, up to 1954, are ignored, the only important departure from a downward-sloping line (most of it traversed in both directions) is the group of remarkably low wage increases between

Chart 8.2.2 *United Kingdom*   Chart 8.2.3 *Japan*

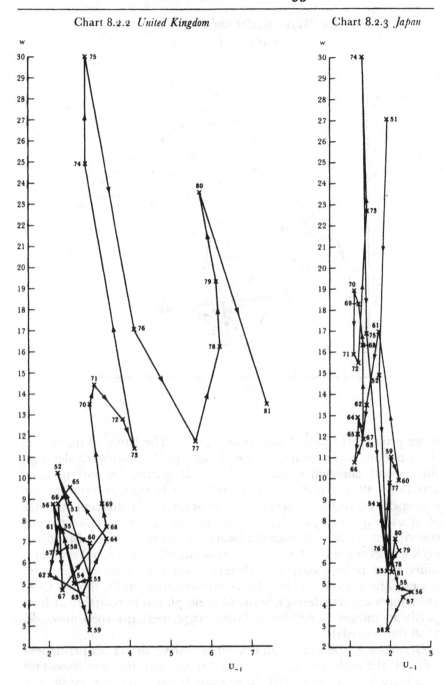

Chart 8.2.4 *Germany*

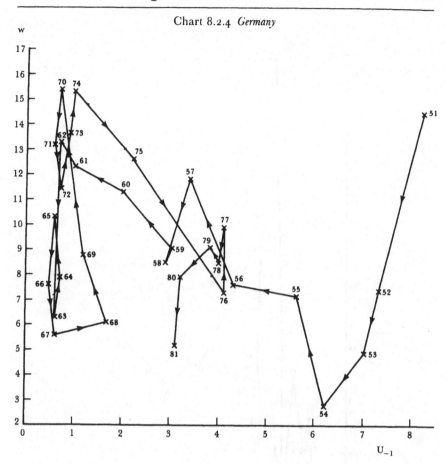

1963 and 1969. The general slope suggests remission of something approaching 2 per cent per year of wage inflation for each percentage point of the unemployment rate.

Italy and the United Kingdom agree in showing reasonably consistent relationships (at least if the year 1951 is ignored), which break down completely in the late 1960s – the British in 1968, and the Italian, after a preliminary wavering in 1967, in the following year, 1969. The British fluctuations between a little over 2 and about 3 per cent of unemployment (Maddison's adjusted figures) are accompanied by variations of three to five percentage points in the rate of wage inflation – a somewhat greater sensitivity than has just been suggested for Germany. In Italy there was little variation of either unemployment or wage inflation from 1952 to 1958, then the line traces a steepening course to the inflation peak of 1962, which is

Chart 8.2.5 *France*

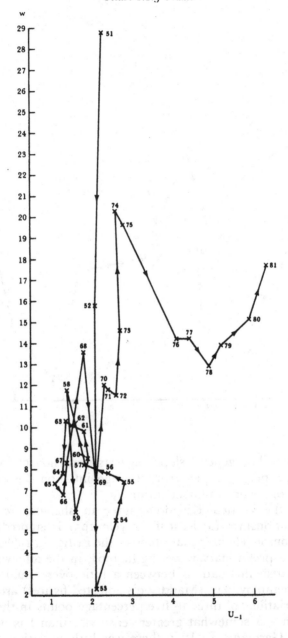

Chart 8.2.6 *Italy*

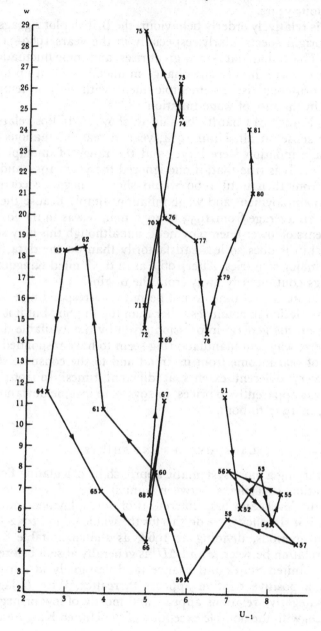

retraced downwards at a slightly lower level of unemployment in the following four years.

After this relatively orderly behaviour, the British plot zigzags away from the origin spectacularly, especially in the years 1969–71, 1975 and 1978. The Italian data show great rises, and some fluctuations, of wage inflation with hardly any change in unemployment up to 1976, then a continuous rise in unemployment with only a temporary reduction in the rate of wage inflation.

Finally, France can hardly be said to show a Phillips relation, in this crude sense, at all. Until 1974, year-to-year fluctuations in the rate of wage inflation were large, and the range of unemployment rates narrow. It is true that, if one ignored the years 1951 and 1952, the data from then until 1969 would show a negative correlation between unemployment and wage inflation, simply beause the latter was lower on average from 1953 to 1956 than it was in the following thirteen years of lower unemployment, but although this may suggest a relationship it does so less satisfactorily than do the data for our other five major countries. After 1969, as in the United Kingdom, the plot zigzags continuously away from the origin.

Available space and time do not permit a corresponding examination of this relation in countries other than the Big Six; but it is worth remarking on the general impression given by the available data for India. There, wages in manufacturing seem to have responded to the deviation of real income from its trend and to the consumers' price index to very different extents at different times. In 1964–6 the response was apparently to prices, in 1973–4 to income deviation (not to prices), in 1977 to both.

LAGS, CYCLES AND SHIFTS

It is worth trying a more systematic approach by calculating Pearsonian correlation coefficients between annual rates of wage inflation and both the levels and first differences of unemployment rate, with some lags. For simplicity, we do this for the whole period 1952–81 and for two sub-periods, dividing at 1968, as shown in table 8.1. An unlagged relation between w and ΔU[1] is generally absent before 1968, but in the United States and France (and vestigially in some other countries) a positive relation appears thereafter. With U lagged a year, only negative relations appear, and mostly of low or negligible significance, with the notable exception of the United Kingdom (both

[1] We continue our convention of using lower-case latters for proportional rates of change, upper-case for absolute quantities. Thus, $w = \Delta W/W$ where W is the level of earnings, and U is the level of unemployment.

Table 8.1 *Wage inflation and unemployment, correlation coefficients*

	$\Delta U, w$	$\Delta U', w_{+1}$	$\Delta U, w_{-1}$	$U, w_{+\frac{1}{2}}$	$U, w_{-\frac{1}{2}}$	$U, w_{-1\frac{1}{2}}$
United States						
1952–81	0.25	−0.05	0.27	0.25	0.43	0.50
1952–68	−0.02	−0.30	0.26	−0.59	−0.62	−0.37
1968–81	0.48	−0.20	0.27	0.23	0.59	0.85
United Kingdom						
1952–81	0.30	−0.15	0.63	0.44	0.46	0.72
1952–68	−0.11	−0.50	0.49	−0.29	−0.41	0.09
1968–81	0.22	−0.52	0.67	−0.05	0.08	0.57
Japan						
1952–81	0.03	−0.22	0.30	−0.65	−0.62	−0.37
1952–68	−0.04	−0.34	0.00	−0.66	−0.66	−0.43
1968–81	−0.12	−0.36	0.68	−0.70	−0.71	−0.32
Germany						
1952–81	0.23	0.00	0.53	−0.53	−0.49	−0.11
1952–68	−0.06	−0.26	0.40	−0.44	−0.51	−0.13
1968–81	0.28	−0.19	0.57	−0.64	−0.47	0.00
France						
1952–81	0.44	0.09	0.58	0.37	0.42	0.46
1952–68	0.14	−0.26	0.50	−0.02	0.07	0.33
1968–81	0.53	−0.16	0.51	0.29	0.38	0.45
Italy						
1952–81	0.17	0.01	0.36	−0.24	−0.15	−0.06
1952–68	0.06	−0.24	0.44	−0.66	−0.65	−0.40
1968–81	−0.10	0.00	0.11	0.19	0.12	0.07

sub-periods). With Δw lagged, the correlations are all positive, apart from one of zero, with high values for the later sub-period in Japan and the United Kingdom, and considerable ones in France and Germany, as also for the earlier sub-period in the United Kingdom, France, Germany and Italy. There is thus a weak tendency (stronger in the United Kingdom) for rising unemployment to be followed by less strongly rising wages, but a stronger one for rising wages to be followed by rising unemployment, with some suggestion that the latter tendency is stronger, or quicker, after 1968 than before.

The 'Phillips' relation between the level of unemployment and (forward-looking) wage inflation can be represented as $U, w_{+\frac{1}{2}}$, since the forward-looking annual first difference leads the absolute figure by half a year. It is negative and significant over the period as a whole only for Germany and Japan, as our examination of the scatter diagrams has already suggested. In Italy, the United Kingdom and the United States it is negative only before 1968, positive or negligible thereafter, and in France positive or negligible in both sub-periods; there, as well as in the United Kingdom and the United States it is positive for the period as a whole. It is noteworthy that the correlations here are generally very like those between unemployment rate and *backward*-looking wage inflation $(U, w_{-\frac{1}{2}})$ which may be taken as suggesting that the relation between the level of unemployment and the rate of wage inflation, where it exists, is a broadly simultaneous one. When a whole year of lag is added to that of wage inflation, so that its total lag in relation to unemployment is a year and a half $(U, w_{-1\frac{1}{2}})$ all the positive correlations become stronger and all the negative ones weaken.

What can we make of all this? The simplest interpretation is that we have, at least for most of the time, a trade cycle, but that there are disturbances. Let us suppose that the cycle has a period of four years (which corresponds pretty well to the facts for the greater part of our period). We have seen that there is evidence, for a good deal of the time (especially before 1968) for a simultaneous, negative, relation between U and w, the Phillips relation. With a perfect Phillips relation and sinusoidal four-year cycles, dW/dt would be a year (a quarter-period) out of phase with dU/dt and thus perfectly uncorrelated with it, (since dU/dt leads U by a quarter period). dW/dt lagged a whole year would be perfectly uncorrelated with U; lagged two years it would show perfect positive correlation with it – a situation which is being approached for some countries in our calculation in which the effective lag is a year and a half. So, for the period up to 1968 in our five major countries other than France, and for the post-1968 period in Japan and Germany, our general picture is consistent with an underlying four-year cycle and an unlagged Phillips relationship. But in regular cycles we cannot distinguish empirically between the latter and negative action of ΔU on w $(U$ on $W)$ with a year's lag – nor for that matter, direct action of w on ΔU operating with a year's lag. So far as the causal mechanism of the cycle goes, there are thus at least three quite appealing possibilities. The amount of excess supply in the labour market, signified by unemployment, may exercise a more or less proportional damping effect on the bidding-up of wages through the collective bargaining process. Or the rate of increase of unemployment may operate in this way on the collective bargaining process, but because of institutional delays the effects on wage inflation do not become fully visible for about a year. (A variant of this, indistinguishable from it empirically, is that the *level* of wage settlements adjusts negatively to the *level* of unemployment, but again that it takes about a year to happen.) Or wage inflation may bring deflationary pressures to bear, with a delay of about a year. This could happen either through its effect on public policy or by producing a balance of payments deficit and thus an outflow of money. All these mechanisms are consistent with each other and with the broad appearance

Chart 8.3 *Average annual increase in wages and average unemployment, per cent*

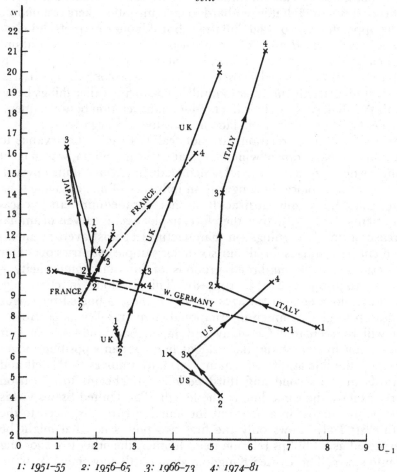

1: 1951–55   2: 1956–65   3: 1966–73   4: 1974–81

we have discerned in much of the experience of our major countries. So far as this appearance goes, any or all of them may have been operating for any or all of the duration of the more or less regular cycles.

Indeed, there is a fourth possible causal mechanism. We noted on page 208 that the Friedman–Phelps 'stale information' hypothesis suggests a negative relation between wage inflation and *frictional* unemployment, because average search time is likely to be reduced if job-seekers meet with wage offers more favourable than they expected.

This effect might contribute to an observed Phillips relation, whether the labour market clears continuously (apart from frictional unemployment) or not – though it is not hard to imagine job-seekers responding in the opposite way to wage inflation. But if labour markets did clear continuously – if *all* unemployment was frictional – then variations in unemployment and in vacancies would presumably be positively correlated. If unemployed job-seekers decide to prolong their searches, they will increase the number of unfilled vacancies, other things being equal. We shall see later that the predominant relation between unemployment and vacancies is, in fact, not positive but negative.

But these cyclical relations are not really of the first relevance to inflation, the basic rate of which, even at cyclical minima, was in most countries never zero or less, and which made important shifts upward. If we want to explore the longer-term influence of unemployment on wage inflation, we must abstract from short- or medium-term cyclical movements. It is instructive, therefore, to plot average levels of annual increase of hourly earnings (in manufacture) against average unemployment percentages for all our six major sample countries over four sub-periods chosen on broad grounds of internal homogeneity – 1951–5, 1956–65, 1967–73, 1974–81. This is done in chart 8.3. The unemployment percentages are again those adjusted by Angus Maddison to give as much international comparability as possible.

It will be seen that Germany and Japan both yield sets of four points lying in something like straight lines. Japan's position moves down, up the line and down again; Germany's moves to the left and upwards in the second and third periods, and begins to return on nearly exactly the same line in the fourth. The United States yields three points almost in a line, but the fourth greatly displaced to the north-east; Italy shows only the first two points in what might be interpreted as a Phillips relation to each other, the other two shooting out into space. The United Kingdom shows little movement between the first two periods, and that suggesting either a very steep Phillips curve or a short-term curve that moved downwards; after that something like the Italian explosion into space occurs. France shows no movement that is not in a south-westerly or north-easterly direction; no sign of a longer-term Phillips relationship at all.

Although the different workings of the national labour market and uncompensated differences remaining between the national methods of measuring unemployment enjoin extreme caution in looking for an international, cross-sectional, relationship, it is worth noting that the six national points for 1951–5 do, in fact, suggest quite a plausible line, flattening towards the right – indeed, flattening out altogether, at a wage inflation rate of about 7 per cent, above 3 or 4 per cent unemployment. In the next period, 1956–65, the 'international line' is rather less convincing; the American and British points have fallen and the Italian has risen; but it is still visible to the eye of faith. In 1966–73, there is really no line at all, though there is a very small negative correlation, the average of the two high unemployment countries, Italy and the United States, being lower than that of the other four countries. In the final period there is again no meaningful line, and the correlation between wage inflation and unemployment is slightly positive.

The general implication is that some influence or influences other than the state of the labour market, as represented by the unemployment rate, has, or have, become progressively more important during our period, but more particularly since the mid-1960s, and that this has been so only to a small extent in Germany and Japan, but to an overwhelming extent in Italy and the United Kingdom and to an intermediate extent in the United States. In France also this has been so, but there it is not possible to see that the unemployment rate, and whatever market forces it represents, ever had any systematic influence.

This brings two questions forward. First, has the unemployment rate's significance as a measure of excess supply in the labour market shifted in such a way as to help in explaining the foregoing facts? Second, what other influences on wage formation can be identified?

UNEMPLOYMENT AS A MEASURE OF EXCESS SUPPLY

Let us consider, first, the significance of unemployment as a measure of excess labour supply. Two chief hypotheses relevant here are, first, that frictional unemployment has increased because of faster technical change, and second, that a higher ratio of unemployment benefits and the like to earnings available in work has increased the number of people who, at any given time, and in a given state of demand, are taking time to search for jobs, or who do not find it worth while to search at all.

The former of these has to contend with the finding by Saunders (1981) that the rate of *structural* change in the west European countries was no greater in the 1970s than in the previous decade – indeed, slightly less great – and with the well-known view, to be considered more fully in a later chapter, that the rate of growth of productivity was also lower. Neither of these facts (if we may take them to be so) implies strictly that the rate of qualitative change in the kinds of skill demanded did not increase in the later part of our period, but together they seem to create a presumption at least that more rapid change cannot have been a major factor increasing the imperfection of the labour market.

The rise of the 'replacement ratio' of unemployment benefits to available earnings is another matter. Most of the discussion of it has related to the United Kingdom, concerning which it has even been claimed (by Benjamin and Kochin, 1979) that the high unemployment between the two world wars was in large part attributable to this cause. The claim has been effectively answered by Ormerod and Worswick (1982), who show that the ratio was poorly (in part negatively) related to unemployment in that period, its coefficient in Benjamin and Kochin's equation, unlike that of the variable used to represent pressure of demand, varying greatly in value and significance with small changes in the period studied. There is, in any case, some room for doubt about the most relevant definition of the ratio, which can be taken, for instance, as benefits payable to a qualifying family with two children, divided by average male manual earnings, or the average actually paid to a person registered as unemployed, divided by the same or some other denominator. In our period (as between the two wars) different formulations give rather different patterns, but all plausible ones show a fairly rapid increase from 1960 to a peak in 1967 or 1968 (see Trinder, 1983). Thereafter there is little change for some years, but a drastic fall (with some indicators to the level of the 1950s) begins at some date between 1974 and 1977. It is, therefore, not unlikely that a rise of the ratio made some contribution to the increase of the United Kingdom unemployment rate in the later 1960s, from 2.5 per cent (average 1950–9 using Maddison's adjusted figures) to 3.3 per cent (average 1967–74). If so, subsequent change in it (a fall) can have made only a negative contribution to the further, much larger, rise to 7.4 per cent, the average over 1977–81.

Survey data show that recipients of earnings-related benefit and substantial redundancy payments, two factors which were suspected of encouraging longer periods of unemployment when they were introduced in the late 1960s, in fact showed no systematic tendency to be unemployed for longer periods than other people of similar age. The long-term unemployed tend to be those with low potential earnings (and thus with high replacement ratios), but this association is largely (not entirely) attributable to low inherent employability by reason of age, ill-health, lack of skill and the like. A high ratio no doubt tends to keep people out of employment, but it is often the case that the high ratio and being out of employment are due to a common cause – low earning capacity.

A considerable amount of econometric work has been done on this subject relating to our period, or part of it. Maki and Spindler (1975), using a two-equation method, in which the possible influence of unemployment on the replacement ratio is allowed for, and with data for 1948–72, find an elasticity of unemployment rate with respect to the ratio of about two-thirds, which would attribute to this cause about half of the rise in unemployment (0.9 points out of 2.1) between, say, 1960 and the peak of 1971–2, with the implication, of course, that benefit-induced unemployment should have fallen rather than risen in the second half of the 1970s, as the ratio fell. Junankar (1981) subsequently challenged the significance of this result, on the ground, among others, that it holds only for Maki and Spindler's whole period, not for parts of it. Maki and Spindler also quote elasticities for the United States of 1.5 and 0.8 (by different methods) and of 0.7 for Canada. The replacement ratio for the United States, however, seems to have changed relatively little; it was only some 10 per cent higher in the decade ending in 1980 than in the 1950s, so that, on this reckoning, its increase should have accounted for only something between a third and a sixth of the two percentage points by which the unemployment rate rose between those two decades. In Canada, the ratio apparently rose sharply in 1972, and from then until 1980 stood about a third above its level of the 1950s. On a similar reckoning this might have accounted for about a third of the rise of 2.8 percentage points since the 1950s.

Holden and Peel (1977) publish estimates of the same elasticity, mostly for 1951–74, obtained in a rather different model, for the United Kingdom, United States, Australia and the Netherlands – they fail to get what they regard as reliable estimates for Canada and New Zealand. For the United Kingom their elasticity is 0.49, lower than that of Maki and Spindler, and a similar value is obtained for the Netherlands. For the United States, a value of 3.26 is obtained, which implies the attribution to this cause of nearly all the unemployment increase between the 1950s and the 1970s. The extreme instability (over a twelvefold range) of the relevant coefficient in the face of different specifications of the estimating equation, all with fairly good overall fits, and its own rather marginal t-value in the chosen specification, coupled with the great difference from other estimates, and those for other countries, suggest that little reliance can be placed upon this figure.

On this limited evidence, therefore, the rise in the replacement ratio seems to have had some effect in raising the unemployment rate, as one would expect. Its contribution to the rise in the United Kingdom in the 1960s was probably quite substantial (perhaps half of 1 per cent of occupied population), but in the United Kingdom subsequently and elsewhere over the period as a whole, its part seems to have been a minor one. For the United Kingdom, indeed, this conclusion is reinforced by the great rise of unemployment in the late 1970s and early 1980s when the ratio was falling.

For the United Kingdom also, there is a further piece of evidence which throws a rather different light on the question. Comparison of the numbers of registered unemployed with Population Census and Labour Force Survey data suggests that over 300,000, or more than half, of the increase in registered unemployment between 1971 and 1979, was due not to an increase in the number out of work, but to a greater propensity of those out of work to register (*National Institute Economic Review*, no. 106, 1983). Improved unemployment benefit may well have had much to do with this, and it is, of course, an important blemish in the most commonly used United Kingdom unemployment series, considered as an index of excess supply of labour; but it also means that the scope for attributing higher total (as opposed to registered) unemployment to the higher benefit ratio of the early 1970s is not as great as at first sight appeared. There is no evidence that completeness of registration by those out of work increased further after 1979, indeed it seems that registration by then was virtually complete.

UNEMPLOYMENT AND VACANCIES

More generally, we can turn to another source of evidence on the change in the degree of imperfection of labour markets, namely change in the relation between measures of unemployment and of unfilled vacancies. In a 'perfect' labour market, with zero search time, a plot of U against V would coincide with the axes – no unemployment so long as there were any vacancies, no vacancies so long as there was any unemployment. As imperfection is admitted into the market, the plotted curve begins to 'cut off the corner' between the axes as pressure of demand for labour varies, but it will be convex to the origin. When vacancies are low and unemployment high, a little extra demand for labour will be likely to reduce unemployment more than it adds to vacancies; when vacancies are high and unemployment low (labour scarce) it will be likely to add to vacancies more than it diminishes unemployment. This convex curve is seen very clearly in the empirical plot for Germany, where, over our period, the curve is traced in both directions. A good approximation to a straight line is obtained by plotting the logarithms of U and V against each other (call these LU and LV).

If, however, pressure of demand for labour remained constant, or if all unemployment was frictional, but the degree of market imperfec-

Chart 8.4 *Vacancies and unemployment*

Chart 8.4.1 *United States*

u = v, i where i is the correction factor applied to recorded v

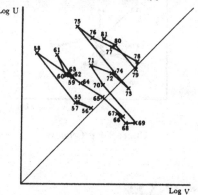

Source: Maddison (1980), OECD Main Economic Statistics, Historical Statistics

Chart 8.4.2 *United Kingdom*

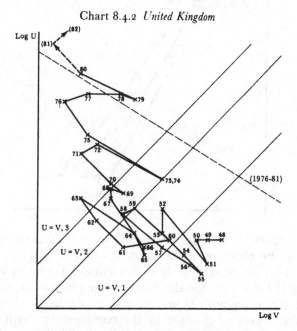

tion varied (e.g. because of variations in the propensity to spend time,
unemployed, in searching or waiting for jobs), then unemployment
and vacancies would increase and decrease together. What we find
in practice is a predominantly negative correlation between these two
variables, though with signs of shifts suggesting changes in degree

Chart 8.4.3 *Japan*

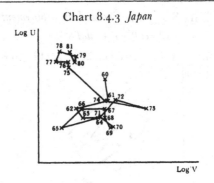

Chart 8.4.4 *Germany*

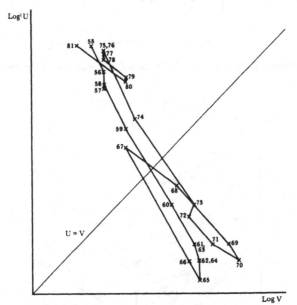

of market imperfection. Demand deficiency unemployment is not eliminated by the clearing of the market; on the contrary, variations in it are more prominent than those in frictional unemployment.

The logarithmic plot for the United Kingdom is shown in chart 8.4.2. The main difficulty of interpreting it consists in distinguishing between the effects of changes in the completeness with which the stock of vacancies was reported, and those of shifts in the schedule due to changes in the imperfection of the market.

The difficulty was discussed very fully by Dow and Dicks-Mireaux (1958) in the course of their attempt to construct an index of excess demand for labour. Reconversion, changes in the extent of official

Chart 8.4.5 *France*

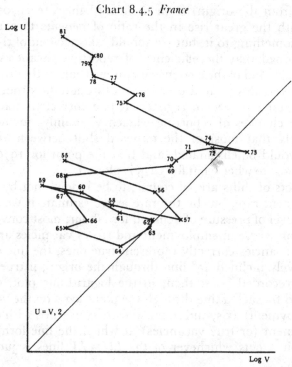

control of engagements in the aftermath of the second world war, and similar controls during the Korean war, probably account for various horizontal shifts of the line, amounting to a net move to the left, between 1948 and 1956. There were certainly considerable changes during our period in the extent to which vacancies were filled through the labour exchange service. It is estimated that the proportion of hirings in manufacturing which took place through labour exchanges, which had been two-thirds in 1949, and nearly half in 1952, fell to one-third by 1956, and probably further thereafter. There is evidence that this proportion (for the whole economy) rose by about 50 per cent between 1971 and 1979 (*National Institute Economic Review*, no. 106, 1983).

It seems that the *stock* of vacancies unfilled at the ends of reporting periods is not very sensitive to variations in the proportion of hirings taking place through exchanges, or to the proportion of vacancies notified during the period, presumably because those not notified are the more quickly filled. Inspection of our diagram, however, does suggest that the apparent leftward shift between the mid-1950s and the early 1960s may have been mainly the result of diminished efficiency of vacancy reporting. On the other hand, the shift back to the right (or away from the origin) from then until the late 1970s coincides in part with the great rise in the ratio of benefits to earnings and may owe something to it, but we should take account of the evidence just mentioned that the efficiency of reporting vacancies increased in these years, and of the evidence mentioned earlier that the efficiency of reporting employment also increased, through the stronger propensity of the unemployed to register. If one corrected chart 8.4.2 for both these changes of reporting efficiency (mainly) in the 1970s, it seems likely that most of the outward shift between 1972–6 and 1976–81 would be eliminated, and that the point for 1979 might be moved almost to where that for 1975 is plotted.

The effects of shifts are, of course, to be judged, not by the actual unemployment rate, but by the rate as we estimate it would be at a standard level of pressure of demand for labour; most conveniently in the situation where unemployment and (true) vacancies are equal. If recorded vacancies correctly represent true ones, the line of equality is a positively inclined 45° line through the origin; if true vacancies are twice recorded ones, then, in the logarithmic plot, equality is represented by such a line through the point log 2 on the vertical (log of unemployment) axis, and so on. We are concerned with the level of unemployment (or true vacancies) at which the line formed by our plotted points cuts whichever of the $LU = LV$ lines is judged to be appropriate.

There are four periods in which the plotted points define fairly distinct lines; 1952–60 (especially if we move the points for 1952 and the next couple of years to eliminate roughly the estimated effects of the Notification of Vacancies Order, of February 1952), 1961–6, 1972–6, and 1976–81. In the first three of these periods, the points describe a narrow cyclical loop or line (in the first a loop-and-a-bit). For the present purpose we have fitted lines to them by eye; there is not much scope for doubt about the general magnitudes of the unemployment rates at which they cut the respective $U = V$ lines. The final collection of points is a looser affair; it seems not unlikely that some shifting was progressing during it, but the best we can do is fit a line by least squares to the 6 points, which have some claim to represent a trough-to-trough sequence.

The outcome is as the table on the facing page.

If one believes that the efficiency of recording vacancies (whatever its actual level) remained constant over the whole period, then the $U = V$ rate fell by some 0.15 or 0.3 per cent between the 1950s and the earlier to mid-1960s, rose by 0.75 or 1.1 per cent from then to the mid-1970s, and then by a further 0.7 or 1.0 per cent by 1976–81. The rise from the lowest (second) sub-period to the final one was in round

U = V Values, per cent

Period	Correction factor applied to recorded V		
	1	2	3
1952–60	1.4	1.9	2.3
1961–6	1.25	1.7	2.0
1972–6	2.0	2.6	3.1
1976–81	2.7	3.5	4.1

figures $1\frac{1}{2}$ or 2 per cent. If one makes the extreme assumption that in 1952–60 vacancy statistics needed no inflation to make them comparable with those of unemployment (as Dow and Dicks-Mireaux believed, on the strength mainly of equality in the seasonal amplitudes of the two series), but that by 1976–81 the stock of vacancies was recorded only one-third as fully as that of unemployment, then the rise in the $U = V$ value is 2.7 per cent, starting from 1952–60, 2.85 per cent starting from 1961–6 (and assuming that all the relative deterioration in vacancy recording came after that), or perhaps 2.4 per cent starting from 1961–6, if one thinks relative recording efficiency had begun to slip by then. But, as we have noted, there is reason to believe that the efficiencies of recording of both vacancies and unemployment increased in the 1970s, so that it seems unlikely that the increase in the *true* $U = V$ value of unemployment from our first sub-period to our final one was more than $1\frac{1}{2}$ per cent.

Germany (see chart 8.4.4) displays a striking approximation to the relation one would expect from the theoretical considerations we have outlined, with very little sign that the degree of imperfection of the market has changed. The most one can discern is a possible shift at the end of the 1960s raising the $U = V$ value by less than half of one percentage point. The United States (see chart 8.4.1) shows considerable regularity in the relationship, but with a zigzagging outwards from the origin which suggests an increasing imperfection of the market – increasing at a fairly steady rate until the mid 1970s, when there are signs of stabilisation. The 'vacancies' (in fact 'Help Wanted') scale is arbitrary. If one relates it to unemployment by a factor implying that only in the late 1960s and in 1973 were vacancies in fact greater than unemployment, then the rise in the $U = V$ value between the mid-1950s and the mid-1970s appears to have been about 2 per cent.

France (see chart 8.4.5) shows, first a zigzagging in towards the origin (suggesting lessening market imperfection) from the mid-1950s to the late 1960s, then a big shift outwards, most of it perhaps before 1973 and after 1975. The vacancy statistics are so small that the proportion reported seems likely to be small, and if one scales them in such a way as to allow them to exceed unemployment in such boom years as 1957 and 1973, then one may deduce a rise in the $U = V$ value between the mid-1960s and the mid-1970s of something under 2 per cent. The ratio by which true vacancies are understated may, however, very well have varied over time.

In Japan (see chart 8.4.3) there is really nothing that looks like movement along a (U, V) curve with constant, or slowly changing, market imperfection except after 1972. In the years 1972–81, the degree of imperfection, judged by this criterion, may well have been about the same as in 1960–1, after which (from about 1962 to 1971) the $U = V$ value was lower by about 0.3 per cent. While this is a not insignificant amount in relation to the low average Japanese level of unemployment, one can perhaps conclude from this evidence that, as in Germany, changes in the degree of imperfection of the labour market in Japan have been small.

Thus, unemployment and vacancy data suggest that the United States, United Kingdom and France suffered increases in the imperfections of their labour markets during our period (in this case running to 1981) which might account, in 'full employment' $(U = V)$ conditions for extra unemployment of the order of 2 percentage points or less, while the corresponding changes in Germany and Japan would account for an extra half of one point, or less. In the United States and United Kingdom estimates of the extra unemployment attributable to a rise in the ratio of unemployment benefits to potential earnings seem to account for only part of this increase. For the United States, the rise of market imperfection seems to be responsible for most, if not all, of the rise in actual unemployment between the early 1960s and 1980–1; pressure of demand (to judge by the combinations of unemployment and vacancies) was much the same in the two periods. If, however, one compares 1980–1 with the late 1960s, when pressure of demand was higher, one can perhaps say that the 3½ per cent increase between the two periods was composed of 1½ per cent due to extra imperfection of the market and 2 per cent due to slacker demand.

In the United Kingdom, the increase in registered unemployment between the 1950s or 1960s and 1980–1 is, of course, much greater (6½ per cent or 7 per cent of which 1–1½ per cent may be attributed to increased propensity to register), and almost 4 per cent must be attributed to demand deficiency rather than additional market imperfections, though the demand deficiency arose mainly after 1979.

Up to then, increased imperfection and propensity to register accounted for most of the $3\frac{1}{2}$ per cent rise in (registered) unemployment rates. The predominance of demand as a cause of the increase of unemployment after 1979 is probably almost as great as this in France and greater in Germany, or, probably, Japan.

It has been noted that the estimated effects of higher ratios of unemployment benefits to potential earnings do not seem generally large enough to account for the whole increases of what we have (rather broadly) called labour market imperfection. What accounts for the rest? We are here treading ground so uncertain that it does not seem profitable to do more than mention possibilities. Even though, as we have noted, increased rate of change of industrial structure cannot generally be demonstrated, it may still be that the rate of change in kinds of occupational skill demanded has increased, and with it the extent of qualitative mismatch between supply and demand. It may be, too, that, with the breakdown of the long period of labour shortage at various times from the mid-1960s onwards, employers ceased to hoard labour temporarily not required to the extent that had previously become habitual, and became more disposed to take their time in finding the best candidates to fill vacancies. It is not unlikely that, quite apart from changes in the support available for the registered unemployed, the propensity to take more time between jobs increased – partly with greater general affluence, partly with changes in attitude – the 'hippie generation' must have counted for something in this connection. It is, however, important to remember that in these speculations we are concerned only with a minor part of the increase of unemployment, especially after 1979. The evidence of vacancies (not to mention common observation) makes it clear that the greater part of the increase stemmed, not from market imperfections, or employers' practices, or employees' dispositions and resources, but from an increasing lack of work on offer.

How far, then, do the changes in degree of labour market imperfection, and similar disturbances, which we have just been discussing, explain anomalies in the simple Phillips relations for the countries in question as shown (in their longer-term manifestation) in chart 8.3? We can dismiss the cases of Germany and Japan, because they have not been afflicted with systematic drifts of their Phillips curves away from the origin, and in any case the amounts of increase in labour market imperfection of which we have found evidence are in their cases very small. For France, the United States and the United Kingdom we found enough increase in labour market imperfection to explain up to two percentage points of unemployment – together with, in the United Kingdom case, another point (or a little more) accounted for by more complete registration. In these three cases, therefore, some part of the outward (or rightward) flight of the Phillips curve is explained; for the United Kingdom perhaps half of it, or even a little more; for France and the United States probably rather less than half. A good deal of the curve's apparently odd behaviour can therefore be put down, in these three countries (we have no comparable data for Italy), to the imperfection of the rate of registered unemployment as an indicator of excess supply in the labour market. But a good deal of it remains unexplained.

EXPECTATIONS

We come back, then, to influences on wage formation other than the excess supply (or deficient supply) of labour. The additional determinant of wage inflation which has been most widely and plausibly identified is, of course, inflationary expectations, generally represented by, and taken to be based upon, more or less recent experience of actual inflation. From early days in the formulation of econometric Phillips curves, an expected inflation term was added on the right-hand side. Frequently it was assumed that the variable in question could be most plausibly cast in the 'adaptive expectations' form, that is to say, as some kind of average, for each year, between what was supposed to have been expected for the previous year and what actually occurred. This amounts to an average of the rates of inflation experienced in all (in practice a finite number) of past years, with weights which decrease as one moves backwards into the past.

One objection to this procedure is that it does not allow expectations ever to catch up with accelerating inflation, whereas rationally-based expectations should be capable of doing so – they may not always be correct, but they should be unbiased, falling on both sides of the target. It will be instructive for us to assume that this is so, that expectations of inflation are expressed by two terms of which one is correct while the other is a random error term of mean value zero, which for our immediate purpose we may ignore. We therefore write the Phillips relation as:

$$w = k(\bar{U} - U) + p$$

where w and p are the rates of change of wages and prices respectively, U is the actual rate of unemployment, and $\bar{U}$ is that rate at which the labour market is in equilibrium, the 'non-accelerating inflation rate of unemployment' (NAIRU), if there is such a thing. Taking p over to

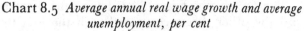

Chart 8.5 *Average annual real wage growth and average
unemployment, per cent*

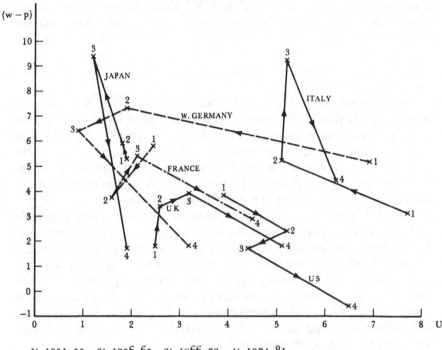

1: 1951–55   2: 1956–65   3: 1966–73   4: 1974–81

the left-hand side gives us the expression for the rate of change of the
real wage rate, so that this extreme assumption that expectations of
inflation are unbiased yields a Phillips curve relating to real, as
opposed to money, wages.

We may now plot the average values of $w - p$ for our four
sub-periods, and for each of our Big Six sample countries, against the
corresponding average unemployment rates (see chart 8.5). Comparison of the result with the previous plotting of w against U provides
some interesting suggestions concerning expectations. For the *United
States*, it will be remembered that the points for the first three periods
lay in a plausible 'Phillips' line in the nominal wage plot, with only
the fourth point shifted upwards. In the real wage plot, the third point
is apparently displaced downwards in comparison with the first two;
the suggestion is that expectations of inflation were hardly any
stronger in the third period than in the first two, and assuming that
they had risen in line with actual inflation amounts to an over-

correction. The fourth point is pulled down into a more plausible relation with the other three; compared with the first two there is some apparent over-correction, and this would be the more so if we shifted this point to the left to correct for the greater labour market imperfection we have diagnosed. In this case, only something like a third of the rise in inflation between periods 2 and 4 would have to have entered into expectations in the latter period to give a plausible modified Phillips curve.

For *Germany*, the four points lay almost exactly in a line with the nominal wage plot. Full correction for actual price inflation displaces the third and fourth points downwards in comparison with the first two; practically all of the correction for extra inflation (in comparison with the first two periods) in respect of the third and fourth point seems to be over-correction. The implication is that very little of the increase in German inflation entered into expectations.

The full price correction for *Japan* produces a more plausible picture for the first three periods, but a suggestion of over-correction for the fourth, when, as in Germany, and nowhere else in our Six, the actual rate of wage inflation was reduced. The suggestion that the degree of incorporation of current inflationary experience into expectations was lower in the fourth period than in the other three is hardly a plausible one, however; we should perhaps look for other influences disturbing the hypothetical relation between wage inflation and the pressure of unemployment.

If we allow that registered unemployment was increased by greater labour market imperfection and higher registration in the *United Kingdom* as much as we have suggested above, then a plausible Phillips curve demands only that something like half of the rate of inflation in the fourth period had entered into expectations (and a smaller proportion in the third period). If, however, we regard much less of the unemployment increase as non-indicative of excess labour supply, then it is possible to make sense of the assumption that the inflation rates of these two later periods had entered fairly fully into expectations.

The French data can be fitted to a regular, negative, relation between unemployment and wage inflation only if it is assumed that experience of price inflation entered into expectations to a large extent in periods 1 and 4, a moderate one in period 3, and in period 2 hardly at all, and this – especially the relatively high confidence in the value of money in 1955–65 – while not entirely incredible, is harder to believe than the hypotheses required in the other countries so far discussed, especially as actual price inflation in the period in question was not very much lower than in those immediately preceding and following it. If we allow that the rise of unemployment rate to period 4 overstated the increase in excess supply of labour, as suggested above, the proportion of that period's inflation that seems likely to have entered into expectations is reduced to perhaps not much more than a half. For *Italy*, the assumption that inflationary experience entered fully into expectations in each period brings the point for the high-inflation period 4 almost exactly into line between those for periods 1 and 2 (when there was little inflation), but most of the leap in wage inflation between periods 2 and 3 is left unexplained. It seems that this leap, largely associated with the 'hot autumn' of 1969, is not explicable by the labour market forces we have been considering.

So far as expectations are concerned, therefore, the suggestion of this rough survey is not out of line with the more direct evidence of general inflationary expectations in chapter 5; there is little evidence that expectation of a continuation of the current rate of inflation was ever fully built into wage settlements in the main OECD countries – Italy, in period 4, when wage indexation was in operation, is an understandable exception. If one makes what seem reasonable adjustments to the unemployment rate, where possible, to make it more representative of the amount of slack in the labour market, one can partially restore a Phillips curve interpretation of wage inflation in most of these countries, granted that current inflation entered partially (often to the extent of about half) into settlements in the late 1970s.

It is, in fact, possible to argue (and Okun, 1981, has done so on the strength of United States evidence) that expectations have not been very important in wage settlements; that demands in particular have been influenced more by a desire to retrieve the real income losses of some recent period than by any peering into the future. Of course, if settlements always fully reflected the inflation of (say) the past year, they would, as between periods each of several years' duration, such as we have been considering, reflect those periods' inflation rates fairly closely. That they fail to do so is no doubt due to the fact that settlements depend on many other variables which we have not been able to take into account – and perhaps particularly to the fact that some of the biggest price increases have been connected with pushes from non-wage costs, and that such pushes do not create favourable conditions for wage concessions. At all events, whether through expectations which only partially reflect the impacts of current experience, or through incomplete success in making nominal wages track the recent movements of consumers' prices, those prices appear to have exercised mostly incomplete influence on the variations of wage inflation, and their strongest influence was manifested only late in our period.

OTHER INFLUENCES

There are, of course, plenty of other factors which may be expected
to have influenced wage inflation. Given the monopolistic character of
much wage bargaining, change in the relative bargaining power of
employees and employers, insofar as it is not already represented by
the level of unemployment or the state of price expectations, might be
considered a candidate, and some systematic studies have, indeed,
tried to take it into account. The trouble is that it is not easily
measured. The bargaining strength, or aggressiveness, of labour –
generally taken as the dominant component of the variable – is not
well represented by trade-union membership (though that is clearly
not entirely irrelevant to it), since the mood of members may be as
important as their number. Nor is it well represented by measures of
strike activity, though they have, perhaps, a stronger claim. Union
bargaining power depends on the effective threat of strike action
rather than on how much there actually is of it, and the connection
between the two is loose. It is, however, possible to identify periods of
especial aggressiveness (the French 'events of May' 1968, and the
Italian 'hot autumn' of 1969, for instance) which at least in their
timing and intensity, are not easily accounted for by market forces of
the kind we have been considering. Moreover, the gradual growth of
unionisation and of enthusiasm for collective bargaining in the United
Kingdom during our period, especially among groups where it had
traditionally been weak or absent, can hardly have failed to affect the
trend of wage and salary inflation.

There are also variations in wage inflation which go with changes in
the mechanisms of wage settlement – official incomes policies and
their collapses, the rise and fall of unofficial arrangements for central
bargaining, the more gradual changes in the shape of dispersed
bargaining arrangements. We shall look later at some econometric
studies of the effects of incomes policies. Among other institutional
factors which may help to explain peculiarities of the relation between
unemployment and wage inflation is the extremely high elasticity of
supply of foreign labour migrating into Germany in the 1960s; this
may well account for the very moderate wage settlements from 1963 to
1970 in the face of low unemployment – the latter did not in the
circumstances reflect a corresponding tightness of the labour-market.
It may, however, also be significant that this was the period in which
central policy was first able to benefit from the reports of the Council
of Economic Experts, and that the formal system of 'concerted action'
whereby negotiations take place in the light of national meetings
between the Council, the Central Bank, the government, and em-

ployees' and employers' representatives, was instituted in 1967. In countries where central bargaining has prevailed (mainly the smaller countries, such as the Netherlands, Denmark, Sweden) and in Australia, with its traditionally quasi-judicial method of wage fixing, the outcome of a particular year's bargaining can show particular sensitivity to its political circumstances and the tactics and accidents of the battle, including the possible breakdown of the machinery in question, with or without the consequent intervention of government. It is particularly relevant for Australian events that the Conciliation and Arbitration Commission system gradually broke down after 1953, and, after widespread alarm at the severe inflation of 1974, was reestablished in the following year.

WAGE EQUATIONS

This broad and cursory inspection of wage changes is perhaps some preparation for a discovery of rather uneven success in the more systematic investigations which have been made by attempting to fit wage equations. It may be useful, before reviewing such attempts, to summarise some features which one may expect to find in equations of this sort.

First, single equations with the level of money wages as the dependent variable may be intended (or, at least, interpreted) as reduced forms of two-equation, supply and demand, equilibrium models in which it is assumed that the market clears – supply equals demand. Anything, such as labour productivity or level of monetary demand, which has a positive effect in shifting the demand curve can appear on the right-hand side with a positive sign; so can anything, such as the level of unemployment benefit, increase of which may be expected to shift the supply curve to the left. The meaning of such equations, on this interpretation, would be muddied by the appearance of unemployment among the explanatory variables, since it is presumed to be voluntary, an equilibrium phenomenon explained by such things as the level of benefit, and to be unaffected by changes in monetary demand, to which the wage level adjusts. An equilibrium equation of this sort could, of course, equally well appear with *all* the variables in the form of first differences, but it would be hard to interpret a mixed (integral and first-difference) version, with explanatory variables such as we have instanced. It is, however, possible to make use of the expression for the equilibrium wage rate in a model which allows deviations from it. All that is necessary is to subtract the actual wage from the expression supposed to give the equilibrium one, and to make the rate of wage change a function of this difference. Practically all the equations we shall note in effect do this.

The simple Phillips curve, the mother of modern wage equations, may be regarded as the most basic instance. The assumption is that rate of wage inflation is proportional to the difference between a 'natural' rate of unemployment, the rate at which, given stable prices (or, at least, the expectation of them), wages would also be stationary, and the actual rate of unemployment ruling. Given that the fixing of wages is for a finite future period, it is reasonable to suppose, further, that if both parties to the bargain have the same, firm, expectation of an increase in prices (let us say both of wage goods and of the products of the industries for which wages are being fixed), then this expectation will be built into the settlement, over and above whatever the state of the market would have produced with prices expected to be constant. A price-expectations term is therefore added, and the logic of the argument suggests that it should have a coefficient of unity. If it is then taken over to the left-hand side of the equation, we have there the difference between wage inflation and expected price inflation, and it is this – not wage inflation by itself – that is now described as varying in proportion to the difference between the natural and actual rates of unemployment.

This (though usually, of course, written with expected price inflation on the right-hand side) is the expectations-augmented Phillips Curve. Estimation of it suffers from the difficulty that neither the natural rate of unemployment nor the general state of relevant price expectations is normally observable; changes in the former have to be represented (if at all) by a term for whatever is thought to affect it, such as the ratio of unemployment benefit to average earnings in work, while expected price change has to be estimated as a confection of past inflation rates, or, occasionally, by figures derived from opinion surveys. The equation, however, suffers even more from the difficulty of economic logic to which Friedman (1968) drew attention, namely, that if the parties learn by experience to expect price inflation equal to current wage inflation, it implies actual unemployment tied to the natural rate, with inflation or deflation indeterminate – the Phillips curve becomes a vertical line with a horizontal intercept representing the natural rate. (The introduction of advancing labour productivity modifies this conclusion without solving the problem).

The third principal kind of equation is derived from a view of money-wage formation as resulting from collective bargaining in which concern is with real wages, and in which the bargaining power of employees is exercised with some effect and to a varying extent, depending on the amount by which real wage has fallen below some target level, which itself depends on the strength of the bargaining position. The target level is taken to be a function of the difference between natural and actual rates of unemployment. It is usual to include also a price-expectations term. The equation may, therefore, be not very unlike an augmented Phillips curve into which the recent level of real wages has been inserted as an additional term. There are, however, numerous possible variations upon this essential theme. They include those in which some measure of trade union bargaining strength, usually union membership or union density (percentage of the workforce who are union members) is included. Hines (1969) was a pioneer of this device.

International wage equations
The principal attempts to fit similar wage equations for a number of countries are those of Gordon (1981), Perry (1975) and Laidler (1976), dealing with the periods 1954–73, 1960–72 and 1954–70 respectively, and a more recent one by Davies (1983). Gordon's investigation is part of a wider one, concerned also with equations of price and of money supply, to which we refer elsewhere. He uses an equation analogous to the augmented Phillips curve, but with the ratio of actual to potential output as the measure of disequilibrium, and changes in money supply and in traded goods prices as the factors bearing on equilibrium wage, and with a lagged wage-inflation term added for 'inertial' effects. Perry's is a form of augmented Phillips curve, with unemployment, various lagged price changes and changes in lagged wages as the explanatory variables (along with some experimental dummies for policy and other influences). Laidler's study is part of a double one, in which price and wage equations derived from what the author puts forward as a more 'sociological' approach (wage change regressed on unemployment and strikes) are tried against other price equations in which expectations based on both world and domestic price inflation are included, along with a measure of the gap between actual and full-employment output, and in the wage equations unemployment rate also.

Some results are summarised in table 8.2. It is not surprising that Perry, and to a lesser extent Gordon, find evidence of inertia in wage inflation (the lagged wage variable significant) in some countries, more so that Gordon finds a significant negative influence for it in Sweden, although the existence of a two-year settlement cycle may be important here. Perry finds lagged domestic prices, as measured by the GDP deflator, more important than lagged wages in the United States and Germany, but not in the United Kingdom, Japan, France or Sweden. Neither is found to be significant in Italy and the

Table 8.2 *International wage inflation equations: signs and statistical significance of selected explanatory variables*

Explanatory variables		United States	United Kingdom	Japan	West Germany	France	Italy	Sweden	Canada	Netherlands
Lagged wage	A)	o*	o	o*	o	o	o	−	o	...
inflation	B)	(+)	+	+	(+)	+	o	+	+ᵃ	o
	C)	...	...	...	...	...	...	...	...	...
Domestic	A)	...	...	...	...	...	...	...	...	...
price	B)	+	...	...	+	...	o	...	...	o
inflation:	C)	...	...	...	...	...	...	...	...	...
current and										
lagged values										
External	A)	o	o	o	o	o*	o*	+**	o	...
price	B)	o	+	o	o	o	o	+	o	o
inflation:	C)	...	...	...	...	...	...	...	...	...
current and										
lagged values										
Output gap/	A)	o	o	o	o	o	o	o	o	...
inverse of	B)	+	o	+	+	o	+	o	+	o
unemploy-	C)	+	+	+	+	...	+	...	...	...
ment rate										
Rate of	A)	+	+	o	o	+**	o*	−**	o	...
change of	B)	...	...	...	...	...	...	...	...	...
money supply	C)	...	...	...	...	...	...	...	...	...
Wage-push	A)	...	+	o	+	+	+	+	...	...
dummy		...	o	o	...	...	+	+	...	...
measure of	B)	...	+	o	+	+	o	+	...	...
strike activity	C)	+	+	−	o	...	+	...	...	...
Incomes	A)	−	o	...	o	o	...	o	...	...
policy		o	−	...	...	...	...	...	...	...
dummy	B)	o	−	...	...	...	...	−	...	...
	C)	...	...	...	...	...	...	...	...	...

Sources: A) R. J. Gordon (1981), Quarterly data 1958:3 – 1973:1.
B) G. L. Perry (1975), Annual data 1960–1972.
C) D. E. W. Laidler (1976), Annual data 1954–1970.

Key: +/−: statistically significant, positive/negative } see notes under.
o: Statistically insignificant
...: not included

ᵃUnited States wages.
Notes: The reader should bear in mind that the results presented above are necessarily in very summary form and that the complexities of the authors' arguments may therefore be obscured. The reader is thus encouraged to consult the original texts for more detailed results.

A) *GORDON* (Equation (4) tables 4, 7–12; equation (3) table 6).

1. Significance is taken to mean significant at the 5 per cent level using a one-tailed test.
2. All coefficients and their t-ratios represent the sum of a series of freely estimated coefficients of up to four lags. In some cases where the sum of coefficients is not statistically significant, individual lagged coefficients may be significant. These are not shown here.
3. The superscript * indicates that the coefficient becomes significantly positive when the equation is extended to 1976:4. The superscript ** indicates that the coefficient becomes insignificant when the equation is extended to 1976:4.
4. The level of the ratio of actual output to potential output (based on Artus' indexes) is the measure of the output gap.
5. M1 is used as the money measure for all countries except Canada and France for which M2 is used.
6. The wage-push dummies refer to the following periods: United Kingdom 1970:1 – 1971:1; [1963:2 – 1964:1, 1970:1 – 1970:4, 1974:2 – 1975:1], re-entry dummy after a period in which an incomes policy is in effect. Japan 1967:4 – 1968:4; 1970:1 – 1970:4. West Germany 1969:4 – 1970:2. France 1968:2 – 1968:3. Italy 1962:1 – 1964:4; 1970:1. Sweden 1969:4 – 1970:2; 1971:3 – 1972:2 [re-entry dummy].
7. The incomes policy dummies refer to the following periods: United States 1963:1 – 1966:2; 1971:3 – 1974:1. United Kingdom [1961:3 – 1961:4, 1966:3 – 1966:4, 1972:4 – 1973:1] freeze dummy; [1962:1 – 1963:1, 1967:1 – 1969:4, 1973:2 – 1974:1, 1975:2 – 1976:4], restraint dummy. West Germany 1967:1 – 1969:3. France 1964:1 – 1965:4. Sweden 1970:3 – 1971:2.

B) *PERRY* (tables 2, 4, 6).

1. Significance here is taken to mean a t-ratio of two or more ($\geq/2/$).
2. Wage inflation is lagged one year, except in the case of Sweden where a two-year lag is imposed.
3. In the cases of the United States and West Germany lagged wage inflation is significant if domestic price inflation is excluded from the regression, but the equation performs somewhat 'better' (that is, higher $\bar{R}^2$ and lower standard error) if domestic price inflation is included and lagged wage inflation dropped.
4. Domestic prices refer to the private, non-farm deflator.
5. The inverse of the unemployment rate is used for all countries except Japan and the Netherlands for which an output gap measure proved superior.
6. The wage-push wage-shares dummies refer to the following years: Japan, France; 1968. United Kingdom, West Germany, Italy, Sweden; 1970.
7. The incomes policy dummies are operative in the following cases; United States 1964–66, United Kingdom 1967, France 1964–65, Sweden 1971.

C) *LAIDLER* (table 3, $\Delta W = \alpha_0 + \alpha_1 y + \alpha_2 S$, where y is the output gap and S is the number of man days lost in disputes).

1. Again, significance has been taken to mean a t-ratio of 2, or more, correctly signed.
2. For Italy, both independent variables are lagged one period.

Netherlands, and in Canada lagged United States wages appear to be an important influence. Lagged traded goods prices are found significant by Gordon in Sweden (although not when the sample period is extended to 1976), but not elsewhere, although they do become significant in France and Italy when the mid-1970s are included in the sample period.

Nor is Gordon's output-gap measure found to be significant in any country. Part of its thunder may, however, have been stolen by his money supply variable (to the extent that money growth is cyclical), which is positively significant for the United States, the

United Kingdom and France, and for Italy when the sample period is extended, as well as negatively for Sweden. Direct effects of money supply on the labour market (or all markets) are not easy to envisage, though money injection may well accompany wage inflation in order to accommodate it, and may also, for the same reason, accompany import-price inflation, as in the United Kingdom and France in 1958–9 and the former also in 1962–3 and 1971–2 and wage inflation may follow.

Perry, however, does find a significant Phillips-type influence of unemployment rate in the United States, Germany, Italy and Canada and also a significant coefficient on an output gap measure for Japan, but not in the United Kingdom, France, Sweden or the Netherlands. Laidler, in contrast, finds the output gap significant in the United Kingdom.

Dummy variables for wage-push, not otherwise explained, are found significant by both Gordon and Perry for the United Kingdom, Germany, France and Sweden and by Gordon for Italy while Laidler finds that working days lost in strikes taken as a measure of trade union pushfulness, is significant in the United States,. the United Kingdom and Italy, but perversely signed in Japan. Finally, so far as these three studies are concerned, Gordon finds dummies representing the effects of incomes policy significant for 1963–6 in the United States, and for various periods in the United Kingdom (see notes to table 8.2). Perry finds significant effects for 1967 in the United Kingdom, 1964–5 in France and 1971 in Sweden.

Differences of methodology and of period covered make these studies hard to compare. All the explanatory variables we have mentioned are found to be significant somewhere, by at least one investigator, but Laidler's finding that a disequilibrium variable as measured by the output gap is significant in all his sample countries is the nearest thing to a discovery of universal validity, and against this, presumably, has to be set off Gordon's failure to find any significant coefficient on this variable. Taking all three studies together, the disequilibrium variable is significant in just under a half of the cases (a 'case' being a particular equation fitted to a particular country), as are lagged wages. Lagged domestic prices, and/or lagged foreign trade prices are significant in a quarter of the cases in which they were tested. The type of variable found significant in the greatest number of cases was that connected with wage-push – either Laidler's strike activity variable or a 'wage-push' dummy inserted to deal with some episode, such as the French 'events of May', associated with well marked labour militancy, not otherwise explained. Such significance occurred fourteen times in the 22 equations relating to our sample countries, although given the nature of these dummies this is perhaps not very surprising. Gordon and Perry also inserted incomes policy dummies where they thought them relevant; one or more of them attained significance in four of their seventeen cases, or, to put it otherwise, four out of the ten in which they were tried.

Davies (1983) has fitted to the 1954–80 data for ten OECD countries four simple equations; an expectations-augmented Phillips equation, and that same equation fortified by the inclusion, respectively, of variables relating to strike frequency, working days lost in disputes, and periods of official incomes policy. He finds that for the United States, the Phillips relation works moderately well, but strike and policy variables do not improve it; that for the United Kingdom the expected sign is obtained in the Phillips relation only if strike frequency is included, and that the policy variables work; that for Japan a Phillips-type relation (using vacancies instead of the inverse of unemployment) works, but strike variables effect no improvement; for Germany a rather similar result, but with some effect attributable to 'concerted action' on wage restraint in the periods 1967–9 and 1972–3 (and that recent price inflation, presumed to represent expectations, had relatively little effect); that for France a Phillips-type relation, using vacancies, works, along with a dummy variable for the events of 1968; and that for Italy unemployment appears not to be significant, but that the price (expectations) term and strikes, especially as represented by working days lost, are. These results are not out of line with our own conclusions from our more cursory examination of the data, except that the emergence of any Phillips-type relation for France is rather surprising – vacancies are perhaps in this case a better indicator of labour market conditions than the unemployment rate is.

These cross-country studies thus provide some evidence of the non-uniformity of wage determining mechanisms as well as the difficulties (largely data difficulties) and the fragility of wage equations of the, broadly, augmented Phillips type. It does, however, appear that the original Phillips (disequilibrium) term refuses entirely to lie down, while supply curve and policy disturbances are shown to play prominent parts in some countries, and important roles for prices, and expectations based upon them, were (as seen from the mid-1970s, at least) very far from universally demonstrable by the methods under review.

There are, of course, also many single-country econometric studies of wage determination. For the United States, it may suffice to consider three, namely those of Nadiri and Gupta (1977), Gordon (1977) and Perry (1980).

Wage equations in the United States
The equation fitted by Nadiri and Gupta resembles their price
equation, which we describe elsewhere. Its intention is to relate the
equilibrium level of hourly earnings in a reduced form of the supply
and demand equations to the variables which should shift it – the
trend rate of change of productivity and the consumers' price index –
and to provide for the geometric adjustment of actual earnings
towards that equilibrium at rates proportional to the disturbances
from equilibrium; signified by departures of productivity from trend,
lagged wages, unemployment, its rate of change, and expectations of
inflation (based on lagged consumer price increases). A dummy
variable is also inserted to represent the effect of the wage and price
'guideposts' of 1962–7. The equation is fitted both to data for the
whole economy and to those for manufacturing for the period 1954 to
mid-1971; also to separate industry group data with which we are not
concerned.

Unemployment (or rather, its inverse) does not prove significant;
rate of change of unemployment, which one might interpret as a
business expectations variable, does, especially in manufacturing,
though with a small (negative) coefficient. So, with a positive
coefficient, does the deviation of productivity from trend. It seems that
wages adjust to price level at all completely only in the longer run, (in
the manufacturing sector the evidence even for this is poor) high
coefficients on lagged wages indicate a large measure of inertia,
especially in manufacturing, and those on rate of price change, an
acceleration term, are well below unity (about 0.5). The 'guidepost'
dummy is significantly negative.

Gordon investigates the performance of a price–wage model which
he originally specified in 1971, to see how well it tracked the inflation
of the 1970s. We consider here his 'structural' wage equation which
may be regarded as a rather unusual version of the expectations-
augmented Phillips type – the price equation is considered elsewhere.

The dependent variable is the two-quarter rate of change in a
private hourly earnings index which is adjusted to exclude the effects
of changes in overtime and of inter-industry employments shifts and
which includes an adjustment for the effects of changes in fringe
benefits. Labour market tightness is proxied by three variables –
unemployment dispersion among demographic subgroups, the 'disguised unemployment rate' (the difference between the actual labour
force and its trend) and the 'unemployment rate of hours' (the
difference between private hours per week and its trend).

Two price variables are included – a distributed lag of past changes
in the personal consumption deflator and the difference between

changes in the 'product price' (the non-farm deflator) and the consumption deflator. A rate of change in the employee tax variable is also included.

Over the period 1954:1 – 1971:2, two of the labour market variables, the disguised unemployment rate and the unemployment rate of hours, are significant and correctly signed. Both of the price variables are significant and the coefficient on each is very close to unity. Since the two coefficients are numerically so close, Gordon concludes that wage change fully incorporates changes in price inflation, but that it is influenced by changes in product prices, not consumer prices. This finding implies that demand conditions in the product market are important in determining wage change and to test this hypothesis the labour market variables are replaced by two product market variables – the gap between actual and potential output, and the first difference in the gap. The standard errors of estimate improve slightly and the predictive ability of the output-gap equation is, in general, superior. Somewhat surprisingly only the rate of change of the output gap is significant and has a far larger coefficient than the output gap itself. One further aspect of Gordon's equations is that post-sample predictions, using alternative price indices, appear to show that none of the 1973–4 inflation in food and energy prices 'got into' wages. It may be that the severity of the subsequent recession mitigated the price feedbacks on to wages, that otherwise would have occurred.

Both equations are extended through to the end of 1976. Dummy variables are included to cover President Nixon's price and wage controls, but these imply not only that controls in 1971–2 did not hold down wages, but that wages increased more than would have been expected in the light of the moderating impact of the controls on price inflation. The other major difference from the pre-1971 results is that the coefficient on the output gap is now also significantly negative and shows a marked increase in size. Gordon argues that this reflects the effectiveness of the 1975–6 recession, in contrast with that of 1970–1, in holding down wage inflation.

Perry's model of wage inflation, estimated in 1980, is an extension of the so-called mainline, or neo-Keynesian model – that is an economy with quantity adjusting markets and involuntary cyclical unemployment, in which the Phillips curve represents the short-run response of wage inflation to cyclical variations in employment. Perry rejects the idea of a natural rate of unemployment identifiable with the point at which inflation neither increases nor decreases. His view of the job market is similar to Okun's in which most firms maintain fairly long-term career relationships with their workers, so that variation in demand makes for variation in employment rather than in wages. However, another, smaller, part of the labour market operates more nearly as an auction market, and wages here are relatively sensitive to firms' employment needs and to the state of the market. Even so, wages in this part of the market are influenced by wage levels in general.

Perry distinguishes between two parts of the nominal wage-setting process: one that is the response of wages to unemployment and demand, the cyclical part associated with the short-run Phillips curve; and one that is the response of nominal wages in individual firms to a wage norm or trend for the economy which, by definition, is unrelated to current employment or demand. The cyclical mechanism he describes makes wage changes depend on both the rate of unemployment and its proportionate rate of change. The idea of a wage norm stems, again, from Okun and represents an extension of the notion of an 'habitual' or persistent rate of wage increase not immediately aimed at particular allocational results. The determinants of changes in this norm are left somewhat vague, although Perry argues that it is at least partly an adaptive response to past rates of wage increase. Thus, for example, the sustained wage inflation that arose from reducing unemployment in the late 1960s did eventually raise the norm. The self-reinforcing character of wage and price inflation where (as in the natural rate hypothesis) wages respond fully and quickly to prices is much modified here.

Unlike those in models which use lagged wages to account for persistent inflation, Perry's changes in norm are episodic rather than continuous. Two norm shifts are identified – the first downward shift after 1961, which allows for the cumulative impact of two quick recessions separated by only an abortive recovery during 1958–61, and the second upward shift starting in 1970 for the reason given above. Each shift is modelled by a dummy variable equal to 1 or zero.

The dependent variable is the quarterly change in the average hourly earnings index. The cyclical effects are accounted for by the (inverse of the) level of unemployment, the change in unemployment and lagged wage adjustment. A demographically weighted unemployment rate is used throughout. A shift dummy on unemployment is used to test whether the Phillips curve 'rotated' in the 1970s. Lagged changes in the CPI are used to incorporate a direct cost-of-living adjustment. A dummy variable, from 1964:1 to 1966:2 is used to account for the effects of guideposts under President Johnson. In order to deal with the period of Nixon controls, which cannot be explained well with a dummy variable, the quarters from 1971:3 – 1975:1 are excluded.

In the period from 1954:1 to 1969:4 both unemployment and lagged unemployment are significant with the coefficient on the latter roughly half the size of the former. (The change in unemployment is excluded here). The lagged consumer price index is significant and enters with a coefficient of one third. Both the guidepost dummy and the 1950s dummy are significant and correctly signed.

When the period is extended to 1980:1, omitting 1971:3 to 1975:1, and a significantly negative slope shift dummy for the 1970s is included, the coefficients on unemployment become larger, indicating a greater response of wages to unemployment than in the 1950s and 1960s. However, when the crucial quarters 1970:1 to 1971:2 are also omitted, the slope shift dummy for the 1970s becomes insignificant and the unemployment coefficients are reduced in size, to become much more consistent with the pre-1971 estimates. In addition, when both the data from 1970:1 to 1975:1 and the slope shift dummy for the 1970s are omitted, the norm shift dummy for the 1970s is substantially reduced in size, although still significant. Perry argues that during the early 1970s the transition to a higher norm was taking place while the economy was in recession. When the data for these quarters are included in the regressions the two shift effects from the norm and the slope are both overestimated, but with offsetting effects on predicted wages.

In a further set of estimates the unemployment variable is given a specific lag structure and the change in unemployment is also included. As in previous studies the latter is significantly negative. The effects of the slope shift dummy for the 1970s are similar to those recorded above, and the omission of this variable and the data from the early 1970s give more consistent results.

The other notable change when the equation is extended through to 1980 is that the coefficient on the lagged consumer price index is reduced in size by a third. This indicates that the very rapid rise in the CPI in the 1970s was not passed through to wages to the extent that smaller previous rises had been. Perry notes that although among major unions indexing became more widespread and, for modest inflation rates, more complete during the 1970s, the proportion of wages covered by major union contracts dropped during the decade.

The norm shifts indicate a decline of about 0.8 percentage points in the rate of wage inflation after 1961 and an increase of about 3.5 points in the late 1970s. When a lagged dependent variable is included, it is not significant.

It is possible to draw some broad conclusions from these three studies. On the labour supply side a feature is the relative lack of importance of changes in consumer prices in influencing wage inflation, particularly in the 1970s. It would appear that between 20 and 40 per cent of any change in consumer prices has been reflected in current wage inflation. (Gordon's more recent estimate (Gordon, 1980), shows a 25 per cent pass-through from consumer prices to wages.) In the light of the rapid price increases in the mid-1970s this meant a sharp decline in real wages at this time. In contrast, the labour demand variables do appear to be important. For example, in the study by Nadiri and Gupta the deviation of productivity from trend is significant and in Gordon's work the coefficient on product prices is significant and equal to one – a similar result to that found by Perry in his international study mentioned above. Both the level of unemployment, or the output gap, and their rate of change affect wage inflation, although the high wage inflation during the 1970–1 recession is not explained by the usual Phillips curve relationship. The effectiveness of the various income policies in the United States is discussed below.

Wage equations in the United Kingdom
For practical purposes wage equations start with the Phillips curve. The original relation between unemployment and wage inflation, calculated by A. W. Phillips in 1958, was, of course, based upon United Kingdom data – in fact on data running back to 1861. It was derived by fitting the logarithms of average rates of wage increase (*plus* a constant determined by trial) which had been experienced in each of a number of ranges of unemployment rate, to the logarithms of the averages of those ranges. No term representative of price inflation or of price expectations was included, though Phillips discussed his results on the basis that his unemployment effect might reasonably be treated as an (inverted) measure of the influence of demand-pull in the labour market, the actual changes in retail prices being taken when a measure of cost-push was required to explain deviations from the line. The implication of his line was that a rise of unemployment from 2 to 3 per cent would lower the rate of wage inflation from about 3.7 to 2.1 per cent a year. In a two-equation model subsequently fitted to the British data for 1946–59, in which the wage equation contained current and lagged price changes as well as a measure of demand pressure in the labour market roughly equivalent to the unemployment rate with its sign changed, Dicks-Mireaux (1961) found a still stronger Phillips effect – a remission of 2½ or 3 per cent in the wage inflation rate for one percentage point rise in unemployment, while the immediate effect of price increase was fairly low; 0.3 per cent rise in wage inflation for a 1 per cent price increase in the year in question, plus a more doubtful lagged effect of 0.16 per cent for each 1 per cent in the year before.

It is worth remembering these early results both as explanations of the practical importance attached to the Phillips curve at the time, and as a marker in assessing the extent to which the world subsequently changed. It was seen from our scatter diagram (chart 8.2.2) that the two-variable relation started to go seriously astray after 1967 – just before the publication of Friedman's 1968 paper pointing out that this relation implies money illusion (or no expectation of inflation), and that if a price-expectations term is inserted to remove this implication, and moves in step with actual prices, the curve becomes vertical at a 'natural' rate of unemployment.

United Kingdom wage equations, since these early days of the simple Phillips curve, have been very largely either expectations-augmented Phillips curves or real wage aspiration relations. The characteristics and degrees of success of these two main types of equation have been discussed by Artis (1981), Artis and Miller (1979) and by Sheriff (1980).

Artis and Miller summarise ten equations developed by different writers for a variety of postwar periods – some ending as early as 1960, some running until 1974. Four of them (Parkin, Sumner and Ward, 1976; Sumner, 1978; Henry, Sawyer and Smith, 1976, and Nordhaus, 1972(1)) are in some versions of the augmented Phillips curve form. Five others (another equation fitted by Henry, Sawyer and Smith, 1976; Apps, 1976; two by Sargan, 1964 and 1971, and Artis, Temple and Copeland, 1977) are real income target equations. That of Johnston and Timbrell (1974) is also of this kind, though with a 'target income' variable summing the failures to reach 3 per cent improvement in real wage (no deduction for greater success) in each of the foregoing three years.

The fits obtained by these models are not, in general, very good. There is, moreover, little sign of consistency in estimates of the effect of unemployment. Artis and Miller remark that only two of the relevant coefficients appear to be significant, (those of Sumner and of Parkin, Sumner and Ward), which give estimates of 1 per cent and 2 per cent respectively for remission of annual wage inflation attributable to a rise of unemployment rate from 2 to 3 per cent. Other estimates vary from 1.6 per cent to virtually zero, and two come out with the wrong sign. The coefficient attached to price expectations is also in some cases non-significant, though in three cases it is both significant and not far below unity. Sumner's unemployment variable is corrected to exclude the estimated effect of the rise in the benefit–earnings ratio over his period (to 1974–5). Since this end point marked the ratio's peak, it is perhaps not surprising that he attributes a contribution of 1.5 percentage points to this cause, even if one suspects that this includes some element more properly attributable to slackening demand. All but one of the real wage target equations succeed in getting significantly negative coefficients on real income, but their values vary widely. In his 1981 paper, Artis investigates the stability of the coefficients in a model in which wage inflation is regressed on current and lagged price inflation, unemployment, lagged real wages, and time. For the whole period (1953–74) only the first two of these coefficients are significant. The period is then broken down into two sub-periods, using various dividing dates between 1966 and 1970. Neither unemployment nor either of the price inflation variables is significant for any sub-period, but the real wage variable is significant for some sub-periods, including earlier periods extending to or beyond 1967, and the later periods beginning in 1969 or 1970. Its coefficient in the later periods is consistently three or four times as great as in the earlier ones, indicating increased speed of adjustment, while the implied 'desired' rate of increase, towards which the adjustment takes place, is more than quadrupled. The general implication is, therefore, that an explanation based upon the pursuit of an advancing real wage becomes valid some time in the later 1960s, and that both the desired rate of advance and the strength of reaction to downward departures from it increase shortly after that, while, for the period .as a whole, expectations based upon recent experience provide the only clue. It must be remembered, however, that this investigation relates to hourly wage *rates* (which may be less sensitive to market forces than are hourly earnings) and that the effects of direct taxation are not deducted from them.

Sheriff, in a later assessment (1980), takes two of the more prominent British wage equations of the middle 1970s, and tests their ability to predict the later course of events. The Parkin, Sumner and Ward equation, based on events up to the end of 1971, is an augmented Phillips relation with expectations terms relating to producers' home and export prices and to consumers' prices, the last-mentioned derived from survey data. For purposes of prediction, actual price indices are employed to continue the estimated (or survey-derived) 'expected' values, used in the fitting of the equation, and the unemployment figures used were adjusted for the effect of changes in the benefit–earnings ratio in the manner of Sumner's 1978 study. The equation thus applied proved to under-predict wage inflation except in the income policy periods of 1973 and 1976–7; it seems to have given to the variations of unemployment, apparently even as adjusted, a wage-influencing power which they no longer possessed.

The other equation tested, that of Henry and Ormerod (1978), is a target real income equation, fitted over the period 1961–77, with dummy variables to deal with periods of income policy and their aftermaths, but with an imposed target rate of real wage growth of 2.6 per cent. Sheriff shows that this was inappropriate to the period 1975–8, when real wages grew much more slowly, and the assumption of catch-up to the norm does not seem to have been justified.

Hope springs eternal in the human breast, and the art of formulating wage equations will no doubt improve. So far, however, every success relating to a particular period seems to have been followed by some change in behaviour, or some intrusion of a new variable, which altered the picture. Our own rough experiment with sub-period averages suggests that, beyond the short run of the four year cycle, the Phillips relation was never wholly valid (since the war) for the United Kingdom without a price inflation term, and that the elasticity of price expectations (or, to put it more neutrally, the extent to which recent price experience modified bargaining behaviour) increased drastically in the late 1960s. Putting this simply in terms of real wage target increases seems to give excessive forecasts when projected into the later 1970s, but the modifying power of unemployment does not appear to have been constant – and changes in the benefit–earnings ratio (especially since that ratio declined from the mid-1970s) may not provide an adequate explanation.

We shall have to come later to the influence of incomes policies, which have been so prominent in the British scene, and must have introduced considerable disturbance, to say the least. For the moment it will be enough to note that, to anyone who has lived through the last thirty years as an observer of the proximate processes by which, and the different atmospheres in which, British wages are actually fixed, the hard time suffered by econometricians seeking to explain them need come as no surprise. Both Artis and Miller (1979) and Blackaby (1978) remark that at their times of writing, none of the three principal British forecasting models (those of the Treasury, the NIESR, and the London Business School) included a money wage equation. The battle was, however, rejoined later.

Wage Equations for Italy
Italy is another country for which the construction of wage equations has been a substantial industry – there being, as we have seen, plenty to explain. A good deal of reliance has been placed upon the expectations-augmented Phillips curve, often with the assistance of dummy variables to represent the fairly well-marked episodes of labour militancy, and sometimes with variables which purport to measure that elusive factor. Such procedures are, of course, open to

attack, and such an attack is launched, in an article reviewing much of the relevant work, by Franco Spinelli (1980). It is clear that there is little, if any, long-term trade-off between inflation and unemployment in Italy after some date which the work of a number of writers suggests to have been the end of the 1950s (half way through the second period which we distinguished in chart 8.3). Our evidence on inflationary impulses suggests that wage-push, acceleration of wage inflation without the accompaniment of symptoms of extra demand pressure in product markets, was unusually frequent in Italy. Neither strikes nor shortening of contracts nor trade union membership (a variable used in some British work) are necessarily good measures of the extent to which employees' bargaining power is exerted, though none of them is without evidential value, and the imitative, self-defensive character of bargaining effort causes it to give an irregularly-amplified response to whatever impulses set it going. There seems to have been some tendency in Italian work to set up 'sociological' models of wage formation, defined as lacking all market-equilibrating content, in order to knock them down. The fact that this is rather an easy task does not disprove the existence of irregular and powerful (and at least partially accommodated) impulses which measurable market indicators cannot easily or accurately explain.

Wage equations and the 'Scandinavian' model
When we come to the smaller, and open, economies, and especially to Sweden, which is its main country of origin, the 'Scandinavian' model of Aukrust (1972) and Edgren, Faxén and Odhner (1973) becomes attractive as the basis of a theory of wages. If it is true that the prices of international goods are given by the world market, and that force of circumstances makes the internationally traded goods sector the wage leader within the economy, then we have not got far to look for the determination of wage rates generally, and internal supply and demand conditions other than anything which affects the productivity of labour in the traded goods sector should be of little importance.

There have been some empirical findings favourable to this model: Gordon (1981), for instance, found lagged prices of traded goods significant in his wage equation for Sweden, and Calmfors (1977) found that wages in the traded and non-traded goods sectors moved broadly in parallel and, in the former sector, were significantly influenced by labour productivity and by the prices of traded goods. Other findings, however, were less favourable. Calmfors also found a measure of Swedish demand pressure significant (as Jacobsson and Lindbeck (1969) had done for an earlier period), and the influence of productivity and of traded goods prices in the Calmfors equation was not as strong as the pure theory of the Scandinavian model would demand.

We have ourselves noted (p. 201) that the detailed course of events in Sweden does not suggest that mainly passive role for prices which the theory seems to require, though it should be added that Maynard and van Ryckeghem (1976) find Swedish export prices to have followed world prices more closely than those of most countries (this is true also of Denmark and Norway) during the period of exchange stability. It may well be that the centralised machinery of wage bargaining in Sweden, despite its vicissitudes, was effective in keeping settlements within the constraints of the world market and the fixed exchange in this period.

ASSESSMENTS OF INCOMES POLICIES

We have already noted that direct controls of varying severity and form have been introduced from time to time in a number of countries in the hope of moderating wage inflation which had accelerated to levels regarded at the time as unacceptable either in themselves or in the context of the country's general economic situation. There have been four fairly well-marked episodes of this kind in the United States; in the United Kingdom some kind of policy with this intention has been in operation for nearly half of the period 1950–81, even if one excludes the years in the middle and later 1950s in which exhortation, diplomacy, and finally the advice of the Council on Prices, Productivity and Incomes were brought into action in the hope that they might influence the course of settlements. For these two countries, there have been several studies seeking, as either their main or an incidental aim, to assess the effectiveness of such incomes policies. For other countries, systematic studies yielding such assessments have been less in evidence, though we have already noted that Perry, in his multi-country study, found significant effects in France (1964–5) and Sweden (1971), as well as for the United Kingdom (1967) and the United States (the 'guidepost' period, 1962–4), and that Davies did so *inter alia* for the United Kingdom (especially the Social Contract 1975–8).

We have already given some account of the United States wage equations of Nadiri and Gupta. The dummy variable which they contain to represent the effect of the government guideposts of 1962–4 proved significant, and its coefficient of similar magnitudes in the equation for the whole economy and in those for manufacturing industry and the durable and non-durable sections thereof. They proceeded to use their wage and price equations in a simulation of wage and price developments in 1971–3 as they might have been in the absence of the first two phases of the Nixon controls of that period, and concluded that the effects of those controls can only have been very small. A somewhat similar investigation, with simpler equations, but separately applied to seventeen sub-groups of manufacturing industry over the years 1959–73 was undertaken by Al-Samarrie, Kraft and Roberts (1977), using dummy variables for the Nixon control period. They conclude that there is no sign of the desired effect from the wage controls – indeed they find, as did Gordon (1977), a very small apparent effect in the opposite direction, though price inflation may have been reduced by about half a percentage point a year. (Some reduction in price inflation by the Nixon controls is implied also by the work of Gordon, of Newton and Blinder (1979) and of McGuire (1976), but it is not our main concern here.)

More recently, Pencavel (1981) has reviewed American experience with incomes policies, and has fitted a simple wage equation of his own, containing dummy variables for incomes policy periods, to data for the whole thirty years 1949–79. In addition to the 'guidepost' and Nixon episodes, so far mentioned, he includes the period of operation of the Wage Stabilisation Board, 1950–3, which operated mainly by exhortation, and that of President Carter's stabilisation programme of 1978–80, of which much the same was, in the event, true. The fit of this equation is not conspicuously good, either over the whole period or when applied to each of its three decades separately, but the general implication is that only the, on the face of it, relatively mild guidepost policy of 1962 onwards can show conventionally significant effects in the desired direction – and even this does not do so when viewed against the background of the 1960s alone.

These investigations are, of course, open to a number of criticisms. We have seen that wage equations in general have proved to be rather fragile creatures, with limited periods of validity, and it follows that, even one that fits a period, or periods, free from incomes policy measures may not give a very reliable yardstick of hypothetical inflation against which to measure the actual inflation of a policy episode. Cagan (1977), comparing the industry equations of Al-Samarrie, Kraft and Roberts with those of Nadiri and Gupta, finds differences large enough to suggest serious lack of robustness. Morley (1977), commenting on the work of the two latter investigators, points out, further, that simulations of the hypothetical 'no-policy' course of events in policy periods may be biased downwards if actual values of, for example, the consumer price index are used as if they were exogenous when, in fact, they may have been affected by the controls.

Wallis (1971) and Pencavel make what is, in some degree, a related point. In so far as incomes policy is represented by dummy variables, or variables of any sort, included in a general equation for periods of varying policy application (or no policy) taken together, and in so far as the application or stringency of policy is correlated with the actual rate of inflation, which is taken as signalling the need for it, estimation becomes hazardous – a supposedly 'independent' variable is systematically related to the supposedly 'dependent' one. Unless we can get some idea of the strength of the feedback from inflation to policy, we cannot measure the effect of policy on inflation. Pencavel finds some evidence for such feedback, though he does not regard United States evidence as sufficient to enable a policy function to be formulated and estimated simultaneously with the wage function.

In the United Kingdom, also, most of the econometric work on this subject has made use of dummy variables to represent policy episodes, usually simple variables taking the value of unity in all 'policy-on' periods and zero otherwise, though the history of policy here is particularly complex, and there is a shortage of periods when it can be said to have been totally absent. The pioneering article was by Lipsey and Parkin (1970), who concluded that policies had not been effective. A later article by Parkin, Sumner and Ward (1976) using an expectations-augmented Phillips curve came to a similar conclusion.

Henry and Ormerod (1978), using different dummies for different policy episodes, and also 'catch-up' dummies for the periods following the lifting of the controls, found some significance in both sets of dummies – controls reduced wage inflation, but it roughly made up for lost time after they were lifted. This work has been updated recently by Henry (1981), using two separate models, one based on an augmented Phillips curve, the other on the target real wage hypothesis. He distinguishes five periods of active policy during 1963–78, the episodes beginning in 1966, 1967, 1972, 1973, and 1975, with catch-up periods following the first four of these. The real wage model is tried in two versions. The dummy for the 'social contract' episode of 1975–7 proves to be consistently significant, those for the 1966–7 and 1973–4 episodes, the former of which involved a statutory wage standstill, are significant in one formulation, but the brief wage standstill of 1972–3 and the voluntary policies of 1967–9 do not register so clearly, though their dummies both have the right sign in at least one formulation of the wage equation.

Of the 'catch-up' dummies, that for 1974–5 is both significant and large in two of the formulations, probably in large part because it catches the effect of the world primary price inflation transmitted by the later stage of the 'threshold' wage indexing instituted as part of the preceding incomes policy. The catch-up of 1967–8 (coinciding with part of the voluntary restraint period of 1967–9) also has a significant and large coefficient in one formulation, a fact perhaps not unconnected with the devaluation of November 1967. The general implication of this study, therefore, is that there is considerable evidence for effectiveness of some phases of incomes policy, and also evidence for a substantial rebound of wages when the restraint is removed, but that, as with wage equations generally, magnitudes of estimated effects vary too much with differences in the form of the equation to inspire much confidence.

The selection of periods for designation as episodes of incomes policy is peculiarly difficult in the United Kingdom, where every phase of policy has differed from every other one in ways that do not lend themselves to quantitative assessment of severity. Surrey (1981) has attempted a solution of this problem by constructing an index of the strength of policy, based on a principal component analysis of five series designed to represent aspects of strength (presence of *any* policy; compulsory, as opposed to voluntary, nature of policy; distance of any 'norm' below the current 'going rate' of wage increase; absence of permitted exceptions; presence of power to delay increases). The index (running from 1960 to 1979) shows two high summits of policy strength, mid-1966 to early 1967 and late 1972 to mid-1974. It fails to give high marks to the 'social contract' phase of 1975–7, the effectiveness of which, one may suspect, was due in the main to a psychological factor of which account has not been taken in econometric work – the fact that the British public was thoroughly frightened by the inflation of 1973–5. Surrey uses his index in competition with the Henry and Ormerod dummies in their 1978 equations, and some variations thereof, and is able to claim superior performance in important respects. One interesting feature of his equations is the absence of significant catch-up effects in the periods of weakened policy, except in 1974–5 when, as we have noted, the special feature of indexed 'threshold' supplements was present. It may be, therefore, that the significance attached to catch-up in much of the econometric work on wages (and perhaps on prices also) owes something to the arbitrary quality of simple dummy variables representing complex variations in the strength of policy constraints.

Finally, the point of Wallis and Pencavel, that bias is introduced in single equation work if strength of policy is affected systematically by a feedback from wage inflation, has been taken in the United Kingdom, and work designed to produce a multi-equation model, including a policy (government reaction) equation, has been undertaken by Desai *et al.*, but full results are not available at the time of writing.

In spite, then, of all the difficulties of measurement and of logic that are involved in econometric assessment of incomes policy, some progress has been made, and one can claim reasonable systematic support for the statement that some episodes of official wage restraint have enjoyed a limited success, at any rate during their currency; but that the extent of the success is far from being great and self-evident (as the success of wage management in many countries in the second world war, for instance, was great and self-evident). Wage determination, as we have seen, is heavily dependent upon the particular institutions and, in the broad sense of the word, political circumstances of national labour markets. Some countries have suffered much more than others from inflationary pressures apparently related to the nature of their labour market institutions. Governmental incomes policies are attempts temporarily or permanently to modify those institutions. One would perhaps not expect them, in non-authoritarian states, to achieve great changes quickly, but international differences suggest that the scope for them to do so in a longer run is far from negligible.

WAGE-PUSH AND FACTOR SHARES

In chapter 4 we made use of the increase in the share of wages in value-added (in manufacturing principally), together with the acceleration of wage inflation, to give *prima facie* indication of wage-push. The year-to-year changes in question were quite largely cyclical, though negative versions of this kind of impulse were somewhat less common than positive ones, among our eleven sample OECD countries, and we found not only that positive wage impulses were very closely associated with rising price inflation (and negative ones with its fall), but that the symptoms of wage-push were especially common at the times of major leaps in the inflation rate, both general and peculiar to particular countries. Nevertheless, they are no commoner in the more inflationary second half of our period than in the less inflationary first half, while their negative counterparts are actually a little commoner. We need to take some account of the magnitudes of these impulses, as well as their numbers, if we are to gauge their effects. Wage inflation was on average more severe in the second half of our period than in the first, just as price inflation was. What was the case with change in the labour share of value-added?

The question is complicated by the great changes which took place over our period in several of our countries with regard to the share of income from self-employment in the total. Estimates with some claim to avoid this difficulty, however, generally agree in showing a rising trend of employees' share (as opposed to gross operating surplus) and, moreover, a steepening trend. T. P. Hill's estimates relating to all non-financial enterprise for the United States, United Kingdom and France, show little change in the United States until the end of the 1960s, then an appreciable rise in the early 1970s, followed by a partial falling back in the second half of that decade. The United Kingdom picture is similar, except that the falling back in the later 1970s is insignificant. France shows some rise in the early 1970s, but a larger one in the later part of the decade. The McCracken Report's estimates relating to the corporate sectors of the main OECD economies (1960 to 1976) shows a sharp rise in the United States between 1967 and 1974, in the United Kingdom from 1968 onwards, in Germany and Italy from 1969 (though with a return in the former by 1976), and in Japan from the early 1970s.

Lindbeck (1983) has made an analysis based on unweighted averages for ten countries (our OECD eleven, minus Australia and Denmark, plus Belgium) from which he concludes that there were two periods – around 1970–1 and 1972–4 – when growth of wage rates measured in terms of real product ran markedly ahead of increase in labour productivity, so that real (product) wages by 1976 stood some 11 per cent higher in relation to productivity than in 1967, and still remained 8 per cent higher in 1979. The periods of running ahead were, of course, periods of accelerating wage inflation which we have already identified, for various countries, as periods of wage-push.

It is obvious that a rise in the labour share of value-added can be looked at in either of two ways; either as an excessive rise of money wages or as an insufficiency of effective demand to maintain the profit share. (Similarly, in a closed economy, 'excessive' real wages may be regarded as another aspect of inadequate final demand, since the deflator used in calculating real wages consists of the sum of unit wage costs and unit profits, and the profit element depends on demand in the product markets.) There is a presumption that higher expenditure can always lower the wage share and the real wage – or, at least, that it can do so if profit margins are lower than sellers consider 'normal'. But monetary and fiscal authorities were pursuing the twin objectives of price stability and full employment; in the late 1960s and in the 1970s the rise of wages (and of import prices) faced them increasingly with situations in which the maintenance of effective demand and employment through raised expenditure meant accelerating inflation. In the main OECD countries they compromised, progressively abandoning full employment, but, partly through the biases and inertias of the labour market, partly through the second oil price shock, with only tardy success in bringing inflation down to the levels of the mid-1960s.

CONCLUSIONS

The first conclusion of this long discussion is that the labour market is extremely unlikely, in any of our sample countries, to behave in the least like an atomistic market for a particular product or material, which clears relatively quickly through the influence of market-flexible prices on amounts supplied and demanded. One reason for this is that the labour market, as a whole, cannot be treated as a microeconomic mechanism; a shift of the supply curve of labour, for instance, shifts both the aggregate supply curve and the aggregate demand curve for final output in the economy, and for that reason alone a fall in the price of labour may not be an efficient way of causing an excess supply of it to be absorbed. A second reason is that the non-homogeneity of labour, and the costs of recruiting and training it for particular jobs, give rise to employers' preferences for a steady evolution of wage rates in the face of fluctuating product demand. A third is that collective bargaining or state regulation of pay and conditions operate widely in such a way as to prevent the kind of bargaining with individual applicants which would be necessary for the simplest kind of market clearing, and that organised labour can influence wage bargains to extents which vary widely with economic, social and political conditions, including the workers' own will to gain.

It is in line with this conclusion that wage inflation is seen to show some cyclical – and some non-cyclical – sensitivity, in a negative sense, to the level of unemployment; a matter of relatively slow movement towards equilibrium rather than its continuous maintenance. The relation is fairly regular in Japan and Germany, but elsewhere shows marked irregularity, especially in the second half of our period. We found evidence that increased imperfection of the labour market, especially the rise in the replacement ratio of unemployment benefit to earnings in work, may explain some of the irregularity, but usually far from all of it. (The replacement ratio nowhere seems to explain the greater part of the secular rise in registered unemployment after 1979). Expectations of price inflation (or movements towards keeping up with its recent rate) can explain some of the remainder, but they seem to have been incorporated into settlements variably and, except in Italy, only very partially.

The econometric wage equations which we have surveyed are

generally fragile; experience with them points to international and intertemporal variation in the nature of wage fixing processes. There is widespread evidence of inertia (high values of lagged dependent variables) and of gradual rather than rapid movements towards equilibrium. What can be interpreted as norms of aspiration with regard to either nominal or real wage increase, in both the United Kingdom and the United States, change from time to time. Incomes policies, though generally only partially successful, have introduced marked disturbances. Institutional differences between countries in bargaining machinery, and identifiable periods of political intransigence have left their marks. In other words, while particular models (especially augmented Phillips curves, or real wage aspiration models, or combinations of the two) have shown short-to-medium-term usefulness, any belief that the labour market has a strong tendency to clear, or is much simpler than the working of the societies in which it is embedded, receives little encouragement.

Some of the episodes of wage-push which we identified earlier seem to have had more than short-term significance, and the profit share of value-added in most OECD countries has been reduced – a phenomenon connected also with increasing official reluctance to accommodate cost-push inflation (partly from wages, partly from key primary materials), which has itself become more severe during the second half of our period.

The question posed at the beginning of this chapter about the possibility of wage-push without an increase in effective demand which might be expected also to maintain the profit share can be answered more fully when we have scrutinised the process of price determination in national economies and the behaviour of the market-flexible world prices; but a partial answer can be provided by what we have seen of the very imperfect market responsiveness of wages under the wide variety of labour market institutions that prevail.

9

WORLD MARKETS AND IMPORT PRICE-PUSH

We come now to the inflationary impulses that reach our sample countries through rises in the prices of their imports. They are not, of course, the only external impulses reaching them; others come by way of the demand for their exports, but these we have chosen to treat as expenditure-pull impulses – they have the immediate effect of raising the profit share, like other impulses which operate by increasing demand for the country's products. Having said this, we must immediately admit that some rises in import prices can have a similar effect. If the elasticity of substitution between the imports and the country's own products is high (that is, if the imports are *competitive* with domestic products), a rise in the price of the former will shift demand to home products and yield the symptoms of demand-pull. This, however, is probably not the most common consequence of a rise in import prices, especially in the short run, though during the great trade liberalisation of our period it is likely to have become more common.

We can start by asking why a particular country's import prices rose on a given occasion. One practically important case is that in which the country's currency has depreciated, or been deliberately devalued, in relation to those of its import suppliers. The other, obviously, is that in which the foreign currency prices of its imports rise. Perhaps it will be useful, before going further, to see what part the former factor – depreciation of countries' own currencies – has played in their import price inflation, using as our sample the Big Six plus India and Australia, as in chapter 1.

INFLATION AND EXCHANGE RATE

One should note that changes in the rate of exchange between two countries' currencies are relevant to their *relative* inflation rate; devaluation is inflationary for the devaluing country, deflationary for its partner or partners. Whether fixed or flexible rates are more likely to assist inflation on a world scale is, as Corden (1977) has argued, by no means certain; fixed rates make it harder for inflation-prone countries to let their inflations proceed without coming up against shortages of foreign exchange reserves and difficulties (or undue expense) of borrowing to bridge external deficits, but they also make it easier for them to ease pressure on their resources by 'exporting' their inflation (by shedding effective demand) to other countries. The first of our sub-periods, 1950–68, was, of course, one in which there was a fairly strong commitment to fixed exchange rates under the Bretton Woods agreement; in the second one, 1968–79, these commitments broke down, leaving in the end a large amount of more or less managed 'floating' in foreign exchange markets. That the second sub-period brought more severe inflation than the first can hardly be cited as even *prima facie* evidence for the more inflationary nature of a flexible rate system – far too many other circumstances were different between the two sub-periods. It is probably nearer the mark to regard the greater flexibility of the second sub-period as a result, partly of the accumulation of the consequences of differences of inflationary pressure in the first sub-period, partly of greater diversity of such pressures operating in the second.

The simplest purchasing power parity theory suggests that, when general price levels in two countries change in relation to each other, equilibrium may be maintained in trade and payments between them by varying the exchange rate proportionately, so as to maintain equality (or, at least, a constant ratio) between the two price levels when expressed in terms of one of the currencies. A more realistic formulation recognises that the constancy of price relations that is required relates, not to some average of the prices of all goods and services, but only to average prices of those which are internationally tradable – the relative prices of tradable and non-tradable goods being apt to change in different ways in different countries, as we have already seen. Does this throw light on experience in our period?

The first of our two sub-periods fell, as we have just recalled, within the Bretton Woods age of mainly constant exchange rates, and five of our eight sample countries did, in fact, maintain constant, or nearly constant dollar values for their currencies throughout it; yet these countries (United States, Japan, Germany, Italy, Australia) showed, as we have seen, consumer price increases ranging from 44 to 129 per cent – the United States at one end of the scale, Japan at the other. How can such disparate rates of inflation over a substantial period be reconciled with exchange stability?

Corden (*op. cit.*) allows that substantial discrepancies of this kind are possible so long as the differences spring from the inflation rates of non-tradable rather than tradable goods and services, though he suggests that a rise in the relative price of non-tradables will tend to

Table 9.1 Indices of CPI, export and import unit values (local currency and dollar) and local currency value of dollar: 1950–79, 1950–68 and 1968–79 (earlier date = 100)

Country	CPI	Local currency unit values		US $ unit values		
		Exports	Imports	$	Exports	Imports
1950–79						
United States	302	345	411	100	345	411
United Kingdom	633	605	560	132	458	428
Japan	567	168	199	62	271	320
Germany	243	245	156	44	558	356
France	566	443	397	121	366	329
Italy	594	376	495	134	280	369
India	427	422	450	170	248	264
Australia	548	198	487	100	198	487
1950–68						
United States	144	135	120	100	135	120
United Kingdom	185	160	137	115	139	119
Japan	229	97	84	100	97	84
Germany	148	144	92	97	148	95
France	227	173	151	137	126	110
Italy	183	92	102	102	90	100
India	213	161	162	156	103	104
Australia	208	71	138	100	71	138
1968–79						
United States	209	210	343	100	210	343
United Kingdom	344	376	409	114	330	359
Japan	248	170	236	62	274	381
Germany	164	168	169	45	373	376
France	249	256	261	87	294	300
Italy	324	404	487	132	306	369
India	201	263	281	111	242	253
Australia	262	280	354	100	280	354

draw resources out of the production of tradable goods, so that they, too, will eventually show higher rates of price inflation. As we have noted, however, it may be that the rate of increase in factor productivity in tradable goods industries exceeds that in production of non-tradables by a larger margin in one country than in another, in which case the former country might continue indefinitely to show a higher rate of inflation of its total output or consumer goods index, while keeping pace with the other country in the costs and prices of tradable goods. There is reason to suppose that Japan showed a very much larger gap between the productivities of its tradable and non-tradable goods industries in the period we are discussing than the United States did. So far, so good.

But when we turn to the rates of price increase in tradable goods, as represented by exports, we find that those of the United States and Japan were not equal; the United States index rose by 35 per cent, the Japanese fell by 3 per cent. Even this could be compatible with fixed exchange equilibrium if the exports of the two countries were qualitatively different; the United States exporting things the world price of which was rising, while Japan sold goods with falling prices. This, however, does not seem likely to have been so to an extent sufficient to explain all of the discrepancy; the products of the two countries were to quite large extents in direct competition with each other.

It seems, then, that given the constant exchange rate Japan was developing an increasing trade advantage in comparison with the United States in the period 1950–68. The confirmation of this is to be found in the exchange rate changes which came soon afterwards. The interpretation of relative price changes in this way, however, is far from straightforward. Germany, with a rise in consumer price index little larger than that of the United States, showed a rise in the unit value of her exports even bigger than the corresponding United States figure. Nevertheless, her competitive strength was manifestly great; like Japan she was on the eve of an upward adjustment in the value of her currency. The high rise in the unit value of her exports must be attributed to improvements in quality within individual classes of goods and to her specialisation on goods with the more quickly rising prices in the world market. Italy, like Japan, had done well with exports of absolutely declining unit value; Australia, on the other hand, showed a drastic cheapening of her exports which was not a source of increased competitive advantage, but a reflection of the reduced world prices of wool and wheat. Different countries' exports, considered as composite commodities, differ a great deal from each other, and one must distinguish between changes in their price due to cost changes and those due to demand changes in order to estimate the direction of the effect on the country's foreign balance and the strength of its currency.

The three countries which did not maintain the dollar values of their currencies in the first sub-period – the United Kingdom, France and India – all showed relatively high increases in the unit values of their exports expressed in domestic currency. Even after allowing for the raised domestic currency price of the dollar, the unit dollar value of United Kingdom exports stood higher in 1968 than in 1950 in relation to those of 'world' manufactures. Both of these years happened to follow immediately after a sterling devaluation; the second devaluation had been less drastic than the first. The French devaluation seems to have kept the dollar prices of the country's exports pretty well in line with the price changes of traded manufactures generally, and India's export prices may well have kept more or less in line with world prices of the kinds of primary products and manufactures which she exported. In all three countries, devaluation had followed increasingly negative external current balances; they may be described in Corden's terms as 'reluctant devaluers', though France was probably the least reluctant of them.

The second sub-period, 1968–79, was characterised by far less strong commitments to fixed exchange rates and, of our present sample of countries, only the United States (by definition) and Australia finished with the same dollar value of their currency with which they began. United States export unit values had, this time, risen a good deal less than the world average for manufactures – and since they contain a substantial proportion of primary products, which generally rose more than manufactures, their relative cheapening is the more marked. Japan was the only other industrial country in our sample to show a rise in her export unit value index less than the 'world' figure (though it was bigger than that of the United States), and this was despite a 38 per cent fall of the dollar in relation to the yen. Japanese competitiveness nevertheless seems to have improved further, whereas that of the United States apparently declined. German export unit values, in dollars, rose more than the world average for manufactures, assisted by the 55 per cent fall of the dollar in Deutschmark terms, but the country's competitiveness seems to have gone on improving. France still kept her dollar export prices near to the world manufactures figure; this time a 13 per cent fall in the franc value of the dollar had been involved in this, and in competitiveness a reasonable judgment would be that she held her own. Italy, with an appreciation of the dollar by about one-third; kept the increase in the dollar unit value of her exports below the world level, but her competitiveness showed signs of slipping from its high point in the later 1960s. The dollar appreciated a further 14 per cent in relation to sterling, but the dollar unit value of United Kingdom exports still rose more than the world manufacturing average; nevertheless, the current balance situation was not less favourable in 1979 than in 1968. Australia and India both experienced increases in the dollar unit values of their exports smaller than the world averages for either primary products (even excluding petroleum) or manufactures. Both may have improved their current balances, on the whole, over the sub-period, India with the help of an 11 per cent appreciation of the dollar, though Australia's share of world reserves fell.

Reduction of the external value of a country's currency produces inflationary impulses from the prices of imports, and these may well induce internal, wage-push, impulses. The origins of currency devaluation, however, may be complex. Greater than average inflation of internal factor prices may bring it about (one thinks of Italy in the second sub-period, and of the United Kingdom throughout), less than average growth of productivity may contribute (the United Kingdom again), and excessive pressure of demand, even if not reflected in prices, may do so also. But the composition of trade, in detail much finer than that of available index numbers, may also be relevant; concentration of exports in categories for which external demand is increasing more slowly than average, or of imports in categories where internal demand is increasing faster, can be a source of exchange weakness, as can a shift towards lower qualities within export categories – the opposite of what seems to have happened, throughout our period, in Germany. While, therefore, one can point to the inflationary consequences of currency devaluation where it has occurred, one has to admit that such devaluations may themselves have been the *consequences* of internal inflationary factors, or of various other circumstances. Purchasing power parity does not explain everything.

MONEY SUPPLY AND INTERNATIONAL PRICES

Just as, in chapter 2, we examined the relations between money supply and prices within each of our sample countries, we may find it worth looking at the relation between world money supply and the indices of 'world' (that is to say, international trade) prices, both expressed in United States dollars. For world prices, we use series of our own (from 1954) compiled for thirteen OECD countries – series for both M1 and M2 – and also the IMF series of M1, both for all countries included in their large compilation and for the countries classed by them as 'industrial'. For our price series, we use the United

Nations indices of primary product and manufactured goods prices, and in the case of the former add a second series from which, after 1971, petroleum is excluded (before that, petroleum prices did not diverge from the general average sufficiently to affect it significantly). In all cases, we are dealing with annual percentage changes. Table 9.2 shows the results of correlating the price and money series. We show results without lags, with money lagged by one year, and with prices lagged by one year. Some of the series in question are shown in chart 9.1.

It is plain that the most impressive correlations, mostly significant at the 1 per cent level, are those for the whole period, and for the second half of it (1968–79), in which money supply changes are lagged by a year – that is to say, the price change is related to the money supply change of the year before. With few exceptions, they are superior to the unlagged correlations, and still more so to those in which price changes lead. It is, however, also striking that, in the first half of the period, up to 1967, we have no correlation significant at even the 5 per cent level, and that, where primary products and M2 are concerned, the correlation with price change leading is superior to either of the others.

As usual, there are considerable differences between the two sub-periods. In the first, the standard deviation of the annual percentage increases in primary product prices was between $1\frac{1}{2}$ times and twice that of the money series (according to which monetary series we use), and that of the prices of manufactures about equal to that of the most volatile of the money series (our M2). In the second sub-period, the ratio of the standard deviations was anything from $2\frac{1}{2}$ to over ten, according to one's choice of money series, and between the primary product series with and without petroleum, while the standard deviation of prices of manufactures was appreciably greater than that of the most volatile of the money series (this time, our M1). World monetary variations thus could not have afforded a simple quantity theory explanation of these international prices in the second sub-period, even if the relevant correlations had been perfect, without the help of large opposite variations in real quantities or concordant variations in velocity of circulation. This is much less markedly true of the first sub-period, but there, as we have seen, the correlations between monetary and price changes are in any case poor.

Prices of manufactures show, as we have already implied, no significant correlation with any of the money series, on any of our lag schemes, in the first sub-period. Their first notable movement (apart from cyclical fluctuations which decrease in amplitude during the 1950s) is an upward jump in 1969 and 1970, early in the second

Table 9.2 *Correlation coefficients between United States dollar world trade prices and money stocks (per cent annual increases)*

	Our money series				IMF money series			
			Lagged		1953–79		Lagged	
	M1	M2	M1	M2	M1	M1 Ind	M1	M1 Ind
1954–79 (IMF 1953–79)								
a) Primary	0.31	0.33	0.81**	0.82**	0.53**	0.44*	0.64**	0.69**
b) Primary excluding petroleum (from 1971)	0.46**	0.51**	0.77**	0.79**				
c) Manufactures	0.60**	0.58**	0.73**	0.75**	0.67**	0.56**	0.76**	0.73**
Lagged (a)	0.27	0.30			0.49*	0.37		
Lagged (b)	0.29	0.31						
Lagged (c)	0.35	0.36			0.63**	0.51**		
1954–67 (IMF 1953–67)								
a)	0.23	0.21	0.44	0.29	0.37	0.39	0.46	0.34
b)	0.23	0.21	0.44	0.29				
c)	0.29	0.05	0.15	0.14	0.14	0.03	0.29	0.12
Lagged (a)	0.33	0.46			0.42	0.26		
Lagged (b)	0.33	0.46						
Lagged (c)	−0.15	0.07			−0.34	−0.35		
1968–79								
a)	−0.04	−0.08	0.76**	0.82**	0.21	0.00	0.50	0.66*
b)	0.21	0.30	0.71**	0.77**				
c)	0.34	0.33	0.57	0.64*	0.35	0.07	0.61	0.61*
Lagged (a)	−0.04	−0.02			0.18	−0.05		
Lagged (b)	−0.02	−0.02						
Lagged (c)	−0.06	−0.05			0.53	0.23		

Source: *International Financial Statistics* and NIESR calculations.

*: significant at 5 per cent level.
**: significant at 1 per cent level.

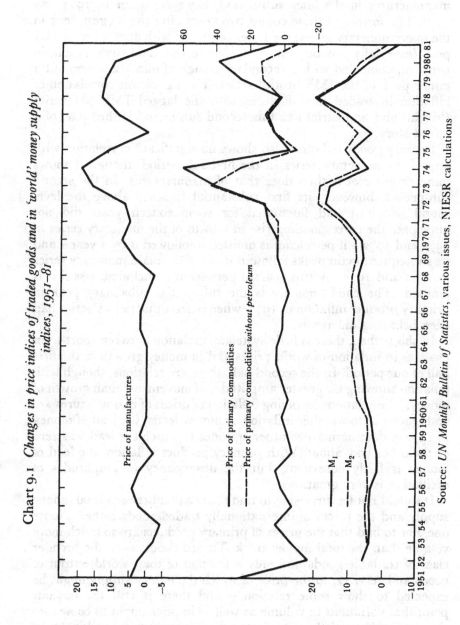

Chart 9.1 *Changes in price indices of traded goods and in 'world' money supply indices, 1951–81*

Source: *UN Monthly Bulletin of Statistics*, various issues, NIESR calculations

sub-period. In this they anticipate the notable rise in the monetary series (1971 and 1972) by two years. The great peaks of inflation in manufactures in the later sub-period, however, occur in 1974 and 1978. The former of these comes two years after the biggest peak in the main monetary series; the latter coincided with another monetary peak (especially pronounced in our M2 series). The 1976 trough, in between, coincided with a secondary trough of our M2 series, but a minor peak of the IMF 'world' series. The significant correlation of inflation in traded manufactures with the lagged IMF M1 series ('world' and 'industrial') in this second sub-period is thus part of a mixed story.

Primary goods inflation also shows no significant correlation with any of the monetary series in the first sub-period, though it shows more promise of it than does that of manufactures. In the second sub-period, however, its first substantial increase above the level round which it had fluctuated for some sixteen years did not anticipate the corresponding rise in growth of the monetary series in 1971 and 1972 – if petroleum is omitted it followed it by a year – and its subsequent main peaks followed those of the main monetary series in 1972 and 1978, by two years if petroleum is included, less if it is omitted. The chief anomaly is the substantial subsidiary peak of primary product inflation in 1977, when different monetary series had been behaving differently.

In short, then, there is little systematic relation between short-term changes in inflation of world prices and in money growth in the first half of our period. In the second half, there are relations, though with inflation showing far greater amplitudes of movements than growth of money. The relations involving inflation of prices of manufactures are ambiguous as to whether inflation or money leads, the lead of money in 1972–3 dominating two other episodes in which the lead was zero or the other way about. With primary product inflation, the lead of money is fairly consistent, but the discrepancy in amplitudes of oscillation is very great.

It should not be surprising to find the relation between total money supply and the prices of internationally traded goods rather a loose one, nor to find that the prices of primary products are so much more volatile than the total money stock. Traded goods, even the broader class of tradable goods, are only a fraction of total world output of goods and services, to the price of which the money supply might be expected to show some relation – and there is still the obvious point that variations in volume as well as in price ought to come into the picture. Nevertheless, it is not without interest to find a hint, even if it can be no more, that changes in the mainly market-determined prices of primary products have some slight tendency to follow changes in world money supply, and that this is less true, or not true at all, of changes in the prices of internationally traded manufactures.

The greater part of all goods entering into international trade consists of manufactures (53 per cent by value in 1959, 60 per cent in 1977; it had been as high as 65 per cent in 1970). By the 1970s there were, indeed, few countries, Japan being the most notable exception, in which manufactures did not dominate the import list. Manufactures are, of course, an enormously heterogeneous class of goods; different countries import considerably different mixes of them. Moreover, even for relatively narrow classes of manufactures the 'law of one price' applies only imperfectly. Nevertheless, because most countries' manufactured imports comprise wide ranges of different goods, and are subject to competition from rival suppliers, it is useful, as a first approximation, to treat the world index of unit prices of manufactured exports as if it were the price of a homogeneous commodity, imported by all countries. The readily available index (United Nations) refers to United States dollar prices. In using it, therefore, we are taking the United States dollar as our *numéraire*. Variations in dollar exchange rates apart, this should give us a first clue to impulses affecting the greater part of the imports of most countries.

As we have already noted, the course of this index from 1951 to 1968 was unspectacular. The net rise between those two years was only 7 per cent; the biggest single-year rises were some 3½ per cent in 1956, and about 2½ per cent in 1957, 1959 and 1965. From 1968 to 1975, however, the index doubled; a rise of about 7 per cent a year in the three years 1970–2, then 21 per cent a year for two years 1973–4, and a year at 11 per cent. After a year's pause, there was another surge of 58 per cent from 1976 to the peak of 1980. To put it slightly differently, the dollar prices of manufactures in international trade underwent two major episodes of double-figure annual inflation in the 1970s, the first of them preceded by three years of more moderate inflation, and a number of very much smaller episodes before the late 1960s which had contributed to only a slight inflationary trend. For the whole period from 1951 to 1980 the price level of manufactured exports had increased more than three-fold.

We must remember our own qualifications about the non-homogeneity of the product and the imperfection of the market. Between 1953 and 1964 the world average price in question rose about

8 per cent, but that of United Kingdom manufactured exports rose some 19 per cent, and those of Italy and Japan *fell* by 12 and 15 per cent respectively. By 1980 the world index, based on 1953, was round about 307, but that for United Kingdom manufactured exports was 421 and that for Japanese 228 – a contrast reflecting, among other things, the heavy overvaluation of sterling in 1980, itself due in part to stronger than average domestic deflation and the impact on the trade balance of North Sea oil; in 1975 the United Kingdom – Japan ratio had been only 1.38, against the 1.85 of 1980.

Broadly, however, it remains true that at least the major surges of inflation in the world dollar prices of manufactured exports can be taken as responsible, proximately, for substantial parts of those episodes or elements of import price-push which are not attributable to the depreciation of the importing countries' own currencies against the dollar. The size of the contribution varies, of course, not only with the degree of openness of the economy in question, but with the proportionate importance of manufactures in its import list. Japan, with its strong competitive position over a wide range of manufactures, is, as we have already hinted, the country in our sample with the lowest susceptibility to this particular inflationary impulse; the proportion of its absorption of manufactures provided from abroad has been estimated at less than 6 per cent in the mid-1970s. For the relatively closed economy of the United States, the corresponding ratio has been put at about 8 per cent, while for the United Kingdom and the larger continental EEC countries it was around 33 per cent, and for some smaller countries (for example, the Netherlands) it was higher still (see Batchelor, Major and Morgan, 1980).

The other source of import price-push is, of course, primary products, and they make up for their rather smaller total weight in world trade by their much wider fluctuations of price inflation. It is perhaps convenient to begin the consideration of their part in the inflationary process by looking, not at their absolute dollar prices, but at these divided by the world unit price of manufactures – the 'real' prices of primary products, or the terms of trade between them and manufactures.

This ratio, in its broadest form, for all primary products, is of great interest in itself, in both short-term and long-term connections. So far as short-term – cyclical – fluctuations are concerned, it would be easy to suppose that primary commodity prices vary with those of manufactures, but with a wider amplitude, so that the terms of trade favoured primary producers at the peaks of world activity and favoured manufacturers in the troughs. This is, however, an oversimplification. Movements in prices of manufactures, like general price movements in manufacturing countries, tend to lag behind those in output. Moreover, the terms of trade in question depend critically upon the weighting systems used, especially for primary commodities, the prices of which follow very different year-to-year courses. If one takes Sir Arthur Lewis's (1978) estimates of the course of industrial production in the 'core' countries (United Kingdom, France, Germany, United States) from 1881 to 1913, and his preferred indices of prices for primary products and manufactures, it appears that only the more pronounced industrial fluctuations which began about 1903 carried the terms of trade approximately with them. Those of the interwar years continued to do so, and the recent wide fluctuations of the 1970s and early 1980s have broadly reestablished the tendency. Year-to-year changes in supply conditions are, and have always been, substantial, even for primary commodities as a whole, and fluctuations in manufacturing production have never dominated the market quite alone.

Nor, as we saw in chapter 1, do the terms of trade entirely follow the long-term variations sometimes formalised as the 'Kondratiev Cycle'. The real price of primary products fell in the economic historians' 'Great Depression' from the late 1870s to the end of the last century, and rose in the first three decades of this one, if a once-for-all downward shift in the first world war (perhaps due to the stimulation it gave to non-European primary production) is allowed for. It showed signs of being on a downward trend in the 1930s. From the early 1950s onwards, however, when the world economy embarked on the most expansionary twenty years in its history, the trend of real primary prices was indubitably downward.

In our period, as in others however, different commodities, or groups of commodities, have behaved very differently. The data have been well analysed by Bosworth and Lawrence (1982) on whose work the following summary account draws freely.

The real price of agricultural products generally followed a strongly falling trend from 1955 to 1972, though with a minor peak of food prices in 1964, after which there came the rise to the very high peak of 1974, and further diminishing fluctuations about a trend which, to judge from the data to 1982, may be a falling one, but lies much above that of pre-1972. Minerals, a class dominated by petroleum, show a smooth falling trend until 1970, then, after a small premonitory rise, the great leap upwards in 1973–4 followed by another one in 1979–80. Non-ferrous metals (not strictly primary products and not included in the general primary index), show no considerable trend over the whole period, but display a number of irregular peaks (notably 1956, 1966, 1968, 1970 and 1974).

On any reasonable system of weighting, an index of the real prices of primary products as a whole was falling, and unsensational, until about 1970. When we remember that the dollar price index of internationally traded manufactures in this period was also fairly smooth and rising only slowly (until 1968, at least), it is clear how even the dollar prices of primary imports can have made little contribution to import price-push. Metals may have been responsible for a small push in 1956, and, with foodstuffs, in the mid-1960s; but these were not serious inflationary impulses. The real questions are why the real price of primary products leapt to such a high peak in 1973–4, and why this leap was bound up with a quasi-permanent move to a higher level.

Both the McCracken Report and Bosworth and Lawrence allot some responsibility to the unusual strength of the 1972–3 upsurge in industrial demand. That the upsurge was unusually large is not in doubt; expansions in the industrial countries were coordinated to an unusual degree, and the world index of manufacturing production rose by nearly 10 per cent in the year, or over 18 per cent in the two years 1971–3, against the background of an annual trend rate of growth of some 6½ per cent in the preceding two decades. One must also, however, take account of the fact that industrial output and demand in 1971 had been considerably below trend. An exponential trend line drawn through the United Nations world manufacturing output index figures for the peak years 1955 and 1969 (with a rate of increase of about 6.62 per cent), passes above the 1973 point; the net annual rate of increase from 1969 to 1973 was about 6.4 per cent. Making all allowance for imperfections of such index numbers, one is left with a strong suggestion that industrial output, and the aggregate use of primary products in 1973 were, to say the least, not much above the trend line of the preceding twenty years.

Something more like a clue emerges from the corresponding calculation about the United Nations primary product index. The average rate of increase of output 1955–69 was about 3.1 per cent (0.47 times that of the manufacturing index). From 1969 to 1973 it was 2.5 per cent, which is 0.39 times that of manufacturing growth. (The index of fuel production alone actually grew rather faster from 1969 to 1973 than from 1955 to 1969 – not too odd a fact if one remembers that the great oil price rise was an administrative act rather than the drift of a free market, and took place late in the year 1973.)

The changed relation between growth rates of manufacturing and primary output is suggestive, but hardly enough to account for so drastic a shift in relative price. The calculation, moreover, takes no explicit account of changes in stock positions. To explain changes in price, Bosworth and Lawrence fit reduced form models, incorporating output (or capacity), stocks, and industrial production, to the data for eleven agricultural commodities and four non-ferrous metals, over various periods up to 1979 with results which are in most cases reasonably good for the period as a whole – a reasonable degree of explanation is generally achieved with plausible and mostly significant values of the coefficients. The exceptions, yielding poor results, are cereals, lead and zinc. An important qualification to the success of even the better equations, however, is that they generally give only a partial explanation of the peak of 1973–4, thus confirming the suggestion of our simple trend calculations, that the supply and demand relations which appear to explain the changes of the previous twenty years reasonably well are inadequate to account for this particular, and spectacular, price boom.

Bosworth and Lawrence discuss possible explanations of this inadequacy. One, which they test and dismiss, is a suggestion by Houthakker that excess supply of cash has a selective effect on demand for stocks of commodities, rather than a uniform effect on all prices. They find, however, a good deal of evidence of exceptional speculative stockholding in the United States and Japan (not, on the whole, in Europe) at the time in question. The simplest explanation of this, in turn, is probably a general awareness or apprehension of scarcity and insecurity of supply, similar to that which, for quite other reasons, had arisen in the Korean war period. Such apprehensions, insofar as they are functions of the statistical situation in markets, are probably non-linear functions, and their relation to the statistics is, in any case, probably not close. The years 1972–3 provide a good deal of evidence of abnormal apprehensions, including the bidding-up of the prices of many industrial exports over the domestic price levels of similar goods. In the field of primary resources, this was the time of the publication of the Club of Rome's doom-laden prophecies, which, even if the flimsiness of their basis was apparent to many economists, must have impressed some people beside their authors. After many years of increasingly plentiful primary resources (despite the unprecedentedly rapid growth of demand for them) the trend was suddenly reversed. This would seem to have given ample reason for some change of attitude towards the holding of stocks.

The changes in output, and in the actual sizes of stocks, which are taken into account in the Bosworth and Lawrence equations, themselves deserve a further comment. It seems likely that, as so often in the supply of primary products, a 'cobweb' process was at work. After many years of falling real price, there had been decisions to reduce both output (or growth of output) and stocks of a number of agricultural commodities. These decisions were no doubt reinforced by the slackening growth of demand after 1969, which had apparently also precipitated a reduction in growth of refining capacity for several metals. The fact that agricultural output and metal-refining capacity cannot be increased overnight made for shortage when demand subsequently rose very rapidly, even though, as we have seen, it probably did not quite reach its old trend line of peaks.

CEREALS AND PETROLEUM

The two primary commodities, or classes of commodity, which bulk largest in the world economy – cereals and petroleum – were, however, involved in special circumstances which rendered their prices not readily explicable by simple market models. We have already noted that the Bosworth and Lawrence equation for cereals does not work well, and that growth of fuel supplies was not checked before 1973 in a way that would help to explain the great subsequent price rise.

World grain production in 1972–3 was below trend by about 3.4 per cent.[1] This negative deviation, however, though not surpassed previously in our period, is not a very startling one, and has been exceeded four times since then. The additional factors that made for a profound effect on price (a doubling) were the low level of stocks in comparison with nearly all previous years of our period, and the decision in the USSR to make up for most of its shortfall (included in the world shortfall just quoted) by importing, instead of by restricting domestic consumption, as had been done in, for instance, 1963–4. It should be added that stocks in the USSR, like those elsewhere, were low, so that the option of drawing upon them, as in some previous years of poor harvest, was restricted. The reason for the reduced level of stocks outside the USSR was, essentially, the breakdown from 1968 of the International Wheat Agreement, under which prices had been kept nearly constant from the beginning of our period at about 2 Canadian dollars a bushel. In the face of increasing productivity large stocks had been accumulated in the course of buying to support this price from time to time, and had served also as a cushion against occasional shortages of output. After the breakdown of the agreement, the exporting countries resorted to downward regulation of acreage, and stocks were run down. The shift from price maintenance by stock

---

[1] The effects of this on total supply of feeding stuffs were exacerbated, though not to a very large extent proportionately, by the collapse of the Chilean anchovy catch. This was the combined effect of over-fishing and of the recurring South Pacific weather phenomenon known as 'el niño'.

accumulation to price maintenance by output restriction left the market unable to accommodate unexpected increases in demand.

Since the peak of 1974, cereal prices have pursued an erratic course. Percentage deficiency of world output below trend was even greater in the crop years 1974–5, 1975–6, 1977–8 and 1979–80 than it had been in 1972–3, a fact for which, on the last three of these occasions, poor harvests in the USSR were mainly or wholly responsible. The impact of these deficiencies on world markets was mitigated to somewhat varying extents by restriction of USSR consumption, but the chief reason why real price of cereals returned to the 1969 level in 1976–7, and has not been much above it since, seems to be the large reduction in consumption, below previous trend, in the exporting countries. In the United States, and probably elsewhere also, there was a massive move away from the grain-feeding of livestock. In the United States grazing largely took its place. The absolute, or dollar, world market price of cereals did, however, move upwards after 1977 roughly in line with that of manufactures – a little further in the bad harvest year 1979–80.

In considering the contribution of rising cereal prices to inflationary impulses in our sample countries, it must be borne in mind that some of them are insulated by domestic or common market policies from the world grain markets. This is true of all members of the EEC, especially Germany and (since 1973) the United Kingdom. It is also true of Japan. Both the mechanisms of the international cereal markets and the impacts of their prices on inflation in individual countries are thus rather complex matters, not easily clarified by straightforward market models.

The same is true of petroleum for different reasons. There, two influences have been dominant; shifts of power within the world market, and changes· in view about prospective reserves and their conservation. In the 1950s, oil production outside the centrally planned economies was overwhelmingly in the hands of seven multinational companies, which collaborated considerably with each other. To a large extent, they had, in principle, the power to fix both the resource price paid to the countries in which the oil was produced, and the selling prices to the public, mostly in the advanced countries. In these circumstances there was at least as much reason to depress the former price as to raise the latter one, so the 'posted price' on which taxation by the producing countries was based was kept low. Margins of profit on the operations of transporting, refining, and marketing were no doubt controlled by considerations relating to competition with other fuels and the avoidance of unfavourable attention from governments of consuming countries.

In principle, the optimum conservation of petroleum resources should have been considered in determining selling prices (which in turn determined output). If the companies had wished to maximise the discounted sum of their profits up to the final exhaustion of oil supplies, they should have charged a price which could be expressed as the sum of two terms. The first is the marginal cost of extracting, processing, and selling the oil. The second is the imputed cost of drawing on the stock of oil in the ground. This latter, imputed, cost (per unit of oil) must be supposed to rise through time at a rate equal to the rate of interest, because a unit of oil left in the ground is an investment, in competition with other investments that might be made. What the price starts at *now* is something which has to be calculated so that, given the demand-curve for oil, the total stock will just be exhausted by sales under the proposed price regime.

It can be shown (see Kay and Mirrlees, 1975) that the size of the second term in relation to the first varies sensitively with the estimated size of stocks in the ground. If, for instance, price elasticity of demand for oil is $\frac{1}{2}$, and the interest rate 5 per cent, then it will be only a fraction of the first term (the marginal extraction cost) with 60 or 70 years' supply, at current extraction rates, supposed to be left in the ground, but will be three or four times the current extraction cost if only 20 years' supply is thought to remain. This example takes no account of the probable rise of real marginal extraction cost as reserves are reduced, but its main point remains valid; as reserves fall their property value per unit rises with increasing rapidity.

Calculations of this kind would have been hard to perform in practice, because, while 'proven reserves' of oil commonly amounted to only a score or less of years' current output, further reserves were always being discovered, sometimes a little faster than the rate of extraction, sometimes a little less fast. In the 1950s, the rate of discovery was rapid, and there was also a good deal of optimism about other (especially nuclear) sources of energy. The presence or prospect of alternative sources sets a ceiling price for oil which makes the calculation of optimum extraction rates and optimum present prices easier, but naturally, the lower the prospective ceiling (or the sooner it is expected to become low) the more it pays to make hay while the sun shines, with low prices and high sales of oil. Moreover, governments taxed sales of petroleum products to consumers quite highly on the average, which both made a substantial contribution to the cause of resource conservation and diminished the scope for the petroleum companies to do so further to their own advantage. All things considered, it is not surprising that, in the 1950s and 1960s (apart from the brief Suez disturbance of 1956–7) the real price of petroleum was low and fell.

Already, however, at the beginning of the 1960s, the Organisation of Petroleum Exporting Countries (OPEC) had been formed as a result of the companies' action in reducing posted prices. Its potential market power increased rapidly as imported oil came to supply increasing proportions of the energy requirements of Japan, Western Europe and the United States. A decade later, it was able to pledge its members to embargo all shipments not conforming to the Organisation's agreed demands.

The ability of OPEC to set terms unilaterally was already apparent by 1972, even though demand was slack. The action of October 1973, during the Arab–Israeli war, which led to a quadrupling of prices in three months, was no doubt in some degree facilitated by the high level to which demand had then climbed, including some induced speculative and precautionary demand for stocks, but for the greater part it seems to have been the result of an exercise of new-found monopoly power which would have had a drastic effect even in a slacker market. Indeed, when slacker demand came, from 1975 onwards, the real price of petroleum merely levelled out, then fell only slightly in 1977–8. After that supply difficulties in the Persian Gulf brought a new doubling despite the near-constancy of world industrial production from 1979 to 1981. Even the slight fall of industrial production in 1981–2 brought only a fall of 2 per cent in real oil prices.

It seems then that the revolutionary rise in the price of oil in terms of manufactured goods – nearly eight-fold since 1970 – is mostly to be attributed to the change from management of price by multinational corporations, subject to pressure in the main consuming countries, and acting in the main on the assumption that reserves, somewhere in the world, would go on being discovered at a rate near to that of consumption, to management of price by combined governments of exporting countries well aware of the finite nature of their own reserves. It has, of course, been a condition of the increase that reserves have not been discovered, either in or out of the OPEC countries, at a substantially faster rate, in relation to consumption, than hitherto; indeed, aggregate proven reserves have fallen since 1973. A further condition was that the supply of alternative sources of energy should not prove elastic. In what may be considered a fairly short run of ten years it has not done so; in the longer run it well may – possibly with disturbing 'cobweb' effects. In relation to the course of world inflation, the rises in real oil prices are best regarded as due to exogenous shifts in the prospects and conditions, including the institutional conditions, of supply.

In relation to the price of manufactures, therefore, any plausible index of primary product prices pursued an unsensational, slightly downward-trending course until about 1970. Thereafter, the courses of the different classes of primary product are so different from each other that the weights appropriate to different importing countries will give markedly different results. The common feature is the great rise from 1972 to 1974; for all the broad classes except fuels that is a peak not subsequently exceeded, and any non-fuel average would show a figure for 1975 only a few percentage points above that for 1970, with a somewhat rising trend from then until 1980, and a sharp descent to 1982. Fuels, after their three-fold increase from 1970 to 1974 (five-fold for crude oil) came down only a little to 1978, more than doubled again by their peak of 1981. The major change in the terms of trade, apart from the sharp, isolated peak of 1974, is that between fuels and everything else.

IMPORT PRICE-PUSH

So far as import price-push is concerned, however, we must look at the nominal, most conveniently the United States dollar, prices of primary products, and these of course show changes which include both those of real primary product prices and nominal prices of manufactures, the latter of which, as we have already noted, follow a continuously and quite steeply rising course (but for a pause in 1975–6) from 1972 to 1980. Through their primary imports, therefore, the presumption is that all industrial countries received very sharp inflationary impulses in 1972–4 and that petroleum importers received another one in 1978–80, the severity of both these shocks depending very much upon the importance of petroleum imports in relation to GDP, since petroleum has risen in dollar price so much more than other things – seventeen-fold in dollar price between 1970 and 1981. It is important in this connection for the United Kingdom that her dependence on petroleum imports fell sharply between the first shock and the second. The United States, on the other hand, became somewhat more dependent on them. The food price boom of 1972–3 had little cost-push impact upon the food-importing countries of the European Economic Community, because their common price level was already well above the previous world level, and much the same was true of domestic prices in Japan. (For the United Kingdom, which joined the EEC in 1973, the cost-push effects of the Common Agricultural Policy levy were largely substituted for those of world food markets.)

Bosworth and Lawrence discuss three approaches to the estimation of the effect which inflation of primary commodity prices had on national price levels. All of them cover more than the effect of import price-push; where the country is a producer, or, indeed, an exporter of primary commodities, the effect of inflation in the price of domestic output is included, along with that of import prices. The first is the highly aggregated approach taken by the United Nations Conference on Trade and Development (UNCTAD, 1975), in which a single equation is fitted to data for the OECD countries as a whole during the years 1952–69. The GDP deflator for the OECD countries is regressed on a measure of their output gap (percentage unused productive capacity), its rate of change, the previous year's GDP deflator, the primary commodity price index, and a dummy variable covering the Korean war years. The model can be interpreted as being built on the assumption that price increases of manufactures and final services display a good deal of inertia, but are based on increase of primary product prices, and on increase of labour costs which tends to accelerate when unused capacity falls. (The part to be attributed to the rate of change of unused capacity is a little more doubtful; it may merely pick up a lag in the unused-capacity effect.) In other words, inflation of the GDP deflator is explained in terms of inertia, a modified Phillips curve and the exogenous inflation rate of primary products.

This simple model is reported to fit its data very well, and also to perform well when used to simulate the events of 1970–5. The coefficient of the primary product inflation term (elasticity of GDP deflator in terms of primary product price) works out at 0.11, which presumably includes indirect effects through stimulation of wage inflation, as well as direct effects. It may also be asked whether the primary product term acts in some degree as a proxy for inflationary expectations, which in a previous chapter we invoked to explain the apparent once-for-all shift of the Phillips curve in the United States at some time in the late 1960s.

The UNCTAD equation, as Boswell and Lawrence point out, ignores several complications which cannot be regarded as unimportant, notably changes in exchange rates and the presence of trade barriers and other imperfections. Nevertheless, its considerable success suggests that something of the essence of the world inflationary process is captured – a combination of primary material cost-push and a Phillips relation. Bosworth and Lawrence follow up this approach by fitting a slightly elaborated version of the equation to ten OECD countries individually, with adjustments for changes in the dollar values of their currencies and with a lagged (as well as a current) primary commodity inflation variable, over the years 1961–

79. The modified equation is also fitted to a weighted average of all the countries together.

The resulting fits are mostly better than that of the original equation to the whole OECD. For the Netherlands, Sweden, the United Kingdom, the United States, Germany and, marginally, France, the lagged primary price variable does more than the unlagged one. Lagged GDP deflator change – inertia – is apparently important everywhere except in Japan and (less markedly) Germany, in line with our observations on the quick reduction of inflation in those two countries. Aggregate demand (the ratio of GDP to its quadratic trend) is significant in half the cases – Germany, the United States, Italy (which we found by inspection to show simple Phillips relations at least up to some point in our period) as well as Sweden and Australia and the OECD total. Change in aggregate demand is significant only for Sweden, and for the OECD total. Its role is thus still more obscure. The sum of the lagged and unlagged primary price coefficients for the whole OECD sample is smaller than the single coefficient in the original UNCTAD equation, and would presumably attribute to primary product inflation only about one-fifth instead of two-fifths of the OECD's GDP deflator inflation rate in the crucial years 1970–4. For the United Kingdom and Japan, in particular, however, the sums of the coefficients are larger, and would have accounted for about a third of the inflation actually experienced at that time. For the United States, also, the contribution of primary prices, from this equation, works out at about a fifth for the years 1970–4; for Germany it is only about half of that.

It must be remembered that, since it is the GDP deflator that is being 'explained' here, the direct effect of primary product *import* price inflation is excluded – this is taken out in calculating the deflator in question – and what we are presumably estimating for single countries is the effect of the rise in world price of primary products on the domestic factor costs of their output. In the case of the United States, in particular, it must also be remembered that the important primary product factor costs are those of domestic output rather than imports, and that we are taking the dollar price of internationally traded primary products as representative of the price of that domestic output.

Such problems as these are largely avoided in the third approach discussed by Bosworth and Lawrence, in relation to the United States, Germany and Japan. The contribution of primary product inflation to the price inflation of final output rather than that relevant to value-added in the country is calculated, starting from price data on domestic primary output and imports of primary materials, and using input–output tables to give the primary content of final output. The primary content of imported intermediate goods is similarly included. In this approach, however, no account is taken of consequential changes in the country's factor prices outside primary production, such as wage inflation related to rise in retail prices, or the absolute increase of profit margins due to the application of constant percentage markups. On this more precise but conceptually restricted reckoning, only 18 per cent of the Japanese inflation in final output prices between 1970 and 1974 is accounted for by primary product inflation, and about 23 per cent of that in the United States. Agricultural products and energy in both cases are responsible in roughly equal degrees for most of the primary commodity push. In Germany the primary contribution – mostly from energy sources – seems to have been responsible, directly, for a slightly smaller proportion of the inflation of these years than in Japan. A rough calculation for the United Kingdom suggests a higher corresponding figure – probably between 25 and 30 per cent.

These separate approaches are to some extent complementary, but they do not add up to an entirely satisfactory assessment of the effect of primary price inflation on either the GDP deflators or the price levels relevant to final expenditure in the main industrial countries. It is, however, plain that there is some evidence for a secondary effect on GDP deflators, operating through factor prices in the non-primary goods industries of those countries, which for some of them is greater than that arithmetical effect on final purchases of the simple 'passing-on' of increased primary material costs. It is likely, too, that the secondary effect was not completed within the four years in question. It may be useful to look briefly, in this connection, at the next important case of inflationary push from primary product prices – that of 1978–80.

Between these two years, dollar export prices of non-fuel primary products rose by about a third, that of petroleum by 143 per cent. On the face of it, these increases would seem adequate to account for about a third of the rise in the price index relevant to final expenditure in the United States. Wage cost per unit in manufacturing rose some 12.8 per cent; if there were similar wage increases, but less growth of productivity, in the service sector, it would not be hard to account for the remaining two-thirds. For Japan (after allowing for exchange rate changes) primary inflation would seem capable of accounting for virtually all the price rise, leaving no room for increases in domestic factor costs outside primary production – a not entirely implausible conclusion, seeing that wage cost per unit of manufacturing output is recorded as having fallen a little, despite a 13.8 per cent rise in average hourly earnings. For the United Kingdom, however, with sterling appreciating at this time, it would seem possible to account for only something like a quarter of the relevant price increase by reference to primary product prices. Wage cost per unit of manufacturing output rose by some 40 per cent, which, together with corresponding rises in other sectors, suggests that much the greater part of the 30 per cent increase in final expenditure prices came immediately from labour costs outside the primary sector. There is clearly a great variety of national experiences here.

In fact, among our Big Six countries, plus Canada, rates of increase of hourly earnings in manufacture showed far from similar courses between the two-year period 1977–8 (before the new primary commodity push) and the period of push itself, 1979–80. Italy and the United Kingdom showed the most notable increases; rate of wage inflation up by nearly half. The others showed only modest increases apart from the United States, where there was a small decrease – though there, as in Canada and Italy, the peak rate of wage inflation which it seems reasonable to associate with this episode was not reached until 1980–1 when dollar prices of many primary products had started to fall.

We come back then, to the nature and mechanism of cost-push by world prices of primary products. On some assumptions, of course, such a phenomenon should not occur. Suppose that a country's nominal expenditure is geared firmly to its money supply, and that prices of primary commodity imports suddenly rise. If the demand for these imports is of less than unit elasticity, expenditure on them will rise, and with constant money supply, that on other things, including home production, will fall. The average price level applicable to final expenditure will be more or less unchanged; the GDP deflator will fall as the price of imports rises. Moreover, it is possible that the extra payment for imports may draw the money stock down, so that total expenditure will fall. This process will cease if and when the extra monetary wealth of the foreign producers of primary goods leads them to increase their expenditure on the country's exports, or as the reduced price level of the country's own products, plus the fact that its demand for primary imports is not completely price-inelastic, brings its external payments into balance again; or – a further channel of adjustment – an increasing shortage of money in the country raises interest rates and brings in loans from abroad, perhaps from prosperous primary producers.

It is even simpler to consider a closed economy (the world economy will do) in which there is a partial harvest failure. If demand for foodstuffs is price-inelastic, then more will be spent on them and less on other things, the price level of which will fall. There is no indication here that the properly weighted price index of all final goods and services will rise, or that it will fall.

How has the real world differed from these simple models? First, the implication that prices are universally flexible is unrealistic. It may well be true of many primary products, especially those that largely depend for their production on self-employed labour, not working for a contractual wage. Manufactures and a great range of services, however, do largely depend on employees at contractual wages and salaries, and on the ability of their producers to discharge other obligations (such as bond interest) fixed in money terms. Contractual factor prices are alterable only gradually. Collective bargaining tends to blur the connection between market pressures and wage movements, and can make resistance to reduction of real wages very strong. Final goods prices may tend to be administratively set in relation to cost, rather than freely market-determined (see chapter 10). Hence the first effect of reducing expenditure on non-primary products, or of holding it below the higher level required to accommodate increases in primary material costs, is largely reduction of profitability, abandonment of plans for expansion, closure of marginal establishments, and thus increase of unemployment. Where rise in primary product prices has lowered real wages (or kept them below the levels to which organised labour aspired) collective bargaining pressures have sometimes generated powerful wage–price spirals. Where the push came from import prices, governments were willing to expand purchasing power and raise domestic prices in order to avoid depression.

The second reason why a rise in primary prices can produce inflation rather than deflation in the non-primary sectors of the economy is that the supply of money, unless rigidly controlled, is in some degree sensitive to demand. Rise of primary prices creates both demand for extra credit to purchase and hold the commodities in question and, unless an early fall is feared, attractive opportunities for additional bank lending. The same is true of price rises in other sectors as the cost increase is passed on. Rigid control of the money stock, in the broad sense, was not generally an aim of policy until the mid-1970s, and where it was then attempted it did not prove easy or accurate. Apart from the internal creation of credit, the raised demand for money in particular economies where primary prices rose, and where confidence in the prosperity of the rest of the economy was not too much damaged, raised interest rates and drew in funds from outside.

In the light of this, the differences between the episodes of the early and the late 1970s, and between these and the episode of the early

1950s, are instructive. In 1972–5 the secondary effects of commodity cost-push were lubricated by abundant money – an abundance not, probably, mainly created in response to earlier price rises, though acceleration of prices of manufactures had preceded the 1970–1 leap in rate of money growth. In 1978–80, the primary price surge was accompanied by *reduced* growth of money stock, though still by accelerated general price inflation, and the succeeding reduction of real growth and increase of unemployment were unusually severe, but on this as in the previous episode national experiences differ widely.

The inflationary episode of 1950–1, which we have so far neglected (mainly because the data relating to it on a world scale are more sparse than those for later years) shows interesting differences both from 1972–5 and from 1978–80. In it, primary price inflation was largely confined to raw materials, and can be attributed mostly to speculative buying, and (so far as imports were concerned) rise of insurance costs, both due to fears that the Korean war would spread. As these fears receded, the price rise was reversed, and the index was down by 1953 almost to its 1950 level. Short though the episode was, however, it occurred at a time when liquidity was still abnormally high in some countries (a legacy of the second world war), and was accompanied by a surge of rearmament. In these circumstances, price–wage spirals in the industrial countries were active. The average rise of the consumers' price index in those countries was two or three times as great as can be accounted for by the 'pass-through' effects of contemporary primary product inflation, even if one ignores any negative effects of the primary price fall after 1951. This ratio of CPI increase to 'pass through' effects of primary product inflation was probably higher, in general, than that of 1972–5 or, *a fortiori*, than that of 1978–80, despite the greater accumulation of inflationary experience available to fuel expectations in the later episodes. But national experiences differ widely.

The two generalisations one can make are, (1) that primary product inflation can take place in widely differing conditions of money supply, and (2) that the size of the secondary inflation which it induces can vary widely between countries not only with differences in their policies of demand management, but with differences in the structure and behaviour of their labour markets.

INFLATION OF PRIMARY PRICES AND ITS REPERCUSSIONS

In conclusion, it may be useful to look at the relation between prices of primary products and those of final output from a slightly different point of view. Final output prices may be represented (adequately though not altogether accurately) by the IMF index of consumer goods prices in the industrial countries, and for this (mainly illustrative) exercise we propose to ignore the deviations between dollar prices and the IMF figures, which are calculated from national currency price indices.

Over the period 1953–81, the United Nations index of primary product prices rose 7.34-fold. If the factor incomes per unit of net output in the industrial countries had remained constant, the 'pass-through' effect of this primary product inflation (assuming zero price elasticity of demand) would have caused something like a doubling of the CPI, whereas, in fact, it virtually quadrupled. This, however, is too crude an approach to the contribution of primary product inflation to that of final product prices. The primary index would not have risen as far as it did if the nominal factor incomes per unit of output in the industrial countries had not risen. To deal with the hypothetical case where they do not rise, the reasonable assumption is that primary prices would have risen just enough to alter the terms of trade between primary and finished goods to the extent actually observed over the period – primary prices rising some 84 per cent in relation to the industrial countries' CPI. This condition, along with the constancy of industrial countries' factor costs per unit of output, gives a rise in primary (nominal) prices by 120 per cent, and of the CPI by less than 20 per cent. The greater (natural and artificial) scarcity of primary products, which changed the terms of trade, can be blamed, on this reckoning, only for about 13 per cent of the inflation actually observed (measured logarithmically) in the CPI – the rest is due to the bidding up of the industrial countries' factor prices in relation to the growth of their factor productivity.

One could, of course, go even further along this road of the imagination by supposing that factor owners' nominal hourly earnings in the industrial countries did not rise in line with factor productivity, but stayed constant. In that case, since total factor productivity probably increased between $1\frac{1}{2}$ and 2-fold, final goods prices would have come down substantially, and primary product prices would have risen only by less than 50 per cent.

But the direct, 'pass-through', effect of primary prices on those of finished goods may not be their only effect. Some of the bidding up of money wages and absolute money profit margins may have been 'real income resistance' to the check which the worsening of the terms of trade imposed on real income growth in the industrial countries. How much, however, it is hard to say; the amount could, in principle, be indefinite. In the fourteen years 1953–67, when there was no price push from primary products (even a slight cheapening), industrial countries' CPI rose by about 2½ per cent a year. In 1967–72, when the pass-through effect of primary inflation on the CPI must have amounted to about 1 per cent a year, CPI inflation rose to 4.8 per cent. In 1972–5, when the pass-through effect had risen to about 6½ per cent, CPI inflation was at 10.7 per cent. So far, the story is consistent with an autonomous rise of inflation due to factor price drift in the industrial countries increasing from 3 per cent to about 4½ per cent after 1967, and the incorporation in CPI inflation of the pass-through effects of 1967–72 and 1972–5 with very little further, secondary, effects added to them.

In 1975–8 matters are a little more complicated. Though the pass-through effect must have sunk to something like 1½ per cent a year (that is, by 5 percentage points), CPI inflation came down only to 8 per cent (by 2.7 points), and when the pass-through effect rose again in the three following years to about 5 per cent, or even more, the rise does not seem to have been fully incorporated in the rate of increase of the CPI. The most obvious explanation is that the primary inflation of 1972–5 left a legacy of price–wage spiraling in the industrial countries which gradually died down. In 1978–81, the rate of CPI inflation was still some 1½ per cent higher than the current rate of primary inflation pass-through might have led one to expect in the light of experience up to 1975.

Further than that we cannot now go; the stories for individual countries differ widely; their rates of upward factor cost drift before 1967, in the absence of stimulus from primary product inflation, varied widely, and the effects of alterations in exchange rates cannot be kept out. The evidence suggests that the secondary effects of primary price inflation on non-primary factor costs may have been substantial in the United States, the United Kingdom and Italy, small in Japan and Germany. What is certain is that the propensity for price shocks to generate a price–wage spiral varies widely between countries and between different times within a given country. But this does not mean that shocks such as those given by the flexible or administered commodity markets in 1951, 1973–4 and 1979 are unimportant. Whether it is easier and less costly to avoid the shocks or to change the constitutional reactions of national economies to them is a further question, but our present point is that the observed outcomes are the products of both these factors.

10

PRICE FORMATION IN NATIONAL ECONOMIES

We have now given some attention to each of the kinds of inflationary impulse distinguished earlier in this book, including those which came to our sample countries from the world market, by way either of prices of (and demand for) exports, or of the prices of those imports for which something like a world market can be said to exist. It remains to look more closely at the process by which prices of final output in our countries were formed. To examine it comprehensively is beyond our scope. Econometric studies of price formation have not been pursued with equal zeal everywhere; they have flourished in the United States and the United Kingdom especially and there are some other single country studies, besides a number of investigations applying relatively simple equations to a number of countries. Some of the United States and United Kingdom studies fit equations separately to a number of industries; some studies seek to explain movements of the GDP deflator as a whole. Some investigations (or parts of them) have applied to the output of manufacturing industry. Some important areas – especially parts of the large final services sector – have received little explicit attention. The general purpose of price equations (apart from the reduced-form Quantity Theory equations, to which we have referred in chapter 2) is to explain prices of final output in terms of prices of factor inputs and a term or terms representing the rate of utilisation of capacity and/or the general pressure of demand. It is on the size and interpretation of this last term that controversy largely turns. How far are prices of manufactures and other kinds of final output in relatively advanced countries directly demand-sensitive? And how far is the issue complicated by cyclical, or other, variations in factor productivity, which often seem themselves to be connected with the pressure of demand on capacity?

PRICES AND WAGES

As a first step, let us see how closely prices are related to wages alone, according to our own data. The test is a crude one, since we are using, for each of the Big Six sample countries, the first differences of

Table 10.1 *Wage and price inflation: correlation coefficients*

		1952–82	1952–79	1952–67	1968–82	1968–79
United States	a	0.69*	0.60*	−0.27 ns	0.54	0.44 ns
	b	0.92*	0.90*	0.35 ns	0.93*	0.92*
	c	0.87*	0.84*	0.61	0.68*	0.65
United Kingdom	a	0.81*	0.83*	0.44 ns	0.68*	0.74*
	b	0.95*	0.94*	0.76*	0.92*	0.91
	c	0.64*	0.63*	0.03 ns	0.38 ns	0.40 ns
Japan	a	0.57*	0.54*	0.27 ns	0.63	0.54 ns
(starting 1954)	b	0.79*	0.77*	0.57	0.83*	0.80*
	c	0.38	0.32 ns	0.10 ns	0.39 ns	0.22 ns
Germany	a	0.54*	0.58*	0.42 ns	0.68*	0.71*
	b	0.75*	0.82*	0.71*	0.82*	0.90*
	c	0.40	0.44	0.27 ns	0.39 ns	0.41 ns
France	a	0.70*	0.69*	0.61	0.73*	0.77*
	b	0.81*	0.78*	0.85*	0.66	0.61
	c	0.42	0.33 ns	0.02 ns	0.56	0.50 ns
Italy	a	0.85*	0.87*	0.85*	0.73*	0.78*
(starting 1953)	b	0.83*	0.84*	0.83*	0.64*	0.69
	c	0.66*	0.62*	0.23 ns	0.42 ns	0.41 ns

Notes: ns = not significant at 5 per cent level.
    * = significant at 1 per cent level.
    a wage inflation leading by one year.
    b no lead or lag.
    c price inflation leading by one year.

logarithms of, respectively, the GDP deflator and average hourly compensation in manufacturing (national currency basis), the latter from the United States Department of Labor, Bureau of Labor Statistics. Any variations in the ratio of manufacturing to other wage rates are therefore sources of error.

The simple correlation coefficients for the whole period (or as much of it as our data cover) and for two sub-periods, dividing at 1967/8, are shown in table 10.1; results for alternative versions of the whole period and the later sub-period extending to 1982 are also shown. In each case, price inflation is related not only to simultaneous wage inflation, but to that of the previous year and that of the succeeding one.

The first impression is that the general level of correlation between the simultaneous movements of price and wage inflation is high, usually well above the 1 per cent point of significance, the exceptions being the United States, 1952–67, and less drastically, Japan, 1954–67. The extent to which the figures support the hypothesis that wage inflation explains price inflation (or *vice versa*) varies, however. In the

United Kingdom, for instance, for the period as a whole, something like 90 per cent of the variance of one variable is explained by the other; for Germany, only 67 per cent (or 56 per cent if the period is extended to 1982). The correlation also varies between sub-periods; it is lower in the earlier one except in France and Italy.

The second point to emerge is that the correlations where w leads p by a year are higher than those where p is in the lead, the sole and striking exception being the United States, for the whole period and both sub-periods, but especially for the first one. The suggestion is that the adjustment of prices to wages is more clear-cut than the opposite adjustment, except in the United States. In most cases, however, the correlation with wages leading is poorer than that where there is no lead or lag, the exceptions being Italy throughout (but most markedly in the later sub-period) and France after 1967.

There is, then, a *prima facie* indication that year-to-year wage movements explain the greater part of those of prices, usually without much time lag, though there are interesting international and inter-temporal variations and some exceptions. We propose first to see what has been made of the contribution of wages and other factor costs in some more systematic multi-country studies. We shall then, for each of the larger economies, summarise a sample of the most illuminating econometric studies, where they are available, and supplement them with our own observations, based on the ground prospected in chapter 3 and other evidence, particularly that relating to changes in productivity.

MULTI-COUNTRY STUDIES

Of the multi-country studies which we shall mention, only one, by Robert Gordon (1977), to which we have already referred for the sake of its wage equations in an earlier chapter, contains price equations of the pure form we have just mentioned, final prices explained in terms of factor prices and demand or similar terms. Gordon uses, as independent variables, quarterly from late 1958 to early 1973, the lagged dependent variable, money supply, wage rates (separating out the contribution of dummy variables found useful in his wage equations), the level of the output ratio (actual output to trend) and an index of prices of internationally traded goods. His eight countries are the United States, the United Kingdom, Canada, France, Germany, Italy, Japan and Sweden. Neither the money supply nor the output ratio are found significant for any of the countries. Traded goods prices is significant positively for Japan, Germany and Italy, but perversely for the United Kingdom. Wages without their dummy element are significant for the United States, the United Kingdom and (in a lower degree) France and the dummy element is also significant (or with France nearly so) in the two last-mentioned.

Laidler's price equations, which we have already noted along with his wage equations, in a previous chapter, apply to the United States, United Kingdom, Germany, Japan, Italy and Switzerland over the years 1954–70. In contrast with Gordon, he finds a measure of excess demand (the output ratio) significant in all his countries in what is designed as the 'sociological' equation; a strike variable in this equation also proves significant in the United States, the United Kingdom and Italy. In his 'monetarist equation', price inflation is related to expectations variables, represented by lagged world inflation and national inflation rates and (again) lagged output gaps. The last-mentioned variable again proved significant in most cases. Lagged world inflation rates seemed to show some explanatory superiority over import price inflation (which was also tried), unless a constant term was included. The general implication of Laidler's findings in this connection is thus that demand forces are at least as strong as supply forces in determining the course of inflation. It must, however, be remembered that these equations relate to the whole process of price determination in a country, including that which takes place in the factor markets as well as that in the product markets, and are thus not comparable with Gordon's price equations just described, which relate only to the product markets. Moreover, the period for which Laidler's equations were fitted was mostly that for which we earlier observed that the Phillips relation remained reasonably valid in wage determination in most countries and it could be this, rather than demand effects in the product markets, that his income ratio term picks up.

The same remarks apply to the price equations (for 1955–68) fitted by Maynard and van Ryckeghem to data on thirteen OECD countries. These are reduced-form equations using lagged inflation rate, unemployment, import price inflation and indirect tax changes as the independent variables. The results are of varying satisfactoriness. They suggest, however, that, insofar as these variables explain the courses of price inflation, the most powerful of them is the unemployment variable in seven cases (United States, United Kingdom, Germany, France, Belgium, Canada and Denmark) and that it is significant everywhere except in Japan and Sweden, where (as in the Netherlands also) import prices are the most powerful. To repeat, however, we are talking here about factor and product markets combined, and about the golden age of the Phillips Curve. Both these authors and Laidler find their equations poor at predicting the inflation of the following few years after those to which they are fitted; they under-predict it.

From these multi-country studies, therefore, we have no positive evidence of the importance of demand factors in the product markets alone, and some (from Gordon) of their unimportance. But we must proceed to single-country studies for more light.

PRICE EQUATIONS IN THE UNITED STATES

In a review of empirical studies of United States price determination undertaken in the 1960s, Nordhaus (1972(2)) found quite general agreement about the structure of the price equation which was used, apart from the reduced-form monetarist model. He listed three main assumptions: (1) prices are set as a mark-up over normal costs, changes which include those in wages, but do not fully reflect short-run fluctuations in productivity; (2) temporary cost changes affect prices less than permanent changes; (3) the mark-up over cost is influenced by the pressure of demand of which various measures are then introduced additively to the equation.

He found that labour costs (either cost per man-hour or cost per unit of product) were invariably highly significant, but with widely varying lag structures and with long-run price elasticities on unit labour costs ranging from 0.37 to 1.8. About half the equations contained a significant term in material (or farm product) costs with elasticities between 0.6 and 0.4. All the studies surveyed by Nordhaus omitted capital costs, although he argues that quarterly changes in this variable may be quite large especially when changes in tax legislation occur. Demand variables, on the other hand, displayed far less uniform effects. Various measures were used, but the most successful appeared to be capacity utilisation, with an elasticity between 15 and 45 per cent. Two of the studies included a guidepost dummy (relating to the period of voluntary price and income policy following 1962) but these gave inconclusive results.

Since then, there have been further major studies, of which we may first note that of Nadiri and Gupta (1977). These authors constructed a model which integrates the long-run determinants of equilibrium price (assuming a Cobb-Douglas production function and profit-maximising firms) with short-run disequilibrium factors operating in the goods market. Firms adjust prices toward their long-run equilibrium levels by a simple geometric adjustment process where the amount of adjustment is assumed to be influenced by a measure of short-run disequilibrium, namely idle capacity.

The short-run reduced-form price equation so arrived at for

estimating purposes sets the price level as a function of hourly earnings, raw material prices, rental price of capital services, a measure of capital services, a measure of capacity utilisation, and past expenditures with a distributed lag to represent expectations of change in expenditure, all measured logarithmically, and a trend rate of productivity growth. Price is thus taken to be a function of variables which influence the long-run equilibrium price on both the cost side (wages, raw materials, capital services and long-run productivity) and the demand (nominal expenditure) side; and also of the short-run adjustment factors (capacity utilisation and lagged prices).

The equation is estimated for the period 1954:1–1972:2 using quarterly data in three applications: for the total economy, the total private non-farm sector and the total manufacturing sector, as well as for various sub-groups within manufacturing on which we do not comment. Money wage rates appear to be a significant determinant of prices in each case, with a short-run wage elasticity of about 0.12 and a long-run elasticity of 0.7 in the total economy and 0.4 in manufacturing. These values are in line with the shares of labour in output as reported by Nordhaus. Long-run productivity growth is also significant in each case, with the expected negative sign. Its coefficient in both the short and the long run, however, is much smaller than that on wages. This may suggest that prices are more regularly, or perhaps more fully, adjusted to wages than to productivity.

The rental price of capital appears to have a positive, but small effect in the aggregate and private non-farm economy, and raw material costs are very important in the manufacturing sector but do not appear so elsewhere. In manufacturing, the elasticities of prices with respect to raw materials exceed those with respect to wages. The expected demand variable, intended to capture long-run changes in demand, is positive and significant in each case, although the long-run elasticity of price with respect to changes in expenditure is well below unity (for the private non-farm economy it is equal to 0.3). Unit changes in aggregate demand thus lead to changes of roughly one-third in prices and two-thirds in output in the long run.

The effect of the utilisation rate is slightly more complex. Nadiri and Gupta find a consistently negative coefficient attached to it, although in all three applications it is significant only when lagged prices are excluded. This, of course, is in contrast to the positive effect of capacity utilisation on price changes reported by Nordhaus. Nadiri and Gupta interpret it as reflecting the effects of short-term changes in productivity. They report that similar results were obtained when a variable measuring the deviation of productivity from its trend was substituted for capacity utilisation. In other words, given some excess capacity, an industry-specific increase in demand, which raises the utilisation rate of existing capacity, results in a movement along a falling unit cost curve which in turn lowers prices. One possible reason for the conflicting signs on capacity utilisation may be the different periods of the two studies. Examination of our data suggests that in 1969–70 and again in 1970–1 pricing showed greater responsiveness to cyclical changes in productivity than in comparable stages of previous cycles.

The other work we note here is one on United States data by Robert Gordon. In 1975 he had published a paper showing relatively strong effects of aggregate demand on the price mark-up, that is on the relationship of the aggregate price level to the aggregate wage level. In a later article (1977) he reestimated his structural price equation and it is to these results that we refer. Gordon takes the view that the price level, net of indirect taxes, is marked up over total cost by a margin which varies with the level of excess demand in the goods market. Total cost in turn consists of unit labour cost, material prices and the user cost of capital. The equation is estimated in terms of quarterly percentage rates of change and technical change is assumed to be labour augmenting. The dependent variable is the rate of change of the deflator for non-food business sector products, net of energy. There are six independent variables: (1) the rate of change of excise tax; (2) the rate of change of the relative price of materials; (3) the deviation of the growth rate of actual productivity from its trend; (4) the rate of change of wages minus the trend growth rate of productivity (trend unit labour cost); (5) the rate of change of the relative price of capital goods; and (6) a proxy for the excess demand for commodities (the 'output gap').

Gordon's results are somewhat similar to those of Nadiri and Gupta. Both find a negative relationship between prices and deviations of productivity growth from trend, although Gordon is working with rates of inflation whereas Nadiri and Gupta are working with the price *level*. Both also find that the level of demand has a separate influence on prices relative to wages, although Nadiri and Gupta take nominal demand whereas Gordon uses the real output gap. Price controls seem to have affected the timing, and hence variation, of inflation although not its long-term average rate. The relative price of materials also seems to have been important and its importance probably increased in the 1970s. Neither of these models tested for changes in the effective exchange rate although later work (Frye and Gordon, 1981) found this had a significantly negative effect. In addition, lagged inflation was not included in Gordon's work although other studies have found strong inertial effects. It is noteworthy that Gordon finds the negative effect of deviation of productivity from its trend much strengthened when the study is extended into the mid-1970s.

Finally, referring to the period between 1971 and 1974, Blinder (1981) has identified the major shocks which hit the United States economy and attempted, where possible, to quantify their effects on the price level. These are as follows: (1) the devaluation of the dollar by about 19 per cent between August 1971 and mid-1973 probably raised the United States price level by about 2.8 per cent (as measured by the CPI) from 1972 to 1973; (2) fiscal and monetary policy actions each raised the annual growth rate of GNP between 1971:1 and 1973:1 by about $3\frac{1}{2}$–4 percentage points, giving a combined net effect of around $7\frac{1}{2}$ percentage points, more than total growth; (3) with respect to the food price shock which began to hit retail prices in early 1973, Blinder's calculations suggest that, from mid-1973 to mid-1975, about 5 percentage points of the annual inflation rate were attributable to food and that this contribution was relatively steady during those two years; (4) the rise in energy prices probably raised the consumer price level by about 3 per cent, $3\frac{1}{2}$ per cent and $4\frac{1}{2}$ per cent by the third quarters of 1974, 1975 and 1976 respectively (the study ends in 1976); (5) Blinder and Newton find that while the Nixon price controls were in effect they slowed inflation modestly; the maximum cumulative deflection of the price level was about 2–3 per cent and it occurred in February 1974. By November 1974 the price level was somewhere between 0 and 1.5 per cent below where it would have been had there never been a controls programme.

Let us see what we can add to this account of price formation in the United States from our own less systematic observations, starting with the quantity–price relations sketched in chapter 3 and adding other relevant data. The story starts with the collapse of the primary commodity boom of 1951, accompanied by a fall in the rate of wage inflation, even though the economy continued for a time to move nearer to full employment, a result which the wage and price controls of 1951–3 may have helped to bring about. In 1954, the end of the Korean war precipitated an absolute fall in real output, which may be seen as the start of a series of fairly regular and moderate cycles for the next dozen or so years, in which the rate of inflation was always positive, but varied relatively little and tended, almost uniquely in the experience of our sample countries throughout our period, to be a little greater when output was growing fast than when it was growing slowly.

It may be remembered from chapter 8 that, during this period, nominal hourly earnings in manufacturing in the United States (as in the other larger OECD countries, except France) broadly followed an unlagged Phillips relation over the cycle. This means that they lagged perhaps a year behind deviations in the *level* of output from trend. From our scrutiny of price and quantity variations (in the economy as a whole) in chapter 3, it appeared that the first difference of the GDP price index moved with, or slightly preceded, deviations of output from trend, which implies that the level of the index (or its deviation from trend) would also follow somewhat behind that of output. It is, indeed, plain from inspection of the United States series that wages and prices, or the first differences of the two, move roughly together. It is also plain, however, that variations in the growth of productivity in manufacturing moved with the cycle in growth of output. They also showed a larger amplitude than that of hourly earnings, which was small. Consequently, growth of labour cost per unit of output, in manufacturing at least, varied on the whole counter-cyclically; it showed minima in 1955, 1959, 1962–3, 1968 and subsequently in 1971–2 and 1976, which were approximate maxima of real output growth. Consequently, change in the profit share of value-added in manufacture varied mainly pro-cyclically, with maxima in 1955, 1959, 1963, 1968 and, later, 1971 (but in 1975 rather than 1976).

This is a combination of circumstances comforting to theorists. It can easily be shown that, in a closed economy, the (proportionate) rate of change of real labour income per person-hour is equal to the sum of the proportionate rates of change of real output per person-hour and of the labour share of value-added (which is, of course, the complement of the profit share). In the United States, in the period in question, the two former variables tended to be of the same sign (the same as that of output growth), the third of the opposite one. Increased output went with increased profit share for firms (which might explain their output increase) and with higher real hourly earnings (even though with decreased share of total output) for employees, which might explain why more of them came forward and/or why they worked longer hours. It is possible to believe that both parties were on their supply curves, though whether that is a realistic or sensible belief is another matter.

We have noted that price inflation varied, in this period between the Korean and Vietnam wars, roughly in step with wage inflation in a pro-cyclical manner, but that the amplitudes of both were small. If much account had been taken of cyclical variations in productivity, the movement of price inflation would have been counter-cyclical and the pro-cyclical variation of the profit share would have been ironed out or reversed. It seems likely that, in this period, manufacturers tended to set prices of their products on the basis of factor prices, making constant rather than cyclically varying allowances for growth of productivity. That factor prices were important, apart from any effects of capacity utilisation or product demand, is suggested by the way in which finished goods prices responded to those of raw materials, with output growth low and falling, in 1956 and 1957. Did mark-ups on cost vary with pressure of final demand? The pro-cyclical variation of profit share is consistent with their having done so but, as we have seen, the wide pro-cyclical variation of productivity growth, if inadequately or not at all allowed for in pricing, is capable of giving the same result.

From the middle 1960s, an intermediate period begins in which the relation between changes in output and price is more liable to upward shifts than in the preceding dozen years. Upward price inflation shifts in 1966 and perhaps 1969 seem to be associated with increased rates of inflation in the United States raw material and farm product markets, partly reflecting world market conditions in non-ferrous metals, though not so clearly those in world agricultural markets. To some extent, therefore, these shifts may be regarded as exogenous but certainly not wholly so. The years in question are ones of high United States output in relation to trend, but it seems to have been through the price sensitive raw material markets rather than through those for finished goods that the high demand operated. In 1968, there was an unusually large wage increase, not counting as a case of wage-push by our criteria of chapter 4, because rising productivity growth enabled the profit ratio to be preserved, but again suggesting that factor prices rather than mark-ups may be blamed for the rise in the GDP deflator. From 1968 onwards, however, it is simplest to view United States price–quantity relations as entering on a new phase, similar to the experience of most other countries, with a negative correlation between changes in output growth and inflation.

It remains broadly true, in the years since the later 1960s, that the real product wage varies with output over the cycle; the main exception to this, in our whole period, is a weakening of the relation between 1961 and 1966. It remains true also, on the whole, that productivity in manufacturing varies with the cycle, and with a wider amplitude than the real product wage. The consequent broadly counter-cyclical variation of labour costs per unit of output, expressed in terms of the product, also continues to be perceptible, though it is perhaps looser than before 1969. Except for a coincidence of maximum labour cost growth with minimum output growth in 1973–4, the turning points of labour cost growth preceded the (opposite) ones of output growth in the 1970s.

In summary then, apart from the exceptional events of 1951–2, when strong reductions in the growth of both costs and expenditure coincided, the United States economy seems to display two main phases, with perhaps an intermediate stage between. In the first, up to the late 1960s, demand fluctuations were associated with fluctuations in the growth of real output, with relatively little variation in the rates of inflation of either factor or product prices (though there was an underlying, basic, rate of inflation of both of these). Gordon (1982) has remarked on the variability of employment, rather than wages, as being characteristic of the United States economy, in contrast with those of the United Kingdom and Japan. In manufacturing, at least, the rate of productivity growth was closely connected with the rate of growth of demand and output. Higher growth of expenditure seems to have provided simultaneously both faster growth of real wages and improvements in the profit share of value-added, presumably raising both the demand for and the supply of labour and other factors and, until the mid-1960s, the supply of factors seems to have been highly elastic. Cyclical variations in productivity seem to have been ignored in pricing output.

The intermediate stage perhaps begins with the fall in supply elasticity of labour as full employment was approached and with development of scarcities in some primary markets and pricing may have become a more year-to-year process, in which changes in productivity could not be ignored. In the second phase, changes in factor cost inflation became major sources of disturbance, affecting capital formation and the growth of output in a degree that had not been apparent in the first phase. To say that they did so because they were not completely accommodated by expenditure, money supply and final product prices, would be an over-simplification, because (while the authorities no doubt stopped short of a perfectly elastic supply of purchasing power in the face of accelerating inflation) firms and final purchasers were also probably deterred from planning expansion of their activities by accelerated price increases which they did not expect to continue.

But, as we have noted in a previous chapter, the apparently most important quantity–price shifts, so far as inflation is concerned, are those in which the whole pattern is moved to a higher level of price inflation, from which it does not return – for the United States, the shifts of 1966, 1967, 1973 and 1977. All of them involve increases in the growth of unit labour cost of output and all but the first one are marked by a significant increase of import price inflation.

The first of these crucial shifts (1966) is mostly explicable from a sharp increase in wage inflation which was not subsequently reversed and which coincided with a decline from a very high level of productivity growth. That of 1967 is similarly, and more completely, explicable, though this increase in wage inflation was not maintained; about half of it was redeemed in the following two years, but they were years of increased inflation of foodstuff and raw material prices. The jump of 1973 was, of course, largely a primary price matter, including some effects of devaluation, but it was followed by a no doubt largely consequential acceleration of wage inflation. The shift after 1976 was traceable to increased primary price inflation again. In fact, the maintenance of the increased inflation rates established in these shifts seems to have been due to an ascending series of wage and primary product inflations alternately, sometimes with obvious reactions of one on the other, sometimes not. When these two sources of cost inflation abated together, there was an abatement of product price inflation, as in 1976, but the second oil shock ended such an abatement in 1979.

On the whole, the conclusion seems to be that the pricing of United States manufactured output, and probably of services that enter directly into the final product, is based mainly on cost calculations, which take account of year-to-year changes in factor prices but mostly treat productivity growth as constant over somewhat longer periods. There may be some sensitivity of mark-ups to demand, but it is of minor importance in comparison with at any rate the larger increases in factor prices. The primary commodity and some intermediate inputs into final output, however, are in a different case. Prices of foodstuffs, raw materials and some metals are sensitive to supply and demand forces, either in the world market or, in some cases, in a partly segregated United States market and in those markets, though supply side influences have been of great importance, variations in United States demand, either by itself or as a large part of world demand, have carried a big weight.

PRICE EQUATIONS IN THE UNITED KINGDOM

Even more than in the United States, the major topic of debate in empirical studies of the United Kingdom price inflation has been whether the pressure of demand has an independent influence on prices or whether its influence comes entirely through its effect upon factor prices, mainly wages, and hence upon costs.

A study incorporating both independent demand effects and a price expectations term was undertaken by Solow in 1969 using both annual data, from 1948 to 1966, and quarterly data, from 1956 to 1966. The two sets of data yield very different coefficients on the variables for unit labour cost and price expectations (a term generated by an adaptive expectations model). This may well reflect the very different characters of the period 1948–55, which is included in the annual equation only and 1955–66 which is included in both. Materials prices, which attain the highest degree of significance among the independent variables of the 1948–66 equation do not appear in that for 1956–66; on the other hand a variable representing capacity utilisation appears significantly in the latter period though not in the former (longer) one.

The suggestion that excess demand (represented by the capacity utilisation variable) exerted an independent effect on inflation was, however, challenged by the results of Godley and Nordhaus (1972) in a study of manufactures excluding food, drink and tobacco. Their work was based on the hypothesis that prices move with normal cost and do not react to temporary changes associated with fluctuations of product demand. Series of weekly earnings, hours, employment and output were purged of all effects of short-term variations in demand (except such as may be incorporated in basic hourly wage rates) and 'trend' rates of unit labour cost calculated. A predicted price series for the period 1955–69 was then constructed on the basis that firms fix their prices as a constant mark-up upon average normal historical current costs, including the costs of materials, fuel, services and indirect taxes, but excluding capital costs and taxes on profits. Tests were then carried out for the presence of independent demand effects upon the mark-up of price over normal historical current average cost. In only four cases out of one hundred were significant coefficients on excess demand found and only one of these was positive. In addition, these authors tested the hypothesis that actual price is a function of predicted price and of a measure of capacity utilisation and found the coefficient on the latter both small and non-significant.

The authors acknowledged certain problems with their assumptions but doubted whether these detracted substantially from their results. For example, it is known that the mark-up on cost declined considerably from 1961 to 1969, which is at variance with the normal cost hypothesis. Further, there is an identification problem. If profit margins increase in booms and fall in depressions, is this because prices are marked up over actual current average cost levels by percentages geared to the level of demand, or because prices are based on standard unit costs, but actual unit costs fall below trend in boom and rise above it in depression?

More recently, Sargan (1980), after extensive study, confirmed that the behaviour of prices from 1951:2 to 1973:4 is well explained by an equation containing a long-tailed Almon distributed lag on normal costs and that there is relatively little evidence for any impact of the general level of demand.

Tests of the normal cost hypothesis have also been extended to industry level. Coutts, Godley and Nordhaus (1978), using a similar approach to that above, studied seven individual industries for the period 1957 to 1973. Although they find slightly more significant demand effects than in the earlier study (about 9 per cent of coefficients significant), a majority of these are negative, suggesting that in the cases concerned final prices decrease with increases in demand, given costs. Their individual results show values for the elasticity of price with respect to demand as lying between 22 per cent and minus 32 per cent, with a mean estimate of zero.

Both the tendency for output increases (and by implication demand) to lower rather than increase prices and that for the net impact of output changes on price to be rather small, were confirmed by Sawyer, Aaronovitch and Samson in a study of pricing in 40 manufacturing industries for the period 1966:1 to 1975:4.

Of course the normal cost hypothesis does not exclude the possibility that demand influences costs and through that route affects prices in manufacturing. The presence and form of demand effects in wage equations are matters of considerable debate as we have seen in chapter 8. The cost of basic materials and food to the United Kingdom is largely determined by import prices, which in turn are thought to be governed by world demand and supply factors, which we have considered in chapter 9. We add here only that purely domestic demand pressure may lead to pressure on the balance of payments and, in turn, on the exchange rate, so that sterling import prices rise and thus also influence the domestic inflation rate.

The normal cost hypothesis may seem vulnerable to the argument that domestic prices are affected directly by those of competing imports; the 'law of one price'. However, Coutts et al. find little significant effect for the behaviour of competitive import prices on the price of domestically produced manufactures. In a study of United Kingdom manufactured exports Ormerod found the following long-run coefficients on world prices and domestic wholesale prices respectively:

Estimation period	World price in sterling	Domestic wholesale price
1964:3–1972:2	0.631	0.369
1964:3–1973:2	0.547	0.453
1964:3–1975:2	0.482	0.518
1964:3–1976:2	0.567	0.433
1964:3–1978:2	0.443	0.606

He argues that not much importance should be attached to small differences in the sizes of the coefficients and concludes that world prices and domestic costs have probably carried roughly equal weight in the pricing of manufactured goods, even since the introduction of floating rates in 1972. The direct conclusion, however, would seem to be that home produced manufactures as a whole, the sample of them which is exported, and the whole body of internationally traded manufactures, while not independent of one another in their price behaviour, are only loosely connected and that the competition prevailing in this area is of a highly imperfect kind.

Finally, we may note the implication of one of the price equations used by United Kingdom forecasters. An example of the type of equation used by the National Institute is given in Ormerod (1981). The equation for consumer prices is based on a model in which firms are operating in oligopolistic markets and set prices so as to ensure that in normal circumstances a profit will be made over current costs. It is a cost-plus mark-up theory of inflation, but one in which the mark-up increases when real demand increases.

The equation estimated over 1971:3–1979:4 implied that the short-term elasticity of consumer price inflation with respect to the output of manufacturing industry is less than 0.1.

It is, indeed, plain from an inspection of annual first differences, as well as from the correlations reported earlier in this chapter, that the relation between change in average hourly earnings and change in the GDP deflator in the United Kingdom is fairly close, especially if one makes some allowance for the lagged effect on price inflation of the major changes in import price inflation, as in 1951–3, 1968–9 and the mid-1970s. For most of the time there are signs of a small lead by wage changes, though this is less in evidence from about 1963 to the mid-1970s and its reappearance after that is unclear because of the interference of import price shocks. Moreover, when one contemplates the negative cyclical relation between price inflation and output growth which prevails throughout our period in the United Kingdom as, indeed, it does in nearly all our sample countries for most of the time, it is not surprising that hypotheses of pricing based on standard (de-cycled) costs do not uniformly accord with a strong positive relation between the mark-up ratio and the use of capacity. Even though prices of non-food manufactures, with which Godley and Nordhaus, for instance, worked, move rather differently in detail from the GDP deflator, they also generally display a negative cyclical correlation with output. If, on the other hand, pricing is related to current, or only slightly lagged costs, varying cyclically, counter-cyclical variation of price inflation can be explained provided that there is either a counter-cyclical variation of wage inflation, or a pro-cyclical variation of productivity growth, or some combination of the two.

On inspection, it proves that manufacturing productivity growth in the United Kingdom, like that in the United States, does indeed vary on the whole pro-cyclically (peaks in 1955, 1959, 1964, 1968, 1972 and 1976). In contrast with United States experience, however, British wage inflation has shown relatively large short-term variability, so that one cannot say unambiguously, as one can of the United States, that so far as short-term fluctuations of unit labour costs are concerned, productivity is the predominant influence. Nevertheless, the main minima in the growth of nominal unit labour cost in manufacturing (wage inflation *minus* productivity growth) seem to fall in 1954, 1959, 1963, 1973 and 1977, all except the last, years of high or rising output growth. So far as manufacturing is concerned, there is some evidence of basically counter-cyclical variation of unit costs which, of course, should help to explain the cyclical variation of output growth by firms, so long as the prices of their products do not vary sufficiently to cancel the implied fluctuation of incentive.

There are two obvious tests of whether this is so. One is to subtract changes in product prices from those in unit nominal labour costs to get changes of unit labour costs in terms of the product. This makes very little difference to the dating of the minima; unit product labour cost variations are clearly counter-cyclical. The second test (which should differ from the first only insofar as sources of the statistics are mutually inconsistent) is to look at the year-to-year changes of the gross profit share in manufacturing. Happily, there is a good deal of agreement; maxima here seem to occur in 1959, 1963, 1967, 1972 and 1977. Prices vary cyclically with unit costs, but to a smaller degree, so the profit share varies negatively with them both. This is consistent with some damping down of cyclical price variations, in comparison with what would happen if they followed unit labour costs pro-portionately, by some use of standard (de-cycled) labour costs. But it is, of course, also consistent with the incorporation in the costs upon which price is based of some elements less volatile than labour.

It may seem extravagant to suppose that prices of manufactures vary from year to year in such a way as to incorporate the effects of short-term productivity variations, productivity changes being largely unpredictable and perhaps not very often measured by firms. Wages are better known and even predictable sometimes for as much as a year ahead. If prices were based upon wages only, however, with the assumption of some standard level or trend of productivity, price variations would still be broadly counter-cyclical, because that is the case with wages (hourly earnings show minima of increase in 1953, 1957, 1963, 1967, 1973 and 1977, at, or more often a year before, output growth maxima). It may be remembered that in chapter 3 we argued that, given a cycle of roughly four years, this timing of events was consistent either with a Phillips relation – maximum wage *inflation* going with maximum output *level* (above trend) and maximum wage level following a year after – or with not instantaneously effective policy measures to reduce growth every time price and wage inflation rose substantially.

Is the picture we have drawn consistent with a pro-cyclical variation of real wages (as in the United States) and therefore with labour being mainly on a stable supply curve? In the earlier part of our period this seems to have been broadly so; the growth booms of the mid-1950s and the early 1960s go with high increase of real wages. After that, however, the relation decays and from about 1965 there is little correspondence between the two series. The growth increases of 1973 and 1976, for instance, were accompanied by reductions in growth of real wages. If the labour market was ever continuously in equilibrium (which is doubtful), it seems at any rate to have ceased to be so by the mid-1960s.

Looking beyond the purely cyclical movements, however, what is there to say about the quasi-permanent shifts to higher levels of nominal income growth – shifts to the north-east as seen on the quantity–price diagram (chart 3.4.2, chapter 3)? The main shifts in question, those not soon reversed, occurred in 1968, 1970, 1973, 1974 and, if one does not look beyond the end of our period, 1979.

The shift of 1968 was a case of wage-push (possibly to be attributed to relaxation of incomes policy) and import price-push, certainly to be connected with devaluation. The same two varieties of cost-push were in evidence in 1970, wage inflation being particularly severe, and their influence on price inflation seems to have continued into the following year. This was the first rise into a region of the diagram not encountered since 1950–1. The great expansion of 1973, though like other cyclical ones in going with a reduction of price inflation, was another landmark on the road to quasi-permanently higher inflation rates insofar as the reduction was smaller than experience of the previous twenty years might have led one to expect. Unlike, for instance, the expansion of just ten years before, it went with a fall rather than a rise in the rate of productivity growth in manufacturing. Since this was by far the biggest annual rate of increase in United Kingdom output in our period and also (perhaps more to the point) the highest summit of real growth in relation to a logarithmic trend over the whole thirty years, one is tempted, as with the United States in the same year (and in the mid-1960s) to suggest decreasing physical returns due to pressure on productive capacity. But there was also a sharp increase of import price inflation. The remaining British fluctuations can be regarded as movements up and down a line representing growth of nominal expenditure by about 14 per cent a year, apart from the great price and wage inflation of 1974–5 and its abatement mainly in the following year, which we have not included in our list of quasi-permanent shifts. (That inflation was accommodated by a temporary increase in money expenditure growth, though at a low and apparently constant level of profit share and a negative rate of real product growth. Although it is obviously to be connected with the surge of wage inflation following the breakdown of incomes policy and its aftermath of threshold payments linked to retail prices, it does not formally qualify as wage-push.) The striking feature of all the quasi-permanent upward shifts is that they qualify as cases of cost-push by import prices, or by wages or by both.

All north-easterly shifts on our diagram involve accommodation of increased rates of expenditure growth. The obvious question is whether the permission of these increased rates cannot simply be regarded as 'the cause' of accelerating inflation. Part, at least, of the answer is that, if the initiative were with expenditure shifts, one would expect them to be accompanied by increases in profit share – to be cases of expenditure-pull, according to our criteria. None of them is. On the contrary, 1968 is, as we have seen, a case of wage-push with decreasing profit share. The north-eastward movement of 1969–71, taken as a whole, goes with a substantial fall in profit share (a big fall in the first year, a smaller recovery in the second) and it was in 1972, with a fall in expenditure growth, but with continuation of the shake-out of labour begun in the preceding year, that profit share regained its 1969 level. Profit share certainly decreased sharply in 1974 and only in the following year does the latest available series of estimates show it recovering very slightly (according to earlier versions it continued to fall). Although it may have fallen again marginally as growth rate of expenditure began to collapse in the following year, over the whole two-year period of growth collapse, 1975–7, it rose very substantially. Cost variations rather than expenditure variations seem to have had primacy in these movements.

JAPAN

In the case of Japan data deficiencies, in the earlier years especially, create some difficulties of interpretation and it must always be remembered that the manufacturing sector may have behaved very differently from the rest of the economy. It seems, however, justifiable to say that, as in the United States, both real wages (in either wage goods or product terms) and the profit share move pro-cyclically, their reconciliation being achieved by a pro-cyclical fluctuation in productivity growth, which in manufacturing is of large amplitude. The fall in price inflation from 1953 to 1955 seems amply explained by reduction of wage inflation, but the rise to 1957, when unit labour cost inflation in manufacturing was apparently still falling and import price inflation steady, appears to have been a matter of demand; the profit share rose. Fall of demand growth, along with a reduction of wage inflation, seems also to have been important in the slump of 1958 (unit labour costs rose with a fall of manufacturing productivity, and the profit share fell).

From this point, the series of substantial cycles in growth rate begins. The expansion of 1958–61, an increase of about 8 percentage points in annual growth rate, brought a roughly equal increase in the price inflation rate. Wage and import price inflation rose, but there was a net fall in the rate of increase of unit labour cost in manufacturing, and probably little if any increase in unit total cost, and the profit share rose very markedly (from about 53 to 58 per cent in manufacturing). In the growth recession of the following year, both price and wage inflation fell by three or four points, though unit labour cost inflation rose (because productivity growth fell too) and the profit share declined. The new expansion of 1962–4 brought little increase in price inflation. Wage inflation actually fell a little, productivity growth rose and profit share in manufacturing probably increased; elsewhere it may well have fallen. This pattern of growth fluctuation with little change in inflation remained until the end of the expansion of 1965–8, during which wage inflation had begun to rise substantially but had been offset by more rapid productivity growth.

It looks as if producers had been learning to live with cyclical variation in productivity growth, perhaps under pressure of increasingly active competition. They do not seem to have been guided entirely by wage rates at this stage, because they did not respond to the very substantial rise in growth of hourly earnings in 1966–9 until 1970, when it had ceased and productivity growth had begun to fall sharply. Thereafter, until the end of our period, the inflation rate of the GDP deflator moves very closely with that of hourly earnings, though with a smaller amplitude. Manufacturing productivity growth continues to fluctuate as much as before, if not more.

The large wage explosion of 1972–4 seems to have affected the economy very much as a supply shock rather than a response to a normal cyclical rise. Price inflation shot up despite a negligible

increase in growth and with total output no further above trend than
it had been in the last four years of the 1960s. In 1974 it rose further,
despite a reduction in the rate of growth of expenditure, and growth of
output fell from nearly 10 per cent a year to a negative value. The rise
in price inflation was somewhat greater than that of wage inflation in
these two years but, since there was an even greater rise of import
prices and a 20 per cent a year fall in productivity growth, the
manufacturing profit share fell sharply. It had made only a modest
recovery by 1979. What the events of 1972–4 amounted to was a 14
percentage point increase in the rate of price (GDP deflator) inflation,
accompanied in manufacturing by a rise of perhaps 23 points in unit
labour cost and accommodated to the extent of only 5 points in
expenditure growth.

The remarkable feature of the aftermath of this episode in Japan
was the speed with which wage inflation fell, not merely to the level of
the mid-1960s, but by 1978 to only 5 per cent a year, with unit labour
cost inflation in manufacturing fluctuating about zero. This was no
doubt much assisted by the collapse of import price inflation into a
(temporary) 15 per cent fall by 1977–8, itself assisted by the 40 per
cent average appreciation of the yen. But, from the domestic point of
view, what is perhaps most remarkable is the fact that this fall of
nominal manufacturing wage inflation brought real (consumer goods)
wage inflation down from about 9 per cent a year during 1967–73 to
about $1\frac{1}{2}$ per cent during 1974–8, while at the same time the
non-labour share of total GDP fell from over 40 per cent to about
one-third. The suppliers of both labour and capital had their situations, or at least their prospects, sharply worsened without an
inflation-exacerbating battle of shares.

In view of the big changes that seem to have occurred in price and
output behaviour between different parts of our period, it is perhaps
not surprising that the multi-country price equation studies have
yielded varying and not very clear-cut results for Japan. Laidler is in a
minority in finding demand a significant variable; we have noted
some cases in which it seems to have been important in the later
1950s. Gordon does not find wages significant. There is, however,
a strong superficial appearance of significance (according to our data)
in the last few years of his period, though not in its first few years.
Maynard and van Ryckeghem find import prices influential, though
it will be recalled that they deal only with the years 1955–68. It will
be recalled that we find a high correlation between wage and price
inflation in the second part of the period, though only a poorer one
in the first.

On the whole, variations of wage inflation seem to supply the most promising single clue to Japanese price variations. The very large year-to-year variations in productivity growth do not seem to have been taken into account in any systematic way, though the steep productivity trend, of course, has. *Prima facie* instances of direct demand influence seem to be confined to the earlier part of the period, for which the data (especially on wages) are weak.

We have already noted that German experience includes a succession of cycles which involve more variation of price inflation than do the United States cycles of the 1950s and early 1960s, but are not negatively tilted in the marked degree that we found in the United Kingdom. Apart from a period in the early 1950s when price inflation was unusually low (negative in 1953), German cycles show a very considerable regularity, those of the early and middle 1970s differed less, both in form and in average inflation level, from their predecessors than was the case in most of our sample countries and by 1979 the inflation level had returned to that of a decade earlier.

Although we found the correlation coefficients between wage and price inflation rather lower in Germany than in other countries of the Big Six, the more striking variations in the rate of price inflation seem nearly all to be related to changes in the increase of factor costs. Of the upward movements, those of 1954, 1956, 1960, 1969, 1970 and in a small degree 1973, satisfy the criteria for wage-push, in the last of these cases assisted by import price-push. In 1955 and 1965 there was increasing wage inflation without a reduction in the profit share. Of the downward movements, those of 1952, 1967 and 1976 are all instances of negative wage-push. The first two of these, and 1953, were also years of diminished import price inflation, and 1959, 1963 and 1972 showed reduced wage inflation without the increase in profit share which would have satisfied our negative wage-push criterion. Changes in productivity growth (in manufacturing) make some contribution to the picture; a fall must have assisted the big increase of price inflation in 1968–70 and a sharp rise helped the moderation of inflation in 1976, for instance, but their relative part, as compared with changes in wage inflation, was smaller than in the United States or, probably, the United Kingdom. German wage inflation varied much more than American, and average productivity growth in manufacturing seems to have varied less from year to year than it did in either the United Kingdom or the United States. Its variations were positively (but rather poorly) correlated with those of output growth; the time series of changes in nominal unit manufacturing labour cost is a somewhat amplified, but otherwise not much changed, version of that of hourly earnings. These show a marked cyclical tendency, with peaks often in the year after that of maximum real growth and troughs in, or just after, the minimum growth year – hence the loops in the quantity–price diagram. But here, too, cyclical movements are far from being the whole story of wage inflation. In particular, there is the unusually big rise of 1968–70 and the combination of reduced amplitude and downward trend thereafter.

We have noted earlier that the multi-country studies which have used price equations to test for demand effects in Germany have in some cases got positive results (Laidler and Maynard/van Ryckeghem), though Gordon's price equation did not; nor did Gordon find lagged wages significant, a fact possibly connected with the compressibility of the profit share, also expressed in our finding of several cases of positive and negative wage-push. Maynard and van Ryckeghem find import prices a significant influence, however.

Change of unit labour cost in terms of product in German manufacturing seems to have varied counter-cyclically, generally with about a year's lead over growth of output (which implies that change in the profit share varied pro-cyclically with this lead), so that increased demand seems to have brought increased profit incentive with it, but real wages (like money wages, to which we have already referred) seem to have followed a loose relation with output, lagging behind it rather more in the peaks than in the troughs. In Germany's case, however, it is hard to believe that the supply of labour, including foreign labour, was not perfectly elastic at any of the going real wage levels of the time; the notion of an aggregate labour supply curve is hardly relevant.

There is no need to explain permanent accelerations of German inflation because, since the recovery from the price fall of 1952–3, no acceleration has gone uncancelled. We have already noted the relation of the relatively large increase in price inflation in 1968–70 to contemporary wage inflation and decline of productivity growth. The pressure of import price inflation after 1972 was moderated by upward valuation of the currency but, in addition to that, there was no wage-push after 1970, except a very mild case in 1973 and the strong fall of wage inflation in 1974–6 (satisfying the criteria of negative wage-push in 1976) brought the rate of increase of unit labour costs down to the level of the 1960s, or lower. This, so different from American or British experience, is a less dramatic version of what happened in Japan.

Gordon, as we have noted, finds only a marginally significant relation between wage and price inflation in France for his period 1958–73. It may be that some wage effect is captured by his lagged price variable. Over our period as a whole, inspection of the data and a correlation coefficient of 0.78 suggest that the relation is a fairly close one, with a few marked exceptions, if one allows for a constant increase in productivity at about 4 per cent a year. The available data on manufacturing show relatively little year-to-year variation in productivity growth, so that the course of change in nominal unit labour cost of manufactures broadly resembles that of hourly earnings. We have also noted (chapter 3, table 3.2) that price inflation shows very little simple correlation with the output gap over either our whole period or the sub-periods we distinguished, which suggests only a limited role for demand variations in altering the short-term course of price formation. On the other hand, wage inflation has varied widely from year to year. A considerable part of this variation seems to have been absorbed by changes in the profit share, notably in the wage-push episodes of 1954, 1956, 1968 and 1973–4; nevertheless the general resemblance between the courses of wages and prices, after some allowance for lag, remains.

The confused nature of the evidence about factor shares in France makes it hard to generalise about its relation to variations in activity, which are themselves both smaller and less conformable to anything like a four-year cycle than in most other countries. The substantial fall in profit share in 1974, suggested by most of the data, went with a collapse of the growth rate and with a wage explosion which, however, did little to increase real hourly earnings, because it was mainly an adjustment to worsening terms of trade. As in Germany, the elastic supply of labour (including foreign labour) makes discussion in terms of an effective rising supply curve of that factor more than usually unhelpful. Over the period as a whole, however, it seems doubtful whether the profit share went at all regularly with the deviation of output from trend.

The relation between wage and price inflation becomes closer (especially in years of rapid change in wages) if one allows for a lag of prices behind wages of about half a year, the price change of each year related to the average wage change of that year and the preceding one. This, in itself, should imply a fall in the profit share in times of accelerating wages and a rise when wage inflation declines, and this implication is broadly verified by the falls of profit share of 1954, 1957, 1968, 1974 and the rises of 1953, 1965 and 1977.

The chief departures from this fairly close, if slightly lagged, relation between movements of wages and of prices are the failure of price inflation to increase in 1954, its somewhat excessive rises in 1963 and in the years after 1976 and, most strikingly, its excessive rise and fall in 1958 and 1959 respectively. The first of these may be explained by expected continuance, or lagged effects on cost, of the fall in import prices of the previous year. The inflation increase of 1963, which would, apparently, have had to be even higher to maintain the profit share of value-added, may have been based on expected continuance of the previous three years' rise in unit money costs. The relatively high price increases in the late 1970s must bear some relation to the resumption of import price inflation; anything like a uniform percentage marking-up of total input costs will cause prices and profit margins to rise faster than wages when import prices do so.

The episode of 1957–9 must be related in this way also to the devaluations of August 1957 and December 1958 but the notable thing about it is the concentration of most of the price adjustment on 1958, though rises of import prices were in fact greater in the preceding and the succeeding years; the second devaluation seems to have been largely discounted in advance.

But with all qualifications, the relation between wage and price movements in France must be judged fairly close as these things go.

ITALY

The most striking feature of Italian experience is the variability of wage inflation. It is not very regularly cyclical, showing a rather broad major peak in the early 1960s, followed by three or four years of a mild nature, then a sharp peak in 1969–70, and a high uneven plateau extending from 1973 to 1977. The fluctuations of Italian economic growth are not very regular either and the relation of wage inflation to them is rather loose; nearly uncorrelated until the later 1970s and then definitely counter-cyclical. The growth of industrial productivity shows, on the whole, shorter-term variations, unusual among those of our sample countries in not being definitely pro-cyclical (in terms of the growth rate) until the 1970s, when its amplitude becomes wider.

As we have already seen in general terms, the changes in the GDP deflator bear a generally positive relation to those in wages, but with a lag and with considerable variations. From 1953 to 1956, the relation is fairly close, but the amplitude of price movement much smaller than that of wage movement. From then until 1961 the changes, down and up again, in price and wage inflation are similar to each other, apart from a drift along the wage inflation axis, as if the fact of rapid productivity growth were increasingly being taken into account. In the burst of wage inflation in 1963, price adjustment seems to lag, perhaps by about half a year and, apart from a rapid initial reaction when the peak of wage inflation is reached in 1964, takes time to settle back, as it does by 1968, to something like the relation to wage change which had existed a decade earlier. At all events, there is the suggestion that wage movements (or the larger ones, at least) lead, and that price change takes a time, not always quite the same one, to adjust. In the big wage increase of 1970, price inflation again seems to have been slow off the mark and to have resumed what in the light of previous experience looks a normal relation to wage increase only in the two following years, when the wage inflation rate had partially receded. Again, most of the price increase corresponding to the even bigger wage inflation of 1973 came only in the following year, together with what may have been a supplement connected with the ascent to phenomenal rates of import price inflation. The incremental wage–price relationship continues, with wages showing much the greater year-to-year amplitude, but with a large constant element in price inflation, apparently unaffected by year-to-year changes of wage increase, until the end of our period; probably the fruit of long experience of high *average* rates of cost inflation. These irregularities, and the influence of traded goods prices, may have been responsible for Gordon's failure to detect a wage effect in his price equation. Laidler detects effects of excess demand, traded goods prices and strikes.

Our own interpretation, unless rise of wage inflation is accompanied strongly and reliably with increases in growth of productivity, suggests rather a variable profit share. In fact, as is implied by what we have already said about the cyclical characteristics of wage inflation and productivity growth, no positive correlation between growth of wages and productivity exists in Italy; indeed, by the 1970s there is a *negative* correlation between them. It is therefore not surprising to find (though the data leave a good deal to be desired) that, after the 1950s at least, the profit share shows more year-to-year variation than that in any country we have so far discussed. In particular, fall of the profit share goes with increased wage inflation, and rises of it quite often with slower wage increase. Italy, even more than the United Kingdom, is the land of wage-push. The symptoms of it, as we have formulated them, are fairly clear in 1954, 1956, 1960–3 (*passim*), 1969–70, 1975 and 1977; its negative counterpart appearing in 1953, 1959, 1965–6, 1976 and 1978. One or the other (that is to say, profit share and wage inflation moving in opposite directions) thus occurs in more than half the years for which we have data.

There is a decided tendency for wage-push to go with rises of price inflation combined with smaller falls in the rate of growth and for its negative counterpart to accompany falls in price inflation with smaller increases of growth, though there are exceptions. Wage-push goes, for instance, with growth contractions in 1954 and 1956, with no price change or only a little. It also goes with the expansion of both growth and price inflation in 1961 and, more oddly, with the great contraction of 1975, which carried a reduction in the rate of price inflation.

The story of quasi-permanent increase of inflation in Italy may be said to start about 1959. Four consecutive years of wage-push, reducing gross profits by some 10 per cent of the whole GDP, took the inflation rate of the GDP deflator up to about 8 per cent. Whether because of the reduced profit share or for other reasons, growth of capital formation and of income then declined and during 1965–6 wage inflation came most, though not all, of the way down towards its 1959 level, allowing the profit share to regain about half its lost ground and the real growth rate to recover. There followed two years of renewed wage-push (1969–70), most of it concentrated in the events of the hot Autumn of 1969; investment growth again collapsed (1971) and real income growth fell to the lowest level, up to then, in our period. Wage inflation fell back by 1972 to 10 per cent; about half its 1970 peak rate. But the cycle did not continue as eight years before. The rise and partial relapse of wage inflation had been very rapid and price inflation took time to adjust itself to the net rise of cost inflation, as we have already noted. There was thus hardly any fall of price inflation before, in 1973, wage inflation leapt again to a point above its previous, 1970, peak.

The great bulk of acceleration in Italian price inflation occurred, however, in the two years 1973–4. The first of these was a boom year, with advancing growth rate and the 13 percentage point rise in wage inflation to which we have referred, though the level of activity was less far above the long-term trend than in the late 1960s and unemployment was a little higher. The following year, 1974, saw some falling off in the growth rate but, at least in manufacturing industry, the profit share of value added seems to have gone on rising, probably because some attempt was made to maintain the mark-up over total direct costs, which in that year included a 73.5 per cent increase in import prices.

The great fall in expenditure growth in 1975 took place at the same time as renewed wage-push, so that the fall of real output growth (to a negative figure of about 4 per cent) was the largest in any of our

OECD sample countries. There was, however, very little fall in wage inflation; over a two year period it even rose further. When it did decline significantly, in 1978, it came down by only half the amount by which it had risen since 1968 and then, in the final year of our period, under the influence of rising import price inflation, started to go up again. By that time, the volume of Italian output was some 9 per cent below its trend (which it had risen nearly 7 per cent above in 1970) and unemployment was substantially higher than in any of the previous twenty years. In the economy as a whole (though it seems to have been less so in manufacturing) these conditions reduced the profit share markedly but that did not prevent prices from reflecting in the main the course of wages.

OTHER COUNTRIES

There are indications from other countries too that prices of manufactures, or of domestic non-farm output generally, are largely cost-determined, though sometimes with the addition of a short-term or adjustment factor related to the departure of output from some normal level and sometimes with an extra effect of import or world prices, beyond what would be justified by the direct and indirect import content of the products in question. But the importance of demand influences is limited. In the Reserve Bank of Australia's quarterly economic model of the economy, for instance, excess capacity enters the price equations in a form calculated to give a sharply increasing effect as full use of capacity is approached, but (according to Challen and Hagger) Argy and Carmichael, in an adaptation of this model used in a simulation exercise, found a price equation without such a term effective for the period 1962–73, though it may be that its role was taken by the cyclical characteristics of the productivity growth term they introduced. For 1947–60, Kmenta had found a demand term significant at the 5 per cent level in an Australian general price index equation in which, however, weekly earnings achieved a very much higher level of significance. For India, however, it is hard to see much relation between the available indices of wages in manufacturing industry and of prices of manufacturers; the latter seem to be more closely related to prices of imports.

The existence of what we may call a demand effect, in addition to a cost effect, of import prices on the prices of a country's output, which may be regarded as implied by a coefficient of import price in the price equation greater than the share of imported inputs in the output in question, brings us near to a version of the 'Scandinavian' model of inflation rates in open economies, referred to in chapter 8. The starting

point is that the price level of all the output of a country which is internationally tradable must move with the world price of such goods,
whether it is in fact traded internationally or not; it is in competition
with traded goods, either at home or abroad. Not all the output of a
country does, of course, consist of tradable goods. Therefore, if the law
of one price (or one rate of inflation) for all tradable goods held
good, the general (tradable and non-tradable goods) rates of inflation
would differ between countries according to (1) the extents to which
the inflation rates of their non-tradable outputs differed from each
other and (2) the differences in relative weights of tradable and
non-tradable goods in their general price indices. The further conten-
tion of this theory is that wages are likely to move similarly, perhaps
with a lag, in the tradable and the non-tradable goods industries
within any one country, so that international differences in inflation
rates of non-tradable goods prices will depend, in anything but the
short run, upon the respective countries showing different gaps
between the rates of productivity growth of the tradable and non-
tradable sectors. A country where there was no gap would necessarily
show a rate of general inflation equal to the world rate for tradable
goods; a country where productivity advanced more slowly in the
non-tradable than the tradable sector would show a higher rate of
general inflation. (This simple formulation requires, of course, that
rates of change of profit shares should not differ between countries in
such ways as to spoil its simplicity.) Given approximate constancy
within each country of its ratio of tradable to non-tradable goods and
the difference between rates of productivity growth in their respective
industry groups, the general price index, as well as that for tradable
goods, would follow the world pattern.

Maynard and van Ryckeghem (1976) tested the applicability of the
Scandinavian model to twelve OECD countries over the period
1954–68. It is immediately plain that the own-currency prices of these
countries' exports followed different courses ranging from a 2.3 per
cent average annual increase in the case of France to a 0.9 per cent
decrease in that of Italy. Dollar exchange rates of the relevant
currencies had in several cases also changed during the period, in
such a way as roughly to compensate for the worst divergences of
own-currency export prices. If these exchange rate changes could be
regarded as exogenous, they might be thought of as *causes* of the chief
own-currency export price divergences. The circumstances of their
occurrence, however, including the continuing prevalence of the
Bretton Woods system, and the balance of payments positions at the
times of alteration, make it much more convincing to treat currency
realignments as the *results* of divergent movements of the prices of

tradable goods and services. Very broadly, it is also true that the larger countries which suffered from a relative increase in the prices of their exports and which devalued their currencies (the United Kingdom and France) showed higher rates of increase of labour cost per unit of output in their international goods industries than did the more successfully competing countries, Germany and still more, Italy and Japan, the last two of which reduced both their unit costs and their export prices in terms of their own currencies. The implication is that neither the export prices nor the related unit costs were kept in line by the mechanism of the world market, though Maynard and van Ryckeghem found some evidence that export prices for these larger countries were governed in their year-to-year movements rather more by world prices than by unit labour costs. For most of the smaller countries included in the study (Belgium, Canada, Denmark, the Netherlands, Sweden, Ireland), the influence of world prices, as compared with unit labour costs, appeared from their data to be more complete and the divergences of their trends from that of world prices were smaller (about a third as great, on average). The trends of the larger countries' unit labour costs deviated from that of world prices appreciably more than did those of their export prices, but those of the smaller countries deviated very much more, not much less than the larger countries' trends did. On this showing, the forces of the world market did something towards keeping the larger countries' export prices in line, rather less towards doing so for their unit labour costs. for the larger countries. It must be remembered that these calculations are performed with index numbers which may not in all cases be ideal for the purpose and using data on productivity which are distinctly fragile. But they suggest that the world markets' control over national unit labour cost levels is weak, while its influence over manufactured goods prices is plainly insufficient to destroy the evidence we have seen of, broadly, cost-plus pricing.

CONCLUSIONS

The chief message of the econometric price equations we have examined is that, where they relate price inflation to factor prices, they tend to support, at least for manufactured goods, a simple mark-up theory of pricing, with relatively little apparent influence of the pressure of demand on the mark-up factor (occasionally even a perverse one).

Our own study of events in the Big Six tends to confirm the existence of short-term relations between general price inflation and inflation of factor prices – wages in particular – with factor prices tending to lead, though with considerable complications, some of them related to the stronger role of materials prices in the early 1950s and since the early 1970s. A further important complication arises from the usually pro-cyclical variation of productivity growth. In the United States and the United Kingdom especially, but also apparently in Japan, these variations have been sufficient to make unit costs of output vary counter-cyclically, and to a larger extent than prices, so that the profit share increased in expansion. At the same time, real wages were enabled to rise faster in expansionary phases of the cycle, even though their share in value-added fell. In Germany, France and Italy, this relation of real wages to the cycle has not been so clear; in Italy, especially, variations of productivity growth have not been regularly pro-cyclical. In all the Big Six, the big extra-cyclical rises in rate of inflation have been connected (as we noted in chapter 4) with wage-push and import (or sometimes internal primary) price-push to disproportionate extents.

The prevalence of mark-up pricing and the limited influence of demand on the size of the mark-up require some explanation. Why do sellers not vary prices (and profit ratios) so as to clear the market? The question is an old one, and the extensive literature on it is well discussed by Okun (1981). For our purposes it will suffice to say that the explanation of relatively rigid prices began fifty years ago with Gardiner Means (1935); the suggestion was that oligopolies have an interest in preserving the joint monopoly element in their revenue by refraining from price competition, and that maintaining stable prices is a device for avoiding relative price changes, which would be likely to ensue, to the detriment of each seller's security, if each attempted to trim prices to his own changing perception of what the market would bear. The 'kinked demand curve' models of Hitch and Hall (1939) and Sweezy (1939) added the thought that oligopolists would see the present price as maximising their profits, because to lower price would invite competitors to do the same, making demand for the individual firm's product relatively inelastic, while to raise it would incur at least the danger that competitors would not follow – in which case the loss of sales would be serious.

What theory has to explain, however, is not only the relative inflexibility of many prices, but why they seem to respond to changes in cost more readily than to changes in demand. On either the 'joint monopoly' or the 'kinked demand curve' line of argument, this requirement can be met, to some extent, by the reflection that firms will see a change in factor costs as something which can be objectively assessed, and which applies to them and their competitors alike, so that they can safely use it as a basis for price adjustment without upsetting market shares and starting a price war – a view taken by many writers, including Brown (1955).

Okun's chief contribution is to point out that, wherever each seller takes the responsibility for setting prices, some degree of attachment between buyers and sellers will suit both parties; sellers because a faithful clientele gives security and reduces selling costs, buyers because regular connections give some security and save buying costs. This at once introduces a positive slope into the individual seller's demand curve; it also probably introduces a kink, because established customers may be frightened off by price increases, but will not be correspondingly increased by price decreases. The situation, therefore, is as the previous lines of thought had suggested, but is not limited to market situations which would be generally recognised as oligopolistic. Moreover, the 'reliability' of a seller, which keeps established buyers loyal to him, includes a reputation for not taking advantage of increases of demand to raise prices and profits – hence the reluctance of sellers to do this on an experimental basis, with the intention of coming down again if competitors fail to follow. It is, indeed, the case, as investigators onwards from the Oxford Economists' Research Group (which provided the data for Hitch and Hall) have found, that price changes in line with cost changes are widely considered 'fair', while others are suspect. All things considered, the failure of prices in most markets to behave like those in auction markets is not hard to understand.

This being so, our conclusions about price formation in general during our period may be summarised thus. The markets for final goods and services have made little direct contribution, in the more advanced market economies at least. They have mostly passed on the costs of factor inputs, and the impact of change in demand in them has mainly been on output rather than price. In the world food-stuffs and raw material markets, on the other hand, changes in demand, and in supply also, have had direct and sometimes drastic price effects – though the most important price shocks of all sprang from institutional upheavals, affecting administered prices. The labour market has in many countries exerted almost continuous upward pressure on costs, by no means insensitive to the state of demand or to cost of living changes, but strongly affected by varying institutional circumstances, not readily reduced to simple economic terms.

These seem to have been the main mechanisms of price formation from which inflation flowed. We turn now to its effects.

11

INFLATION, WELFARE AND GROWTH

EFFECTS IN THEORY

What light, if any, does the experience of our period throw upon the effects of inflation? Have they been good or bad? At the time of writing, the general views of governments and electorates are highly unfavourable to inflation. Its reduction has been given high degrees of priority – in the United Kingdom overriding priority – and electorates in many OECD countries seem to have found success in that endeavour a substantial, if not an entirely adequate compensation for depression, slow growth and high unemployment such as had not been experienced for well over a generation.

To the great majority of people, inflation is clearly, in itself, a bad thing. Most people sell only their services, at a price fixed, at any time, in terms of money. They, or their households, buy a wide range of goods and services, approximating to one or other of the 'baskets' of goods and services in general with reference to which inflation is defined and measured. It therefore presents them, in most cases, with cause for continuing anxiety lest the prices of their particular services should fail to keep up with it. Adequate revision of money rates of wage or salary is widely seen as something that has to be fought for. There is probably a great deal in John Flemming's observation that people whose pay is revised annually are aware of the achieved revision only on one day in the year, and of the gradual decline of the purchasing power of their receipts throughout the other 364. (His ingenious conjecture that inflation may cause trouble in the home, because husbands are aware primarily of rising pay, and wives primarily of rising prices, is less substantial, but still not to be lightly dismissed.) What is quite certain is that all holders of money and of assets denominated in terms of it stand to lose more the higher the rate of inflation goes, that inflation necessitates troublesome revision of all pecuniary valuations, and that, for many people, including some politicians, decline in the real (and perhaps still more the foreign exchange) value of the national currency is an affront to their patriotism.

The practical strength of all these grounds for objection is, of

336

course, very much increased by the fact that inflation, and not its opposite, has prevailed for as long as most people can remember. In the last two decades of the 19th Century, and in the early 1930s, it was price *deflation* and its supposed effects that attracted attention, as witness in the former time the fear that mankind might be 'crucified upon a cross of gold', and, in the latter, the New Deal's 'price codes'. Perhaps the moral is that approximate stability of the general price level in the long term is the most popular regime – at least for the reason that it is not a sufficiently noticeable phenomenon to attract widespread public attention.

All this, however, relates to popular perceptions of the direct effects of trends in the general level of prices. Attempts to assess the effects of different trends on the total working of the economy, or on the consequences of that working for the general level of welfare, are another matter. We have already noted in chapter 5 that it is possible to imagine an economy in which a given rate of inflation is both universally expected and realised, and in which the only effects of the inflation (and expectation of it) will be (a) that rates of interest will exceed by the rate of inflation the levels they would have under constant prices, and (b) that the quantity of cash in circulation (notes and coin, on which it is not practicable for the holders to receive interest) will be smaller, in real terms, and in relation to income, than it would be in a steady price regime. Provided that *all* prices are sufficiently flexible, it is not clear that the performance of such an economy would differ from what it would be with a constant price level, except for the inconvenience costs of people carrying less than the real amount of cash that would be optimal without inflation, and the extra costs of altering price-lists, vending machines and the like. Universal expectation of the established inflation-rate would probably ensure that wages and salaries were adjusted to it in such ways as to give their recipients little more cause for anxiety about the real outcome than they would have with a zero inflation rate. The real value of savings would be protected against the effects of inflation by the higher rate of interest. It would be more troublesome in such an economy than in a non-inflationary one to use one's memory of past prices of particular goods in assessing present levels, or in estimating for the future, and members of it would be up-staged by foreigners from less inflationary countries; but short of a very high inflation-rate, the material effects of such an inflation would not be important.

The relevance of this to the real world is limited by the closely interrelated trinity, price inflexibility, imperfect foresight and uncertainty. When a changed expectation of the future course of the general price level is formed, even if it is correct, some prices are slow for

institutional reasons to adjust. The great fall of real wages in the
inflation of the 16th Century is perhaps an extreme case in point,
though increasing population pressure may also have had something
to do with it. The cases of expenditure-pull in our period may be taken
as relatively minor examples of delayed wage adjustment, those of
wage-push, with some qualifications, as possible instances of delayed
price adjustment. For anyone who has entered into contracts on the
basis of a false expectation of the course of prices (say a lower inflation
rate than that which actually occurs), the higher realised rate can
obviously be a very serious matter indeed. Even our hypothetical
period of universally expected inflation would be likely at its beginning to have inherited bond-holders, for instance, who bought their
bonds before they, at least, expected the inflation in question, and
who suffer capital loss when interest rates rise to match what has now
come to be expected. Holders of equities since before the change in
expectations make corresponding windfall gains.

With changes in the general level of prices, as with changes in
relative prices; the bigger they are, the more likely it is that
individuals, or whole sections of society, will enjoy big gains or suffer
big losses through being right or wrong, respectively, in their anticipations, or simply lucky or unlucky in the choices they happen to make.
In so far as anticipations are based on past experience, there is some
presumption also that the more complex the course of inflation over
time is, the more likely it is that a lot of people will be wrong about it.
High inflation and, still more, variable inflation might therefore be
expected to alter the general distribution of income.

The nature and effects of such an alteration are, however, dependent upon other things. The windfall loss, or series of windfall losses,
of wealth by fixed-interest debt-holders, as general price rises which
they had not anticipated take place after their acquisitions of the debt,
will make for a less unequal distribution of income and wealth if
fixed-interest borrowers are poorer than fixed-interest lenders; it will
make for a higher growth rate if the borrowers have a higher
propensity to invest out of marginal changes in their income than the
lenders have. The former (equality) effect is problematic; the latter
(investment) effect rather less so – Keynes's (1923, 1930) bias towards
moderate (under-anticipated) inflation was based on its presumed
transfer of resources to the enterprising. There is also a possible effect
on saving, not taken into account in the earlier discussion of the
subject. If the money-denominated assets whose real value is reduced
by unanticipated inflation are regarded primarily as part of necessary
reserves against emergency, their depreciation will prompt efforts to
rebuild the reserves by extra thrift.

Insofar as under-anticipated inflation leads to lags of wage adjustment and increases the profit share, it also transfers resources to
entrepreneurs and encourages productive investment, though in this
case there is some presumption that distribution of incomes is made
more unequal. In all these connections, however, it must be remembered that *more variable* inflation may well mean that some inflation is
over-anticipated, which would lead to a reversal of the transfers, and
consequent effects, that we have mentioned.

The other point to be borne in mind in connection with wage lag
and the like is that it is not a universal phenomenon. In fact, it is plain
that the effects of inflation on the distribution of income and wealth,
and on the probability of enterprise and growth, will depend on where
it comes from. We have, indeed, taken as an indicator of wage-push,
or more generally, cost-push, the reduction of the profit share in
company with accelerated inflation of the cost in question. If wages,
or other cost items, take the lead in inflation, it is to be expected that
profit margins, the saving ratio, and thus both the incentive and the
capacity to invest will be at any rate temporarily reduced, while in the
short run the incentive to produce may also suffer. Certainly this is to
be expected if it is from import costs that the push comes; if it comes
from higher wages, they may provide some compensation in the form
of higher demand for consumers' goods. Cost-push inflation is thus
inimical to activity and growth, though wage-push may make immediately for a rather more egalitarian distribution of income.

On the other hand, demand-pull, from whatever source, is almost
certain to stimulate the level of activity to some extent, even if, in the
presence of labour shortage and/or other production bottlenecks the
additional expenditure goes mainly into raised prices at home and
increased net imports from abroad. It is also likely, though not certain,
to raise the profit share, directly augmenting both the motive and the
means for increased domestic investment. If the expenditure pull
takes the form of expenditure on additional domestic capital formation, then almost *ex hypothesi* any additional inflation that results goes
with faster growth. On the face of it, this is a case of a push for faster
growth *causing* inflation rather than of inflation (from some unstated
cause) turning out to favour growth, but we have noted that a
structuralist might put it differently. In countries where it is politically
difficult to cut private consumers' expenditure further by taxation,
credit-financed inflation may be the chosen *instrument* by which resources
for urgently required extra growth are obtained. Expenditure-pull inflation, at all events, seems *a priori* likely to be *associated* with growth,
as well as with high levels of activity in relation to capacity.

We have not yet touched on the third member of the unholy trinity, uncertainty. Whatever the effects of realised inflation on the expectations entertained of its continuance or modification, and whatever its effects in transferring real income from one section of society to another, its occurrence, and more particularly its variability, are likely to induce uncertainty about the future of prices, which influence economic behaviour very differently from positive expectations that inflation will continue or not continue, its rate rise or fall.

If uncertainty about the future of prices is general, people will wish to avoid commitments in money terms for the future, the more distant future especially, either as borrowers or as lenders. Long-term investment projects, insofar as fixed interest borrowing is the preferred way of financing them, thus tend to be avoided in favour of shorter-term investment. A switch to equity borrowing or to repeated short-term borrowings helps, but does not provide a perfect substitute for greater confidence in the price level (see Flemming 1976, chapter 11). There is thus some bias towards shorter-term investment; some indeed, against investment altogether. The effect on the propensity to save is more problematic. There is perhaps some presumption that increased uncertainty impels people to desire bigger reserves, in some form, which implies real saving related to the *rate of increase* of perceived uncertainty – more likely to be significant for short-term variations in it than for its general level.

Finally, it is suggested (Friedman, 1977) that the 'noise' introduced into economic signals by varying inflation, and by varying and uncertain expectations of it, has the effect of causing more mistakes to be made than in a situation of steady general price levels, so that the effectiveness of the investment is reduced and the marginal capital–output ratio raised. This effect may be taken as comprehending the bias towards shorter-term investment, just mentioned, but as being broader.

EFFECTS IN PRACTICE

Out of all these effects of inflation on welfare and economic growth that theory suggests, how much can be distinguished in practice? We must be prepared to find little easily discernible, since the influences on welfare and growth are numerous, and inflation is only one of them. Some things are easily seen. The misfortunes of money and bond holders and the corresponding windfall gains of equity holders are obvious. At least in the advanced countries, however, measures have been taken which have in some degree mitigated personal hardship from excessive faith in the value of money, as from other sources. State insurance benefits, financed out of current income and largely indexed to costs of living, have been initiated or greatly extended in scope and real magnitude. Supplements out of current revenue have in some cases been paid to repair the ravages of inflation on the real value of fixed nominal benefits from occupational pension schemes. Much disappointment of previously held expectations by those holding assets denominated in money terms has no doubt remained but, apart from observing an absence of evidence that it has been socially catastrophic, it is beyond our scope to evaluate it.

People are not so innocent about the safety of the value of money as they used to be. Keynes, in the *Tract on Monetary Reform*, written in the shadow of the great European hyperinflations, gives an eloquent account of their traumatic effects in victimising those who, according to all previous conventional wisdom had been most cautious. But by the later 1920s the lesson that equities might be safer in real terms than bonds or money was being widely proclaimed, not least by Irving Fisher (1928, 1930). These warnings and the events of the succeeding generation must have done something to diminish the extent to which wealth holders allowed themselves to be caught out by the inflation of our period and perhaps more to diminish their sense of shock when they were caught out.

If we are to try rather more systematically to look for associations of inflation with observable economic magnitudes which may be presumed to have a bearing on welfare, we should perhaps do well to focus on three such magnitudes or classes of magnitude; measures of the degree of inequality of distribution of income and/or wealth, levels of real income, and rates of growth of real income. The first of these classes of magnitude presents difficulties because there is no single, unambiguous, measure of degree of inequality which can be shown to be the right one for our purpose, but we must make do with the measures available. The *absolute level* of real income, even *per capita*, is hardly likely to be worth studying comparatively, between countries, for clues to the influence of inflation on it in our period, since countries' average real incomes already differed very greatly at the beginning of our period for reasons relating to their previous history. So far as the relation of a particular country's income level to varying inflation rates is concerned, probably the best we can do is to examine the relation (if any) to inflation of deviations of real income from its long-term trend. Whether there is an association, positive or negative, of inflation with *rate of growth* of real income (especially *per capita* real income) is a rather more straightforward question. In all these cases, we must be cautious about inferring causal connections from empirical associations, but it may be useful to look for associations for a start.

INFLATION AND DISTRIBUTION OF INCOME AND WEALTH

We may start with the factor distribution of income. We noted in a previous chapter that, within our period, the generally more inflationary second half was marked in all the Big Six by a shift of factor incomes towards wages and salaries and away from gross profits, as compared with the less inflationary first half. It may be that the gross profit share was rather high in the first half of the period in comparison with earlier times, it being a time of high prosperity and full use of capacity; precise comparisons of this kind over any considerable number of years are, however, confused by the changing relative size of incomes from self-employment, which form an intermediate, mixed, category. The category of income that, in some countries, had traditionally shown some, inverse, relation with inflation is rent, partly because of statutory controls, partly because contracts are long. In the United Kingdom its proportion of the whole dropped sharply with (and just after) the second world war but subsequently it made a gradual and partial recovery; experience and expectation of inflation had shortened contracts, and new property slowly replaced old.

When we come to the degree of inequality of personal (pre-tax) incomes, the evidence is clear for the more advanced countries that our period showed a very substantial decrease in comparison with the 1930s or, where evidence is available, with earlier times. Champernowne (1973) has made interesting comparisons by means of income-ratio curves (aggregate income distributed by size-class, both measured logarithmically) for the United States, United King·dom, Sweden, Holland, Norway, Denmark and Australia between the distribution in 1967 or 1968 and that in a pre-war year. Among the highest incomes, the share of the total and the degree of inequality are in every case greatly reduced, though the United States, United Kingdom, Sweden and Australia show relative increases in the amounts of income somewhat, but not very far, above the modal class.

Williamson and Lindert (1980) quote estimates of the percentage of United States national income received by the top 5 per cent of recipients, according to various authorities, which show a fall from 26–30 per cent in the 1930s to about 20 per cent between 1952 and 1965, with signs of a very small rise (about 1½ percentage points) in the later 1960s. Champernowne charts in detail the changes in the slope of four separate sectors of the income-ratio curve for the United Kingdom from 1912 to 1966. All these measures of inequality of distribution over particular income ranges trend downwards between the two world wars and plunge during the 1940s. Thereafter, the curves for the broader intermediate classes of rich persons (between the 3,200th and the 51,200th from the top) continue to fall steeply until 1966; those for the more select few above them make some recovery to the early-to-middle 1960s and then fall back. A rough calculation (depending on some hazardous interpolations) of the share of United Kingdom income going to the top 1 per cent of income receivers in sample years shows no marked trend over our period; the only departure from figures around 5 ahd 6 per cent is a slight hump in the mid-1960s.

All this suggests strongly that the trend towards greater equality of personal income distribution has not been in any serious way reversed during our period, though it may have been checked. To some (though in advanced countries now a minor) extent, distribution of income depends on that of personal wealth. Phelps Brown (1983) quotes various estimates for Great Britain and the United Kingdom which suggest that the proportion owned by the top 1 per cent of holders probably continued to decline during most of our period, though it may have stabilised (at about a quarter) in the later 1970s. Williamson and Lindert quote somewhat similar estimates for the United States (up to 1972) which suggests, again, a reduction of inequality between 1939 and 1945, but little change after that, except for a hint of temporarily greater inequality in the mid-1960s. One cannot say from all this what the effect of inflation on the general inequality of distribution of income and wealth in our period was, but in the United States, the United Kingdom, and some other advanced market economies, at least, it can hardly have been sensational.

INFLATION AND INCOME LEVEL

If by 'income level' we are to mean, as suggested in the last section, the deviation of real income from a long-term trend, then the reader may recall that we have already given some attention to this subject for the Big Six in chapter 3. With regard to the more regular cyclical variations, generally with periods of about four years, we there found, for the United States, United Kingdom and Germany in particular, that appearances are consistent with the hypothesis that rises in the rate of inflation go with the putting of a brake on the level of activity (from trend) sometimes with, sometimes without a short lag. We noted that they are equally consistent with a Phillips-type relation, high activity being followed by a rise in the inflation rate, and that these two relations probably coexist as part of a cyclical process. So far as causal implications are concerned, however, we are at present interested only in the former relation; that raised inflation rates are accompanied or followed by (and may cause) a cutting-back of activity in relation to the longer-term trend line of its growth.

If we look at the major (as opposed to the gentler, cyclical) reductions in the level of activity in relation to trend in the Big Six, it is plain that such reductions everywhere follow, mostly overlap with, the major accelerations of inflation starting in 1972 or 1973 (in Germany 1969). Extraordinary recessions from trend also follow jumps of the inflation rate in 1968, 1969 or 1970 and from around 1979 in the United States, United Kingdom and Italy; in France as well, on the last of these occasions. Most of these contractionary episodes are associated, in their beginnings at least, with negative monetary impulses and/or negative budgetary impulses and those in the 1970s very generally with import price-push; in some cases also with sharp negative changes in current external balance. Extraordinary inflation inspires deflationary measures; in some cases of cost-push from abroad the deflationary pressure on income tends to come automatically with the inflation of prices. In short, accelerations of inflation seem to have *caused* depressions of income below its growth trend by one means or another, some by the direct action of cost-push, some by inducing anti-inflationary turns of monetary and budgetary policy. The accelerations of inflation themselves were, of course, in turn attributable to some cause; some of them to alterations of worldwide demand and supply conditions in world markets, some to internal factor prices which, as we have seen, tend to respond to internal demand with some delay and respond also to bursts of import price inflation. We come back to the proposition that the levels of real income, in relation to trend, depend a great deal on the balance between demand-pull and cost-push elements in inflation. The two elements show some tendency to alternate within any country in the course of the trade cycle, but in addition less regular instalments of demand-pull and cost-push either enter the country from abroad by way of the demand for exports and the prices of imports or seem to arise within it. At various times, mostly in the late 1960s, the internal balance in most of our sample countries seems to have swung in the cost-push direction, perhaps partly (though by no means entirely) because of the cumulative growth of inflationary expectations in the labour market. In the 1970s, for most countries other than the oil exporters, external factors made contributions strongly biased towards cost-push and the general effect of inflation became less favourable to high levels of activity, even apart from the fact that there was more of it. Output ran, on average, further below either its trend or its full capacity level than in the earlier part of our period, because there were bigger slumps and weaker booms.

There is, however, as we noted earlier, another way in which inflation, this time regardless of where it came from, may have influenced the susceptibility of economies to depression; through its influence on the propensity to save. In the simplest Harrodian (or Hicksian) theory of macroeconomic equilibrium, an increase in the proportion of national income saved increases the 'warranted rate of growth', since it raises identically the proportion of income which must be invested if the economy is to stay on an equilibrium growth path. With a capital market which cleared instantaneously through the working of the rate of interest alone, any increase in thriftiness (which we are supposing to connote an increase in the amount which people will save at any given income and any given rate of interest) would ensure an equal increase in intentional investment, though the fall in interest rate would probably also make the increase in saving smaller than it would otherwise have been and the economy would proceed to grow smoothly along a path now tilted rather more steeply upward.

In the real world of time lags in the revision and implementation of investment decisions, not to mention stickiness of interest rates, any sudden diminution of expenditure on consumption will lead to unintended investment in the form of unsold stocks of goods and thus to the cutting-back of orders and of longer-term investment plans – in fact, to a cumulative recession. The process by which such recessions may be expected to reverse themselves need not concern us. What matter for our purpose are two points. First, any increase of thriftiness, unless offset in some way, may be expected to throw the economy temporarily (though perhaps to a considerable extent and for a considerable time) in a downward direction from its 'warranted' or equilibrium growth path, by making the path suddenly steeper. Second, the higher the warranted rate of growth needed to absorb full-employment savings into intentional investment, the more likely it is that this rate will be above the 'natural' rate at which the economy can grow without a fall in the real rate of return on investment, which, unless saving is highly sensitive to interest rate, will also tend to initiate a recession. Greater thrift, in the sense just defined (higher saving not induced by higher income or higher returns) is likely to increase the instability of the level of activity and (at least in comparison with a previous situation of fairly high employment), the average extent to which capacity is unused.

The possible relevance of this to our present concerns arises from the increase in thriftiness, especially in the personal sector, of a number of economies from the late 1960s or early 1970s. The United Kingdom is the most striking case. In the two years 1969–70 the net surplus (net acquisition of financial assets) of the household sector was estimated at about $2\frac{1}{2}$ per cent of GDP; the borrowing by companies brought the figure for the whole private sector down to not much over 1 per cent. The public sector in these years showed surpluses of about the same amount; there was therefore a surplus of about 2 per cent to be divided between overseas investment and a residual error. By 1979, the net surplus of the personal sector was put at 8 per cent of GNP, which covered the 2 per cent deficit of the company sector and the 5 per cent public sector deficit, leaving something over for foreign investment. To judge from either the unemployment rate or the deviation of real GDP from trend, however, there was considerably more slack in the economy than ten years earlier. It may be argued that the creation of this slack was a consequence of the adjustment to a higher degree of household thriftiness, the increased borrowing by companies and the public sector notwithstanding.

In some other countries also, the private saving ratio rose at this time. In Germany it had done so by 1970; in the United States, France and Japan it reached a peak in 1974 or 1975. So far, this seems to suggest a correlation with the rate of inflation, but the United States ratio failed to rise further as inflation there rose in the later 1970s, whereas the United Kingdom ratio did rise in the later part of the decade, even though the rate of inflation was well below its previous peak. A considerable amount of empirical work has been done on the reasons for such changes. Howard (1978) made a study of personal saving in the United States, United Kingdom, Japan, Germany and Canada in the dozen years ending in 1976, in which he detected a significant effect of inflation through its erosion of real values of liquid asset holdings and other effects interpreted as differing from country to country; expected inflation is presumed to act through increase of uncertainty in some cases. Von Ungern-Sternberg (1981) made the more precise assumption that saving should be related, not to disposable real income as usually defined, but to that magnitude *minus* an allowance for decreases in the real value of private sector holdings of money-denominated public debt. He found this relation to work tolerably well for Germany during 1962–77 and to go a long way to explain the peculiarities of the savings ratio in the United Kingdom, but to help hardly at all with the United States data. Subsequently, in the early 1980s, the British ratio has fallen considerably in the wake of decreasing inflation. On the whole, it looks as if the higher inflation of the 1970s did have the effect in a number of countries of increasing private thriftiness, presumably to make good the erosion of real values of debt held as a nest-egg or reserve. If that is so, then it may well, through this route as well as others, have destabilised the level of activity and depressed it further than before, on average, below the full capacity level. But this relates to the 1970s. One has to remember that the inflation of the 1950s and 1960s, severe by previous peacetime standards, was accompanied by an unprecedentedly high and stable level of activity in relation to capacity and trend, in sharp contrast with the interwar period, which was, on the whole, one of deflation.

INFLATION AND GROWTH

We noted in chapter 1 that, on the whole, for the more highly developed countries taken together, the Kondratiev cycle seemed to prevail in regard to both inflation and growth in the last hundred years, up to a point. Growth was probably slower from the 1870s to the 1890s, when prices fell, than from then to the first world war, when they rose; certainly slower in the two deflationary interwar decades than in the 1950s and 1960s. So far, the suggestion is of a mild association between growth and inflation, similar to that which has traditionally been familiar in the shorter-term trade cycle. It is, however, a fragile association, not holding for all the principal countries individually and not always conspicuous even where it does hold. The United Kingdom grew less fast from 1896 to 1913 than in the generation before 1896 and for the United States the decade-by-decade alternations of the Kuznets cycle, up to the second world war, are much more impressive than contrasts between Kondratiev phases.

The initial generalisation is dented too by the fact that, for primary materials and metals, the 1950s and 1960s do not really qualify as an inflationary period, though they were not deflationary in the firm sense in which that was true of 1870–95, or of the interwar period. We noted, moreover, in chapter 1 that any regularity that we may have discerned apparently broke down in the 1970s, a decade of undeniable, though severely fluctuating inflation, and of a conspicuous and general fall in rates of economic growth. Of these long-term fluctuations, perhaps all we can say is that faster growth in the industrial countries tends to pull world prices (mainly those of primary materials and metals) up, and that rising world prices, on the scale on which they were encountered in these peacetime periods up to 1970, were not decisively less favourable to industrial growth than falling prices. We shall have to look at our period more carefully presently.

Can we do any better with cross-section studies? Are the countries with higher inflation over our period (or any period) on the whole those with faster or with slower growth rates? There have been several simple investigations of this question, but it will be enough to refer only to that by Thirlwall and Barton (1971) who deal with 51 countries over the period 1958–67, making use of rates of growth of total output.

Their conclusions are, in brief, that among the seventeen countries with relatively high *per capita* incomes and with moderate inflation (3 to 8 per cent a year), there was a significant positive correlation of inflation with growth. Among the 34 poorer countries, as a whole, there was no significant correlation between the two variables, but among the seven members of this group in which inflation exceeded 10 per cent a year, the correlation was negative. The authors take this as suggesting that moderate inflation rates may favour growth, higher ones impede it.

Before commenting on this, it may be worth looking at the record for a later period, after inflation rates generally had increased. An examination of average inflation rates and average growth rates of *per capita* real GDP (chosen because it seems desirable to eliminate the direct effects of differences in rates of population growth) for 28 countries between 1973 and 1979, shows a positive correlation, but not a significant one. The positive element in the correlation is due almost entirely to two countries with high growth and high inflation, Turkey and Brazil. For our Big Six by themselves, the correlation is negative, though not significant.

Perhaps we can get a little nearer to comparing like with like by taking as our 'growth' variable, not the rate of increase of output per head in the economy as a whole, but that in manufacturing industry, bearing in mind that productivity increase in other sectors and much of the structural change in the economy, are thereby left out. Chart 11.1, based on data from Capdevielle and Alvarez (1981), shows how, among eleven OECD countries, a positive and significant correlation for the period 1960–73 turns into a negative, though not significant one for 1973–80. The rank order of countries by rate of productivity growth changed little between the two sub-periods, but there was some tendency for the countries with the fastest growth rates (Japan, Belgium and the Netherlands) to show the smallest increases in rates of inflation, while the relatively slow growers (United States, United Kingdom, Canada) showed the largest.

When we seek to interpret these empirical observations and to comment upon Thirlwall's and Barton's interpretation of their work, we are brought sharply up against the facts that the causal connections here are not all in one direction, and that the environments of the earlier and later sub-periods which we have just compared differed

Chart 11.1 *Productivity growth and inflation, average rates, 1960–73 and 1973–80*

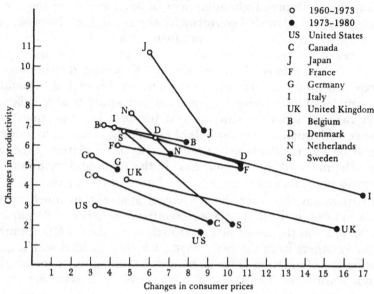

Source: Capdevielle and Alvarez, *US Monthly Labor Review*, December 1981

in ways relevant to our results.[1] The years of the Thirlwall–Barton study and of our earlier sub-period, were mainly years of fixed exchange rates for most of the more advanced countries. As we have seen in chapter 9, this did not mean that their tradable goods moved entirely parallel with each other in price, but their price divergences were to an important extent restrained. The countries with the highest rates of productivity growth in tradable goods industries enjoyed the highest wage increases; they also suffered, for that reason, the highest price increases in those sectors of the economy in which their productivity had smaller scope for increasing. Their general price indices (including the consumers' index) thus tended to show the largest rises. Even in those years, however, the countries in the Thirlwall–Barton sample with the highest rates of inflation (South Korea and six of the more inflationary Latin American countries) had abandoned fixed exchange rates; their wage inflation was freed from any gearing to the rise of productivity in their traded goods industries and, under the pressures which form the chief subject matter of the

[1] In connection with the main points in this and the following paragraph I am grateful for suggestions from Moses Abramovitz and Robin Matthews.

doctrine of 'structuralism', there was perhaps some tendency for inflation to be greatest where the obstacles to progress were greatest.

With the widespread abandonment of fixed exchange rates, even among the more advanced countries, in the 1970s, their links between wage inflation and traded goods productivity also snapped. Instead of differences in productivity growth in traded goods industries impinging directly upon domestic wage inflation, they tended to impinge on the external values of currencies, so that under this regime it would be the countries of low productivity growth that would tend to suffer the higher rates of inflation – in the first instance by importing them. These considerations seem capable of explaining much, at any rate, of the positive correlation between productivity and inflation (especially among the more advanced countries) in the 1950s and 1960s and the change to poor, mainly negative, correlation in the 1970s.

Attention has, however, been concentrated not so much on the correlation, or lack of it, across countries, between inflation and growth, as upon the slowdown of growth in all the OECD countries and many others from the early 1970s, which coincided with a great exacerbation of inflation. This is, indeed, a striking phenomenon, but it is not worldwide. The World Bank's *World Development Report 1981* shows domestic absorption as having grown as fast in a group of 60 middle income countries during the 1970s as it had during the 1960s. In Brazil, South Korea, Turkey, Malaysia, Singapore and Indonesia (as well as in Uruguay, where growth was slow in both decades and in Nigeria where the civil war of 1967–70 must have affected the issue) growth seems to have been faster in the later decade. India's growth rate rose in the planning period beginning in 1973. Prais (1983) points out that, even for the world as a whole, whether the United Nations index of industrial output per person employed shows a slowdown or not depends on precisely how one chooses, for the comparison, periods which can be claimed to be similar in regard to phases of the trade cycle.

However, it is hardly deniable that there was a slowdown in much of the world, including the OECD countries. There was also a great increase in unemployment. The question what, if anything, accelerated inflation had to do with these events is not easily separated from more general discussion of the reasons for their occurrence and these, in turn, include some attention to the exceptional nature of the unprecedented secular boom of the postwar generation. We cannot enter in detail into these wider questions, but we cannot ignore them either.

THE SECULAR BOOM AND ITS COLLAPSE – FACTORS OTHER
THAN INFLATION

Angus Maddison (1980) lists among the special circumstances which
enhanced economic performance in the 1950s and 1960s the liberalisation of trade, government promotion of buoyant demand and the
existence of a backlog of growth possibilities. Other writers, including
Giersch and Wolter (1983) and Lindbeck (1983), have also put
forward some or all of these, with variations of interpretation and
emphasis and especially cheap capital has been added by the
McCracken Report (1977) and Sargent (1982). Maddison also men-
tions the moderation of inflation during the period as a factor
permitting fast growth; but we come to that later.

What weights should be attached to these factors, how far were they
special, in the sense of necessarily temporary, and what was their
relation to inflation? The increase of foreign trade in relation to output
is clearly an outstanding feature of the 1950s and 1960s; it took place
more or less continuously through that period, so that the increase in
gains from trade would also be continuous. Denison, in his classic
book published in 1967, allocated to these gains only an amount
which he calculated from reductions in average import duties, without
including that part of the total gain from economies of scale which was
assignable to this source. Maddison (1972) modified and revised
Denison's estimates in a form which included scale returns with the
other gains from increased international trade. For the United States
and eight European countries, over the period 1950–62, he put this
gain at 0.29 per cent of real income per annum, or about 7 per cent of
the total increase in real income. One should not, of course, assume
that this gives an accurate measure of the contribution of increased
international trade to the growth of the world economy, or of the
OECD countries, or of any of our samples, over the two decades
under discussion; but it can perhaps be taken as suggesting the order
of magnitude to be attributed to that contribution – appreciable, but
hardly to be classified as major. The possibilities of a more open world
economy were clearly not all exploited in these twenty years; after
1970 and, still more, after 1973, world trade continued to grow faster
than output, but both growth rates were lower than before.

The role played by government promotion of buoyant demand
lends itself even less to quantitative assessment. There can, as we saw
in chapter 1, be no doubt as to the *fact* of buoyant demand; the low
level of unemployment and the rarity of year-to-year declines of real
output, even for single countries in the sample which Maddison
(1977) examined, were both unprecedented so far as the historical

record goes. The two questions that arise are; how much did this level of demand have to do with the (also unprecedented) rapid growth rate of real income and how far was it attributable to government policies?

It seems likely *a priori* that high demand in relation to plant capacity stimulated the growth of that capacity and also the high rate of absorption into generally urban employment of labour previously attached to agriculture. Matthews *et al.* (1982) point out, however, that high demand can have ambiguous relations to structural change, because it may keep labour and other resources in trades which they would otherwise leave as well as providing stronger attractions elsewhere.

Historically, the medium run relationship between demand pressure, measured inversely by the unemployment rate, and rate of growth either of productivity or of total output, is not always clear. In the United Kingdom, for instance, data on the five major trade cycles between 1872 and 1913 show no particular relation between average unemployment and annual growth of real GDP (especially if one allows for both being reduced at the turn of the century by the South African war). The United States gives rather better promise over this period of a negative relation between unemployment and productivity growth but still an imperfect one. But, for both countries, the stronger contrasts between the interwar years and 1950–70 are more suggestive.

More generally, it can hardly be an accident that, even despite the widespread subsidisation of agriculture (in the EEC especially) the period of high demand went with the most rapid urbanisation on record in many countries. Worswick (1982) quotes evidence from C. T. Saunders to show that, within manufacturing industry also, the rate of structural change (shifts between classes of the standard industrial classification) was faster in the 1960s than in the 1970s. This is not in conflict with the view that slack demand also brings its own brand of pressure for growth of productivity, mainly through closure of the less efficient plants (see the study by Bowers, Deaton and Turk, 1982), but the pressures of high demand are real enough, as anyone acquainted with, for instance, the labour shortage in the West Yorkshire textile industry in the 1960s can attest and the EEC and other evidence just referred to suggests that, contrary to the argument of Paish (1962), they have shown greater structure altering power.

It is also fairly clear that high pressure of demand was connected with the greatly increased drawing of immigrants and guest workers into the countries of north-western Europe, which made an important contribution to the growth of aggregate output in them during the two decades in question. Insofar as this increased growth took place in the manufacturing sector, there is a presumption that, along with the shift of labour from agriculture already mentioned, it contributed to increase of output *per head* in that sector, through the scale economies and the faster introduction of design improvements which between them are responsible for the Verdoorn effect, the correlation which is observed between rates of growth of total output and of output per head. Nor does the drawing of workers into north-western Europe seem to have done much damage to growth in the countries from which they came. Southern Europe and Turkey were among the areas with the highest growth rates. Altogether, therefore, there appears to be good reason for supposing that the high demand of the years 1950–70 made an important, though a not easily measured, contribution to the fast rate of increase in both *per capita* and aggregate output at that time.

How far is that high level of demand ascribable to government policies? We may start with the fact that it was a declared object of policy in a number of countries, starting with the United Kingdom White Paper of 1944 (*Employment Policy, Cmnd* 6527) and the United States Full Employment Act of 1946 and including later on the German Stabilisation Law of 1967 and the spirit and assumptions implicit in French indicative planning. A number of observers have suggested that this, reinforced progressively by the experience of rapid growth and modest fluctuations, had an important effect in generating entrepreneurial confidence, quite apart from whatever acts of official policy may have achieved. We have noted that in France, where the process of indicative planning took the reassurance of private entrepreneurs a stage further than the mere adoption of a governmental commitment to seek high and steady employment, the courses of investment and income growth were noticeably steadier than in the other main OECD countries. So far as the performance of government as a regulator is concerned, we have seen that budgetary impacts on our sample countries' economies during the two decades were predominantly in a stabilising direction. The great extension of public sectors during the period must have increased the leverage of the built-in stabilisers inherent in the systems of taxation and of transfer expenditure. (Even on the most radical assumptions of the rational expectations school, the power of built-in stabilisers to reduce the effects of unpredicted random shocks has to be allowed.) In monetary policy, the record is rather more mixed; but we have seen that in the United States, by far the largest of national economies in terms of real income, it was predominantly stabilising, apart from the external repercussions of events at the very end of the period we are discussing. All in all, it would be hard not to allow a substantial part to

governments (and monetary authorities where the latter are independent) in maintaining the high and stable level of activity which was
itself a major factor in the rapid growth of the 1950s and 1960s.

How far were official policies responsible for the collapse of the
boom? The average net first round impact of budgetary changes from
1974 to 1979 was less expansionary (or more contractionary) than
in the previous decade in the United States, United Kingdom, and
Italy, as well as in Sweden and Canada (Maddison, 1980), but
more expansionary in France and Germany (and in Japan and the
Netherlands in comparison with the previous quinquennium). The
picture is not, therefore, an unmixed one of absolutely more restrictive
government fiscal policy. One has, however, to remember that the
deflationary impact of the oil shock on most of the countries just
mentioned would have called for a considerably more expansionary
policy in the later 1970s to maintain the demand pressure of the
previous ten or twenty years (in the United Kingdom and Germany
the increase in private thrift reinforced this requirement). It is
probably a fair generalisation to say that budgetary policies in the
later 1970s either became absolutely more restrictive or failed to
respond to the challenge of other forces making more strongly for real
income deflation. Monetary policy came increasingly under the
influence of attempts to limit the rate of growth of the money stock in
the face of tendencies to price inflation which were stronger than in
the preceding golden age. Policy was thus less supportive of, or at
least did not rise to the task of continuing to support, as effectively as
in the past, a high and stable level of activity; and one of the factors to
which we have attributed a significant part in promoting rapid growth
was undermined.

The backlog of growth possibilities which is given some credit for
faster growth presumably includes the accumulation during the
second world war of knowledge not yet exploited for peacetime
purposes and of both normal capital depreciation and wartime
damage waiting to be made good. All major wars leave such a
backlog; indeed, it might be claimed that the relatively weak booms of
the late 1930s in some of the main industrial countries had also left
possibilities unexploited which, with greater confidence and the
further passage of time, fuelled the postwar surge. These elements,
however, would hardly be enough to account for a twenty-year boom
of such magnitude. The factor on which most emphasis has been laid
is the opportunity which existed for other countries, mainly other
OECD countries, to catch up with the best technical practice, which
might be taken as that of the United States.

It has been plausibly argued by Marris (1982) that the growth rates of *per capita* real GDP in OECD countries in the period 1965–73 can be explained by their investment rates, the growth of their exports and, negatively, the *levels* of their real *per capita* GDPs at the beginning of the period. (Allowance is made for the facts that exports are affected by the domestic inflation rate and that investment is itself influenced by the lowness of the starting income and thus the size of the technology gap to be filled.) The details of the model and some criticisms made of its exact form (Feinstein, 1982), need not concern us. The argument that technological catching-up was a very important element in the secular boom is a strong one. The question which remains and has been put by Matthews is why did so much catching-up happen at this particular time?

It was not the case that the technology gaps to be filled were newly created (for example, by the war), though, at least in the cases of France, Germany, Italy, Japan and the United Kingdom, they had been enlarged by it. If we take Maddison's (1977) figures for *per capita* GDP in these countries at United States prices in the selected years 1870, 1913, 1929, 1950 and 1970, we find that all of them fell continuously, as percentages of the corresponding United States figure, until 1950, except that Japan showed a small increase between 1913 and 1929. In the great catching-up time 1950–70, France got back to about where she had been in 1890, Germany to a ratio above that of 1870 (which had been lower than France's), Japan to almost twice her low 1870 ratio. Italy and the United Kingdom did not regain their 1870 positions; Italy's improvement on the 1950 relative position, however, was very substantial, whereas the United Kingdom's was small and she finished little more than half as high, relatively, as in 1870, when she had been the only member of the group above the United States.

The fact is, of course, that different countries have generally had different times of spurting in relation to their competitors – either catching up with them or going ahead. The United Kingdom went ahead of the other countries just mentioned most notably in the mid-19th Century. The United States was ahead by 1913, but continued to forge ahead further until about 1950, with the aid of the greater handicaps imposed on her competitors by the two world wars. From 1950 to 1970, the United States rate of growth of *per capita* income was a trifle better than it had been in the generation before 1913 and much better than from 1929 to 1950; the great catch-up was not assisted by any slowing down on the United States' part, it was a genuine spurt, remarkable for being so widespread.

Some plausible reasons why it was so widespread readily present themselves. Many countries were, so to speak, gathered at the starting line with wartime (and perhaps older) backlogs of replacement and modernisation waiting to be undertaken. The United States was the great available source of capital, equipment, technical knowledge and of direct investment which combined all three. Marshall Aid was very important; it primed all the receiving countries' national pumps simultaneously and involved the United States in the economy of western Europe. Occupation involved her with that of Japan. There was some resemblance to the situation after the first world war, but on that occasion there had been no Marshall Aid, a great deal of quarrelling over reparations and war debts, United States experience in overseas investment had been small, much of the lending had been by portfolio investment and the stream was sharply cut off by the depression of the 1930s. After the second world war, moreover, the accumulated experience of reconstruction, of the war itself, of the depression before it, and perhaps some influences emanating from the example of planning in the USSR, generated a conviction that economic growth could be promoted by the public authorities; not only by directive planning, which had been widely established for war and reconstruction purposes, but by various forms of exhortation and education and a more conscious search than had existed before for the best technical practices. Among economists, 'growth' became so far the leading specialism that it was hard to remember that, before the war, it had scarcely existed as a subject at all. This preoccupation both reflected and produced attitudes of mind which make the almost worldwide surge of faster growth easier to explain.

Insofar as the growth-surge consisted of other countries, or many of them, catching up with the best United States practice, productivity growth was bound to decelerate, in principle asymptotically, to the rate at which productivity advances at the technological frontier; on recent experience about $2\frac{1}{2}$ per cent a year, or about half the average rate recorded for the OECD countries as a whole in the 1950s and 1960s. In the later 1970s, their average rate of productivity growth had, indeed, come down most of the way towards that figure. The strength of the claim that this was entirely the inevitable result of catching-up was, however, diminished by various considerations. One of these was the suddenness with which the fall in productivity growth took place between 1972 and 1974 (see Lindbeck, 1983), more like a step function than an asymptotic decline. Another is the fact that United States productivity growth also fell by more than half, which fits ill with the general hypothesis unless (see Matthews, 1982) it is supposed that United States progress had consisted to quite a large extent of internal catching-up with the best practice and, even then, the suddenness of the decline presents difficulties.

Nevertheless, so far as any sample of active catchers-up is concerned there must be something in this hypothesis. As they succeed in getting nearer to the leader, the technological gain from every fresh adoption of his practice is bound to diminish. Unless some country (or some set of practitioners not necessarily all in one country) succeeds in pushing the technological frontier ahead faster than it has hitherto been pushed ahead, mainly in the United States, most of the OECD countries may not again have a chance to gain by modernising themselves as fast as they did in the two golden decades.

For the world as a whole, this argument is hardly valid. We have noted that the torch of rapid growth was taken up, with effectiveness which in some cases increased in the 1970s, by middle income countries. Unlike most of the original OEEC countries, they achieved political and social conditions (and perhaps the economic infrastructure) favourable to rapid development mostly at various later times and there remains, of course, a large reserve of other countries which have not yet achieved such conditions, or have done so only partially. Even within the old OEEC ranks there were anomalies, especially the remarkably slow rate of gap-closing achieved by the United Kingdom. The world economy showed, and shows, no sign of running out of gaps to be narrowed. But for the great growers of the 1950s and 1960s, some part of the slowdown in the 1970s may be credited to diminished opportunity.

It has been suggested that the slowdown in the OECD countries also owed something to increased competition from the less industrialised world, notably the very middle income countries to which we have just referred. Certainly the non-exporters of oil in the less industrialised world showed an increased rate of growth in the volume of their exports in the 1970s, when growth of exports from the industrialised countries was slowing down and it is a matter of common observation that they captured significant markets from the older industrial countries. But, of course, their imports also grew faster. The short-term impact on the older industrial countries would depend on how much deflationary pressure they had to suffer in order to maintain, or re-establish, external and internal equilibrium; the long-run effect would depend on what the loss of comparative advantage turned out to be between the old trade pattern and the eventual, viable, new one.

In the event, at least the short-term problems, for both the older industrial countries and their new competitors, were swamped in the 1970s by the massive disturbance they suffered from the oil shocks. Both of them were subjected to deflationary pressures mitigated by borrowing, the latter being easier for the old industrial countries, which (or some of which) were the inevitable first repositories of OPEC surplus funds. All one can easily say about the impact of increased competition on the more developed manufacturing countries is that it certainly imposed additional tasks of structural adaptation on them but, once again, this has to be assessed in relation to the *total* burden of such adaptation. That burden had been increased much more by the very rapid change of trade patterns *between* the established industrial countries, and up to the end of the 1960s, at least, there was little sign that it had not been smoothly carried. As Matthews (1982) suggests, the pains of adjustment seem to be inversely related to the general pressure of demand.

THE SECULAR BOOM AND ITS COLLAPSE – THE PART OF INFLATION

Our discussion of the causes, other than the operation of inflation itself, which various writers have suggested for the boom of 1950–70 and its subsequent partial collapse, seems to point to the following conclusions. The great liberalisation of trade made an appreciable contribution to rapid growth, but cannot be given credit for more than a fraction of it. Nor, since trade went on expanding faster than income in the 1970s, does it seem realistic to treat the collapse of the boom as to any large extent a result of slower extension of international division of labour. High pressure of demand seems to have been of major importance in promoting rapid growth (including structural change) and its decline to have been important among the causes of the slower growth after the early 1970s. Government policies seem to have been of importance in promoting the high and steady level of demand while it lasted and to have been absolutely less supportive to it and/or to have failed to rise to the stronger challenges facing them afterwards. For the OECD countries (other than the United States) as a whole, the simultaneous exploitation of opportunities to catch up with the best technological practice may account for a considerable amount of the fast growth, and for some of the subsequent fall in growth rate, but by no means for all of it, and for the world as a whole it is not clear that the contribution of catching-up to total growth has necessarily fallen. The contribution to the slowing down in the OECD countries made by additional competition from the advancing middle income economies is minor.

All this has nothing directly to do with inflation. The theoretical considerations mentioned at the beginning of this chapter suggest the following questions: (1) has uncertainty about the course of inflation diminished the efficiency of investment decisions and, in particular, has greater uncertainty since 1970 caused investment to be less efficient than before? (2) Have changes in the form and the severity of inflation affected growth either directly or through their impacts on policy?

The first of these questions relates, it will be recalled, to an argument by Friedman. It is not easy to test the efficiency of investment. The crude test presented by the ratio of gross capital formation to increase of output suffers from the twin weaknesses of high sensitivity both to the distribution of the capital formation in question between different sectors of the economy and to changes in the degree of utilisation of capacity over the period of measurement. Some adjustment is also required for differences in the amounts of cooperating factors which go with the extra capital.

For what it is worth, however, this crude ratio does indeed rise sharply after 1970 (or 1973) in all the main OECD countries, the change being due directly to fall in income growth, not rise in investment; but the rise was not related to how much inflation increased. It was high in Germany and Japan, where the rise of inflation was mildest and most temporary. In Brazil, the ratio was low throughout, in spite of high and fluctuating inflation and in the United Kingdom it was, if anything, lower in the 1950s and 1960s (when there was, of course, already a good deal of inflation) than it had been between 1929 and 1937, when the trend of prices was downwards. It is perhaps more to the point that the net rate of return on fixed capital in manufacturing (see Sargent, 1982) fell between 1960–72 and 1973–8 in each of the five biggest OECD countries but again there is not much obvious correlation with the worsening of inflation (the United Kingdom shows the biggest fall but Germany and Japan also do rather badly). For the results of both of these tests, fall in demand is likely to have been important.

The argument that uncertainty about inflation is bad for growth does not, of course, imply that inflation itself is bad for it unless there is a presumption that more inflation means more uncertainty about its course. On the face of it, this seems to be a commonsense presumption. It cannot, however, be taken for granted, and it happens that the increases of inflation between 1960–73 and 1974–9 were virtually uncorrelated with changes in standard deviations of year-to-year inflation, whether across the Big Six or across a sample of eleven OECD countries. All these countries (see Brown, 1982) showed higher mean inflation rates in the second sub-period than the first, but the standard deviations of those rates (from year-to-year) in the United States, France and Italy were lower in the second sub-period; their inflation, though faster, was smoother. One clearly cannot generalise from this to other episodes, but it is a fact that has to be taken into account in comparing the sub-periods which most invite comparison within the years of our study. (Incidentally, the standard deviation of year-to-year inflation rates in the United Kingdom was no greater during 1953–73 than it had been between 1929 and 1938, though the mean inflation rate had been −0.2 per cent in the earlier period and had risen to 4¼ per cent in the later one). There seems, in general, to be little evidence for the importance of uncertainty about inflation in adversely affecting growth in our period.

The effects of inflation itself and of the *kind* of inflation are other matters. Let us consider first the suggestion, made in slightly different forms both by Sargent (1982) and by Giersch and Wolter (1983) that during the 1950s and 1960s the real rate of interest had fallen below its equilibrium level and so induced a boom which could not be maintained. At first sight, one thinks of inflation as the likely culprit but the reference should, of course, be to the *ex ante* real rate of interest, the nominal rate minus the *expected* rate of inflation. We have reviewed the evidence on expectations of inflation in chapter 5. Taking Carlson's interpretation of the Livingston survey data on wholesale price anticipations in the United States, we may see that, from 1950 until 1968, the expected rate of inflation (about a year ahead) was some 0.8 per cent. For that period as a whole, therefore, the *ex ante* real interest rate (nominal rate minus expected inflation rate) works out at about 2.9 per cent. (Using expectations of *retail* prices would give 2.6 per cent.) This may, by historical standards, be on the low side. The nominal rate had averaged about 2¾ per cent from 1939 to 1950, in which period there must have been some expectations of continuation of the inflation already in progress, so that it is possible that the *ex ante* real rate as then perceived was lower than in the period under discussion; but in the 1880s and 1890s, and from 1924 to 1929 for instance, when expectations must have been non-inflationary (if not actually deflationary), rates had been in the 3¼ to 5 per cent range. The possibility that capital appeared abnormally cheap in the 1950s and 1960s cannot be entirely dismissed.

Had inflation anything to do with this? The expectations that made real interest look low to borrowers should have made lenders push the nominal rates up. Were governments and monetary authorities alone (or, at least, different from other borrowers) in being unable to entertain (or admit to) expectations of inflation, or were their interest rate policies influenced by the existence of a particular group of borrowers (for example, house purchasers) whom they did not believe to share the perception that the real rate was low? If we make some of these assumptions, then we can say that it was the fact of inflation and the selective entertaining of expectations that it would continue, that made capital look unusually cheap to those who did entertain them, but the assumptions would have to be justified. It may be added that those who believe that over-investment took place in this period often blame it on the subsidisation of investment, largely by tax concessions. These, in themselves, should presumably have raised the nominal rate of interest.

The area is rather murky; it is clear enough that either perception by entrepreneurs of an abnormally low real interest rate or subsidisation of investment might produce a boom which would eventually lower the real return on capital and that investment and growth would then slow down unless either the lowering of perceived real interest rates or the increase of subsidisation continued. But the existence of inflation is not unconditionally a basis for such a story.

We have already seen that the *kind* of inflation may be more important in relation to the level of activity than its mere existence; demand-pull inflation favours high activity, cost-push inhibits it. What is true in this context of the level of activity is also (as, again, we have seen) likely to be true in this period of the rate of growth. A salient feature of our period is that, after some fifteen or so years in which a mixture of demand-pull and cost-push influences produced little inflation in international markets and mostly medium degrees of it in national markets for finished goods and services, severe international market inflation supervened, which impinged on most national markets in our sample as cost-push. In those economies, raw material and fuel costs rose, rising cost of living and real wage resistance amplified the inflationary effect, governments and monetary authorities refused full monetary accommodation, or deflated income to limit the inflation, profits fell and so did both activity and investment. The ultimate beneficiaries of the changed terms of trade, the oil exporters, did not provide enough effective demand to match the rest of the world's cost increases.

Bruno's cross-section study (1982) of the causes of the diminished rate of growth of total factor productivity in the business sectors of the economies of OECD (and some other) countries, 29 in all, between 1960–73 and 1974–9, supports this diagnosis. On average, rise in real import prices and slowdown of domestic public expenditure growth seem to be about equally important, the former more so in the United Kingdom, Belgium and Sweden, the latter in France, Germany and Japan. In a supplementary study of the service sectors, where such information is available, the import shock drops out and the changed growth rate of total absorption of goods and services proves to be a good explainer of productivity changes.

Bruno goes on to provide a formal analysis of the conditions in which a shock to relative prices within an economy can have real effects on measured income and productivity; we may apply it to the world economy as a whole. The condition in question is, straightforwardly enough, imperfect mobility of the factors of production between sectors after the shock. He points out that the primary effects of the shock in the countries where terms of trade worsened combined with the induced secondary effects of anti-inflationary measures to bring this mobility down. It is the combination of relative price change and the policy reaction to absolute price inflation that seems to have been deadly. Some newly industrialised countries which accepted higher inflation instead of trying to throttle it managed to avoid any slowdown of real output growth; though it may well be that they were less troubled by real wage resistance to the initial change in the terms of trade than the older industrial countries were. But, in most of the established industrial countries, the experience of higher inflation caused its containment and reduction to be given priority over high activity and growth, themselves already dented by the cost-push shock. It was this double blow of inflation against prosperity, directly by cost-push against profit margins and indirectly through public policy, that seems to have been its most important effect on the working of most national economies and of the world economy as a whole.

INFLATION, UNEMPLOYMENT AND WELFARE

It seems, then, that some of the slower growth of productivity, and some of the increased unemployment since about 1973 and most after 1979 in the OECD countries is attributable to the shocks to their terms of trade, or to shifts of their policy aims from full employment to the reduction of inflation. (The terms of trade shocks, mainly the oil shocks, also, of course, involved direct losses of gain from external trade, amounting to something like 5 per cent of GDP for the OECD countries as a whole, up to 1981, which may be regarded as offset by the gains of their trading partners.) Unemployment in these countries was two percentage points higher in 1975–9 than in the 1960s, and had risen a further $3\frac{1}{2}$ points by 1983. Growth of output per head was some $2\frac{1}{2}$ per cent a year lower in the later 1970s than in the 1960s, and came down a little more in the early 1980s. Over the later 1970s, as a whole, the real output of the OECD countries was probably some 10 per cent lower than it would have been if the unemployment rates and the productivity growth rates of the previous decade had persisted. How much of this can be regarded as due to the indirect effects of the primary price inflations and to the policy changes induced by the promotion of inflation in general to the rank of Public Enemy Number One, it is impossible to say with any precision. Certainly some of it is due to other causes which we have touched on in this and previous chapters. It would not, however, on the face of it be absurd to attribute half of the shortfall – 5 per cent of GDP over the five years 1975–9 as a whole – to these two indirect consequences of inflationary events and pressures.

Still less can one say what rates of inflation would have been if policies had been more accommodative, and if some part of the extra unemployment, and some part of the loss of growth, had been avoided, as apparently happened in some less highly industrialised countries, which had also been exposed to the stormy weather of the world markets. Even if one could do so, one would still be faced with the problem of balancing loss of material output and employment against inflation in welfare terms.

We have seen that the welfare losses connected directly with inflation are elusive. In its milder degrees it is no more than an annoyance, though a widely-felt one. Even at very high rates, it has proved compatible with a remarkable growth performance in Brazil (until the combination of over-borrowing, recession, and high world interest rates brought disaster) and at rather more modest levels, still well above the world average over our period, it has gone with outstanding development in South Korea and impressive sustained performances in Spain, Portugal, Greece and Turkey. Among the OECD countries, where attitudes to inflation have been generally more inhibited, it is not obvious that, for instance, France, with her 5.7-fold price increase, has suffered any great disadvantage in the development of her economy in comparison with Germany, with a 2.4-fold one. Up to very high levels, it seems that inflation is just inflation.

On the other hand, slow growth and high unemployment, which seem to be the penalties for monetary and fiscal resistance to cost-push, carry rather obvious costs. According to the usual calculus in which real consumption serves as a proxy for welfare, the cost of slow growth is the discounted present value of the future consumption foregone, *minus* the value of the current consumption that would have had to be foregone to get it. To the extent that resources are idle, the second, negative, term may be reduced, even to zero. In fact, expenditure which draws otherwise idle resources into use for capital formation is likely to increase both current consumption and the prospect of consumption to come. The simple, and obvious point is that involuntarily unemployed resources signify lost opportunities for present and/or future consumption.

Nor is that the end of the matter. Since the incomes of the unemployed are in the great majority of cases lower than those which the people in question would receive if employed in their normal occupations, and since the lower-paid occupations tend to be those most prone to unemployment, unemployment increases the inequality of distribution of total personal income, as well as diminishing its amount. But that is not the end of the matter either. Experience of a new period of heavy unemployment reinforces the conclusion stated by Beveridge (1944, p. 248) on the basis of earlier experience: 'The greatest evil of unemployment is not the loss of additional material wealth which we might have with full employment. There are two greater evils: first, that unemployment makes men seem useless, not wanted, without a country; second, that unemployment makes men live in fear and that from fear springs hate.'

It is for this reason that, given the mode of operation of labour markets, the cure of inflation by control of expenditure may rather easily prove worse than the disease. But people are in general unwilling to contemplate two evils at the same time, and tend to concentrate on the one of which they have more recent experience. Throughout the 1970s, commitments to high and stable employment were being eroded by experience of serious inflation, and theoretical views were being formed which discounted the possibility of massive unemployment that was, in a proper sense, involuntary. It was, however, only in the early 1980s that unemployment approached the levels last seen before the second world war. To this episode we now turn.

12

THE RECESSION OF THE EARLY 1980s

A COMPARISON

In the foregoing chapters we have discussed, in the main, a period ending in 1979, though, on occasion, we have made use of data from later years where they were available and appeared to throw light on relationships which were under consideration. The years immediately following 1979, however, can best be regarded as the beginning of a new period, marked by a world recession, which many people have found uncomfortably reminiscent of events exactly half a century earlier. For our purpose, it may throw light on the inertia, or durability, of the inflationary processes which we have been studying.

The parallel with the 1930s having been mentioned, it may be best to examine it a little further, if only to see how far the ghosts of that time can be exorcised, and how far they remain as bearers of still valid warnings from the disasters of a world which most of those now active in economic affairs no longer remember.

On even a superficial inspection, however, the differences between the two episodes are very striking. The first difference is that of magnitude. Between 1929 and 1932, the real gross domestic product of the United States and the League of Nations index of world manufacturing output both fell by about 30 per cent. German real gross product fell by some 20 per cent, and those of Italy and some of the smaller Central European countries may have done about the same. Even the Soviet Union, hit by its collectivisation crisis, and despite a soaring index of industrial production, suffered a fall in real income variously estimated between 7 and 14 per cent. Japanese income may have continued to grow, or hardly dipped, but otherwise the United Kingdom, with a 5 per cent fall, sustained one of the smallest reductions among the countries for which estimates exist. World agricultural output is estimated to have remained roughly constant; a reasonable estimate of the fall in world real income would probably lie between 15 and 20 per cent. Moreover, the volume of international trade fell more than that of output; probably about 25 per cent overall, 40 per cent for manufactures. Apart from its huge scale, the depression was like most others before it in that it went with

365

a fall of prices, ranging so far as internationally traded goods were concerned, from some 56 per cent for raw materials to 37 per cent for manufactures.

Compared with this, the world indices for 1979–82 are not impressive. The United Nations Index of Industrial Production merely stagnated for three years within 1 per cent of its 1979 level, and began to rise again in mid-1983. The corresponding index of agricultural production stagnated from 1978 to 1980, and began to rise again in 1981. The real GDP of the OECD countries failed to rise in only one year – it fell by less than 1 per cent between 1981 and 1982. The volume index of total world exports fell, on an annual basis, only 2 per cent from its 1980 peak, starting to rise again in 1983, that of manufactured exports likewise fell only 2 per cent, in this case from a peak in 1981. Dollar prices of traded goods again fell – but only by some 8 per cent for all categories together and also for manufactures (prices of primary products excluding petroleum fell by 16 per cent between 1980 and 1982).

Unemployment statistics tell roughly the same story. A weighted average of rates for the main industrial countries (excluding France and Japan) between 1929 and 1932 gives a rise from just over 3 per cent to 16½ per cent of the labour force (based on Maddison's adjusted figures); the broadly comparable OECD increase from 1979 to 1982 was from 5.1 to 8.2 per cent (the rate rose further to 8.7 per cent in 1983). This rise in the early 1980s was not very much greater than that from 3.2 per cent to 5.3 per cent which had been experienced between 1973 and 1976. Part of the alarm and distress which it caused, however, was due to the fact that there had been little reduction of unemployment in the industrial countries between 1976 and 1979, so that the rate stood some 5 percentage points higher in 1982 (5½ in 1983) than in 1973. The depression of the early 1930s, in the industrial countries as a whole, did not arrive in two separate instalments in this way; 1929 can reasonably be taken as the peak year in use of capacity, as well as the peak in real income, from which the subsequent descent is to be reckoned. Nevertheless, from whatever reasonable datum line one chooses to measure the rise in unemployment rate to 1982 (or 1983), that rise is not appreciably more than a third of the increase from 1929 to 1932, and the absolute level of unemployment rate in the main industrial countries, together, in 1983 was probably not much more than half the corresponding figure for 1932.

For particular countries the comparisons were different. While the United States and central Europe, the heaviest sufferers in the 1930s, have escaped comparatively lightly since 1979, the United Kingdom which, as we have observed, was one of the lightest sufferers in the 1930s, has contrived in the 1980s to have a depression earlier and deeper than that in any other industrial country, with a proportionate fall in real income very similar to that of 1929–32; and with both her unemployment rate in 1982 (and 1983) and its increase since the previous minimum not much smaller than fifty years before. A number of the Latin American countries, caught in a crisis of over-borrowing and worsened terms of trade, also find themselves, at the time of writing, in a situation reminiscent of many primary producers fifty years ago; the aggregate dollar value of Latin American imports was cut by more than half between 1981 and 1983. But in the world economy generally, the apocalyptic character of the early 1930s has, happily, not been repeated; though it is wise, as always, to take the Duke of Wellington's advice: 'Don't halloo 'til you're out of the wood'.

THE ORIGINS OF THE RECESSION

Where did the recession of the early 1980s come from? If one looks at each of the Big Six separately, it is plain that increased import prices (especially of oil) were a depressing factor, starting to be substantial already in 1979 and continuing to be so (except in the United States) in 1980, in which year Japan, Germany, France and Italy all experienced severe deterioration in their external balances of visible trade. Italy received a further import price shock in 1981, with the depreciation of the lira. Exports seem to have been a source of depression, in that they fell in relation to total expenditure, in Italy (in 1980) and to a smaller extent in the United Kingdom; but they pulled in the other direction in Germany, Japan, France and (until 1982) the United States.

Negative expenditure impulses (to some of which exports contributed in the way we have just mentioned) seem to have occurred in most of the Big Six in most of the years 1980–2, inclusive; decelerations of the growth of nominal expenditure are clearly visible, and most of them were accompanied by reductions of the profit share. To judge from changes in its ratio to total GDP, gross fixed capital formation was a major immediate element in these impulses. It fell sharply in the United States in 1980 and 1982, the two years of absolute reduction in real output, with stock accumulation reflecting the same pattern. It fell steadily in the United Kingdom from 1980 to 1982, but there the turnround in stock accumulation from a positive to a negative figure in the first two of those three years was a bigger influence in the same direction. It fell also in Germany and Japan in the last two of those years, and in Germany a turnround of stock accumulation in 1981 was important. Italy enjoyed a rise of domestic fixed capital formation up to 1981, then there was a fall; but the rise of 1981 was overshadowed by a sharp decrease in stock accumulation.

The other notable active element in domestic expenditure was public consumption. Generally speaking, as a percentage of GDP, it tended to move counter-cyclically, rising throughout 1980–2 in Japan, Italy and the United States and, until 1981, in the United Kingdom, Germany and France. In assessing the impact of public finance, however, the influence of taxation has also to be considered, and for our immediate purpose it will suffice to bring it into the story by looking at public sector surpluses or deficits. The stabilising tendency is for the deficit to rise, or the surplus to fall as a proportion of GDP in depression, as tax revenues vary rather more than income, and/or expenditures vary rather less – or actually rise when total income falls. This happened in the United States in the recession years 1980 and 1982, in Germany, especially in 1981, the first year of actual recession there, in France also in 1981, the year of slowest growth, and in Italy in 1981 and 1982, the years when growth was falling sharply.

The outstanding exception is the United Kingdom, where the deficit fell throughout the depression, from more than 5 per cent of GDP in 1979 to less than 3 per cent of it in 1982. A recent study by Artis, Bladen-Hovell, Karakitsos and Dwolatzky (1984), using both the National Institute and the Treasury models of the British economy to simulate its performance on alternative assumptions about policy variables, suggests that policy changes accounted for at least twice as much of the fall of GDP below trend as did the changes in world trade conditions (fiscal policy and exchange rate variations both being important). Public statements of policy intentions are also consistent with a deflationary course having been pursued in the United Kingdom more consistently and vigorously than elsewhere. It seems likely that this is the main cause of the unusual depth of the country's depression, in comparison with those experienced by the other countries we have been considering.

The part played by monetary impulses in the recession is not immediately clear. For the industrial countries as a whole (according to IMF indices) the annual rate of growth of M2 did not vary a great deal; in 1980 it fell from about $11\frac{1}{2}$ per cent, its value of the previous two years, to $9\frac{1}{2}$ per cent. From 1977 to 1979, the rate of growth of nominal income had been fairly steady around 12 per cent, but with a slightly upward trend in inflation of final goods and services prices and a slightly falling one in real income growth. In 1980, the fall in money growth was accompanied by a jump of price inflation by 3 per cent, partially offset by a 2 per cent fall in real growth. Growth of velocity accordingly increased by nearly 3 per cent. It increased by 2 per cent in 1981, when money growth had declined a little further, and the inflation rate had come down by 2 per cent; it fell by more than 3 per cent in 1982, when both inflation and growth rate declined further (the latter to a negative figure) and the growth rate of the money stock rose again to more than 10 per cent. There was thus, in the terms of our previous analysis, a strong *prima facie* negative monetary impulse in 1980, coinciding with a decline of real growth, but also with a larger upsurge of inflation. This was followed in 1982 by a positive impulse, just when the rate of inflation had come down again to its pre-1979 level, and real income growth to a negative value. On the face of it, the negative impulse of 1980 looks like a quick response to increased growth of prices and nominal income, made despite the incipient decline of real growth, and the fall of both inflation and output growth after 1980 might be attributed in part to the monetary squeeze – subsequently relaxed when inflation had returned to somewhat lower levels and the recession had become serious.

On a closer view, taking account of interest rates as indicators of monetary conditions, however, events are more complicated. We have seen that, in 1979, there were what we called 'confirmed' negative monetary impulses only in Germany and France. On a somewhat cursory inspection of the indicators, there seem to have been such negative impulses in 1980 in all the Big Six except the United States and the United Kingdom, and another in the United States in 1981. Positive impulses, broadly confirmed by the interest indicators, appeared in the United States, Japan and Germany in 1982 (in Japan already in 1981). But it is noteworthy that in the United Kingdom, where the depression was deepest, the indicators of changes in monetary conditions were ambiguous throughout. The signs of increased stringency in 1979 and 1980 and greater ease in 1981 and 1982 were not unanimous – in particular, *ex post* real interest rates point the other way. The study by Artis *et al.*, quoted above, finds the effects of monetary policy, alone, small and unclear when exchange rate is taken as fixed, though their effects *via* exchange rate and changes in competitiveness may have been more substantial. Our own inspection suggests considerable shifts of the demand schedule for money, which render this ground uncertain. The size of the contribution made by monetary policy to the production of this particular depression (and later on to limiting it) is hard to assess, but its importance perhaps lies largely in its timing – monetary stringency was used to fight rising inflation, and the inflation in question, especially the element in it derived from the second oil shock, came just at the point when the stabilisation of *activity* would have required an easing of monetary conditions. This has been largely true of the surges of cost-push inflation throughout our period, including the first oil shock of 1974; but by 1979 or 1980 inflation had come to be considered more dangerous than before in comparison with depression, and there was less inclination to accommodate it. This brings us to the main question, for our purpose, that arises in connection with the recession; what were its effects on inflation?

RECESSION AND INFLATION

We have already noted that the stagnation of industrial production and the 2 per cent fall of world trade in 1979–82 went with an 8 per cent fall in the dollar price index of traded goods. What is relevant here may be not so much the size of the falls in output, as the extent of deviation from the trend of full capacity outputs. Even if one makes the generous assumption that world manufactured output was on this trend in 1979 as well as (more plausibly) in 1973, the implied nearly 4 per cent per annum rise in the trend would have left actual output some 10 per cent below it by 1982, and since there was almost certainly more excess capacity in 1979 than in 1973, this is likely to be an underestimate; the true one probably lies in the range 10–15 per cent. What is still more to the point is the fact that this dip of manufacturing output below trend went with a cheapening of primary products, other than oil, by some 16 per cent between 1980 and 1982, but that the rising price of oil until 1981, and the modesty of its fall until after 1982, meant that there was less cheapening of the non-labour inputs into manufacturing as a whole – as we have noted, the United Nations world index of primary prices, including oil, came down by only 8 per cent. That the prices of manufactures came down by about the same percentage clearly implies some fall in unit labour costs (in dollar terms) or some squeezing of profit margins, or both; since, however, the 'effective rate' of the dollar against other currencies rose by some 25 per cent during the relevant period, neither internationally traded manufactures nor primary products necessarily cheapened in terms of most other currencies. Indeed, in terms of Special Drawing Rights, manufactures and traded goods generally both rose by about 7 per cent; non-petroleum primary products fell by only 2 per cent. We must return to this shortly, looking at the main countries separately. The immediate point is that the events of 1979–82 were in this respect intermediate between those of 1973–5, when primary materials as a whole rose in price by about 75 per cent, and manufactures by about 35 per cent, alongside a reduction in manufactured output of perhaps 8 per cent in relation to trend, and those of 1929–32 when, as in most depressions, manufactures fell in price, but primary commodities fell much more. The element of cost-push from oil prices was present in 1979–82, though not in such an extreme form, in percentage terms, as in 1973–5. One may reasonably say that 1929–32 was a classic demand depression, 1973–5 a cost-push depression with some restraint of demand, 1979–83 a demand depression with added cost-push complications.

In fact, the domestic wholesale prices of manufactures had not begun to decrease in any of the main OECD countries by 1982, though they had nearly stopped rising in Japan, and decreased marginally there in 1983. Nor had consumer prices or the GDP deflator stopped rising; the IFS 'world' index of consumer prices rose 7.5 per cent in that year, compared with its most recent peak increase of 11.9 per cent in 1980. An extension to these years of the q, p diagram in chapter 3 for the Big Six shows a considerable variety of experience (see chart 12.1). In Japan, small falls in real growth rate have gone with even smaller falls in the already low rate of inflation; in Germany increasing falls in growth to small negative values have gone with almost constant (if anything, slightly rising) inflation rates. France, while true to her tradition of comparatively low variability of real growth rates, experienced an even smaller fluctuation of inflation, with a rise in it accompanying her main growth reduction in 1980, and a fall continuing through the partial growth recovery of 1982. In Italy, the gradual reduction in growth rate to a small negative value had not, by 1982, brought inflation down below its 1979 starting point, above which it had been jerked sharply in 1980. It was in the United States and the United Kingdom that inflation rates came down substantially; in the former not until the second, and larger, episode of negative growth in 1982, in the latter, much more strongly, in the second consecutive year of substantial real income decline, 1981, and continuing in the following year despite the resumption of some growth.

Some further light is thrown on these changes by the simple Phillips relation between unemployment and wage inflation (increase of hourly earnings in manufacture). Lagging unemployment slightly (unemployment rate of 1978 with change of earnings from 1978 to 1979), we find some very presentable relationships over this limited period (see chart 12.2). The United Kingdom relationship, in particular, appears as a Phillips curve of almost blameless character, after its gross misbehaviour of the preceding dozen years, though with signs of a temporary upward displacement in 1980, perhaps attributable to

Chart 12.1 *Quantity–price relations, 1979–82*

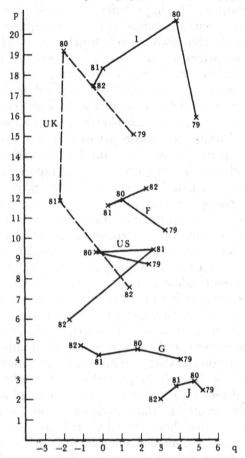

Source: *International Financial Statistics*

import prices and indirect taxation. The other countries, except France, also show broadly Phillips-like relations, dependent mainly on the values for 1982 and 1983 – the depression hit them later than it hit the United Kingdom. France maintains its record, for our period, of showing no signs of a Phillips relationship at all.

For all the Six, or all except France, one must of course remember that what we have here is a cyclical relationship, and a dynamic one, in which wages and prices interact. In all six countries, import price-push played a large part in these years. We saw in a previous chapter that (as defined for our purpose – an increase in the weighted rate of inflation of import prices sufficient to cause a 1 per cent

Chart 12.2 *Phillips relations, 1979–83*

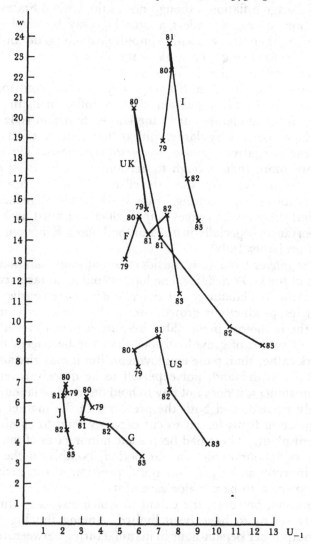

increase in the rate of inflation of final output prices by its 'pass-through' effect) it was present in all six countries in 1979. In all except the United States, there was a further push in 1980, which helps in varying degrees to account for the rise in their rates of wage inflation in that year. There were negative versions of this same impulse in the United States, United Kingdom and Japan in 1981, which in the second and third of these countries may help to account for the reduction of wage inflation – though not in the United States (where wage inflation increased) unless a time lag may be invoked. Italy suffered yet another strong positive impulse, which no doubt helps to account for 1981 being her peak wage inflation year. The even stronger negative impulse of 1982 must have made a substantial contribution to the big fall of her wage inflation; the contribution of import prices to the big remission of wage inflation in the United Kingdom and the moderate one in the United States in 1982 cannot, however, have been very large, unless the lagged effects of the previous year's negative impulses were still significant. The negative impulses are more than enough to account for the easing of wage inflation in Germany. Altogether, the effects of import price changes go some way towards accounting for the variations of wage inflation at this time, but the growth of excess supply of labour must have been of major importance, especially in 1982 in the United Kingdom, United States and probably Italy.

When one moves back from consideration of wage inflation to that of inflation of the GDP deflator, one has, of course, to take account of the rate of growth of labour productivity. We have seen earlier that, in most countries, productivity growth rises with cyclical increases in the growth of the economy, presumably because it pays to meet at least some part of surges of growth steeper than the long-term trend by harder work rather than more employment. But it may rise also when there are falls in demand, not expected to be quickly reversed. In those circumstances, it does not pay to hold on to more labour than is immediately needed, and both the pressures of the market and the rational choice of firms forced to cut capacity tend to eliminate the least efficient plants. There had been some minor cases of this kind of 'shake-out' of labour earlier in our period, notably in the United Kingdom in 1967 and 1971; but the depression of the early 1980s might be expected to be a major case of it.

On inspection, however, the extent to which adversity stimulated productivity seems to have been limited. Among the Big Six, the growth of output per person-hour in manufacturing between 1979 and 1983 was greater than that in the generally (though rather disappointingly) upward phase of output, 1975–9, only in the United States and the United Kingdom – the two countries in which growth during 1975–9 was slowest. There, it exceeded the growth in the earlier quadrennium by between a quarter and a half; in the other four countries of the Six, however, and in Canada the productivity growth of the earlier quadrennium had been between twice and four times that of the later one. Generally speaking, therefore, changes in productivity growth in the depression cannot be said to have contributed greatly to bringing down the rate of inflation, though absolute improvement in productivity continued. Reduction of wage inflation and reduction in world prices of primary products – both arriving rather late in the day, after exhaustion of the effects of the second oil shock – seem to have been the chief agents.

In a general way we may start from the proposition that the traditional effect of depression on inflation has been two-fold; first, the fall (in relation to trend) of income as a whole has shaken down the prices of primary products, or such of them as are sold in flexible price markets, and this has reduced inflation of prices of manufactures *via* their raw material costs. Then both this reduction in inflation of final goods prices and the slack in the labour market have gradually reduced wage inflation, and prices of manufactures (and services) have responded. The recession of the early 1980s fails to follow this pattern in that, like that of the mid-1970s, it starts, not simply with a reduction of industrial activity, but with a cost-push, mainly from fuels, which is the product of supply-side factors.

The first of our two traditional lines of action on prices is thus largely blocked; the dollar price index of primary products as a whole (including fuels) nearly doubled between 1978 and 1981, and came down only by some $5\frac{1}{2}$ per cent in the following year; though prices of primary products other than petroleum, as we have noted earlier, peaked in 1980 and came down by 16 per cent in the succeeding two years – not a very big fall, as such things go, but then, on the world scale, it was not a very big depression. In those two years, non-petroleum primary prices did the traditional thing by falling also in relation to those of manufactures (by about 8 per cent). The 8 per cent fall in the prices of (internationally traded) manufactures can, however, hardly be taken as being a response to the cheapening of material inputs, because, if fuels are included, these were still a little higher in 1982 than in 1980.

We have seen that wage inflation did, in fact, come down (except in France). How far this was a slide down a reborn, stable, Phillips curve, how far a slide down a curve that was itself falling with the expectations of inflation, is a matter into which we cannot here enter at length. It must suffice to remark that, both in the United States and the United Kingdom, professional forecasts of inflation rates up to a year ahead (the Livingston and Holden and Peel series) came down by six or seven percentage points between 1980 and 1983 – more than the total fall in wage inflation in that period in the United States, but less than that in the United Kingdom. Actual inflation experienced over the previous year came down considerably more than the forecasts. It is reasonable to suppose that either anticipation of inflation to come, or wish (and willingness) to catch up with inflation past, or both, must have exerted diminishing forces on settlements over these years. In fact, the fall in nominal hourly earnings inflation (in manufactures) in the United Kingdom failed to adjust fully to the fall in consumers' price inflation, and real wages grew faster than in the years immediately before the depression – an exception to the general experience over our period as a whole that growth of real earnings moved pro-cyclically. In the United States, the experience was the opposite; hourly earnings (perhaps because of the prevalence of longer-term wage contracts) failed to rise as much as consumers' prices in the three years 1979–81. In this respect, Japan's experience resembled that of the United Kingdom, with counter-cyclical real earnings growth, Germany's and Italy's came nearer to that of the United States, with very little or no growth of real earnings in the recession years.

By the end of 1983, wage costs per unit of output in manufacturing had ceased to rise in the United States, Canada, Japan and Germany, and seemed to be approaching a halt in the United Kingdom, France and Italy, though, in keeping with the general tendency for the CPI to rise in relation to the prices of manufactures, the inflation rate of consumers' prices was still over 5 per cent for the OECD as a whole. The disturbing feature of this otherwise satisfactory situation was the high level of unemployment, which, by the summer of 1984 had been above 8 per cent in the OECD for more than two years, and was not expected to change much for a year or more to come. In the United Kingdom, the rate stood at 13.3 per cent (on the OECD definition) and was expected to rise further. For the OECD as a whole, output was, as we have noted, probably more than 10 per cent below the trend of capacity established in the years 1973–9. The still incomplete remission of inflation had been dearly bought, and there was little to suggest that, with the eventual progress of recovery, rates of inflation would not rise again. On the face of it, prospects of anything like inflation-free recovery seemed to require considerable further moderations of the wage settlements going with any given level of unemployment.

13

CONCLUSION

In seeking to bring the conclusions of this study together, the writer is tempted to start from the views which he expressed, thirty years ago (Brown, 1955) in an effort to describe the main mechanisms of inflation operating in the world between 1939 and 1951. So far as the postwar world was concerned, the story went like this. Most finished goods, especially in the advanced market economies, were priced mainly by a mark-up over cost, the mark-up being relatively insensitive to pressure of demand. Cost varied in the short run mostly with the prices of labour and primary material inputs. Primary material prices were to a large extent flexible and market-determined. Labour markets operated with sticky prices, the rates of change of which were to some extent sensitive (negatively) to the amount of slack in the market, of which unemployment rates could be taken as broadly representative; and also sensitive, though probably not linearly, to the current or recent rate of inflation of prices of consumers' goods.

Inflation in a given industrial country therefore varied with the tightness of its labour market and (through the channels both of raw material and of labour markets) with the relative growth rates of physical supply of primary materials in the world markets, and of monetary demand in them. Growth of monetary demand in these markets depended on the rate of increase of factor incomes in all the market economies together. These incomes, in turn, depended on the rate of inflation of the prices of the hired factors and on growth of employment, the latter of which was the more sensitive, at least in the short run, to any check to the growth of accommodating monetary demand.

A ratchet was built into this mechanism, since, while primary product prices were sensitive downwards, as well as upwards, to world market forces, nominal wages and salaries, at least in the advanced countries, were insensitive downwards (money-illusion would operate to provoke resistance to nominal reductions, even if real rewards were rising). Fluctuations of primary product prices would therefore tend to generate an upward trend of prices generally, except insofar as the growth of factor productivity was sufficient to

377

offset this tendency by itself, or insofar as depressions occurred in which unemployment was sufficiently high to hold the growth of nominal factor prices down to that of factor productivity on average.

A scrutiny of the interwar record in the United States and the United Kingdom suggested that the former might be able to keep the inflationary trend down to a tolerable level (say not much more than 1 per cent a year) with average rates of unemployment which were also tolerable; but, mainly because of the lower rate of productivity growth that it was assumed to achieve, the United Kingdom was viewed less hopefully – unless new wage-fixing machinery, requiring drastic changes in the attitudes and functions of trade unions, could be introduced. The final, hardly sensational, conclusion was: 'The dilemma which the first sustained period of full employment in the history of industrial civilisation has revealed seems likely to remain with us for some time'.

For a decade or more after this was written, it might have been taken as reflecting a good deal of the current perception of the worldwide inflationary process. This was the golden age of the Phillips curve; the key to the rate of inflation was located in labour markets. Complications arising from the world primary product markets, as in 1939–41 and 1951, were notably absent, but memories of the events of 1951–2 were fresh. How have subsequent events modified these perceptions?[1]

In the course of the 1960s and the first three years of the next decade the basis for a simple Phillips curve interpretation decayed. From the side of practical experience, it was weakened by the outward shifts of the curve in the United States after 1967, and in the United Kingdom and Italy, most notably in 1970. From the side of theory and interpretation, it was undermined by Friedman's perception that the logical consequence of the complete adjustment of expectations to the actual, average rate of inflation was the natural, or non-accelerating-inflation, rate of unemployment. It was also complicated, to say the least, by the introduction, from various sources, of the 'search' theory of unemployment rate, which could be seen as demoting that variable from its previous status as a measure of demand deficiency in the labour market. At the same time, the whole approach was eroded by the transfer of attention to the supply of money as the crucial variable. The key was to be sought, not in the labour market, but in the banking system. Finally, the development during the 1970s of Muth's (1961) exploration of the consequences of the rational ex-

---

[1] Among the leading accounts of the evolution of thought during our period are those by Gordon (in Lundberg (ed.) 1977), Laidler (1981) and Tobin (1981).

pectations hypothesis strengthened belief in the self-adjusting powers of the market economy.

Meanwhile, the placid weather in the world market economy had come to an abrupt end, first with the boom of 1973, quickly, and very greatly, complicated by the first oil shock, then with the second oil shock in 1979. There was not much, essentially, about the immediate impact of these primary price increases – except their scale – that was different from what had already been experienced in 1951. They produced cost-push inflation and a net external draining of purchasing power in the OECD countries, and, in varying proportions, elsewhere in the oil-importing world. The rises in consumer prices started price–wage spirals, and the inflation of nominal incomes, and of the prices of non-primary goods and services, which all this produced, tended to prevent the nominal prices of primary products from falling back afterwards. (On these occasions, however, unlike 1951, the managed character of the rises in petroleum prices did even more than the ratchet mechanism of the labour market to make the rise of prices in general irreversible.)

What the events of 1973–5 did in most countries (with Germany as a partial exception, its sharpest inflation having occurred earlier) was to raise inflation to levels that caused major alarm. To some extent this found expression in renewed attempts to establish incomes policies of, broadly, the kinds that had been tried earlier in our period. In the new theoretical atmosphere which we have described, however, it was natural, first, that control of the money supply should come to be selected as a main – in some cases *the* main – instrument of anti-inflationary policy; second, that fiscal (or, indeed, monetary) policy for the fine-tuning of the level of activity should pass out of favour; and, third, that there should be a tendency to regard unemployment in a new light, as a manifestation of willingness to prolong the average period of search for jobs, either because what was foregone by staying out of work had become smaller than before, or because of temporary over-optimism about the real wage that might be found by waiting. 'Targeting' of the rate of growth of the money supply became fashionable from the mid-1970s, despite the fact that unemployment rates were considerably higher than in the 1960s. Outside the United States (where the reasons for it were somewhat unorthodox, and where countervailing monetary policy was correspondingly severe) there was little sign in the main OECD countries of discretionary fiscal action against the further rise of unemployment after 1979 – in some of them (for example the United Kingdom) quite the contrary.

The changes that experience, in fact, produced in the view of inflation, and how to deal with it, which prevails in the quarters where policy is decided are thus profound. At the end of our main period of study there had been a shift in influential quarters in many countries towards the doctrine, chiefly associated with Milton Friedman, that the price level is uniquely determined by the quantity of money along with the level of real income, and that the latter is determined by other forces – is unaffected by the quantity of money in all but the short run. Keeping the average growth rate of the money supply down to the rate at which productive capacity is expanding will therefore yield a zero average rate of inflation. The view is expressed, moreover, that the less money growth varies, from year to year, about its constant average value, the better; monetary authorities are not sufficiently well-informed to operate a reliably counter-cyclical policy of supply variations, and expectation of a steadily growing supply will tend to stabilise economic behaviour. The more extreme view is that, once governments have done their best for stability (of both price level and real growth rate) in this way, they should not worry about unemployment, which is always voluntary and normally transient. Broadly, the real economy is satisfactorily self-adjusting through market forces, given an appropriate, steady growth of the money supply.

How far does our own survey require us to abandon or modify the 1955 picture of the inflationary process and how far to endorse the views just described as being in the ascendant in 1979? First, what has it suggested about the processes of price formation? So far, at least, as finished goods in the more highly developed countries are concerned, it does, indeed, seem to be confirmed by most of the relevant studies that they are priced on the basis of a percentage mark-up over average cost, usually reckoned at some conventional level of capacity utilisation, and that the mark-up percentage is not very sensitive to the state of demand. The profit share tends to increase when demand is high, not so much because the mark-up is raised as because, with fuller use of capacity, fixed overheads are more widely spread.

The formation of wages is more complicated. The institutional setting within which it occurs varies greatly from country to country, and from time to time. In none of our sample countries does it approximate to an atomistic, competitive market in which unemployed workers can effectively bid wage rates down. Established notions of 'the rate for the job', employees' and employers' organisations, bilateral monopoly in bargaining, governmental regulation, and the exercise of political power by employees and employers all make for situations in which the response of price to changes in supply and demand conditions is different from a simple, market-clearing one, and in many cases the convenience of relatively long-term contracts makes the response sluggish. The simple Phillips relation between the tightness of the market and the *rate of change* of hourly earnings remains as a fairly persistent, though not universal, constituent of wage equations. Variables designed to represent expectations of price inflation (but which may well refer more realistically to recent inflation still to be caught up with) also generally occur, as do, with varying strengths, indicators of effective desire to maintain some conventional rate of real income growth. But other factors – episodes of incomes policy, rebounds from them and otherwise unexplained wage explosions – have been prominent and widespread. Our own exploration of 'wage-push' impulses, in which acceleration of wage inflation has gone with a reduction of the profit share (so that it is unlikely to have been the product of a spurt in the growth of demand) has found them to be fairly common, and especially associated with the major accelerations of inflation.

The 1955 picture of the labour market as having a tendency to move in the direction of an equilibrium, rather than to be usually in one, is thus largely confirmed, though with the addition of much evidence of complicating circumstances. It gives no reason to suppose that the long-term equilibrium position implicit in the Phillips relation (which may never be reached) is one in which the labour market is cleared, in the sense that everyone willing to take a job at the current rate has one, or has one waiting for him which he has not yet found, as one would expect it to be in an atomistic, competitive market. It is simply the situation in which the bargaining organisations which want wages to go up are in balance with those which want them to come down; the unemployed, for whom there are insufficient jobs on offer at present rates, having no vote in the matter. It is not 'full employment', even with an allowance made for friction.

This view that the labour market does not automatically clear is in conflict with attempts which have been made to show that large variations in unemployment can be explained by changes in the ratio of unemployment benefit rates to average earnings in work and/or other sources of alteration in the degree of imperfection of the labour market. Our study of the evidence presented, and of unemployment-vacancy relations in a number of countries, suggested that some unemployment changes can be attributed to such causes; perhaps a considerable part of the increase between the more prosperous years in the 1960s and those in the 1970s in the United States, United Kingdom and France (much less in Germany or Japan); but it indicates strongly that part of that increase, and virtually all of the greater increases in the early 1980s, cannot be accounted for by market imperfection. They were due to demand deficiency.

Does our evidence throw any light on the relevance to our period of the proposition that, with unbiased expectations of inflation, the Phillips curve will vanish in a puff of smoke, leaving us with a unique non-accelerating inflation rate of unemployment? Were expectations unbiased, as opposed to downward-biased (as would be the case if they were adaptive when the trend of inflation rates was upwards)? We have found that expectations of inflation, as deduced variously from surveys of professional opinion, general opinion, and the behaviour of security markets, tended to be substantially downward-biased. In these circumstances, the Phillips curve in principle survives, and is steepened. Our examination of national data has suggested that, if expectations of inflation were the main causes of shifts of the simple curve, they foreshadowed actual experience to very different extents in different countries and at different times, tending to do so much more seriously in the second half of the period than in the first.

In fact, to attribute all the shifts to expectations of price inflation is probably incorrect. Institutional and political changes contribute heavily to the complicated story of wage-push. Apart from them, it is clear (as was noted in 1955) that spectacular price changes usually make an immediate mark on wage inflation, as in 1919–22 and 1951 and, as we have seen more recently, in 1972–5 and 1978–80. Inertia, the sense of a norm to which wage increases should approximate, is itself a matter of wage rather than price expectations, though the two are not easy to disentangle. The norm rose in several countries in the late 1960s for reasons which purely economic analysis has not altogether elucidated; in some countries, though not in others, it was raised further in the 1970s by experience of sharp inflation originating in the primary product markets. The difficulty of bringing it down in the early 1980s has varied greatly from country to country. These aspects of wage behaviour are not adequately summed up by anything so simple as a 'change of gear' of price expectations. Through the changes of wage norms, the intrusions of impacts from the primary product markets and other complications, however, some sensitivity of wage inflation to pressure of demand seems to have remained.

When we come to primary (and some intermediate) commodities, it is obvious that we should not treat their world market prices, collectively, as being formed mainly by free market forces; it is important to distinguish between those for which this is broadly true (with some important qualifications concerning prices which are managed within particular national or regional areas, as many agricultural prices are) and those – pre-eminently of petroleum – which are managed on a world scale. Apart from petroleum, and with a qualification about the influence of the World Wheat Agreement and its demise, primary product prices generally responded to the forces of supply and demand in markets which in some sense 'cleared'. The boom of 1951 had been due mainly to a war scare and the consequent rush to accumulate stocks. That of 1973 was due in large part to the coincidence of what one may call bad (but not phenomenally bad) luck on the supply side with a major (but not phenomenally high) peak of demand. The only suggestion of a systematic cause, otherwise, is that of an element of delayed cumulative reaction of supply (for example in non-ferrous metal refining capacity and, perhaps, in the dismantling of the Wheat Agreement) to a long period in which, surprisingly in view of the great secular industrial boom, the relative prices of primary products had declined. A mechanism of this kind, akin to the familiar 'cobweb', was sometimes suggested as a major intensifier, working in an opposite sense, of the great depression of the 1930s. Perhaps this source of world disequilibrium deserves more attention. But there can be no doubt that the oil shock, probably a greater dislocating influence than the booms in all the other primary products put together, cannot be treated as a response to world supply and demand in any simple quantitative sense. Oil must be classed as having an administered price, and the price rise of 1973 was a result of a change in the identity of those exercising power over it, combined with a change in the general outlook concerning world energy supplies. The further shock of 1979–80 was partly a consequence of the Iranian revolution – an unusually large-scale example of a more familiar class of supply-side disturbance – but partly an administrative adjustment of the OPEC monopoly price to the perceived demand situation.

So far as the machinery of price formation is concerned, therefore, the modifications that seem to be required to the 1955 view are not very drastic. The prevalence of cost-plus pricing of finished goods is confirmed, the Phillips relation survives in something more than a vestigial form in the labour market, though it is plain that much else besides the pressure of demand is involved there. At all events, the market does not clear in the sense of eliminating involuntary unemployment, and reduction of demand produces such unemployment which can be persistent – as the experience of the United Kingdom between the wars, and of the United States throughout the 1930s, should have made clear.

Our investigation of price–quantity relations provided a picture in agreement with this. Changes in expenditure in the earlier part of our period (after the Korean disturbances had subsided) tended to have their immediate effect on output rather than its price, which responded (usually later) to changes in factor prices. In the second half of the period primary commodity prices were more apt to lead the dance, taking finished goods prices with them, but exerting an opposite influence on output; larger movements of wage rates (some of them apparently in response to import price movements) also became more prominent, again taking finished goods prices with them and applying a brake to output – or causing governments to apply it. The short-term correlation between growth and inflation was everywhere (except in the United States in the earlier sub-period) negative, not positive as one would expect it to be if varying monetary demand impinged directly on both price and output; and the growth rate of output was nowhere very near to constancy – over most individual cycles in many countries it was more variable than the rate of inflation.

Postwar macroeconomic policy in most advanced countries aimed to avoid either positive or negative inflationary gaps by controlling nominal expenditure. This turned out to be far from a simple task, partly because some elements of expenditure on the national product are exogenous (for example exports), partly because the response of costs and prices to pressure of demand, as we have seen, is both gradual and changeable. The instrument most favoured at first was budgetary and fiscal policy – the United Kingdom and the United States in particular began with a tradition of accommodative monetary policy, derived in part from the wartime borrowing needs of the governments, in part from the Keynesian fear of high and variable interest rates as destructive of the inducement to invest.

The main questions that arise about fiscal and budgetary policy, as pursued in our period, are whether it was stabilising or destabilising of the level of activity, and whether, on average, it was inflationary. As to the first, we have seen that the built-in stabiliser property of the public finance system was generally clear. In most of the Big Six, the positive and negative expenditure impulses which we have identified (arising mostly from capital formation, sometimes from exports, sometimes, in a negative sense, from rises of import prices) were generally opposed by it. (The United Kingdom is something of an exception, especially in 1951 and 1963). In the later part of our period, at least, the discretionary element in budgetary impacts on the economy proves to be broadly neutral as regards stabilisation – it is the structural properties of the systems that seem to be responsible for their stabilising effect.

As to the second question, one can, of course, answer that, since inflation seems to be related, though irregularly, to the level of activity at which economies are run, and since it occurred, pressure from the public sector can be said to have been excessively high. That, however, does not necessarily mean that it was higher than in previous times. We have not made the comparison for most of our sample countries, but in the United Kingdom it is not clear that this pressure (taking account of both sides of the budget) was any greater than it had been before the war; domestic capital formation was the great source of additional pressure. In the United States, on the other hand, public finance probably was a main source of additional pressure, though there the period with which comparison is made was one in which additional pressure of this kind, from some source, was manifestly very desirable. Whether one regards the pressure of demand as having been 'excessive' in a broader sense, of course, depends on how one values the extra inflation which a marginal unit of it caused against the real income that would have been lost, through higher unemployment and slower capacity growth, in its absence. To this we return later.

Money supply and monetary policy generally raise larger questions. It is probable that money supply increased over our period as a whole by a factor of the same general order of magnitude as that by which nominal income increased (both 11–13-fold for the industrial countries combined). Did the expansion of money supply 'cause' that of nominal income, which (if for the moment we take the $3\frac{1}{2}$-fold growth of real income for granted) carries the roughly 3.7-fold price inflation with it? It is plain that something like this increase in money supply was a necessary condition of such an increase of nominal income and (again, given the real expansion) of prices. Moreover, if all the extra money had been showered on to the earth (from a helicopter?) in some durable form, it is probable that something like the observed increase in nominal income would have taken place, much as inflation took place in Western Europe after the Spanish acquisition of New World gold and silver in the 16th Century.

But the analogy is misleading. Modern increases in the money supply are the results of additional loans by banks, made because someone wants to borrow and thinks it worthwhile to do so at the interest rate offered. Money created in this way, moreover, is not everlasting; it vanishes whenever it is transferred to recipients who use it to repay their own debts to the banking system or to buy securities from it (a point made by Kaldor, 1983). Increase in the stock of money in these conditions seems likely to be the consequence of changes in the demand for it as well as of changes in the conditions of supply. In all of the Big Six, the greater part of bank lending was to the private sector rather than to governments; most of the demand that was relevant here was private.

In dealing with the net change over a period of nearly thirty years, we are more concerned with the transactions demand for money than with the speculative and precautionary demands for it, important though variations in those may be, especially in the somewhat shorter run. The demand for bank loans to finance increases in employment and output raises no inflationary problem; it is the extra demand to finance dearer imports, increases in wage rates, and increased unit costs of intermediate and final goods that is immediately relevant – though the two are, of course, along with speculative and precautionary balances, all part of a single, undifferentiated total, in the sense that, for instance, inability to borrow to cover higher costs may lead to purchases of smaller physical quantities and/or to sales of securities.

Can we distinguish between the effects of demand-side factors and those of supply-side factors in bringing about the great increase in money stock? Our concept of the monetary impulse (positive or negative) was an attempt to identify occasions on which supply-side changes 'led the dance' – when money growth accelerated to the accompaniment of an easing of the financial situation, or decelerated to the accompaniment of a tightening. We saw that, in the Big Six, less than a fifth of the total increase in the money stock took place during episodes of positive impulse; less than a quarter against the resistance of negative ones. More than half of the total expansion everywhere (three-quarters in the United Kingdom, Japan and Italy) took place in conditions which can be described as 'accommodative'. Supply-side impulses seem to have been mainly counter-cyclical in terms of both growth and inflation; though the great inflationary surge of 1973–4 had the assistance of unusually large monetary impulses, except in Germany. The impression is that monetary systems were responsive to demand, with variations in that responsiveness designed (though not always with success) to be of a stabilising tendency. At the higher level of the supply mechanism, the data suggest that the supply of reserve money was trimmed to fit the commercial banks' and the public's demands for it about as often as the adjustment was in the other direction.

In any case, the meaningful question is not what single factor 'caused' the inflation, which, like any other event, was the product of a great complex of factors, but what alteration in which of those factors would have served to avoid it, and how difficult or costly the alteration would have been. If one sets the avoidance of inflation as an objective, the responsiveness of the monetary systems to demand for loans was clearly excessive. What would have happened if the terms on which bank loans were offered had been, on average, stricter than they were to a sufficient extent to prevent a rise in, say, the GDP deflator for each of the industrial countries over our period as a whole? Broadly, we are back with the question that we asked above about the results of running the industrial economies at a rather lower level of activity in relation to capacity. Monetary stringency might have caused employees' organisations to make smaller demands, and would probably have caused employers to concede less; but it would have done so mainly by creating a situation in which profits and jobs were seen to be more precarious. A greater denial of monetary accommodation would have operated mainly by cutting the average level of activity to a point where the average level of wage and salary settlements was less inflationary, or not inflationary at all. There would also, presumably, have been a once-for-all reduction of the flexible prices of primary products (in comparison with what actually happened) at the point at which the more restrictive policy was embarked upon.

An attempt to construct a more detailed zero-inflation scenario on these lines, however, would not be very useful; the machinery involved is too complex. Expectations of inflation and/or awareness of its recent occurrence, and the existence in the pipeline of anomalies and grievances left over from past settlements, all came to play increasing parts in the inflationary process as time went on. Without inflation in the 1950s and 1960s, its containment in the 1970s would no doubt have been easier. But the inflation was far from being simply a self-reinforcing process, which could easily have been nipped in the bud. It was, as we have seen, a series of more or less separate inflationary episodes, the earlier of which apparently contributed to more inflationary attitudes and reactions later on. It is significant that, even in the relatively calm period from 1953 to 1968, no market economy escaped inflation of its GDP deflator and consumers' price index which was, by historical standards, very considerable – in the industrial countries following the more austere policies, 30–60 per cent. (This was true even of Austria, where, according to Professor Scitovsky, 'the governor of the central bank, secretary of the general committee of trade unions and the head of the federation of Austrian industries had all been in the same concentration camp' and 'had met once a week for dinner ever since' (Worswick and Trevithick, 1983, p. 254).) Convincing wage equations relevant to the longer term are scarce, but it seems likely that, without some change in the mode of operation of their factor markets, the industrial economies (and the world economy) would have had to be run at considerably lower pressure, even then, to achieve zero inflation. One has to remember that lower pressure might have been partially self-defeating, through an adverse effect on the (in the event) phenomenal productivity growth of that time. (Experience since 1979 is not at variance with this. For the Big Six as a whole, the rate of growth of output per person-hour in manufacturing during 1979–83 was not much more than half of what it had been during 1975–9.)

We have noted that the course of events since 1979 has not been a simple matter of reduction in pressure of demand bringing down the rate of inflation; it was complicated by the second oil shock which, while it reduced activity in the oil-importing countries, also gave price inflation in general an upward push. But, as the effects of the oil push died away and non-oil primary prices came down, wage inflation too was brought down in the Big Six, to the point at which, by 1983, wage costs per unit in manufacturing had either ceased to rise or seemed to be approaching a halt. At this point, however, the rate of unemployment in the OECD countries was 8.7 per cent, or nearly twice its average level for the 1970s, and not far below three times that of the 1960s, and there was still a substantial positive inflation rate of the wage costs of final goods and services as a whole.

One cannot, of course, deduce that this (or some higher) level of unemployment, maintained indefinitely, is the price of zero wage cost inflation in manufacturing. Nor, on the other hand, can one say that it is only a temporary cost of changing attitudes in the labour market in such a way that a cautious recovery of activity could be allowed, or engineered, without excessive inflation. The truth probably lies in between. The general implication of the last thirty years' experience, however, is that, given the labour market institutions of the advanced countries (with Japan, latterly, perhaps the nearest thing to an exception), high and steady levels of employment induce excessive wage inflations, and that non-inflationary levels of demand go with serious unemployment and slow growth.

That is the central problem. There are, of course, others. If one considers the doctrine, popular in recent years, that the control of the money supply is the key to that of inflation, or even the more reasonable view that it is one of the keys, one is bound to take account of the experience, in the decade since it began to be attempted, of its very considerable difficulty. Variations in demand (including non-transactions demand) for money are too important to allow a rigid quantitative control (if that were possible) to succeed without creating problems; the existence, and invention, of substitutes for whatever is treated as money for the purposes of such control make it hard for it to succeed at all without repeated extensions of its scope. The evidence, including that derived from our study of monetary impulses, suggests in any case that the connection between money supply and expenditure is loose; the direct evidence (such as it is) on the effect of interest on expenditure continues to point to its limitations. The control of expenditure that has been achieved seems, in fact, to owe more to budgetary than to monetary policy – witness the apparent victory of the former over the latter in the United States at the time of writing.

The other outstanding problem, of course, is that posed by inflationary shocks from the primary product markets. Ideally, the need is for more effective cooperative, international action to anticipate, and deal with, major mismatches between the growth of demand and that of supply. That is a tall order, though in the spirit which inspired the international postwar monetary and trade organisations it should not be thought impossible. More modestly, the possible role of buffer stock schemes (not at present in fashion) needs reinvestigation. The admitted difficulties of such schemes are rather similar to, though probably smaller than, those attending control of the supply of money (which *is* at present in fashion). The death of the International Wheat Agreement was the prelude to one of the major inflationary disturbances of our period. Prevention of disturbances of the nature and magnitude of the two oil shocks is outside the scope of economic management as normally understood; more might perhaps be done to anticipate their possible occurrence and make precautionary plans (including buffer stock arrangements) to mitigate their effects. But accidents will happen, and national economies (and the international economy) need flexibility to cope with their impacts.

This brings us back to the rigidity in the responses of industrial countries to rising primary prices – the secondary inflation induced through the mechanism of the price–wage spiral – and so to the general problem of labour market spirals of which it is a part. The central problem is that, even without any such nudges from the flexible price markets of the world, labour markets tend, in widely varying degrees, to put an upward pressure on unit costs of final goods, even when the economy is some way off what an atomistic labour market would register as a general shortage of labour. And upward nudges from the flexible markets, also in widely varying degrees, jerk these spirals into further action. Control of the supply of money, if it can be done sufficiently comprehensively (and with or without the help of budgetary and fiscal policy), may well be capable of holding this upward pressure in check, but, given existing labour market institutions, only at the cost of running the economy at considerably less than its full-employment capacity.

If that were the last word on the subject, we should be left with the problem of balancing the alternative evils of inflation and unemployment (the latter coupled with lower real output and slower growth than would be possible in its absence). All such balancings of costs or benefits are difficult. Inflation, which is at least annoying to everyone, and imposes a tax on some kinds of property income, is at the time of writing weighing heavily in the scales of popular disapproval. Unemployment, which is disastrous for a minority, deeply troubling for many more, and threatening to the social fabric, is widely viewed with some degree of fatalism, and also widely blamed (as happened also fifty years ago) on technical progress – ironically, at a time when the application of technical progress is slower than it has been for more than a generation. Most of the unemployment results from deficiency of effective demand, imposed by governments (in important part collectively rather than individually) mainly because they fear inflation, partly, in some cases, because they have been persuaded, contrary to the fairly plain evidence of history, that effective demand is relevant to the level of activity only in the short run, if then.

But the statement of the dilemma is not the last word. In a long series of *ad hoc* policy episodes during our period, some attempt has been made in a number of countries to curb the demand for transactions money (rather than the supply of it) by influencing, or temporarily constraining, the working of the labour market. Success has been varying, partial, and temporary. But it is plain that differences in the structure and working of national labour markets have been a main – probably the main – source of differences in success in combining high activity and growth with the moderation of inflation, and this should give hope that modifying the institutions can improve the performance. A considerable literature has grown up on possible reforms of the wage-fixing process (Blackaby, 1980, Okun and Perry, 1978, Meade, 1982). Their mechanisms, and appraisal of them, lie beyond the scope of this book. The main conclusion which we can draw from our survey of inflation since 1950 is that, while the control of money supply, or of interest, has an important part to play, along with budgetary and fiscal policy, in the management of expenditure, the relation between increase in expenditure and increase in activity is another matter, the main key to which is, after all, in the labour market. The problem of how to use it has presented itself in all the industrial countries, in varying forms, since the end of the war. It is with us still.

Akerlof, G. 'The case against conservative macroeconomics', Inaugural lecture, *Economica N.S.*, vol. 46, no. 183, August 1979.

Al-Samarrie, A., Kraft, J. and Roberts, B. 'The effects of Phases I, II and III on wages, prices and profit margins in the manufacturing sector of the United States' in J. Popkin (ed.), 1977, *op cit.*

Apps, R. 'Real wage equations: some further results and further problems' (mimeo), University of Manchester, 1976.

Argy, V. *Postwar International Monetary Crisis: an analysis*, London, Allen and Unwin, 1981.

Argy, V. and Carmichael, J. 'Models of imported inflation for a small country – with particular reference to Australia' in Kasper, W. (ed.), *International Money – experiments and experience*, Australian National University, Canberra, 1976.

Argy, V. and Kouri, P. 'Sterilization policies and the volatility in international reserves' in R. Aliber (ed.), *National Monetary Policies and the International Financial System*, University of Chicago Press, 1974.

Artis, M. J. 'Is there a wage equation?' in A. S. Courakis, 1981, *op. cit.*

Artis, M. J., Bladen-Hovell, R., Karakitsos, E. and Dwolatzky, B. 'The effects of economic policy: 1979–82', *National Institute Economic Review*, no. 108, May 1984.

Artis, M. J. and Lewis, M. K. 'The demand for money in the U.K. 1963–73', *Manchester School of Economic and Social Studies*, vol. 44, June 1976.

Monetary Control in the U.K., Oxford, Philip Allan, 1981.

Artis, M. J. and Miller, M. H. 'Inflation, real wages and the terms of trade' in J. Bowers (ed.), 1979, *op. cit.*

Artis, M. J., Temple, P. and Copeland, L. 'Wage equations' (mimeo), University of Manchester, June 1977.

Aukrust, O. 'Wage-price interdependencies in open economies', processed, Oslo, *Central Bureau of Statistics of Norway*, 1972.

Bain, G. S. and Price, R. *Profiles of Union Growth: a statistical portrait of eight countries*, Oxford, Basil Blackwell, 1980.

Balassa, B. 'Economic reform in China', *Banca Nazionale del Lavoro Quarterly Review*, no. 142, September 1982.

Bank of England, 'A note on real short-term interest rates', *Quarterly Bulletin*, vol. 23, no. 4, December 1983.

Batchelor, R. 'Expectations, output and inflation: the European experience', *European Economic Review*, vol. 17, no. 1, 1982.

'Rational expectations market efficiency and economic policy', *Annual Monetary Review*, Centre for Banking and International Finance, London, City University, no. 2, December 1980

Batchelor, R. A., Major, R. L. and Morgan, A. D. *Industrialisation and the Basis for Trade*, Cambridge University Press, 1980.

Benjamin, D. K. and Kochin, L. A. 'Searching for an explanation of unemployment in interwar Britain', *Journal of Political Economy*, vol. 87, no. 3, June 1979.

Beveridge, W. H. *Full employment in a free society*, London, Allen and Unwin, 1944.

Blackaby, F. T., 'Incomes policy', in *British Economic policy 1960–74*, National Institute of Economic and Social Research, Cambridge University Press, 1978.

(ed.) *The Future of Pay Bargaining*, London, Heinemann, 1980.

Blinder, A. S. *Economic Policy and the Great Stagflation*, London, Academic Press Inc., 1981.

Blinder, A. and Newton, W. 'The 1971–74 controls program and the price level: an econometric post-mortem' (mimeo), Princeton University, October 1979.

Bosworth, B. P. and Lawrence, R. Z. *Commodity Prices and the New Inflation*, Washington, Brookings Institution, 1982.

Bowers, J. (ed.) *Inflation, economic development and integration: essays in honour of A. J. Brown*, Leeds University Press, 1979.

Bowers, J., Deaton, A. and Turk, J. *Labour hoarding in British industry*, Oxford, Blackwell, 1982.

Bresciani-Turroni, C. *The Economics of Inflation*, London, Allen and Unwin, 1937.

Broughton, J. M. *Demand for money in major OECD countries*, Organisation for Economic Cooperation and Development, *Economic Outlook*, Occasional Papers, Paris, 1979.

Brown, A. J. *The Great Inflation 1939–51*, Oxford University Press, 1955.

'Interest, prices and the demand schedule for idle money', *Oxford Economic Papers*, no. 2, May 1939.

Brown, A. J. 'Friedman and Schwartz on the United Kingdom'. Bank of England Panel of Academic Consultants, *Panel Paper 22*, October 1983.

'Accelerating inflation and the growth of productivity' in R. C. O. Matthews (ed.) *op. cit.*

Brown, W. A. 'Antipodean contrasts in incomes policy' in J. Bowers (ed.), 1979, *op. cit.*

'The structure of pay bargaining in Britain' in F. T. Blackaby (ed.), 1980, *op. cit.*

Bruno, M. 'World shocks, macroeconomic response and the productivity puzzle' in Matthews (ed.), *Slower Growth in the Western World, op. cit.*

Cagan, P. 'The monetary dynamics of hyperinflation' in M. Friedman (ed.), *Studies in the Quantity Theory of Money*, Chicago University Press, 1956.

'Comments on Al-Samarrie, Kraft and Roberts' in J. Popkin (ed.), 1977, *op. cit.*

Calmfors, L. 'Inflation in Sweden' in L. B. Krause and W. S. Salant (eds.), *Worldwide Inflation*, Washington D.C., The Brookings Institution, 1977.

Capdevielle, P. and Alvarez, D. 'International comparison of trends in productivity and labour cost', US Bureau of Labour Statistics, *Monthly Labor Review*, December, 1981.

Carlson, J. A. 'A study of price forecasts', *Annals of Economic and Social Measurement*, vol. 6, no. 1, Winter 1977.

Carlson, J. A. and Parkin, M. 'Inflation expectations', *Economica*, vol. 42, no. 166, May 1975.

Challen, D. W. and Hagger, A. J. *Modelling the Australian Economy*, Melbourne, Longman Cheshire, 1979.

Champernowne, D. G. *The Distribution of Income between Persons*, Cambridge University Press, 1973.

Clegg, H. A. *Trade unionism under collective bargaining*, Oxford, Blackwell, 1976.

Coghlan, R. T. 'A transactions demand for money', *Bank of England Quarterly Bulletin*, vol. 18, no. 1, March 1978.

Corden, W. M. *Inflation, exchange rates and the world economy*, Oxford, Clarendon Press, 1977.

Courakis, A. S. (ed.) *Inflation, depression and economic policy in the West*, London, Mansell, 1981.

Coutts, W., Godley, W. A. H. and Nordhaus, W. D. *Industrial Pricing in the United Kingdom*, Cambridge University Press, 1978.

Darby, M. R. and Stockman, A. C. (eds.) *The Mark III International transmission model*, Cambridge, Mass., National Bureau of Economic Research Working Paper, no. 462, 1980.

Davies, R. J. 'The comparative political economy of wage determination' (Paper read at the 6th World Congress of the International Industrial Relations Association, Kyoto, 1983).

Dean, A. J. H. 'Roles of governments and institutions in OECD countries' in F. T. Blackaby (ed.), 1980, *op. cit.*

Denison, E. F. *Why Growth Rates Differ*, Brookings Institution, Washington, 1967.

Dicks-Mireaux, L. A. 'The interrelationship between cost and price changes 1946–1959: a study of inflation in post-war Britain', *Oxford Economic Papers*, vol. 13, no. 3, October 1961.

Dow, J. C. R. and Dicks-Mireaux, L. A. 'The excess demand for labour', *Oxford Economic Papers*, vol. 10, no. 1, February 1958.

Edgren, G., Faxen, K. and Odhner, C. *Wage formation and the economy*, London, Allen and Unwin, 1973.

Fallick, J. L. and Elliott, R. F. (eds.) *Income policies, inflation and relative pay*, London, Allen and Unwin, 1981.

Feinstein, C. 'Comments on Chapter 8' in Matthews (ed.), *Slower Growth in the Western World*, *op. cit.*

Fisher, I. *The purchasing power of money*, New York, Macmillan, 1911.

The Money Illusion, New York, Allen, G., 1928.

The Theory of Interest, [1930], Clifton N. J., A. Kelley, 1974.

Flemming, J. S. *Inflation*, Oxford University Press, 1976.

Friedman, M. Nobel Lecture: Inflation and Unemployment, *Journal of Political Economy*, June 1977.

'The role of monetary policy', *American Economic Review*, vol. 58, no. 1, March 1968.

Friedman, M. and Schwartz, A. *Monetary trends in the United States and the United Kingdom: their relation to income, prices and interest rates, 1867–1975*, Chicago University Press, 1982.

Frye J. and Gordon, R. J. 'Government intervention in the inflation process: the econometrics of 'self-inflicted wounds', *American Economic Review*, vol. 71, no. 2, May 1981, Papers and Proceedings.

Giersch, H. and Wolter, F. 'Towards an explanation of productivity slowdown: an acceleration-deceleration hypothesis', *Economic Journal*, vol. 93, no. 369, March 1983.

Godley, W. A. G. and Nordhaus, W. D. 'Pricing in the trade cycle', *Economic Journal*, vol. 82, no. 327, September 1972.

Goldfeld, S. M. 'The case of the missing money', *Brookings Papers on Economic Activity*, no. 3, 1976.

'The demand for money revisited', *Brookings Papers on Economic Activity*, no. 3, 1973.

Goodhart, C. A. E. 'Monetary trends in the United States and the United Kingdom: a British review', *Journal of Economic Literature*, vol. XX, December 1982.

Goodhart, C. A. E. and Crockett, A. D. 'The importance of money', *Bank of England Quarterly Bulletin*, vol. 10, no. 2, June 1970.

Gordon, R. J. 'Can the inflation of the 1970s be explained?', *Brookings Papers on Economic Activity*, no. 1, 1977.

'International monetarism, wage push and monetary accommodation' in A. S. Courakis (ed.), 1981, *op. cit.*

'Comments on Perry', *Brookings Papers on Economic Activity*, no. 1, 1980.

'Recent developments' in E. Lundberg (ed.), 1977, *op. cit.*

'Why US wage and employment behaviour differs from that in Britain and Japan', *Economic Journal*, vol. 92, no. 365, March 1982.

Haberler, G. von, *Prosperity and Depression*, Geneva, League of Nations, 1937.

Hacche, G. J. 'The demand for money in the United Kingdom: experience since 1971', *Bank of England Quarterly Bulletin*, vol. 14, no. 3, September 1974.

Hall, R. L. and Hitch, C. J. 'Price theory and business behaviour', *Oxford Economic Papers*, no. 2, May 1939.

Hamburger, M. J. 'Behaviour of the money stock: Is there a puzzle?', *Journal of Monetary Economics*, vol. 3, no. 3, July 1977.

Hendry, D. F. and Ericsson, N. R. 'Assertion without empirical basis: an econometric appraisal of Friedman and Schwartz', *Monetary Trends in the United Kingdom*, Bank of England Panel of Academic Consultants, *Panel Paper 22*, October 1983.

Henry, S. G. B. 'Incomes policy and aggregate pay' in J. L. Fallick and R. F. Elliott (eds.), 1981, *op. cit.*

Henry, S. G. B. and Ormerod, P. 'Incomes policy and wage inflation: empirical evidence for the UK 1961–77', *National Institute Economic Review*, no. 85, August 1978.

Henry, S. G. B., Sawyer, M. C. and Smith, P. 'Models of inflation in the United Kingdom: an evaluation', *National Institute Economic Review*, no.77, August 1976.

Hickman, B. G. and Schleicher, S. 'The interdependence of national economies and the synchronisation of economic fluctuations: evidence from the LINK project', *Weltwirtschaftliches Archiv*, vol. 114, no. 4, 1978.

Hicks, J. R. *The theory of wages*, (2nd edn), London, Macmillan, 1935.

Hieser, R. O. 'Wage determination with bilateral monopoly in the labour market: a theoretical treatment', *Economic Record*, vol. 46, no. 113, March 1970.

Hill, T. P. *Profits and rates of return*, Paris, OECD, 1979.

Hines, A. G. 'Wage inflation in the U.K. 1948–62: a disaggregated study', *Economic Journal*, vol. 79, no. 313, March 1969.

Holden, K. and Peel, D. A. 'Forecasts and expectations: some evidence for the U.K.', *Journal of Forecasting*, vol. 2, no. 1, January–March 1983.

'Unemployment and unanticipated inflation: some empirical results for six countries', *European Economic Review*, vol. 10, no. 4, November 1977.

Howard, D. H. 'Personal saving behaviour and the rate of inflation', *Review of Economics and Statistics*, 60(4), November, 1978.

International Bank for Reconstruction and Development, World Development Report, 1981.

Jacobsson, L. and Lindbeck, A. 'Labour market conditions, wages and inflation – Swedish experiences 1955–67', *Swedish Journal of Economics*, vol. 71, no. 2, June 1969.

Johnston, J. 'A model of wage determination under bilateral monopoly', *Economic Journal*, vol. 82, no. 327, September 1972.

Johnston, J. and Timbrell, M. 'Empirical tests of a bargaining theory of wage rate determination' in D. E. W. Laidler and D. Purdy (eds.), *Inflation and Labour Markets*, Manchester University Press, 1974.

Judd, J. P. and Scadding, J. L. 'The search for a stable money demand function: a survey of the post-1973 literature', *Journal of Economic Literature*, vol. XX, September 1982.

Junankar, P. N. 'An econometric analysis of unemployment in Great Britain 1952–72', *Oxford Economic Papers*, vol. 33, no. 3, November 1981.

Kaldor, N. 'Keynesian economics after fifty years' in D. Worswick and J. Trevithick (eds.), 1983, *op. cit.*

Kay, J. and Mirrlees, J. 'The desirability of natural resource depletion', in Pearse, D. W. (ed.), *The Economics of Natural Resource Depletion*, London, Macmillan, 1975.

Keynes, J. M. *The general theory of employment, interest and money*, London, Macmillan, 1936.

Treatise on money, London, Macmillan, 1930.

A Tract on monetary reform, London, Macmillan, 1923.

Kmenta, J. 'An econometric model of Australia, 1948–1961', *Australian Economic Papers*, vol. 5, 1966.

Knoop, D. and Jones, G. P. *The Medieval Mason*, Manchester University Press, 1933.

Laidler, D. E. W. 'Inflation-alternative explanations and policies: tests on data drawn from six countries' in K. Brunner and A. H. Meltzer (eds.), *Institutions, policies and economic performance*, Amsterdam, North Holland Publishing company, 1976.

'Monetarism: an interpretation and an assessment', *Economic Journal*, vol. 91, no. 36, March 1981.

Laney, L. O. 'National monetary independence and managed floating exchange rates', Federal Reserve Bank of Dallas Research Paper, no. 7905, 1979.

Laney, L. O. and Willett, T. D. 'The international liquidity explosion and worldwide inflation: the evidence from sterilization co-efficient estimates', *Journal of International Money and Finance*, vol. 1, no. 2, August 1982.

Lewis, W. A. *Growth and fluctuations 1870–1913*, London, Allen and Unwin, 1978.

Lindbeck, A. 'The recent slowdown of productivity growth', *Economic Journal*, vol. 93, no. 369, March 1983.

Lipsey, R. G. and Parkin, M. 'Incomes policy: a reappraisal', *Economica N.S.*, vol. 37, no. 146, May 1970.

Lundberg, E. (ed.) *Inflation theory and anti-inflation policy*, (International Economic Association), London, Macmillan, 1977.

McGuire, T. W. 'On estimating the effects of controls' in K. Brunner and A. H. Meltzer (eds.), *The economics of price and wage controls*, Amsterdam, North Holland Publishing company, 1976.

Maddison, A. 'Explaining economic growth', *Banco Nazionale del Lavoro Quarterly Review*, September 1972.

'Phases of capitalist development', *Banca Nazionale del Lavoro Quarterly Review*, no. 121, June 1977.

'Western economic performance in the 1970s: a perspective and assessment', *Banca Nazionale del Lavoro Quarterly Review*, vol. 33, no. 134, September 1980.

Maki, D. and Spindler, Z. A. 'The effect of unemployment compensation on the rate of unemployment in Great Britain', *Oxford Economic Papers*, vol. 27, no. 3, November 1975.

Marris, R. 'How much of the slowdown was catch-up?' in Matthews (ed.), *Slower Growth in the Western World, op. cit.*

Matthews, R. C. O. 'Introduction: a summary view' in Matthews (ed.), *Slower Growth in the Western World*, London, Heinemann Educational Books, 1982.

Matthews, R. C. O., Feinstein, C. and Odling-Smee, J. C. *British Economic Growth, 1856–1973*, Oxford, Clarendon Press, 1982.

Maynard, G. and Van Ryckeghem, W. *A World of Inflation*, London, Batsford, 1976.

Meade, J. E. *Stagflation, Vol. I Wage-fixing*, London, Allen and Unwin, 1982.

Meade, J. E. and Andrews, P. W. S. 'Summary of replies to questions on the effects of interest rates', *Oxford Economic Papers*, no. 1, October 1938.

Means, G. C. 'Industrial prices and their relative inflexibility', Senate Document Q 13, 74 Congress, 1st session, 1935.

Meek, R. (ed.) *Central Bank views on monetary targeting*, Federal Reserve Bank of New York, 1982.

Miller, N. C. 'Sterilization and offset co-efficients for five industrial countries and the monetary approach to the balance of payments' (Consultant Paper to U.S. Government Interagency External Research Group), October 1976.

Morley, S.A. 'Comments on Nadiri and Gupta' in J. Popkin (ed.), 1977, *op. cit.*

Muth, J. F. 'Rational expectations and the theory of price movements', *Econometrica*, vol. 29, no. 6, 1961.

Nadiri, M. I. and Gupta, V. 'Price and wage behaviour in the U.S. aggregate economy and in manufacturing industries' in J. Popkin (ed.), 1977, *op. cit.*

National Institute of Economic and Social Research, 'The Economic Situation', *National Institute Economic Review*, no. 106, November 1983.

'The National Institute's forecasts of inflation 1964–82', *National Institute Economic Review*, no. 107, February 1984.

Nolan, P. and Brown, W. 'Competition and workplace wage determination', *Oxford Bulletin of Economics and Statistics*, vol. 45, no. 3, August 1983.

Nordhaus, W. D. 'The worldwide wage explosion', *Brookings Papers on Economic Activity*, no. 2, 1972(1).

'Recent developments in price dynamics', in Eckstein, O. (ed.), *The Econometrics of Price Determination*, Washington, Board of Governors of the Federal Reserve System, 1972 (2).

Okun, A. M. *Prices and quantities: a macroeconomic analysis*, Washington D.C., Brookings Institution, 1981.

Okun, A. M. and Perry, G. L. (eds.) *Curing chronic inflation*, Washington D. C., Brookings Institution, 1978.

Organisation for Economic Co-operation and Development. *Budget financing and financing and monetary control*, Monetary studies series, Paris, 1982.

Historical Statistics 1960–82, Paris, 1984.

'Budget Indicators', *OCED Economic Outlook*. Occasional Studies, July 1978.

Towards full employment and price stability (McCracken Report), Paris, 1977.

Ormerod, P. 'Manufactured export prices in the UK and the law of one price', National Institute of Economic and Social Research, Discussion Paper nq. 27, 1978.

'The maintenance of large macro-economic models: a case study with the NIESR model of the UK economy', *Applied Economics*, 13, pp. 431–47, 1981.

Ormerod, P. A. and Worswick, G. D. N. 'Unemployment in interwar Britain', *Journal of Political Economy*, vol. 90, no. 2, April 1982.

Paish, F. W. 'Output, inflation and growth', in *Studies in an Inflationary Economy*, London, Macmillan, 1962.

Parkin, M., Sumner, M. and Ward, R. 'The effects of excess demand, generalised expectations and wage-price controls on wage inflation in the UK: 1956–71' in K. Brunner and A. Meltzer (eds.), *The Economics of Price and Wage Controls*, Amsterdam, North Holland Publishing Company, 1976.

Peacock, A. T. 'A note on the balanced-budget-multiplier', *Economic Journal*, vol. 66, June 1956.

Pencavel, J. H. 'The American experience with incomes policies' in J. L. Fallick and R. F. Elliott (eds.), 1981, *op. cit.*

Peebles, G. 'Inflation in the People's Republic of China 1950–1982', *Three Banks Review*, no. 142, June 1984.

Perry, G. L. 'Determinants of wage-inflation around the world', *Brookings Papers on Economic Activity*, no. 2, 1975.
'Inflation in theory and practice', *Brookings Papers on Economic Activity*, no. 1, 1980.
Phelps, E. S. 'Phillips curves, expectations of inflation and optimal unemployment over time', *Economica N.S.*, no. 34, August 1967.
Phelps Brown, E. H. 'Egalitarianism and the distribution of wealth and income', *Industrial Relations*, vol. 22, no. 2, Spring 1983.
Phelps Brown, E. H. and Hopkins, S. V. 'Seven centuries of the price of consumables, compared with builders' wage rates', *Economica*, no. 23, November 1956.
Phillips, A. W. 'The relation between unemployment and the rate of change of money wage rates in the United Kingdom 1861–1957', *Economica N.S.*, vol. 25, no. 100, November 1958.
Pigou, A. C. *The theory of unemployment*, London, Macmillan, 1933.
Popkin, J. (ed.) *Analysis of Inflation 1965–1974*, National Bureau of Economic Research, Cambridge, Mass., Ballinger Publishing Company, 1977.
Portes, R. 'The control of inflation: Lessons from East European Experience', *Economica*, vol. 44, no. 174, May 1977.
Prais, S. J. 'The recent slowdown in productivity growth; comments on the papers', *Economic Journal*, vol. 93, no. 369, March, 1983.
Price, L. D. D. 'The demand for money in the United Kingdom: a further investigation', *Bank of England Quarterly Bulletin*, vol. 12, no. 1, March 1972.
Price, R. W. R. and Chouraqui, J. C. 'Public sector deficits: problems and policy implications', *OECD Economic Outlook*, Occasional Studies, June, 1983.
Robbins, L. *The Great depression*, London, Macmillan, 1934.
Sargan, J. D. 'Wages and prices in the United Kingdom: a study in econometric methodology' in P. E. Hart, G. Mills and J. K. Whitaker (eds.), *Econometric analysis for National Economic Planning*, Colston papers, 16, London, Butterworths, 1964.
'A study of wages and prices in the U.K. 1949–1968' in H. G. Johnson and A. R. Nobay (eds.), *The Current Inflation*, London, Macmillan, 1971.
'The consumer price equation in the post war British economy: an exercise in equation specification testing', *The Review of Economic Studies*, 47, pp. 113–136, 1980.
Sargent, J. R. 'Capital accumulation and productivity growth', in Matthews (ed.), *Slower Growth in the Western World, op. cit.*
Saunders, C. T. (Consultant), Draft note for Senior Economic Advisers G.E.C.E. Governments, August 1981 (Ec. Ad. (XVIII) Ac.1/R1).
Sawyer, M. C., Aaronovitch, S. and Samson, P. 'The influence of cost and demand changes on the rate of change of prices', *Applied Economics*, 14, pp. 195–209, 1982.
Scitovsky, T. 'The demand-side economics of inflation' in D. Worswick and J. Trevithick (eds.), 1983, *op. cit.*
Seers, D. 'A theory of inflation and growth in under-developed countries based on the experience of Latin America', *Oxford Economic Papers*, no. 2, June 1962.
Shackle, G. L. S. *Expectations in Economics*, Cambridge University Press, 1949.
'The nature of the bargaining process' Chapter 19 in J. Dunlop (ed.), *The theory of wage determination*, London, Macmillan, 1964.
Sheriff, T. D. 'The lessons of wage equations' in F. T. Blackaby (ed.), 1980, *op. cit.*
Shuford, H. L. 'Subjective variables in economic analysis: a study of Government expectations', (PhD dissertation), Yale University, Wachtel, *loc. cit.*
Sims, C. A. 'Money, income and causality', *American Economic Review*, vol. 62, no. 4, September 1972.

Sinha, R. P. 'Labour in India – market and institution' in J. S. Uppal (ed.), *India's economic problems*, New Delhi, 1975; 2nd edn, India, Tata McGraw, 1978.

Solow, R. M. *Price Expectations and the Behaviour of the Price Level*, Manchester University Press, 1969.

'On theories of unemployment', *American Economic Review*, February 1980.

Spinelli, F. 'Wage inflation in Italy: a reappraisal', *Banca Nazionale del Lavoro Quarterly Review*, vol. 33, no. 135, December 1980.

Sumner, M. T. 'Wage determination' in M. Parkin and M. T. Sumner (eds.), *Inflation in the United Kingdom*, Manchester University Press, 1978.

Surrey, M. 'Measuring the effectiveness of incomes policy', Discussion paper, School of Economic Studies, University of Leeds, 1981.

Sweezy, P. 'Demand under conditions of oligopoly', *Journal of Political Economy*, vol. 47, August, 1939.

Thirlwall, A. P. and Barton, C. A. 'Inflation and growth; the international evidence', *Banco Nazionale del Lavoro Quarterly Review*, September, 1971.

Tobin, J. 'The monetarist counter-revolution today – an appraisal', *Economic Journal*, vol. 91, no. 36, March 1981.

Trinder, C. 'Income in work and when unemployed: some problems in calculating replacement ratios', *National Institute Economic Review*, no. 103, February 1983.

Tyrrell, R. J. 'World growth', *National Westminster Bank Quarterly Review*, August 1976.

Ungern-Sternberg, T. von, 'Inflation and savings; international evidence on inflation-induced income losses', *Economic Journal*, vol. 91, no. 364, December 1981.

United Nations Conference on Trade and Development (UNCTAD), 'Inflationary processes in the international economy and their impact on developing countries, UN Document TD/B/AC. 18/2, 1975.

United Nations Organisation, Department of Economic and Social Affairs, *Economic Survey, 1969–1970*, New York, 1971.

Wachtel, P. 'Survey measures of expected inflation and their usefulness', in J. Popkin (ed.), 1977, *op. cit.*

Wallis, K. 'Wages, prices and incomes policies: some comments', *Economica N.S.*, vol. 38, no. 151, August 1971.

Weintraub, S. *An approach to the theory of income distribution*, Philadelphia, Chilton Company, 1958.

Williams, D., Goodhart, C. A. E. and Gowland, D. H. 'Money income and causality: the U.K. experience', *American Economic Review*, vol. 66, no. 3, June 1976.

Williamson, J. G. and Lindert, P. H. *American Inequality: a Macroeconomic History*, New York, Academic Press, 1980.

Worswick, G. D. N. 'The relationship between pressure of demand and productivity' in Matthews (ed.), *Slower Growth in the Western World, op. cit.*

Worswick, D. and Trevithick, J. (eds.) *Keynes and the modern world*, Cambridge University Press, 1983.

Wren-Lewis, S. W. 'Employment' in A. Britton (ed.), *Employment, output and inflation*, London, Heinemann, 1983.

'The role of money in determining prices: a reduced form approach', *Applied Economics*, vol. 16, no. 4, August 1984.

INDEX

France (*contd*)
quantity–price relations, 52–85 *passim*, 88–91
recession of early 1980s, 367–76
savings, 345–6
vacancies, 259
variability and rate of inflation, 359–60
wage equations, 255–9
wage inflation, determinants of, 232–52 *passim*
wages and unemployment, 230–1
French revolutionary and Napoleonic wars, 3
Friedman, M., 16, 38–9, 44, 208, 254, 265, 340, 359, 378, 380
Frye, J., 312

Germany, East, 12, 13
Germany, West,
capital–output ratio, 359
'catch-up', 354–7
cereals, 293
competitiveness and exchange rate, 278–82
'concerted action', 252, 259
consumers' prices and prices of traded goods, 6–10 *passim*
'crowding-out', 179
cyclic and basic inflation, 85–8
demand for and supply of money, 138–76 *passim*, 386 (*see also*, monetary impulses; money, demand for; money supply)
depression of 1930s, 365–7
employment policy, 353–4
expectations, evidence on, 120–9
expenditure effects, 190, 204
factor shares, 274
Fisher identity, 25–44 *passim*
foreign labour, effects of, 252
growth and inflation, 363, variability of, 55, 56
hyperinflation, 3
impulses, inflationary and disinflationary, 101–6, 107, 110, major movements, 110–12
income and inflation, 343–4
labour market, 217–18, 381
Phillips relation, 229, 233, 236, 372
price formation, 306–9, 324–6
primary product and general prices, 298–300
quantity–price relations, 55–84 *passim*, 89–91
rate of return, 359
recession of early 1980s, 366–76
savings, 346, 354
Stabilisation Law (1967), 353
wage equations, 255–8

wage inflation, determinants of, 229–53 *passim*
wages and unemployment, 221
Ghana, 1
Giersch, H., 351, 360
Godley, W. A. G., 317, 318
Godfeld, S. M., 142
Goodhart, C. A. E., 41, 44, 141
Gordon, R. J., 255–9, 261–3, 264, 268, 270, 307, 311, 315, 324, 326, 378n
Goulart, regime in Brazil, 202
Gowland, D. H., 41
'greatest depression', in tropical countries, 15
Greece,
growth and inflation, 363
hyperinflation, 2, 3
gross domestic product (GDP) deflator,
and consumer price index, 18–19
continuity of change in, 4–6
definition, 24
increase of, relations between countries, 25
and primary commodity prices, 296–8
variability of changes in, 55–6, 88–90, 175, 371
see also, episodes, inflationary and disinflationary; quantity–price relations
growth,
inflation and, 347–51
less developed countries, 14–15
OECD countries, 14, 14n, 17–18
variability of, 55–6, 88–90, 174, 371
Gupta, V., 259, 260, 264, 269, 270, 309–11

Haberler, G., 106
Hacche, G. J., 141
Hagger, A. J., 331
Haiti, 6
Hall, R. L. (Lord Roberthall), 334–5
Hamburger, M. J., 143
Harrod, R. F., 345
Hendry, D. F., 38
Henry, S. G. B., 265, 267, 271–2
Hickman, B. G., 169
Hicks, J. R., 212, 345
Hieser, R. O., 212
Hill, T. P., 96, 274
Hines, A. G., 255
Hitch, C. J., 334–5
Holden, K., 120, 239, 375
Hopkins, S. V., 4
Howard, D. H., 346
Hungary, 1
hyperinflation, 2, 3
repressed inflation, 13
hyperinflation, 2–3, 341
hysteresis loops, in quantity–price relations, 50

THE NATIONAL INSTITUTE OF ECONOMIC
AND SOCIAL RESEARCH
PUBLICATIONS IN PRINT

published by
THE CAMBRIDGE UNIVERSITY PRESS
(available from booksellers, or in case of difficulty from the publishers)

ECONOMIC AND SOCIAL STUDIES

XIX *The Antitrust Laws of the USA: A Study of Competition Encorced by Law*
By A. D. NEALE and D. G. GOYDER. 3rd edn, 1980. pp. 548. £35.00 net.

XXI *Industrial Growth and World Trade: An Empirical Study of Trends in Production, Consumption and Trade in Manufactures from 1899-1959 with a Discussion of Probable Future Trends*
By ALFRED MAIZELS. Reprinted with corrections, 1971. pp. 563. £22.50 net.

XXV *Exports and Economic Growth of Developing Countries*
By ALFRED MAIZELS, assisted by L. F. CAMPBELL-BOROSS and P. B. W. RAYMENT. 1968. pp. 445. £20.00 net.

XXVI *Urban Development in Britain: Standards, Costs and Resources, 1964-2004*
By P. A. STONE. Vol. I: *Population Trends and Housing*. 1970. pp. 436. £22.50 net.

XXVII *The Framework of Regional Economics in the United Kingdom*
By A. J. BROWN. 1972. pp. 372. £22.50 net.

XXVIII *The Structure, Size and Costs of Urban Settlements*
By P. A. STONE.1973. pp. 304. £18.50 net.

XXIX *The diffusion of New Industrial Processes: An International Study*
Edited by L. NABSETH and G. F. RAY.1974. pp. 346. £22.50 net.

XXXI *British Economic Policy, 1960-74*
Edited by F. T. BLACKABY. 1978. pp. 710. £40.00 net.

XXXII *Industrialisation and the Basis for Trade*
By R. A. BATCHELOR, R. L. MAJOR and A. D. MORGAN. 1980. pp. 380. £25.00 net.

XXXIII *Productivity and Industrial Structure*
By S. J. PRAIS. 1982. pp. 410. £25.00 net.

OCCASIONAL PAPERS

XXV *The Analysis and Forecasting of the British Economy*
By M. J. C. Surrey. 1971. pp. 120. £8.50 net.

XXVI *Mergers and Concentration in British Industry*
By P. E. HART, M. A. UTTON and G. WALSHE. 1973. pp. 190. £11.50 net.

XXVII *Recent Trends in Monopoly in Great Britain*
By G. WALSHE. 1974. pp. 156. £10.50 net.

XXVIII *Cyclical Indicators for the Postwar British Economy*
By D. J. O'DEA. 1975. pp. 184. £12.50 net.

XXIX *Poverty and Progress in Britain, 1953-73*
By G. C. FIEGEHEN, P. S. LANSLEY and A. D. SMITH. 1977. pp. 192. £12.95 net.

XXX *The Innovation Process in the Energy Industries*
By G. F. RAY and L. UHLMANN. 1979. pp. 132. £9.50 net.

XXXI *Diversification and Competition*
By M. A. UTTON. 1979. pp. 124. £10.50 net.

XXXII   *Concentration in British Industry, 1935–75*
By P. E. HART and R. CLARKE. 1980. pp. 178. £13.50 net.
XXXIII   *State Pensions in Britain*
By J. CREEDY. 1982. pp. 112. £12.50 net.
XXXIV   *International Industrial Productivity*
By A. D. SMITH, D. M. W. N. HITCHENS and S. W. DAVIES. 1982. pp. 184. £15.00 net.
XXXV   *Concentration and Foreign Trade*
By M. A. UTTON and A. D. MORGAN. 1983. pp. 150. £15.00 net.
XXXVI   *The Diffusion of Mature Technologies*
By GEORGE F. RAY. 1984. pp. 96. £13.50 net.

NIESR STUDENTS' EDITION

2. *The Antitrust Laws of the U.S.A.* (3rd edition, unabridged)
By A. D. NEALE and D. G. GOYDER. 1980. pp. 548. £11.50 net.
4. *British Economic Policy, 1960–74: Demand Management* (an abridged version of *British Economic Policy, 1960–74*)
Edited by F. T. BLACKABY. 1979. pp. 472. £10.95 net.
5. *The Evolution of Giant Firms in Britain* (2nd impression with a new preface)
By S. J. PRAIS. 1981. pp. 344. £8.95 net.

REGIONAL PAPERS
(a series of working papers arising from the study of regional economic development produced in near-print)

1. *The Anatomy of Regional Activity Rates*, by JOHN BOWERS, and *Regional Social Accounts for the United Kingdom*, by V. H. WOODWARD. 1970. pp. 192. £8.50 net.
2. *Regional Unemployment Differences in Great Britain*, by P. C. CHESHIRE, and *Interregional Migration Models and their Application to Great Britain*, by R. WEEDEN. 1973. pp. 118. £8.50 net.
3. *Unemployment, Vacancies and the Rate of Change of Earnings: A Regional Analysis*, by A. E. WEBB, and *Regional Rates of Employment Growth: An Analysis of Variance Treatment*, by R. WEEDEN. 1974. pp. 114. £8.50 net.

THE NATIONAL INSTITUTE OF ECONOMIC AND
SOCIAL RESEARCH

publishes regularly

THE NATIONAL INSTITUTE ECONOMIC REVIEW

A quarterly analysis of the general economic situation in the United Kingdom and overseas, with forecasts eighteen months ahead. The last issue each year usually contains an assessment of medium-term prospects. There are also in most issues special articles on subjects of interest to academic and business economists.

Annual subscriptions, £30.00 (home), and £40.00 (abroad), also single issues for the current year, £8.50 (home) and £12.00 (abroad), are available direct from NIESR, 2 Dean Trench Street, Smith Square, London, SWIP 3EH.

Subscriptions at the special reduced price of £12.00 p.a. are available to students in the United Kingdom and Irish Republic on application to the Secretary of the Institute.

Back numbers and reprints of issues which have gone out of stock are distributed by Wm. Dawson and Sons Ltd., Cannon House, Park Farm Road, Folkestone. Micofiche copies for the years 1959–83 are available from EP Microform Ltd., Bradford Road, East Ardsley, Wakefield, Yorks.

Published by
HEINEMANN EDUCATIONAL BOOKS
(distributed by Gower Publishing Company and available from booksellers)

THE UNITED KINGDOM ECONOMY
By the NIESR. 5th edition, 1982. pp. 119. £2.25 net.

DEMAND MANAGEMENT
Edited by MICHAEL POSNER. 1978. pp. 256. £6.95 net.

DE-INDUSTRIALISATION
Edited by FRANK BLACKABY. 1979. pp. 282. £6.96 (paperback) net.

BRITAIN IN EUROPE
Edited by WILLIAM WALLACE. 1980. pp. 224. £6.50 (paperback) net.

THE FUTURE OF PAY BARGAINING
Edited by FRANK BLACKABY. 1980. pp. 256. £16.00 (hardback), £6.50 (paperback) net.

INDUSTRIAL POLICY AND INNOVATION
Edited by CHARLES CARTER. 1981. pp. 250. £16.00 (hardback), £6.95 (paperback) net.

THE CONSTITUTION OF NORTHERN IRELAND
Edited by DAVID WATT. 1981. pp. 233. £15.00 (hardback), £7.50 (paperback) net.

RETIREMENT POLICY. THE NEXT FIFTY YEARS
Edited by MICHAEL FOGARTY. 1982. pp. 224. £15.00 (hardback), £6.95 (paperback) net.

SLOWER GROWTH IN THE WESTERN WORLD
Edited by R. C. O. MATTHEWS. 1982. pp. 182. £16.00 (hardback), £6.95 (paperback) net.

NATIONAL INTERESTS AND LOCAL GOVERNMENT
Edited by KEN YOUNG. 1983. pp. 180. £15.00 (hardback), £7.50 (paperback) net.

EMPLOYMENT, OUTPUT AND INFLATION
Edited by A. J. C. BRITTON. 1983. pp. 208. £19.50 net.

THE TROUBLED ALLIANCE. ATLANTIC RELATIONS IN THE 1980s
Edited by LAWRENCE FREEDMAN. 1983. pp. 176. £16.50 (hardback), £6.50 (paperback) net.

EDUCATIONAL AND ECONOMIC PERFORMANCE
Edited by G. D. N. WORSWICK. 1984. pp. 152. £15.00 net.